REWARD

GW00382575

Upper-intermediate

Teacher's Book

Simon Greenall

MACMILLAN
HEINEMANN
English Language Teaching

Macmillan Heinemann English Language Teaching
Between Towns Road, Oxford OX4 3PP
A division of Macmillan Publishers Limited

Companies and representatives throughout the world

ISBN 0 435 242369

Text © Simon Greenall, 1996
Design and illustration © Macmillan Publishers Limited 1998
Heinemann is a registered trademark of Reed Educational & Professional
Publishing Limited

First published 1996

All rights reserved; no part of this publication may be reproduced,
stored in a retrieval system, transmitted in any form, or by any means,
electronic, mechanical, photocopying, recording, or otherwise,
without the prior written permission of the publishers.

Designed by Stafford & Stafford

Cover design by Stafford & Stafford
Cover illustration by Martin Sanders

Illustrations by:
Adrian Barclay (Beehive Illustration), pp42,43, 66
Hardlines, pp2, 5, 45
Martin Sanders, pp22/23, 24/25, 32, 37, 38/39, 41, 44, 45, 48/49, 54,
68, 72, 74, 75, 82, 86/87, 90
Simon Smith, pp3, 12, 57

Commissioned photography by:
Chris Honeywell pp50, 51, 68, 70/71.

Note to teachers
The four tests at the back of this book may be photocopied for use
in class without the prior written permission of Macmillan
Publishers Limited. However, please note that the copyright law,
which does not normally permit multiple copying of published
material, applies to the rest of this book.

Author's Acknowledgements
I am very grateful to all the people who have contributed towards
Reward Upper-intermediate. Thank you so much to:
- All the teachers I have worked with on seminars around the world,
  and the various people who have influenced my work.
- James Richardson for the happy and efficient work he has done on
  producing the tapes, and the actors for their voices.
- The various schools who piloted the material.
- Philip Kerr, for his comments on the material, which are especially
  helpful and well-considered.
- Helen O'Neill, Mike Sayer, Sue Bailey and Elizabeth Fulco for their
  reports on the material. I have tried to respond to all their
  suggestions, and if I have not always been successful, then the fault
  is mine alone.
- The Lake School, Sue Kay and Ann Lee for allowing me to observe
  classes.
- Simon Stafford for his usual, skilful design.
- Jacqueline Watson for tracking down some wonderful photos.
- Helena Gomm for helping me out during a particularly busy period
  of writing.
- Chris Hartley for his good faith in the Reward project.
- Catherine Smith for her support and advice and her sensitive
  management of the project.
- Angela Reckitt for her attention to detail, her contribution to the
  effectiveness of the course, and her calm, relaxed style which
  makes work such a pleasure.
- and last, but by no means least, Jill, Jack, Alex and Grace.

Acknowledgements
The authors and publishers would like to thank the following for
their kind permission to reproduce material in this book:
BBC Worldwide Limited for an extract from the chapter 'Santos to
Santa Cruz' by Lisa St Aubin de Terán from *Great Railways Journeys*;
The Independent Newspaper Publishing plc for extracts from
'Foreigner at Sie over what to do about an intimate problem' by
Steve Crawshaw (*The Independent,* December 19930);
'I'd like to teach the world to sell 'by Jonathan Glancey
(*The Independent,* January 1993); 'Growing Trends 'by Paul Barker
and Steve Connor (*The Independent on Sunday,* March 1995);
The Observer for an extract from 'Passion Play 'by Beverley Glick;
Vivienne Rae-Ellis for extracts from *True ghost stories of our own time*
published by Faber and Faber Ltd; Random House UK Ltd on behalf
of the Executors of the Estate of F Scott Fitzgerald for an extract from
Tender is the Night published by The Bodley Head, and for an extract
from *Beyond Belief* by Ron Lyon and Jenny Paschall, published by
Stanley Paul and Company; Reed Consumer Books Ltd for an extract
from *The Lost Continent* by Bill Bryson, published by Secker and
Warburg; Octopus Books Ltd for an extract from

Times Newspapers Ltd for an extract from 'Meals on Wheels 'by
Robin Young © Times Newspapers Ltd, 1994; Clive Anderson for
illustrations from *Patent Nonsense* published by Michael Joseph;
Gillette Management Inc, Fiat, Kellogg's Company of Great Britain
Limited, H J Heinz Company Limited, for the use of their logos;
Classic FM for the recordings of radio advertisements; an extract
from *Lend me Your Alphorn* by Eugene V Epstein, published by
Benteli Verlag, Zurich; an extract from *The Ridgeway* by Richard
Ingram, published by Phaidon Press Ltd; an extact from *The Lost
Continent* by Bill Bryson, published by Secker and Warburg.

Photographs by: © BBC pp20/21, 22; Colorific p60(b); Kevin
Cummins pp10/11; Mike Southern/Eye Ubiquitous pp31(r), 84(m);
Robert Harding Picture Library pp31(l), 60(t), 84(l); Hulton Deutsch
pp47, 64 (t&b); Images Color Library p84(t);
David S Silverberg/Impact Photos p16(b); Magnum p16(t);
Simon Marsden pp34/35; The Photographers Library pp62/63, 77,
84(b); William Robinson p52; Royal Army Medical College p26;
Science Photo Library p46; Matthew Sherrington p40; Tony Stone
Images pp28/29, 30, 80; Telegraph Colour Library pp58, 88; Zefa
pp6, 15, 78/79.

The publishers would also like to thank Jean Winter, Andy Garnett
and Matthew Sherrington.

While every effort has been made to trace the owners of copyright
material in this book, there have been some cases when the
publishers have been unable to contact the owners. We should be
grateful to hear from anyone who recognises their copyright material
and who is unacknowledged. We shall be pleased to make the
necessary amendments in future editions of the book.

Printed and bound in Spain by Edelvives

2003 2002 2001 2000

12 11 10 9 8 7 6 5

Contents

Introduction

Course organisation

Reward is a general English course which will take learners of English from their first introduction to English up to a fully proficient use of the language. British English is used as the model for grammar, vocabulary, spelling and pronunciation, but other varieties of English are included for listening and reading practice. The course components for each level are as follows:

For the student	For the teacher
Student's Book	Teacher's Book
Practice Book	Class cassettes
Practice Book cassette	Resource Pack
	Business Resource Pack

The Student's Book has twenty teaching lessons and five Progress check lessons. After every four teaching lessons there is a Progress check lesson to review the language covered in the preceding teaching lessons and to present new language work relevant to the grammar, functions and topics covered so far. Within the teaching lessons the main grammar or language functions and the most useful vocabulary are presented in boxes which allow easy access to the principal language of the lesson. This makes the focus of the lesson clearly accessible for purposes of presentation and revision. Each lesson will take between 90 and 120 minutes.

The Class cassettes contain all the listening and sounds work in the Student's Book.

The Practice Book has twenty practice lessons corresponding to the twenty teaching lessons in the Student's book. The activities are designed for self-access work and can be easily used to provide extra practice for the language presented in the Student's Book, either in the class or as self-study material. Each lesson will take between 60 and 80 minutes to do.

The Practice Book cassettes contain all the listening and sounds work in the Practice Book.

The Resource Packs provide extra teaching material to practise the main language points of the teaching lessons. There is a general Resource Pack for learners of general English and a business Resource Pack for learners with language requirements of a more professional nature. The material is photocopiable. *Reward* is designed to be very flexible in order to meet the very different requirements of learners and the course. So the Resource Packs can be used to extend a core teaching lesson of 90 – 120 minutes from the Student's Book with approximately 45 minutes of extra material for use in the classroom.

The Teacher's Book contains a presentation of the course design, methodological principles, detailed teaching notes interleaved with pages from the Student's Book and four photocopiable tests. The teaching notes for each lesson include a step-by-step guide to teaching the lesson, a discussion of some of the difficulties the learners may encounter, and more detailed methodological issues arising from the material presented.

Course design

The course design is based on a broad and integrated multi-syllabus approach. It is broad in the sense that it covers grammar and language functions, vocabulary, reading, listening, speaking, writing, and sounds explicitly, and topics, learner training and socio-cultural competence implicitly. It is integrated in that each strand of the course design forms the overall theme of each lesson. The lessons always include activities focusing on grammar and language functions, and vocabulary. They will also include reading, listening, speaking, writing and sounds. The inclusion of each strand of the syllabus is justified by its communicative purpose within the activity sequence. The methodological principles and approaches to each strand of course design are discussed below.

Methodological principles

Here is an outline of the methodological principles for each strand of the course design.

Grammar and language functions
Many teachers and learners feel safe with grammar and language functions. Some learners may claim that they want or need grammar, although at the same time suggesting that they don't enjoy it. Some teachers feel that their learners' knowledge of grammar is demonstrable proof of language acquisition. But this is only partly true. Mistakes of grammar are more easily tolerated than mistakes of vocabulary, as far as comprehension is concerned, and may be more acceptable than mistakes of socio-cultural competence, as far as behaviour and effective communication is concerned. *Reward* attempts to establish grammar and language functions in its pivotal position but without neglecting the other strands of the multi-syllabus design.

Vocabulary
There are two important criteria for the inclusion of words in the vocabulary boxes. Firstly, they are words which the upper-intermediate learner should acquire in order to communicate successfully in a number of social or transactional situations. The revised Threshold Level (1990)[1] has been used to arbitrate on the final selection. Secondly, they may also be words which, although not in Threshold Level, are generated by the reading or listening material and are considered suitable for the upper-intermediate level. However, an overriding principle operates: there is usually an activity which allows learners to focus on and, one hopes, acquire the words which are personally relevant to them. This involves a process of personal selection or grouping of words according to personal categories. It is hard to acquire words which one doesn't need, so this approach responds to the learner's individual requirements and personal motivation. *Reward* Upper-intermediate presents approximately 950 words in the vocabulary boxes for the learner's active attention, but each learner must decide which words to focus on.

Reading
The reading passages are generally at a higher level than one might expect for learners at upper-intermediate level. Foreign language users who are not of near-native speaker competence are constantly confronted with difficult language and to expose the learners to examples of real-life English in the reassuring context of the classroom is to help prepare them for the conditions of real life. There are always an activity or two which encourage the learner to respond to the passage on a personal level or to focus on its main ideas. *Reward* attempts to avoid a purely pedagogical approach and encourages the learner to respond to the passages in an authentic way before using it for other purposes.

Listening
Listening is based on a similar approach to reading in *Reward*. Learners are often exposed to examples of natural, authentic English in order to prepare them for real-life situations in which they will have to listen to ungraded English. But the tasks are always graded for the learners' particular level. Furthermore, a number of different native and non-native accents are used in the listening passages, to reflect the fact that in real life, very few speakers using English speak with British or American standard pronunciation.

Speaking
Many opportunities are given for speaking, particularly in pairs and groupwork. Learners are encouraged to work in pairs and groups, because the number of learners in most classes does not allow the teacher to give undivided attention to each learner's English. In these circumstances, it is important for the teacher to evaluate whether fluency or accuracy is the most important criterion. On most occasions in *Reward* Upper-intermediate speaking practice in the *Grammar* sections is concerned with accuracy, and in the *Speaking* sections with fluency. In the latter case, it is better not to interrupt and correct the learners until after the activity is ended.

Writing
The writing activities in *Reward* are based on guided paragraph writing with work on making notes, turning notes into sentences, and joining sentences into paragraphs with various linking devices. The activities are quite tightly controlled; this is not to suggest that more creative work is not valid, but it is one of the responsibilities of a coursebook to provide a systematic grounding in the skill. More creative writing is covered in the Practice Book. Work is also done on punctuation, and most of the writing activities are based on real-life tasks, such as writing letters, newspaper articles, a report of a debate etc.

---

[1] The Threshold Level 1990, J. A van Ek and JLM Trim, Council of Europe Press, 1991

Sounds

Pronunciation, stress and intonation work tends to interrupt the communicative flow of a lesson, and there is a temptation to leave it out in the interests of maintaining the momentum of an activity sequence. In *Reward* there is work on sounds in most lessons, usually just before the stage where the learners have to use the new structures orally in pair or group work. At this level, it seems suitable to introduce work beyond the straightforward system of English phonemes, most of which the learners will be able to reproduce accurately because the same phonemes exist in their own language. So activities which focus on stress in words and sentences, and on the implied meaning of certain intonation patterns are included. The model for pronunciation is standard British.

Topics

The main topics proposed by the Threshold Level 1 are covered in *Reward* Upper-intermediate. These include personal identification, house and home, daily life, leisure activities, travel, relations with other people, health, education, shopping, food and drink, geographical location and the environment. On many occasions the words presented in the vocabulary box all belong to particular word fields or topics.

Learner training

Implicit in the overall approach is the development of learner training to encourage learners to take responsibility for their own learning. Examples of this are regular opportunities to use mono- and bi-lingual dictionaries, ways of organising vocabulary according to personal categories and inductive grammar work.

Cross-cultural training

Much of the material and activities in *Reward* create the opportunity for cross-cultural training. Most learners will be using English as a medium of communication with other non-native speakers, and certainly with people of different cultures. Errors of socio-cultural competence are likely to be less easily tolerated than errors of grammar or lexical insufficiency. But it is impossible to give the learners enough specific information about a culture, because it is impossible to predict all the cultural circumstances in which they will use their newly acquired language competence. Information about *sample* cultures, such as Britain, America as well as non-native English speaking ones, is given to allow the learners to compare their own culture with another. This creates opportunities for learners to reflect on their own culture in order to become more aware of the possibility of different attitudes, behaviour, customs, traditions and beliefs in other cultures. In this spirit, cross-cultural training is possible even with groups where the learners all come from the same cultural background. There are interesting and revealing differences between people from the same region or town, or even between friends and members of the same family. Exploring these will help the learners become not merely proficient at the language but competent in the overall aim of communication.

Level and progress

One important principle behind *Reward* is that the learners arrive at upper-intermediate level with very different language abilities and requirements. Some may find the early units very easy and will be able to move quickly onto later lessons. These learners can confirm that they have acquired a certain area of grammar, language function and vocabulary, consolidate this competence with activities giving practice in the other aspects of the course design, and then move on. Others may find that their previous language competence needs to be reactivated more carefully and slowly. The core teaching lesson in the Student's Book may not provide them with enough practice material to ensure that the given grammar, language functions and vocabulary have been firmly acquired. For these learners, extra practice may be needed and is provided in both the Practice Book (for self-study work) and the Resource Packs (for classroom work). If learners return to language training at upper-intermediate level after a long period of little or no practice, it is hard to predict quite what they still know. *Reward* is designed to help this kind of learner as much as those who need to confirm that they have already acquired a basic knowledge of English.

Interest and motivation

Another important principle in the course design has been the intrinsic interest of the materials. Interesting material motivates the learners, and motivated learners acquire the language more effectively. The topics have been carefully selected so that they are interesting to adults and young adults, with a focus on areas which would engage their general leisure-time interests. This is designed to generate what might be described as authentic motivation, the kind of motivation we have when we read a newspaper or watch a television programme. But it is obvious that we cannot motivate all learners all of the time. They may arrive at a potentially motivating lesson with little desire to learn on this particular occasion, perhaps for reasons that have nothing to do with the teacher, the course or the material. It is therefore necessary to introduce tasks which attract what might be described as pedagogic or artificial motivation, tasks which would not usually be performed in real life, but which engage the learner in an artificial but no less effective way.

Variety of material and language

Despite the enormous amount of research done on language acquisition, no one has come up with a definitive description of how we acquire either our native language or a foreign language which takes account of every language learner or the teaching style of every teacher. Every learner has different interests and different requirements, and every teacher has a different style and approach to what they teach. *Reward* attempts to adopt an approach which appeals to differing styles of learning and teaching. The pivotal role of grammar and vocabulary is reflected in the material but not at the expense of the development of the skills or pronunciation. An integrated multi-syllabus course design, designed to respond to the broad variety of learners' requirements and of teachers' objectives, is at the heart of *Reward*'s approach.

RESEARCH

Heinemann ELT is committed to continuing research into coursebook development. Many teachers contributed to the evolution of *Reward* through piloting and reports, and we now want to continue this process of feedback by inviting users of *Reward* – both teachers and students – to tell us about their experience of working with the course. If you or your colleagues have any comments, queries or suggestions, please address them to the Publishing Director, Adult Group, Heinemann ELT, Halley Court, Jordan Hill, Oxford OX2 8EJ or contact your local Heinemann representative.

Map of the book

Lesson	Grammar and functions	Vocabulary	Skills and sounds
1 *English ... at home and abroad* Signs in English from around the world	Questions: basic rules	Words used in English from other languages	**Reading:** reading signs from around the world; reading and answering a questionnaire; reading for main ideas **Speaking:** talking about hopes and expectations for an English course; asking questions about ***Reward*** Upper-intermediate **Writing:** writing questions about ***Reward*** Upper-intermediate
Discussion about learning; learning styles	Question tags; negative questions; imperative questions; suggestions and reply questions	Vocabulary to describe language errors and parts of speech	**Sounds:** intonation in question tags; using a model dialogue for guided speaking practice **Listening:** listening for main ideas; inferring **Writing:** writing a composition *The best way to learn English*
2 *Friends and relations* Customs and rituals in different cultures	The indefinite, definite and zero article	Gestures and movements of the body	**Speaking:** talking about ways of greeting and addressing people; using a model dialogue for guided speaking **Reading:** reading for main ideas; understanding text organisation; focusing on topic sentences; inferring
Customs in different age groups			**Sounds:** /ðiː/ and /ðə/ **Listening:** listening for main ideas; interpreting information; talking about customs and rituals **Writing:** text organisation in an informal letter; writing an informal letter about customs and rituals
3 *Passion play* Italian football	Tense review: present tenses		**Speaking:** exchanging information on hobbies and leisure activities; a commentary of a sporting event **Reading:** reading for main ideas; linking ideas; dealing with unfamiliar words **Writing:** preparing a commentary of a sporting event
Hobbies and leisure activities	Criticising behaviour and habits; agreeing and disagreeing	Sport and leisure activities	**Speaking:** talking about hobbies and leisure activities; a discussion about hobbies **Listening:** listening for main ideas; listening for specific information **Sounds:** stressed words in sentences of complaint **Writing:** writing a report of a discussion on hobbies
4 *Twenty-four hours in your town* Arranging a day out in Boston, USA	Tense review: talking about the future; making suggestions and responding to them	People, places and types of entertainment	**Listening:** identifying context and purpose; listening for specific information **Speaking:** planning a day out in Boston; making suggestions **Writing:** identifying the difference between formal and informal expressions; writing a formal business letter
Planning a tourist guide of a town or region	Tense review: talking about the future with *will*	Features of city life	**Reading:** reading for specific information; evaluating a text **Sounds:** polite and friendly intonation **Speaking:** describing different aspects of a town or region **Writing:** note-taking; writing a tourist guide for a town or region
Progress check lessons 1 – 4	Revision	Using a monolingual dictionary; learning vocabulary	**Sounds:** /ɔː/ and /ɜː/; /ə/; stressed words in sentences **Speaking:** talking about plans for a penfriend's visit **Writing:** writing a letter giving advice about greeting people and arrangements for a stay
5 *Achievements and ambitions* An extract from *Great Railway Journeys* by Lisa St Aubin de Teran	Tense review: present perfect simple and continuous	Important life events	**Speaking:** talking about personal achievements and ambitions; exchanging information about biographies **Reading:** predicting; reading for main ideas; reading for specific information; evaluating a text; inferring **Writing:** writing questions to obtain biographical information
Personal achievements and ambitions	Tense review: present perfect simple and continuous		**Sounds:** weak form /bɪn/ **Listening:** listening for specific information **Writing:** writing a biography for a newspaper article

Lesson	Grammar and functions	Vocabulary	Skills and sounds
6 *Trust me – I'm a doctor* Truth and deception; *Sister Coxall's revenge,* a short story in two parts	Tense review: past tenses		**Speaking:** talking about truth and deception **Listening:** predicting the order of events; listening for main ideas; listening for specific information **Writing:** rewriting the story from a different point of view
The story of a doctor in the 19th century	Describing a sequence of events in the past	Words connected with medical matters	**Sounds:** syllable stress; stress in compound nouns **Reading:** reading for main ideas; inferring; dealing with unfamiliar words **Speaking:** talking about different jobs
7 *Wish you were here?* An extract from *The Lost Continent* by Bill Bryson	Adjectives		**Speaking:** talking about features of a holiday; discussing holiday preferences **Writing:** writing statements about holiday preferences **Reading:** reading for main ideas; inferring; understanding writer's style; distinguishing between fact and opinion
Talking about holidays	Describing position	Geographical description	**Listening:** listening for specific information; inferring **Sounds:** linking sounds /y/, /w/ **Writing:** writing a description of a town or region using fact and opinion adjectives
8 *Strange sensations* Four stories from *True ghost stories of our time*	Participle (*-ing*) clauses	Words connected with the senses	**Reading:** reading for main ideas; reading for specific information; dealing with difficult vocabulary **Speaking:** talking about ghost stories
A ghost story set in Scotland	Verbs of sensation	Words connected with sounds	**Sounds:** pauses, word stress, intonation for dramatic effect **Listening:** predicting; listening for specific information; inferring; dealing with difficult expressions **Speaking:** talking about a ghost story **Writing:** writing a ghost story; linking words *meanwhile, eventually, finally*
Progress check lessons 5 – 8	Revision	Positive and negative connotation; adjective suffixes	**Sounds:** /ɔɪ/ and /əʊ/; stressed words in sentences **Listening:** listening and note-taking **Speaking:** retelling a story
9 *Impressions of school* An extract from *Jane Eyre* by Charlotte Brontë	Talking about memories: *remember* + noun/*-ing*	Education and school	**Speaking:** talking about early schooldays **Reading:** predicting; reading for main ideas; dealing with unfamiliar words; inferring
An interview with an English teacher in Sudan	*Used to* and *would* + infinitive; *be/get used to* + noun/*-ing*		**Listening:** listening for specific information; inferring **Sounds:** /j/ in British and American words **Writing:** interpreting and writing a school report
10 *Rules of law* Strange laws around the world	Modal verbs: *must, have to, have got to, can't, mustn't*	Words connected with crimes	**Sounds:** syllable stress **Reading:** reacting to a text; reading for main ideas; reading for specific information **Speaking:** talking about new laws **Writing:** writing new laws
The legal system in Britain	Modal verbs: *don't need to /needn't, needn't have/didn't need to, should/shouldn't*	Words connected with law and order	**Listening:** listening for main ideas; listening for specific information **Reading:** reacting to a text; reading for main ideas **Writing:** writing a letter to a newspaper expressing an opinion; linking words and expressions for opinions
11 *Discoveries and inventions* The story of the inventor and traveller, Francis Galton	Clauses of purpose		**Speaking:** talking about inventions; talking about tips for everyday situations **Reading:** reacting to a text; reading for main ideas; dealing with unfamiliar words **Writing:** writing practical advice
Strange inventions	Noun/adjective + *to* + infinitive	Household items and actions	**Speaking:** guessing the purpose of different inventions **Listening:** listening for main ideas; listening for specific information **Sounds:** assimilation of /t/ and /d/ in connected speech **Writing:** writing a product description

Lesson	Grammar and functions	Vocabulary	Skills and sounds
12 *Food, glorious food* What your choice of food reveals about you	Conditionals (1): zero, first and second conditionals; *if* and *when*	Food and drink	**Speaking:** talking about different ways of cooking and preparing food; talking about typical food and drink **Reading:** reading and answering a questionnaire; reading for main ideas **Listening:** listening for specific information; inferring **Sounds:** stressed words in sentences
Car-engine cooking	Conditionals (2): *unless, even if, as long as, provided (that), or/otherwise*		**Reading:** predicting; reading for main ideas; reading for specific information **Speaking:** talking about car-engine cooking **Writing:** writing advice on eating in different situations, such as picnics and barbecues
Progress check lessons 9 – 12	Revision	*Remember, forget, try, stop, regret + -ing* or infinitive; opposite or negative meanings with prefixes	**Sounds:** /ɔː/, /aʊ/ and /ɔː/; different ways of pronouncing *-ough*; stressed words in connected speech **Listening:** listening and note-taking **Writing:** rewriting news stories
13 *High-tech dreams or nightmares?* A computerised home	The passive	Words connected with technology	**Reading:** predicting; reading for specific information; inferring **Writing:** writing a letter of complaint
Items of new technology	Passive infinitive; passive gerund	Words connected with different kinds of communication	**Listening:** listening for specific information; inferring **Sounds:** stress in compound nouns **Speaking:** a discussion about technology and communication **Writing:** writing a summary of a discussion
14 *Lifestyles* The Amish people of Pennsylvania	Relative clauses	New words from a passage about the Amish people	**Speaking:** talking about lifestyles; talking about changes in lifestyles **Reading:** reading for specific information; inferring
Living in California	Relative and participle clauses	Lifestyle in California	**Listening:** predicting; listening for specific information **Sounds:** pauses in defining and non-defining relative clauses **Writing:** writing a diary of a day in the life of an Amish family or in a Californian community
15 *Lucky escapes* Talking about lucky escapes	Third conditional	Positive and negative feelings	**Speaking:** talking about lucky and unlucky situations **Listening:** listening for main ideas; listening for specific information **Reading:** reading for specific information **Writing:** writing a summary
Stories about good and bad luck	Expressing wishes and regrets	Opinions	**Reading:** predicting; reading for main ideas; understanding text organisation **Sounds:** /s/ and /ʃ/; stressed words in sentences expressing wishes and regrets **Speaking:** talking about the stories
16 *All-time greats* The story of the song *The Girl from Ipanema*	Phrasal verbs	Types of music and words connected with music	**Speaking:** talking about different types of music; talking about national characteristics of music **Reading:** reading for main ideas; inferring; linking ideas
Favourite music and books	Phrasal verbs	Words connected with music and books	**Sounds:** stressed words in sentences with phrasal verbs **Listening:** listening for main ideas; listening for specific information **Writing:** completing a book review using attitude words or phrases; writing a review of a favourite piece of music or book **Speaking:** talking about favourite pieces of music and books

Lesson	Grammar and functions	Vocabulary	Skills and sounds
Progress check lessons 13 – 16	Revision	Phrasal verbs	**Sounds:** /ə/ and /ð/; silent consonants; being aware of speaker's attitude **Writing:** preparing for a game called *If things had been different* **Speaking:** playing a game called *If things had been different*
17 *Spending money* An extract from *Tender is the Night* by F Scott Fitzgerald	Countable and uncountable nouns	Shopping items; new words from a story	**Speaking:** talking about shopping; discussing humorous sayings **Reading:** predicting; understanding the writer's style; reading for main ideas; reacting to a text **Sounds:** timing and intonation in jokes; different ways of telling a joke
Different shopping habits	Ways of expressing quantity	Words connected with money	**Speaking:** talking about words connected with money **Listening:** predicting; listening for main ideas; listening for specific information **Speaking:** talking about shopping habits **Writing:** writing a questionnaire about people's shopping habits
18 *Trends* How to survive the 21st century	Future continuous and future perfect		**Reading:** predicting; reading for main ideas; dealing with difficult vocabulary; inferring **Speaking:** talking about future trends **Writing:** writing advice about future trends
Future trends and party politics	Future in the past	Words connected with politics	**Listening:** listening for main ideas; listening for specific information **Sounds:** syllable stress **Writing:** looking at words and phrases often used in discussions; writing a composition about the 21st century
19 *Legendary Britain* The legend of King Arthur and the Knights of the Round Table	Passive constructions with *say, believe* etc		**Reading:** reading for main ideas; reading for specific information **Speaking:** talking about legends
Legendary places	Speculating about the past: *may have, might have, must have, can't have*	Words connected with legends	**Listening:** predicting; listening for specific information; listening and note-taking; inferring **Sounds:** stressed words in a dialogue **Writing:** writing a guide to legendary people and places
20 *The real thing?* Characteristics of different brands and products	Reported speech	Adjectives to describe different products	**Speaking:** talking about well-known brands and products **Listening:** predicting; listening for main ideas; listening for specific information **Sounds:** understanding different tones of voice
Global advertising	Reporting verbs		**Speaking:** talking about advertising; using a model dialogue for guided speaking practice **Reading:** reading for main ideas; linking ideas; distinguishing between main ideas and examples **Listening:** predicting; understanding text organisation **Writing:** writing a dialogue complaining about an advertising claim
Progress check lessons 17 – 20	Revision	Idioms; slang and informal language	**Sounds:** homophones; homographs **Speaking:** planning a stay in a foreign country

1 *English... at home and abroad*

Questions: basic rules

VOCABULARY

1 Here are some words from other
languages which are used in English.
Are there any which you also use in your
language? Are there any words which
come from your language?

> sushi pasta pizza salon samba alpha
> sauna karate boutique mascara drama
> panorama fez delicatessen kindergarten
> delta concerto kebab glasnost junta
> samovar siesta piano bungalow route

2 Work in pairs. Say what the words in the
box mean and where they come from.

3 Write down five English words which you
often see in your country.

READING AND SPEAKING

1 Look at the signs written in English from
around the world. Read them and decide
where you might see them. Choose from
these places:

  – in a hotel   – in a zoo   – in a laundry
  – in a restaurant   – in a street

2 Work in pairs. The English in the signs is
grammatically correct but each sign has a
different meaning from what it intends
to say. Say what each sign intends to say
and what it really says.

3 Which sign do you find the most
amusing? Have you come across any
similar confusing signs in English or in
your language?

The lift is being fixed for the next
day. During that time we regret
that you will be unbearable.

Visitors are
expected to
complain at the
office between
the hours of
9 and 11am daily.

Please do not feed the
animals. If you have any
suitable food, please give it
to the guard on duty.

Please leave your
values at the front
desk.

STOP – DRIVE
SIDEWAYS

Ladies are
requested not
to have children
in the bar.

Our wines leave
you nothing to
hope for.

1

GENERAL COMMENTS

Course design

This lesson contains activities and exercises in all the main syllabus strands to be found in *Reward* Upper-intermediate: *Vocabulary, Grammar, Functions, Reading, Writing, Speaking, Listening* and *Sounds*. Every two pages corresponds to about 60 minutes' classroom time and usually ends on a writing activity which can be finished for homework, or a speaking activity which can be adapted to fit the time remaining in the lesson, if necessary.

If this is the first time the students have seen the book, ask them to look through and find examples of the different syllabus strands. Point out that the grammar and vocabulary boxes contain the target structures and words for each lesson, which will make revision much easier.

Starting the course

This lesson concerns some useful learner training strategies, and is designed to equip the students with the language they need to talk about the learning process.

VOCABULARY

1 Aim: to present or revise some *loan words*.

● *Loan words* are words borrowed from other languages.
Ask the students to see if there are any words in the vocabulary box which come from their own languages.

2 Aim: to practise using the words; to practise *nationality* and *language* words.

● Ask the students to work in pairs and to say what the words mean and where they come from.

Answers
sushi – Japanese   pasta – Italian   pizza – Italian
salon – French   samba – Brazilian Portuguese
alpha – Greek   sauna – Finnish   karate – Japanese
boutique – French   mascara – Spanish
drama – Greek   panorama – Greek   fez – Turkish
delicatessen – German   kindergarten – German
delta – Greek   concerto – Italian
kebab – Turkish   glasnost – Russian
junta – Spanish   samovar – Russian   siesta – Spanish
piano – Italian   bungalow – Hindi
route – French

● It may be a good opportunity to revise *language, nationality* and *people* words. For more information, see *Reward* Intermediate Progress Check 1–5, activity 1.

3 Aim: to draw students' attention to English words in their own country.

● Ask the students to write down five English words which they often see in their country.

● Ask them to work in groups of four and to compare their lists.

● Turn the checking process into a competition. Ask one student in each group to call out their list and in turn write them on the board. The group with the most words is the winner.

READING AND SPEAKING

1 Aim: to practise reading for main ideas.

● Explain that the signs come from all around the world. Although each sign is grammatically correct, they do not actually say what they mean. Consequently, there is an element of humour attached to each sign. Ask the students first to read and enjoy the signs, and to decide where they might see them.

Answers
in a hotel: The lift is being fixed for the next day
in a zoo: Please do not feed the animals
in a hotel: Visitors are expected to complain at the office
in a hotel: Please leave your values at the front desk
in a street: Stop – drive sideways
in a restaurant: Ladies are requested not to have children in the bar
in a hotel: Our wines leave you nothing to hope for

2 Aim: to practise speaking; to practise looking for mistakes.

● Ask the students to suggest what each sign is meant to say, and what it literally says.

3 Aim: to practise speaking.

● Ask the students to talk about the signs and to say which ones, if any, they found amusing. Have they ever seen similarly amusing signs in their own language?

4 Aim: to practise answering a questionnaire; to present the target structures for the grammar section.

● Explain that the questions concern the students' feelings and attitudes towards learning and using English both in and out of the classroom. Ask the students to read the questions and think about their answers.

5 Aim: to practise speaking; to check reading comprehension.

● Ask the students to work in pairs and talk about their answers to the questions. Go round and listen to each pair, and note down any mistakes you hear. Go through any mistakes you've heard and ask students to suggest corrections.

6 Aim: to practise speaking; to help the teacher identify the class's expectations.

● This activity will be particularly useful if this is the first time you have met the class. Spend time with each group discussing why they want to learn English, and if necessary, helping the less motivated students identify a real need to learn English.

● Ask the students to tell you about their hopes and expectations, and either write them on the board or make a class list in the form of a wall poster.

GRAMMAR

1 Aim: to focus on the basic rules for forming questions.

● Ask the students to read the information in the grammar box.

● Explain that one of the most common mistakes that students make is in the formation of questions. Ask the students to look at *Reading and Speaking* activity 4 and find another example of each rule for the formation of questions in the grammar box.

> **Answers**
> **Sentences 1, 4:** You put the auxiliary verb before the subject. You put the rest of the verb after the subject.
> **Sentences 2, 3, 10:** You don't use **do** in questions with modal verbs or the verb **be**.
> **Sentences 5, 6:** When you use a question word (**who, what, where, when, how**) you put an auxiliary verb before the subject.
> **Sentences 7, 8:** When a verb has no auxiliary you use the auxiliary **do**, followed by the infinitive without **to**.
> **Sentence 9:** When **who, what** or **which** is the subject of the sentence you don't use **do**.

2 Aim: to practise forming questions.

● Ask the students to work in pairs and to think of questions that they could ask their fellow students. This is the opportunity for a class which has never worked together before to get to know each other. Encourage them to think of questions about family, friends, homes, jobs etc.

● Ask the students to work with another pair and ask their questions.

● Ask the students to report back on what they've learnt about the others.

WRITING AND SPEAKING

1 Aim: to practise forming questions in written English.

● Make use of the students' natural curiosity to explore their new textbook. Ask them to look through the book and to write down questions that they could ask about it. Go round and check they are forming questions correctly. Correct any mistakes you have seen with the whole class. This stage of the activity should focus clearly on accuracy.

2 Aim: to practise forming questions in written English.

● Ask the students to ask and answer the questions they wrote in 1. Encourage them not to read their questions aloud, but to learn them by heart before they ask them.

4 Here are some questions about using English at home and abroad. Read them and think about your answers to them.

1 Have you ever been to an English-speaking country?
2 Can you meet English-speaking people in your country?
3 Where can you hear English spoken or written in your town?
4 Have you ever spoken English with a native speaker?
5 How long have you been learning English?
6 What do you like most and least about learning English?
7 Do you ever use your own language during your English lessons?
8 Do you usually ask questions during your lessons?
9 Who speaks to you most often in English? Your teacher or your fellow students?
10 Are you looking forward to your Upper-intermediate English course?

5 Work in pairs and talk about your answers to the questions.

I've been to the States a couple of times, and...

6 Work in groups of three or four and make a list of your hopes and expectations for your English lessons. Use these phrases:

We hope we'll... We'd like to... We expect we'll...
When you have finished, share your ideas with the rest of the class and make a class list. You could put your hopes and expectations on a wall poster to remind you.

GRAMMAR

Questions: basic rules
Here are some rules for forming questions.
You put the auxiliary verb before the subject in written questions and usually in spoken questions.
You put the rest of the verb after the subject.
Have you ever studied another foreign language?
When a verb has no auxiliary, you use the auxiliary do in the question, followed by an infinitive without to.
Do you write down every new word you come across?
You don't use do in questions with modal verbs or the verb be.
Can you guess what a word means from the context?
Are you looking forward to working in groups?
When you use a question word (who, what, where, when, how) you put an auxiliary verb before the subject.
How long have you been in this class?
When who, what or which is the subject of the sentence, you don't use do.
What gives you most help, your textbook or your dictionary?

1 Read the rules for making questions in the grammar box. Find one more example of each rule in *Reading and speaking* activity 4.

2 Work in pairs and think of questions that you could ask your fellow students. Work with another pair and ask your questions. Then tell the rest of the class some of the things you have found out about your partners.

WRITING AND SPEAKING

1 Look through *Reward* Upper-intermediate. Write five questions about the book to ask your partner.

Where's the pronunciation guide?

2 Work in pairs and exchange questions. Can you answer your partner's questions?

The pronunciation guide is at the back of the book.

Question tags; negative questions;
imperative questions; suggestions; reply questions

SOUNDS AND SPEAKING

1 Read the dialogue. Decide where Pat's sentences a–g
below go in the dialogue.

PAT (1) ____

DON Yes. In fact, I speak French and Russian.

PAT (2) ____

DON Yes, when I was seventeen, I did Russian for a
couple of years.

PAT (3) ____

DON No, I've almost forgotten it. It's easy to forget a
language if you don't practise.

PAT (4) ____

DON No, I practised when I was in France.

PAT (5) ____

DON For the day?

PAT (6) ____

DON Does it? I didn't know that. Aren't you worried
about the cost?

PAT (7) ____

a You speak French, don't you?
b Why not? It only takes three hours by train now,
doesn't it?
c Russian! You didn't learn Russian at school,
did you?
d I've got an idea. Let's go to Paris, shall we?
e Well, say something in Russian, will you?
f No, it'll be good fun. And there'll be plenty of
opportunities to speak French, won't there?
g And what about your French? You haven't forgotten
that as well, have you?

2 📼 Now listen to the dialogue. Write R if you
think the intonation is rising on Pat's question tags
and F if you think the intonation is falling.
For more information on the intonation of
question tags, see the Grammar review at the back
of the book.

3 Work in pairs and act out the dialogue.

LISTENING

1 Look at these statements about English and decide if
you agree with them. Work in pairs and compare your
answers with a partner.

You'll forget a language if you don't use it.

You can learn a language outside the classroom.

The best way to learn a language is to go to the
country where it is spoken.

You should always use the dictionary if you don't
understand a word.

Don't worry about making mistakes; it's more
important to make yourself understood.

Learning about grammar is very useful.

Listening, especially to native speakers, is the most
difficult skill to develop.

Children find it easier to learn a foreign language.

2 📼 Listen to Hazel, Michael and Janet talking
about how they learned a foreign language.
Find out where and when they first started learning
the language.

3 Work in pairs. Put the name of the speaker by the
statements in 1 that you think they would agree with.
📼 Now listen and check.

GRAMMAR

Tags after affirmative statements
*You speak French, **don't you**?*
*There'll be opportunities to speak French, **won't there**?*
Tags after negative statements
*You haven't forgotten that as well, **have you**?*
*You didn't learn Russian at school, **did you**?*
Negative questions
***Aren't you worried** about the cost?*
Imperative questions
***Say** something in Russian, **will you**?*
Suggestions
***Let's** go to Paris, **shall we**?*
Reply questions
*It only takes three hours.   **Does it?** I didn't know that.*
*He doesn't like grammar.   **Doesn't he?** I thought he did.*
**For more information, see the Grammar review at the
back of the book.**

SOUNDS AND SPEAKING

1 Aim: to prepare for listening; to present the target structures for the grammar section.

The *Sounds* work in *Reward* Upper-intermediate focuses more on the pronunciation, stress and intonation of whole sentences, rather than on individual sounds. Ask the students to read the dialogue and decide where Pat's missing sentences go.

> **Answers**
> 1a 2c 3e 4g 5d 6b 7f

2 Aim: to focus on intonation.

● 📼 Point out that more information about intonation in question tags is given in the Grammar review. They may like to read this before they do the activity. Play the tape, pausing after each speaker. Rewind and check students answers.

> **Answers**
> aF bR cR dF eR fF gR

3 Aim: to practise speaking.

● The activities in this section establish the dialogue as a model for some guided speaking practice. Ask the students to act out the dialogue.

● If there is time, ask the students to write a similar dialogue and act it out in front of the class.

LISTENING

1 Aim: to prepare for listening.

● Ask the students to read the statements about learning a foreign language and decide if they agree with them. When they have finished, ask them to compare their answers with their partners.

2 Aim: to listen for specific information.

● Before you play the tape explain that the speakers are all talking about how they learned a foreign language. Ask them to find out where and when they first started learning the language.

> **Answers**
> **Hazel:** learned at school, a long time ago.
> **Michael:** learned by living in the country as a child.
> **Janet:** learned by playing cassettes in the car, two years ago.

3 Aim: to listen for main ideas; to listen and infer.

● Ask the students to work in pairs. Explain that it isn't necessary to understand everything the speakers say, but that they can infer which statements the speakers would agree with.

> **Answers**
> **Hazel:** You'll forget a language if you don't use it.
> **Janet:** You can learn a language outside the classroom.
> **Michael:** The best way to learn a language is to go to the country where they speak it.
> **Janet:** You should always use the dictionary if you don't understand a word.
> **Michael:** Don't worry about making mistakes; it's more important to make yourself understood.
> **Hazel:** Learning about grammar is very useful.
> **Janet:** Listening, especially to native speakers, is the most difficult skill to develop.
> **Michael:** Children find it easier to learn a foreign language.

● You may want to play the tape a second time before checking their answers.

GRAMMAR

1 Aim: to focus on question tags, negative questions, imperative questions and reply questions.

● Ask the students to read the information in the grammar box.

● Explain to the students that it isn't essential to use these target structures, but if they do, they'll sound more fluent.

> **Answers**
> 1 with a negative tag using the auxiliary
> 2 with a positive tag using the auxiliary
> 3 with the auxiliary **will**
> 4 with the auxiliary **shall**
> 5 with a negative auxiliary followed by the subject
> 6 by using the positive auxiliary verb and personal pronoun after a positive statement and a negative auxiliary verb and personal pronoun after a negative statement

2 Aim: to practise using question tags, negative questions, imperative questions and reply questions.

> **Answers**
> 1 will you   2 have you   3 shall we
> 4 have you   5 can't you   6 Isn't it
> 7 Didn't you   8 Are you

3 Aim: to practise using question tags.

● Ask the students to look back at the statements in *Listening* activity 1 and rewrite them with question tags.

> **Answers**
> wont't you?   can't you?   isn't it?   shouldn't you?
> isn't it?   isn't it?   isn't it?   don't they?

● Ask them to work in pairs and ask each other the questions. Encourage them to talk about their opinions about different ways of learning English.

WRITING AND VOCABULARY

1 Aim: to analyse mistakes.

● Explain that the composition has a number of mistakes. It is sometimes easier to spot other people's mistakes, but it's important to develop the ability to spot one's own.

● Ask the students to look at the first four mistakes, which have been marked, and to analyse what's wrong.

> **Answers**
> **Since** - wrong word
> **have trying** - missing word
> **learning** - wrong word/verb form
> **language foreign** - word order

● Now ask the students to read the whole composition and to use the symbols to analyse the other mistakes. They need not correct the composition at this stage.

2 Aim: to analyse mistakes; to present words in the vocabulary box.

● Ask the students to work in pairs and to use the words in the box to analyse the mistakes in the composition.

● Ask the students to discuss the mistakes, and correct them.

> **Answers**
> **For** many years, people have **been** trying to find the best way **to learn** a **foreign** language. For me, the best way is to **stay for** a long time in the country, such as England or **the** United States. Listening **comprehension** is extremely **hard** and you **need** to **listen** to **authentic** English. **It** is good to **listen** to the radio and **watch** television in English. **Grammar** is important as **well**, so you must spend **a** long time **learning** the rules. **Finally,** the most important thing to do is **take** the opportunity to talk **to people** as much as you can. Do you agree?

3 Aim: to practise writing.

● Ask the students to write a composition with the same title. Go round and make sure they are avoiding the same mistakes. When they have finished their first draft, ask the students to read it through and check they have avoided the types of mistake mentioned in activity 2.

4 Aim: to analyse mistakes.

● When the students have finished checking their composition ask them to give it to their partner. Can their partner find any mistakes? Do the students share the same ideas as to the best way to learn English?

1 Look at the grammar box. How do you form the following?

1 question tags after affirmative statements
2 question tags after negative statements
3 question tags after imperatives
4 question tags after *let's* to make a suggestion
5 negative questions
6 reply questions

2 Complete the sentences with a suitable question word or tag.

1 Pass me your book, _____ ?
2 You haven't been waiting long, _____ ?
3 Let's finish now, _____ ?
4 You haven't got a pen, _____ ?
5 'We must go.' 'Oh, _____ you stay longer?'
6 '_____ dreadful weather?' 'Yes, it is.'
7 'I didn't like the film.' '_____ ? I did.'
8 'I'm tired.' '_____ ? You don't look tired.'

3 Choose four statements from *Listening* activity 1 and rewrite them with question tags.
Work in pairs and ask each other your questions.

WRITING AND VOCABULARY

1 This composition was written by a learner of English. It contains twenty-three mistakes. Mark the mistakes in the following ways.
– Underline any words which are wrong.
– Circle and arrow any words which are in the wrong position.
– Insert any words which are missing.
The first four have been done for you.

2 Work in pairs. Use these words to analyse the mistakes in the composition.

punctuation   spelling   word order   missing word   wrong word   preposition   verb form   noun   adjective

Are there any mistakes which you often make?

3 Write a composition with the same title. When you have finished your first draft, read it through and check that you have avoided the types of mistake mentioned in activity 2.

4 Work in pairs and exchange your compositions. Do you both agree on the best way to learn English?

The best way to learn English

Since many years, people have been trying to find the best way to learning a language foreign. For me, the best way is to last a long time in the country, such as England or United States. Listening comprehension is extremely hardy and you needed to hear to English auhtentic. it is good to hear to the radio and wacth television in English. Gramer is important as wel, so you must spend long time to learn the rules. At last, the most important thing to do is seize the opportunity to talk at peple as much as you can. Do you agree?

2 *Friends and relations*

The indefinite, definite and zero article

SPEAKING AND READING

1 Work in groups of three or four and discuss the following.

1 Does your language have a familiar and a formal way of addressing people? If so, do you think this is better than the neutral *you* in English?

2 How long do you usually take to use the familiar form with people?

3 How long do you usually take to use their first names?

4 Do you ever use first names at work?

5 Do you kiss people to greet them? If so, how many times, and when?

2 Read the article and decide which of the following statements describe the writer's problem. (For the moment, ignore the gaps in the text.)

1 He doesn't know how to greet people.

2 He doesn't know how to address people.

3 He's never made any social mistakes.

4 He doesn't like using first names.

(1) ____. Should you kiss friends and acquaintances once, twice, three times or not at all? On the hand or the cheek? Should I kiss only women when saying hello or am I supposed to give men a kiss (or a bear hug) too? Am I expected to shake hands when saying goodbye, or only when saying hello? I've more or less given up getting it right and comfort myself that foreigners' mistakes are forgivable. But I usually make a little effort to crack the code. Getting your handshakes or bear hugs right can be another way of getting your verb endings straightened out. Even if you know you're getting it wrong most of the time, you can at least give a nod towards the local grammar of etiquette.

(2) ____. Thus, in Russia earlier this year, my heart sank when my companions in the couchette compartment I was travelling in addressed me, the moment they saw me, with the familiar *ty* instead of *vy*. My experience is that *ty* from a stranger usually means trouble. I am uncomfortable too, with the idea – apparently introduced in Sweden some years ago – that the polite *ni* form should be abandoned, even in banks or formal interviews with the Prime Minister, in favour of the intimate form.

(3) ____. It's not just a matter of familiar *du* versus formal *Sie*. If you call somebody *Sie*, you are also expected to call them *Herr* and *Frau*. And you may go on calling them *Herr Braun* and *Frau Schmidt* for years. A friend in Bonn described how her mother and a male neighbour sometimes go on holiday together. The relationship is close, but the two of them call each other *Herr B* and *Frau L.*

(4) ____. It sounded such a good idea and I decided to follow her example. But then she confessed that she had been reprimanded for breaking the rules. (She used to live in the United States, which may be part of the problem.) I was pleased when a friendly acquaintance, who is a civil servant, suggested, after we had met only a few times, that we should move away from the *Herr Crawshaw – Herr X* routine. But he, too, admitted that he was more likely to be on first name terms with foreigners than with Germans – even those he knew well.

(5) ____. A politician confessed that he did not know the first name of his press assistant. Then he suddenly remembered. His wife commented, wryly: 'Knows her first name, eh? A bit suspicious, don't you think?'

Adapted from an article by Steve Crawshaw, *The Independent*

2

GENERAL COMMENTS

Level and correction

Your learners are now at upper–intermediate level, and may be experiencing a *plateau,* at which they feel they are making little or no progress. Some learners may need help in becoming more fluent, but generally now is the time to put the focus of learning more on accuracy, especially if they intend to take an examination, such as Cambridge First Certificate in English, at the end of this course.

You will need to explain at this stage what your policy on correction will be. Tell the students that you will not necessarily correct every mistake they make, as this will impede the development of their fluency. But you may need to correct them a little more frequently than they have been used to so far. In longer discussion activities, rather than interrupt the students you may like to note down their mistakes, and talk about them at the end of the activity.

Cross-cultural training

If you have used other levels of *Reward*, you will be aware that cross-cultural training constitutes a discreet but important part of the course design. Much of this training involves exposure to foreign cultures and opportunities to become more aware of one's own culture. It may be useful to point out that the concept of culture is defined not simply by its geographical origin (North America, Western Europe, East Asia) but also by professional and social context, generation and gender. For example, as a teacher of English as a Foreign Language, you will probably have much in common with a similar teacher from a culture which is geographically distant from your own.

SPEAKING AND READING

1 Aim: to practise speaking; to prepare for reading.
● This lesson is about cultural and generational differences. Ask the students to discuss their answers to the questions. Then one student from each group should give feedback to the class on answers to the questions.

2 Aim: to read for main ideas.
● Ask the students to read the passage and to decide which statement best describes the writer's problem. The correct statement reflects the main idea of the article.

Answer
2

3 Aim: to read and evaluate the text.

● At this level, you should be encouraging the students to look at the style of a passage, and to evaluate why a passage was written and who it was written for. This kind of information will also be useful when the student is confronted by a particularly difficult passage.

● Ask the students to decide what type of article it is. If you have time, give the class some newspapers and ask them to find examples of different kinds of articles.

4 Aim: to read for text organisation.

● Topic sentences are relevant in helping students not only to read and understand, but also to write well-planned compositions. You may need to explain that some writers choose not to use topic sentences at the beginning of a paragraph for reasons of personal style. However, there is usually a topic sentence somewhere in most paragraphs.

● Ask the students to read the passage again and to decide where the sentences go.

Answers
1 b   2 e   3 f   4 a   5 c

● You may like to encourage the students to look for topic sentences in other newspaper passages or articles.

5 Aim: to read for specific information; to read and infer.

● A writer sometimes does not state directly but merely implies what he or she wants to say. Ask the students to decide if these statements are true or false.

● Ask the students to work with another pair and to check their answers.

Answers
1 True   2 True   3 False   4 False

6 Aim: to practise speaking; to read and evaluate the passage.

● Ask the students to talk about their answers to the questions. Here are some suggested answers for 1 - 3.

Possible answers
1 Because it suggested that they were going to be too friendly towards him or talk to him a great deal when he wanted peace and quiet.
2 Probably because he normally maintains the distinction between formality and informality.
3 He thinks it's too strict.

VOCABULARY AND SPEAKING

1 Aim: to present the words in the vocabulary box; to practise speaking; to revise parts of the body.

● This kind of categorisation activity continues the discussion of the topic raised in the reading passage. It also creates an opportunity to revise parts of the body.

Answers
2 cuddle hug kiss laugh smile
3 beckon - hand, blow - mouth, lips, bow - body, waist, chew - mouth, teeth clap - hands, cuddle- arm, body, frown - forehead, grin - mouth, hug - body, arm, kiss - mouth, lips, kneel - knees, laugh - mouth, nod - head, nudge - elbow, pat - hand pinch - fingers, point - finger, scratch- finger, shrug- shoulder smile - mouth, stare - eye, stoop - body, shoulders, stretch - arm, leg, wave - hand, arm, wink - eye, yawn - mouth

2 Aim: to provide a model for guided speaking practice; to read for text organisation.

● This activity focuses on behaviour in offices. In Britain and America, it is very common for the atmosphere to appear quite informal, with everyone using first names. It is sometimes difficult for people from other cultures to understand that despite the appearance of informality, relationships between people still follow a fairly formal code. Ask the students to read the conversation and to put the sentences in the right order.

● Make sure everyone realises that George is a new employee, Jane is a more senior member of staff and Bob is the boss.

● 🖵 Play the tape and ask students to check their answers.

Answers
a f c e b d g h

3 Aim: to use a model dialogue to give guided speaking practice; to examine cultural differences.

● Ask students if the conversation would take place in their country. If not, what would be different?

● Ask the students to rewrite the dialogue so that it's suitable for their country. They may want to insert more complex names and honorifics (sir, doctor, comrade etc), so help them translate these into English if you can.

● Ask the students to act out the dialogues in front of the class.

3 Work in pairs. The article is from a newspaper. Decide what kind of article it is. Choose from the following:

– front page news   – latest news   – political news
– foreign correspondent's diary   – social news

Can you say explain why? Does this kind of article appear in newspapers in your country?

4 A topic sentence is one that begins a paragraph by introducing the main idea. The rest of the paragraph adds further information and examples to develop the topic sentence. Five topic sentences have been removed from the passage. Choose from the sentences a–f the one which fits each gap 1–5. There is one extra sentence which you do not need to use.

a Another friend said she likes to use first names, whenever possible.

b Social norms are impossible to get right when they vary so radically across European borders.

c At work, first names are sometimes non-existent.

d For example, you shake hands when you say hello.

e Every European language has a *tu* and a *vous* form, but I am not a radical when it comes to the familiar form.

f But I find the conventions in Germany quite strict.

5 Work in pairs. Decide if these statements about the passage are true or false. Then work with another pair and compare your answers.

1 The writer thinks that people are not worried by foreigners' mistakes.

2 Knowing the social code is like knowing the grammar of a language.

3 A 'radical when it comes to the familiar form' would be someone who abandons the familiar form.

4 The writer was pleased when the companions in the couchette used the familiar form.

6 Work in pairs and answer the questions.

1 Why did the writer's heart sink when the companions in the couchette compartment used the familiar form?

2 Why does the politician's wife think it is suspicious that her husband knows his press assistant's first name?

3 What does the writer really think about the social code in Germany?

4 How would you see the writer as a travelling companion, a dinner guest or a work colleague?

VOCABULARY AND SPEAKING

1 Work in pairs. Look at the verbs in the box and answer the questions.

> beckon blow bow chew clap cuddle frown
> grin hug kiss kneel laugh nod nudge pat
> pinch point scratch shrug smile stare stoop
> stretch wave wink yawn

1 Are there any verbs which describe actions that are socially unacceptable to perform in public in your country?
You shouldn't yawn in public.

2 Which verbs describe gestures which are warm and friendly?
cuddle

3 Which part of the body do you use to perform the actions of the verbs?
beckon: hand

2 The following conversation takes place in an office. Put the sentences in the right order.

a **JANE** You must be George Dennis.

b **JANE** I'll introduce you to everyone. Let's go and meet your boss. Ah, there he is. Bob, this is George Dennis, it's his first day. George, this is Dr Robert Crewe.

c **JANE** Hello, George, pleased to meet you. Welcome to the company! My name's Jane and I'm going to show you around the office.

d **GEORGE** How do you do, sir.

e **GEORGE** Hello, Jane. Thank you very much.

f **GEORGE** Yes, that's right.

g **BOB** Call me Bob, George. Everyone calls me Bob. Welcome to the company.

h **GEORGE** Thank you, Bob.

[🔊] Listen and check.

3 Work in groups of three. Would a similar dialogue take place in your country?

Adapt the dialogue so that it is suitable for your country.
Now act out the dialogue.

The indefinite, definite and zero article

GRAMMAR

The indefinite and definite article

Here are some rules for the use of articles.

You use *a/an*:

– when you talk about something for the first time.

*I was pleased when **a** friendly acquaintance,...*

– with nouns, especially jobs, after *be* and *become*.

*...**a** friendly acquaintance who is **a** civil servant, suggested...*

You use *the*:

– with nouns which are defined by a phrase or clause.

*...when my companions in **the** couchette compartment I was travelling in...*

– when you talk about something again.

*Then he suddenly remembered **the** woman's name.*

The zero article

You don't use any article:

– with plural, abstract or uncountable nouns when you talk about something in general.

Social norms are impossible to get right.

– before the names of most countries, towns and streets.

Thus, in Russia earlier this year,...

For more information, see the Grammar review at the back of the book.

---

1 Work in pairs. Use the rules in the grammar box to explain the use of the articles or zero article in these sentences from the article on page 6.

1 Should you kiss friends and acquaintances...?

2 I am not a radical when it comes to the familiar form.

3 Should I kiss only women when saying hello?

4 A friend in Bonn described how her mother and a male neighbour...

5 ...the two of them call each other *Herr B* and *Frau L.*

6 ...he was more likely to be on first name terms with foreigners...

2 Complete the passage with the indefinite or definite article. On some occasions, both may be possible. Can you say why?

(1) ____ kiss as (2) ____ form of social greeting is, of course, no longer reserved for women. Indeed, men often exchange kisses in countries where it would be considered insulting to kiss (3) ____ woman in public. Except in (4) ____ few countries, it is now regarded as quite normal for men and women to exchange (5) ____ cheek-to-cheek salutation. There was a time, when (6) ____ custom was (7) ____ sign of fairly close friendship; nowadays it has become so pervasive that to shake hands with (8) ____ woman at (9) ____ end of (10) ____ party is regarded as (11) ____ silent equivalent of Groucho Marx's famous remark, 'I've had (12) ____ marvellous evening, but this wasn't it.'

SOUNDS

Which articles in the following noun phrases will be pronounced /ðə/ and which ones will be pronounced /ði:/? Put them in two columns.

the article   the smile   the head   the elbow   the arm   the finger   the body   the eyes

[cassette icon] Listen and check. As you listen, say the phrases aloud.

LISTENING

1 You're going to hear Mary Davies and her grandson Peter talking about how certain social customs in Britain have changed over the last fifty years. First of all, look at the social customs in the chart below. Think about how they have changed in your country and write notes in the column.

	Your country	**Mary Davies**	**Peter Davies**
Behaviour of children			
Head of the family			
Age for getting married			
Manners and ways of addressing people			
Living with parents and grandparents			

2 [cassette icon] Work in groups of three.

Student A: Turn to Communication activity 8 on page 94.

Student B: Turn to Communication activity 13 on page 95.

Student C: Turn to Communication activity 21 on page 96.

GRAMMAR

1 Aim: to present and practise using the article.

● Ask the students to read the information in the grammar box and then do the exercises. There is not enough space within the lesson to explore all the rules governing the use of the article. If students need more information, ask them to turn to the Grammar review at the back of the book. The rules which are focused on in this lesson are the ones which can be used most often.

Answers
1 Zero article with plural nouns when you talk about something in general.
2 Indefinite article after the verb **be**.
3 Zero article with plural nouns when you talk about something in general.
4 Indefinite article when you talk about something for the first time.
5 Definite article when you talk about something again.
6 Zero article with plural nouns when you talk about something in general.

2 Aim: to practise using the article.

● Ask the students to complete the passage using the indefinite or definite article. When they have finished, ask the students to work in pairs and discuss the reasons for their decisions.

Answers
1 The, a 2 a 3 a 4 a 5 a 6 the 7 a
8 a 9 the 10 a 11 the 12 a

SOUNDS

Aim: to focus on the two ways of pronouncing *the*.

● Write the word *the* on the board and elicit the two ways of pronouncing it. Ask the students if they know the rule for pronouncing it in the two different ways. If they know, ask them to do the exercise. If they don't know, ask them to listen and work out the rule.

● 🔲 Play the tape. Ask the students to say the words aloud and check their answers.

Answers
/ði:/: the article, the elbow, the arm, the eyes
the is pronounced /ði:/ as it is followed by a vowel.
/ðə/: the smile, the head, the finger, the body
the is pronounced /ðə/ as it is followed by a consonant.

LISTENING

1 Aim: to prepare for listening.

● This activity focuses on the generational aspect of cross-cultural training. Ask students to predict what the speakers are going to say about the topics in the chart.

2 Aim: to practise listening for specific information.

● Explain that you're going to play a tape in which two people, Mary and Peter Davies, talk about the topics in the chart. Ask the students to work in threes and to turn to the relevant Communication activity. They should listen and find the answers to their particular questions.

● 🔲 Play the tape.

3 Aim: to check comprehension; to practise speaking.

● This is the first time that note-taking of listening material has been practised in the *Reward* series. It is a skill which will become increasingly relevant to the students. They should build up their confidence gradually by working together and by making notes from memory and not at the same time as they are listening, which is difficult to do, especially if your students' first language has a different script (Greek, Cyrillic, Japanese etc). Ask the students to work together and check their answers. They should try and remember as much as they can and complete the chart with as much detail as possible.

● 🔲 Play the tape again.

Answers

	Mary Davies	**Peter Davies**
Behaviour of children	Discipline strict	Less discipline
Head of the family	Father	Discussion by all family
Age for getting married	21–22	Early thirties
Manners and ways of addressing people	Formal	Informal often first names
Living with parents and grandparents	Children left home when they got married	Children leave home when they go to college/ university

4 Aim: to practise speaking.

● The students may not be old enough to have experienced such changes for themselves, but perhaps parents or older members of their family have. Ask them to try and remember if these people have talked about changes in customs over the last fifty years.

WRITING

1 Aim: to read for text organisation; to prepare for guided writing practice.

● This is the first of several letter-writing activities in *Reward* Upper-intermediate. Tell the students that the letter is from a grandmother to her granddaughter and ask them what kind of letter they expect it to be. Ask the students to put the parts of the letter in the right order.

Answers
A F C E B D

2 Aim: to check reading comprehension.

● Ask the students to compare the information about customs in Britain in Mary's letter with those in their own country fifty years ago.

3 Aim: to focus on the layout of informal letters.

● It may be necessary for the students to lay out letters in the English way, especially if they are going to take an exam such as Cambridge First Certificate of English. If this is not the case, you may simply want to draw their attention to the English style, but not oblige them to adopt it themselves. However, you should discourage them from attempting to translate into English any formulae which are peculiar to letter-writing conventions in their own language.

Answers
1 The person sending the letter places their address at the top right-hand corner of the letter.
2 The date is placed below the address.
3 **Dear ...**
4 **Lots of love, Grandma**

The way in which Mary writes the answers to the questions suggests a conversational, informal style. The concluding *Lots of love* suggests that it is an informal letter.

4 Aim: to use the letter as a model for guided-writing practice.

● Ask the students to use the letter as a model for their own letter. They should write about one of the customs they made notes about in *Listening* activity 2. You may like to ask the students to do this activity for homework.

3 Work together. What do Mary and Peter say about the social customs? Complete the chart in as much detail as possible.

[tape] Now listen again and check.

4 Work in pairs. Talk about how customs have changed in your country in the last fifty years. Compare them with the customs in Britain.

WRITING

1 Mary Davies is writing to her granddaughter, Helena, who is doing a history project at school about changes in social customs. Helena has asked her grandmother about social customs when she was young. Put the sections of Mary's letter in the right order.

2 Decide if the customs Mary describes were similar to those in your country fifty years ago.

3 In groups, discuss the way English people write informal letters.

1 The address on the letter is Mary's. Where has she placed her address?
2 Where is the date?
3 How does the letter begin?
4 How does the letter end?

Do you write informal letters in a similar way? What else tells you that it is an informal letter?

4 Write an informal letter to a penfriend about one of the social customs you made notes on in *Listening* activity 2. You can use Mary's letter as a model.

A

8, Meadow Grove
Nottingham NG6 7HF

B

Some people had a boyfriend when they were eighteen or nineteen, but I met my first boyfriend when I was twenty-one. Some people got married at eighteen or nineteen, but most of us waited until we were in our twenties.

C

Thanks for your letter. It was good to hear from you and to hear about the friends you have made at your new school. The history project you are working on sounds very interesting and I hope that this information will be helpful.

D

If you have any more questions, let me know and I will try to answer them.

Lots of love,

Grandma

E

You asked about how I made friends when I was a teenager. Well, when I was your age, I had lots of friends too and I saw them at school or at the weekends. They didn't all know each other as I knew people from the tennis club, from school and from lots of other places. Sometimes I met people at dances and other social occasions.

F

May 26th

Dear Helena,

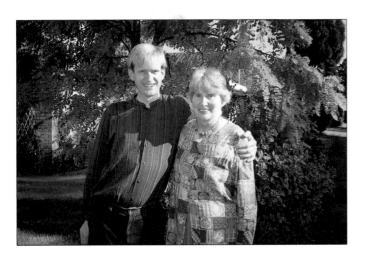

3 *Passion play*

Tense review: present tenses

SPEAKING

1 Work in pairs. Make a list of popular hobbies and leisure activities which people in your country enjoy.

Now answer these questions.

Do the activities involve teamwork or individual skill?
Do they involve or interest both men and women?
Do any of the activities involve collecting things?
Do you have a strong passion for them, a mild interest or no interest at all?
If there are any that you have little or no interest in, do you think people who enjoy them are strange?
How much time do you spend on your hobby or leisure activity?

Our taxi driver has just discovered that one of his passengers supports AC Milan. As he hears the name of his team's deadly rivals he holds up his Internazionale Football Club season ticket and kisses it as if it were a religious icon. The San Siro stadium appears in the distance, a sight as awe-inspiring as Milan's beautiful cathedral. Our driver cries: '*San Siro – la Scala de calcio*! A temple!'

This story illustrates the relationship between Italy's three great loves: religion, opera and football. It's not just a game. Even a moderate sports fan cannot fail to be moved by the spectacle of Italian football and its faithful supporters.

We come as pilgrims in search of the divine sporting experience: a *Serie A* match at the 80,000 capacity San Siro, home of Milan's twin giants, Inter and current champions, AC Milan. Today, Inter is playing at home to Parma. If Parma win today, they can replace Milan at the top of the league.

The *Gazetta dello Sport* is building up the match in dramatic style; the Milan sporting newspaper is comparing it to a battle of operas; it is being played under floodlights, the two cities have great opera houses, and the virtuoso performers are the players.

The majority of the crowd at the San Siro are well dressed, with a high percentage of women. In Milan, the women sit in the expensive seats in their dark glasses, and in winter wear their fur coats. Football attracts the rich and powerful in Italian society. It's big business, one of Italy's most profitable industries. Being seen in the right place at the San Siro is as important as attending the first night of an opera at *La Scala*.

It is no coincidence that the game is played on the holy day, Sunday, because football is Italy's sacred pastime. Italians call it *la Giornata* – the Day – as if the rest of the week is a mere preparation. On Sunday afternoons, a million Italians go to watch football, while 25 million listen to match reports on the radio or watch the frantic commentary of TV reporters describing action from games which cannot be broadcast until the evening.

Before kick-off, the Parma fans are shouting at the Inter fans, who are replying just as loudly. When the teams arrive on the pitch, the Inter fans let off flares, turn up the volume and wave flags, producing the most electric atmosphere I've ever experienced at a sporting event.

Inter starts well, but after ten minutes, Parma scores a beautifully simple goal. Then Inter equalises, but their captain is sent off after a deliberate handball. Inter scores again after thirty-seven minutes from a free kick. Parma gets close again just before half time, but Inter scores their third goal. The fans start singing and whistling again. Parma scores again, but it's Inter's day at the end of the match.

The Italians call *Serie A* 'the most beautiful league in the world.' And they're right.

Adapted from *Passion Play* by Beverley Glick, *The Observer*

3

GENERAL COMMENTS

Revision

Despite the relatively high level of English which students using *Reward* Upper-intermediate will have, it may be helpful to go back over some areas to consolidate or clarify form or use. Much of the work in the early part of *Reward* Upper-intermediate focuses on tenses which the student will already have come across, but either the uses may be new, or there is a comparison of two or more tenses. Everyone will have come across the two present tenses, but in the first grammar box in this lesson, their uses are compared. In the second grammar box, the function of the present continuous for criticising behaviour and habits is presented, probably for the first time. If you think the students have successfully acquired all these uses, then spend less time in this lesson working on the grammar, and more on skills.

SPEAKING

1 Aim: to practise speaking; to introduce the theme of the lesson.

● This activity introduces the topic of the lesson, which is different leisure activities and whether they are a hobby or an obsession. Ask students to work in pairs and to discuss their answers to the questions.

● Ask the students to report on their discussions to the rest of the class. Find out which group has the most surprising or extreme opinions.

2 Aim: to practise speaking.

● These statements are meant to present controversial or extreme opinions. Ask the students to discuss them in pairs and then compare their answers with another pair.

READING

1 Aim: to prepare for reading.

● Ask students to discuss if their country has a national sport. Is football a popular sport? If so, why do they think it is so popular? Who does it appeal to, both men and women? The students can either discuss the questions in pairs or as a whole class.

● There may be students who are not interested in football. However, the subject of football was chosen to explore both passion for and lack of interest in the sport, as well as discovering people's leisure activities in general.

2 Aim: reading for main ideas.

● Ask the students to read the statements and then to read the passage. They should choose the statement which best describes the main idea of the passage.

● Point out that all the statements are true, but the writer is trying to make a link between religious, operatic and sporting passion.

3 Aim: to read and link ideas; to understand complex sentences.

● Sometimes it's hard to keep the thread of a writer's argument or description, so this activity encourages the student to take a closer look at more complex sentences. Ask the students to read and answer the questions.

Answers
1 AC Milan 2 yes 3 the match 4 for the match

4 Aim: to evaluate the writer's style.

● Ask the students to look at the sometimes colourful language the writer uses to describe the passion of the fans.

Answers
... kisses it as if it were a religious icon
... a sight as awe-inspiring as Milan's beautiful cathedral.
Even a moderate sports fan cannot fail to be moved by the spectacle ...
... football is Italy's sacred pastime.
... frantic commentary of TV reporters.
... producing the most electric atmosphere I've ever experienced ...
The fans start singing and whistling again.

GRAMMAR

Aim: to focus on the uses of the present simple and continuous tenses.

● Ask the students to read the information in the grammar box and then do the exercises.

Answers
1 present simple for a general truth or state
2 present simple for an event in a story
3 present continuous for a temporary action
4 present continuous for the background in a story
5 present simple for an event in a story
6 present simple for a fact

● The uses of the two tenses overlap, so as long as students recognise the tense itself, other answers may be acceptable.

WRITING AND SPEAKING

1 Aim: to practise using the present simple and present continuous tenses in a writing context.

● Ask the students to imagine they are watching an important sporting event. Tell them to take notes on the key events to prepare for their commentary.

2 Aim: to practise using tenses.

● Ask the students to work in groups of four or five. Tell them that they are going to give their commentaries to the rest of the group. Explain that they must not tell the group what sport the commentary is focusing on. As they give their commentary the other students in the group have to guess the sporting activity.

2 Work in pairs. Discuss these statements about leisure activities. Do you agree with them?

1 Collecting things like stamps or coins is boring.
2 It is better to enjoy a range of activities than to concentrate on just one.
3 Most people prefer to watch sport on television rather than take part themselves.
4 Some sports can only be played by men.
5 Football is popular with both men and women.

Now work with another pair and compare your answers.

READING

1 Work in pairs. You're going to read a newspaper article about football in Italy.

Does your country have a national sport? What is it? Is it popular only with men or with women as well? Can people become obsessive about a national sport?

2 Read the article and decide which of the following statements best describes why the writer calls it *Passion play*.

1 Football is a game which is played with passion.
2 A *passion play* is a religious drama, and the writer is suggesting that football is similar.
3 The fans are passionate about the way their team plays.

3 Read the sentences from the article and answer the questions.

1 *...the name of his team's deadly rivals.* – Who are his team's deadly rivals?
2 *Even a moderate sports fan cannot fail to be moved by the spectacle...* – Is he moved or not?
3 *...the Milan sporting newspaper is comparing it to a battle of operas; it is being played under floodlights...* – Who or what does *it* refer to?
4 *...as if the rest of the week is a mere preparation.* – A preparation for what?

4 Write down any words or phrases which the writer uses to describe the *passion* of the spectators of football.

Even a moderate sports fan cannot fail to be moved by the spectacle.

GRAMMAR

> Tense review: present tenses
> **You use the present simple to talk about:**
> **– a general truth, such as a fact or a state.**
> *On Sunday afternoons, a million Italians* **go** *to watch football.*
> **– something that is regular, such as a routine, custom or habit.**
> *In Milan, the women* **sit** *in the expensive seats, and* **wear** *their fur coats.*
> **– events in a story or a commentary on a game.**
> *...after 10 minutes, Parma* **scores** *a beautifully simple goal.*
> **You use the present continuous to talk about:**
> **– an action which is happening at the moment or an action or state which is temporary.**
> *Today, Inter* **is playing** *at home to Parma.*
> **– the background in a story.**
> *Before kick off, the Parma fans* **are shouting** *at the Inter fans.*

Look at these sentences from the article. Decide which present tense they use and why.

1 ...one of his passengers supports AC Milan.
2 The San Siro stadium appears in the distance...
3 The *Gazetta dello Sport* is building up the match...
4 ...the Parma fans are shouting at the Inter fans who are replying just as loudly.
5 When the teams arrive on the pitch...
6 The Italians call it 'the most beautiful league in the world'.

WRITING AND SPEAKING

1 Think of an important sporting event, such as the opening of the Olympic Games, or the final of the World Cup. Imagine you're giving a commentary of the scene to radio listeners. Makes notes on what you can 'see'.

2 Work in groups of four or five. Give your commentaries to the rest of the group but don't mention the name of the sport. Can the others guess the sporting event you are describing?

Criticising behaviour and habits;
agreeing and disagreeing

VOCABULARY AND SPEAKING

Work in groups of three or four.
One student chooses one of the
leisure activities in the box. The
other members of the group have
to ask questions to guess the leisure
activity you have chosen. You can
only answer their questions with
yes or *no*. Use the following
questions to find out about
the leisure activity or make up
your own.

Do you do it on your own?
Do you do it outside or inside?
Does it need any special equipment?
Do you have to be fit to do it?
Is it usually done by both men
and women?
Does it involve collecting
something?
Is it a sport?
Is it dangerous?

> baseball hunting bullfighting
> motor racing surfing tennis
> riding golf athletics boxing
> chess knitting dancing
> mountaineering gambling pottery
> fishing yoga jogging

SPEAKING AND LISTENING

1 What hobbies do other students in
the class have? Find out who has:

– the most interesting hobby
– the most expensive hobby
– the most dangerous hobby

2 You're going to hear Dave,
Jane, Sarah and Tim talking about
their hobbies. Listen to a section of
each of the four interviews and try
to guess what their hobbies are.

3 Listen to the whole of each interview. Did you guess the hobbies
correctly? Make notes about their hobbies and how long they have been
doing them.

4 Work in pairs. Discuss whether Dave, Jane, Sarah and Tim are describing
hobbies or obsessions.

5 Here are some of the things that the speakers' friends and families have said
about their hobbies. Put the name of the speaker referred to next to each
comment.

1 'If only she'd do something different as well – at least at the weekend!'
2 'He's always watching them. If only he were interested in something a bit
   more up-to-date.'
3 'It's definitely an obsession. You know he even watches it on the TV when
   he's seen it live!'
4 'It can't be good for you to do it so often.'
5 'It's boring. All they do is kick a ball around. I wish he spent more time
   with me.'
6 'I wish it were more exciting. I just can't see the point of digging up the
   past.'
7 'She looks great! I just wish I could be that disciplined.'
8 'He's absolutely right. They <u>are</u> the best things on TV.'

Compare your answers with your partner.

6 Now listen to the tape and check your answers.

VOCABULARY AND SPEAKING

1 Aim: to present the words in the vocabulary box; to practise speaking.
● Many of the words in the vocabulary box will be known or recognisable to the students, but ask them to look at the words and to check they understand them. If there are any unfamiliar words, ask other students to explain them or mime them. Ask the students to work in groups of three or four and to follow the instructions for the *yes/no* question game.

SPEAKING AND LISTENING

1 Aim: to practise speaking; to prepare for listening.
● Ask the students to think about their own hobbies, and decide if these are interesting to others, expensive or dangerous. Set a limit of three or four minutes and ask the students to go round finding out who has the most interesting, expensive and dangerous hobbies in the class.

● Ask the students to write the hobbies on the board. As a class, decide which ones are the most interesting, expensive or dangerous.

2 Aim: to listen and infer; to prepare for listening to a longer passage.
● Explain that the four speakers are talking about their hobbies but without mentioning the name of the hobby. Ask the students to listen and guess what the hobby is.

● 🔲 Play the tape but don't check the students' answers until after the full listening in activity 3.

3 Aim: to listen for main ideas.
● This activity checks the students' answers to 2, but it also makes them listen to the main ideas of what the speakers say and find one extra piece of information – how long they've been doing their hobby.

● 🔲 Play the tape and ask students to check their answers.

> **Answers**
> **Dave:** football fan, since the age of five
> **Jane:** working out in the gym, for five years
> **Sarah:** looking up family history, started three years ago
> **Tim:** watching B movies, since he was a teenager

4 Aim: to practise speaking.
● You may find that some students disagree on whether the speakers have hobbies or obsessions. Of course, many people admit to a hobby but few admit to an obsession, so the distinction is very subjective. At the very least, ask the students if they think the hobbies are strange or not.

5 Aim: to present the target structures; to prepare for listening.
● Ask the students to read the extracts from the next listening passage and decide to which speaker, Dave, Jane, Sarah or Tim, they refer.

● Ask the students to work in pairs and to compare their answers. Don't correct the students answers until they have listened to the extracts in the next activity.

6 Aim: to practise listening for specific information.
● 🔲 Play the tape and ask the students to listen and check their answers.

> **Answers**
> 1 Jane 2 Tim 3 Dave 4 Jane 5 Dave
> 6 Sarah 7 Jane 8 Tim

FUNCTIONS

1 Aim: to present expressions used for criticising someone's behaviour.

● You may need to explain that these expressions are all quite strong ways of criticising people. It is not acceptable in British and American English to criticise people to their face unless you know them very well or unless they are public figures. It may be different in the students' culture, but you may need to explain that they may cause offence if they assume their customs of criticising can be transferred into other cultural contexts.

● 🔲 Rewind the tape so that students can hear the expressions from the functions box.

> **Answers**
> Oh, I couldn't agree more.
> Oh, I disagree.
> Oh, so do I.
> Yes! He's absolutely right.

2 Aim: to practise using the target functions.

● Ask students to think of family and close friends or public figures whose behaviour they are critical of. Ensure that the activity remains light-hearted!

3 Aim: to present expressions for agreeing and disagreeing; to be aware of culturally sensitive expressions.

● It is important to remember that disagreement in British and American English is done fairly indirectly. In other cultures it may differ. For example, it would be very rare for anyone to say in a British English context *I completely disagree* as it would appear rude. The aim of this activity is to help the students become sensitive to language and culturally influenced behaviour. You may like to point out that some cultures will verbalise this expression, while others will use a gesture, for example, a shake of the head to register their disagreement.

4 Aim: to practise using expressions for criticising behaviour and agreeing and disagreeing.

● Ask the students to turn to the relevant pages in the Communication activity and follow the instructions.

SOUNDS

Aim: to focus on sentence stress for criticism.

● Explain that criticism can be made stronger or weaker according to the stress and intonation used. Ask the students to predict which words are likely to be stressed.

● 🔲 Play the tape and ask the students to listen and check. Pause the tape to allow students to repeat each sentence aloud. Make sure they use marked stress and intonation. Remind them that, usually, the stronger the stress and intonation, the stronger the criticism.

SPEAKING AND WRITING

1 Aim: to practise speaking.

● This activity is a structured discussion activity which may take fifteen to twenty minutes to do properly. Ask the students to work in two groups. It doesn't matter if the students do not agree with the view they are meant to support.

2 Aim: to practise note-taking.

● Ask the students to do this activity in their two groups, working on their arguments in favour or against the statement. Ask them to choose a representative to put forward their arguments.

● The representative from each group should talk for about one minute stating the views of the whole group. Encourage a debate and take a vote.

3 Aim: to practise writing reports.

● Ask the students to use the framework in this activity and the results of the discussion to write a report about it. You may like to ask students to do this activity for homework.

FUNCTIONS

Criticising behaviour and habits	
keep + *-ing*	She *keeps going* to the gym.
present continuous + *always*	He's *always watching* football on TV.
present simple + *just*	He *just watches* movies all day.
If only + past simple	*If only* it *were* more exciting.
I wish + past simple	*I wish* he *spent* more time with me.
All they do is + infinitive	*All they do is kick* a ball around.

Agreeing	Disagreeing
I couldn't agree more. Exactly.	*I completely disagree. Do you really think so?*
I agree. Absolutely.	*I'm not sure. That's rubbish.*
So do I. (in answer to *I think...*)	*Do you? I don't.* (in answer to *I think...*)
Nor/Neither do I. (in answer to *I don't think...*)	*Don't you? I do.* (in answer to *I don't think...*)

1 Which of the expressions in the functions box for criticising behaviour and habits or agreeing and disagreeing did you hear in *Speaking and listening* activity 6? Can you think of other sentences the speakers might say using the expressions in the box?

I wish they would only play football one day a week.

2 Think of someone you know well, and make a list of his or her annoying behaviour or habits. Tell a partner about this person using some of the expressions in the functions box.

My father is always leaving the lid off the toothpaste.

3 There are some expressions in the functions box which speakers of English might use to agree or disagree. Can you use their equivalents in your language? If not, what do you say?

4 Work in pairs.

Student A: Turn to Communication activity 1 on page 92.
Student B: Turn to Communication activity 19 on page 96.

Do you know anyone who behaves like these people? Tell the class about them.

SOUNDS

Look at these sentences. The speakers are making complaints about other people's behaviour. Underline the words you think the speaker will stress to emphasise the complaint.

1 'They keep fighting each other.'
2 'All they do is kick a ball around.'
3 'He's always watching TV.'
4 'He just spends the whole time playing music.'
5 'I wish it were more exciting.'
6 'If only he spent more time with his family.'

🔊 Listen and check. As you listen, say each sentence aloud.

SPEAKING AND WRITING

1 Work in two groups. You're going to take part in a discussion about the following statement:

Hobbies are a necessary and important part of your life. People without hobbies are boring.

Group A: You agree with the statement. Make a list of points to support this view.
Group B: You disagree with the statement. Make a list of points against this view.

2 Choose two people from each group to present the arguments agreeing or disagreeing with the statement. Prepare to talk for about one minute.

Your teacher will organise the discussion.

3 A magazine is publishing a series of reports on *Hobbies are a necessary and important part of your life. People without hobbies are boring.* Write a report on your discussion for the magazine. Introduce the subject and say what it's about.

The discussion was about the statement that hobbies are a necessary part of your life and that people without hobbies are boring.

Say what the arguments of people who agreed with the statement were and give some examples.

People who agreed with the statement argued that...

Say what the arguments against the statement were and give some examples.

The arguments against were...

Describe the result of the vote.

The result of the vote was five people agreed with the statement and two people disagreed.

4 *Twenty-four hours in your town*

Tense review: talking about the future; making suggestions and responding to them

VOCABULARY AND LISTENING

1 Work in pairs. Look at the words in the box and decide what you could use them to talk about. Put them in groups of your own choice.

> aisle *a la carte* box office café
> cash desk circle guided tour
> cloakroom course opening hours
> department store display
> escalator exhibit foyer interval
> menu reservation row scenery
> sculpture service shelf snack
> stage stalls stroll till tip

Theatre/cinema: aisle, circle...

Think of other words which can go in these groups.

2 🔲 Listen to five telephone conversations. Put the number of the conversation by its purpose.

a an enquiry about opening and closing times ☐
b making a complaint ☐
c making a reservation ☐
d information about services ☐
e an enquiry about starting and finishing times ☐

3 Work in pairs and write down the times mentioned in each conversation.

🔲 Now listen again and check.

GRAMMAR AND FUNCTIONS

> Tense review: talking about the future
>
> | | *will* | *going to* | **present continuous** | **present simple** |
> |---|---|---|---|---|
> | **predicting the future/ future hopes** | * | * | | |
> | **an intention** | | * | | |
> | **a decision taken at the moment of speaking** | * | | | |
> | **a definite arrangement** | | | * | |
> | **fixed times, such as timetables** | | | | * |
>
> Making suggestions and responding to them.
> *How about going to the theatre on Friday?* *That's a great idea.*
> *We could take Tony to the museum on Saturday.* *I'm afraid I'm busy on Saturday.*
> *Why don't we have lunch in the Union Oyster Bar?* *Yes, that would be wonderful.*
> *Let's go to the cinema tonight.* *I'm sorry I'm having dinner with my parents tonight.*
> *Shall I get the tickets?* *Yes, please.*

1 Look at these sentences. Decide which future tense is used and why. Use the information in the grammar box to help you.

1 It's going to rain.
2 I'm sure it'll rain.
3 It starts at eight.
4 I'm going to be there to meet you when you arrive.
5 I'm taking the train at ten o'clock.
6 I'll give you a lift if you like.

2 Look at these sentences from the conversations you heard in *Vocabulary and listening* 2. Which tense do the speakers use to talk about something they decide as they speak? Which tense do they use to talk about something which is already planned?

1 'We open at 10 in the morning, except on Saturdays, when it's midday.'
2 'OK, Mr Stein, we'll see you tomorrow, Friday June 7th at 8pm. Bye.'
3 'Good, I'll try and get there this evening. You're open until 7, aren't you?'
4 '...but last night and tonight it stays open until 4.'
5 'So it's going to be just the same tonight?'
6 'How about in row D?' 'Yes, that'll do fine.'

3 Work in pairs. Talk about your intentions for the weekend. Use *going to* for plans, and *I think I'll...* or *I'll probably...* for anything you're not sure about.

On Saturday I'm going to a tennis match, and on Sunday I think I'll stay at home.

4

GENERAL COMMENTS

British and American English

Reward Upper-intermediate is a course in British English. The spelling is standard British English and the model for *Sounds* work is British received pronunciation. However, because English is used as a means for international communication and because American English is likely to be read and heard more often than British English, there are several lessons which use an American English context. The main differences between British and American English spelling and pronunciation were presented in *Reward* Pre-intermediate Lesson 24, and you may like to remind your students of these differences. It is important to remind students that despite certain differences, British and American English are varieties of the same language and speakers of either are mutually intelligible. If confusion does arise between a British person and an American, it is likely to be a socio-cultural difference rather than a linguistic one.

VOCABULARY AND LISTENING

1 Aim: to introduce the theme of the lesson; to present the words in the vocabulary box.
● The theme of the lesson is entertainment. Elicit different forms of entertainment and write them on the board. Make sure they include the following categories – *theatre, cinema, restaurant, sightseeing, art galleries, shopping*.

● Ask the students to work in pairs and look at the words in the box and decide to which category of entertainment they refer.

Possible answers
theatre/cinema: aisle, box office, circle, cloakroom, foyer, interval, row, scenery, stage, stalls
restaurant: *à la carte*, café, cloakroom, course, menu, opening hours, reservation, service, snack, tip
sightseeing: guided tour, stroll, tip
art galleries: cloakroom, display, exhibit, foyer, opening hours, sculpture
shopping: cash desk, department store, escalator, opening hours, shelf, till

● Ask the students to think of other words which can go in these categories.

● Ask the students to work with another pair and check their answers.

● Check the answers to activity 1 with the whole class.

2 Aim: to practise listening for main ideas.
● 📼 Explain that you're going to play five short conversations a - e. Ask the students to listen to the five conversations and to put the number of the conversation in the boxes according to the purpose.

Answers
1 a b 4 c 2 d 3 e 5

3 Aim: to practise listening for specific information.
● Ask the students to work in pairs and discuss the times the speakers mention.

Answers
Conversation 1: 10 o'clock in the morning, 7 o'clock in the evening, 10 o'clock on Thursdays
Conversation 2: 8 o'clock
Conversation 3: 7 o'clock
Conversation 4: 2 o'clock, 4 o'clock
Conversation 5: 7.30, 10.30

● 📼 Ask the students to listen again and check their answers.

GRAMMAR AND FUNCTIONS

1 Aim: to focus on ways of talking about the future.
● Ask the students to read the information in the grammar box and then do the exercises.

Answers
1 predicting the future based on evidence
2 predicting the future
3 fixed times
4 an intention
5 a definite arrangement
6 a decision at the moment of speaking

2 Aim: to focus on ways of talking about the future.
● Ask the students to use the grammar and functions box to explain why the different tenses in 2 are used. Sometimes there may be more than one possibility.

Answers
1 fixed time	4 fixed time
2 predicting a future certainty	5 predicting the future
3 future hope / promise	6 a decision taken at the moment of speaking

3 Aim: to practise using the target structures for talking about the future.
● This is a more informal activity in which the students use what they have learnt to talk about their own plans and intentions.

● Ask the students to talk about their plans for the weekend. Encourage them to use the target structures suggested in the Student's Book.

LISTENING AND SPEAKING

1 Aim: to listen for main ideas.

● This activity is designed to distract the students' attention from the detail of what is said and to encourage them to focus on the main ideas, namely, the things the speakers are planning to do. Ask them to read through the activities first. Find out if anyone has been to Boston, USA.

● ▭ Play the tape and ask the students to tick the activities which are mentioned.

> **Answers**
>
> a walk along   lunch at Union Oyster Bar ✓
> Commonwealth Avenue ✓
>
> breakfast on   finish the evening in
> Harvard Square ✓   Quincy Market ✓
>
> shopping in the   drinks at the Hyatt
> Back Bay ✓   Regency ✓
>
> a stroll around   dinner at Joseph's
> Beacon Hill ✓   Aquarium ✓
>
> sightseeing in   visit the Public Garden ✗
> Cambridge ✓

2 Aim: to practise listening for specific information.

● Ask the students to work in pairs and discuss the times Angela and Graham decided to do the things on their list.

● ▭ Play the tape and check their answers.

3 Aim: to practise speaking; to practise using expressions for taking decisions.

● Ask the students to work in pairs and to plan a day's sightseeing in Boston. Make sure they are using the future simple for decisions taken at the time of speaking.

WRITING

1 Aim: to focus on conventions in fairly informal letter-writing; to practise using the target structures.

● This is the second occasion in *Reward* Upper–intermediate in which letter writing has been practised (see Lesson 2). Explain that in a professional context it's common to send a letter confirming arrangements. Point out that between people who know each other, the style of the letter is likely to be informal, although there will be expressions which you wouldn't normally see in a letter between friends or members of a family.

● Ask the students to underline any words/expressions which are not appropriate to Angela's letter.

> **Answers**
>
> Saltonstall Building
> 13 th floor, 100 Cambridge Street
> Boston, Mass 02178
>
> Monday, 5 September
>
> Dear Sir,
> Further to our conversation the other day, it was good to hear from you and to sort out the arrangements for Tony's visit. I have attached the schedule for his visit to Boston.
> With reference to the aforementioned visit, I'm writing to say that I'll pick Tony up from the airport on Saturday night and take him to his hotel. I'll see him on Sunday at his hotel at 8. Can you fax him and let him know what's happening when he arrives and on Sunday? I would be grateful for your help in this matter.
> See you then,
>
> Yours faithfully,
>
> Angela

2 Aim: to focus on formal and informal letter-writing conventions.

● Ask the students if they are more likely to see these expressions in formal or informal letters. Some of them can be used in both types of letter, but the final degree of formality will depend on other expressions contained in the letter.

> **Answers**
>
> 1 F   2 F   3 F   4 F or I   5 I   6 F   7 I   8 F

3 Aim: to practise writing informal professional letters.

● Ask the students to rewrite the letter in more appropriate language. There is of course more than one satisfactory way of rewriting Angela's letter, so accept any suitable answers the students may give for the underlined phrases above.

4 Aim: to practise writing fairly informal professional letters.

● Ask the students to discuss how formal the letter to their boss should be. They may decide that in their own culture, it will be very formal. However, they should write *Dear Mr Baxter,* rather than *Dear Sir,* as they obviously know their boss and should finish with *Yours sincerely,* rather than *Yours faithfully.*

● Ask the students to include in their letter details of the visit they planned for Tony Baxter in *Listening and speaking* activity 3.

LISTENING AND SPEAKING

1 🔲 Listen to a conversation between Graham and Angela who are going to spend a day with their boss, Tony Baxter, showing him around Boston.
Put a tick (✓) beside the activities they mention.

a walk along Commonwealth Avenue ☐

lunch at Union Oyster Bar ☐

breakfast on Harvard Square ☐

finish the evening in Quincy Market ☐

shopping in the Back Bay ☐

drinks at the Hyatt Regency ☐

a stroll around Beacon Hill ☐

dinner at Joseph's Aquarium ☐

sightseeing in Cambridge ☐

visit the Public Garden ☐

2 Work in pairs. Write down the times they decide on and compare your answers with your partner.

🔲 Now listen again and check.

3 Work in pairs. One of you is Angela and the other Graham. Plan a day's sightseeing in Boston for your boss. Make suggestions about what you'll do and at what time. Think about what other arrangements you need to make and decide who will do them.

How about having lunch at the Union Oyster Bar?
OK, I'll ring them and book a table. At what time?

WRITING

1 Work in pairs. Angela is going to send Graham a letter confirming the arrangements they discussed on the phone. Decide if the letter is likely to be very formal or fairly informal.
Now read Angela's letter below. There are some expressions which aren't appropriate to the letter. Can you decide what they are?

Saltonstall Building
13th floor, 100 Cambridge Street
Boston, Mass 02178

Monday 5 September

Dear Sir

Further to our conversation the other day, it was good to hear from you and to sort out the arrangements for Tony's visit. I have attached the schedule for his visit to Boston.

With reference to the aforementioned visit, I'm writing to say that I'll pick Tony up from the airport on Saturday night and take him to his hotel. I'll see him on Sunday at his hotel at 8am. Can you fax him and let him know what's happening when he arrives and on Sunday? I would be grateful for your help in this matter. See you then.

Yours faithfully, *Angela*

2 Decide if these are opening or closing remarks for a formal or informal letter. Write F for formal and I for informal in the box.

1 Thank you for your letter of 20 August. ☐
2 It was good to speak to you the other day. ☐
3 Further to our conversation of 13 August,... ☐
4 Please give my best wishes to... ☐
5 Looking forward to seeing you on Saturday. ☐
6 I look forward to seeing you on Saturday. ☐
7 It was good to hear from you. ☐
8 I look forward to hearing from you. ☐

3 Rewrite Angela's letter above in more appropriate language.

4 Write a formal letter to Tony Baxter. Think about:
addresses, greetings, opening remarks, closing remarks, conclusion.

Make sure you include information about the arrangements for Saturday and Sunday.

Tense review: talking about the future

Cambridge, Massachusetts.

Cambridge, Massachusetts, lies over the Charles River opposite Boston. A university town since shortly after its 1630 founding, site of the only college in the Americas until nearly the eighteenth century, Cambridge has a worldwide reputation as a respected seat of learning. Nearly half its 95,000 citizens are connected in some way to Harvard, Massachusetts Institute of Technology or the smaller colleges in the city.

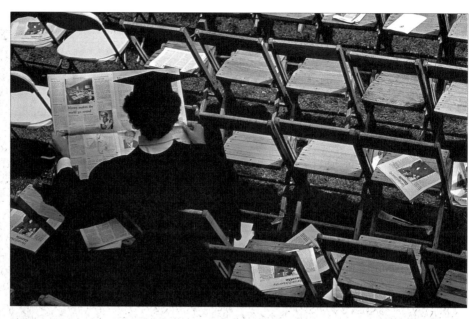

Sights to see

The heartbeat of Cambridge is *Harvard Square*, where life revolves around the many bookstores, coffee shops, boutiques and newsstands. No one would come to Cambridge without taking a walk through *Harvard Yard*. A stroll through the yard's winding paths, stately trees, grassy quadrangles and handsome brick buildings is a walk through a long history of higher education.

Six US Presidents have graduated from Harvard. The *Longfellow National Historic Site* is the house where the poet Henry Wadsworth Longfellow lived for 45 years and wrote most of his famous works. In the house you will find many fine Victorian furnishings, among them Longfellow's desk, pen and inkstand. A few miles east of Harvard Square lies Cambridge's other famous university, the *Massachusetts Institute of Technology* (MIT) which has offered a premier education in engineering and technology since 1865.

Museums

Harvard is also home to a number of museums. The *Busch-Reisinger Museum* is noted for central and northern European works of art from the Middles Ages to the present, and for its collection of musical instruments. The *Fogg Art Museum* holds European and American art, with a notable Impressionist collection.

Shopping

In the very center of Harvard Square you will see the *Out of Town News and Ticket Agency* kiosk, a Harvard Square landmark for many years, famous for its thousands of national and foreign periodicals. Visitors will find a wealth of shopping in *Harvard Square*, with everything from boutiques to chain stores. Most notable are the many bookshops surrounding the square.

Yet another Harvard institution is the *Harvard Co-op*, formed in 1882 by several Harvard students as a cost-saving measure. The Co-op holds three floors of clothing, gifts, computers and calculators, games and toys, records, art prints, posters and books.

Nightlife

Ryle's features nightly jazz, rhythm-and-blues, Latin music and swing in a casual atmosphere. At the *Mystery Café*, the audience participates in solving a murder over a four-course dinner. Harvard's professional theater company, American Repertory Theater, produce world premieres and classical works, often taking a non-traditional approach. *Catch a Rising Star* showcases rising young comics seven nights a week in a dark and cosy basement club.

Restaurants

East Cambridge is a treasure chest of colorful and ethnic restaurants. A 50's style decor of diner stools, neon and a black-and-white tiled floor enlivens the *East Coast Grill*. Southern cooking is represented by the *Cajun Yankee* which serves seafood gumbo, Cajun popcorn and shrimp remoulade. It would be hard to find a friendlier place than the *Casa Portugal*, one of only a handful of Boston Portuguese restaurants, and serving spicy dinners of marinated pork with potatoes or mussels, and squid stew. The family-owned *La Groceria* looks like an Italian trattoria and is famed for its hot antipasti and homemade pasta. *Troyka* is a real Russian restaurant, and serves excellent caviar and blinis. Its hearty peasant fare includes borscht, piroshki, meat-potato pie and Russian dumplings.

VOCABULARY AND READING

1 Aim: to present the words in the vocabulary box; to prepare for reading.

● The words in the box all appear in the passage and may hinder the other comprehension activities if the students are unfamiliar with them. Since they are nevertheless often used in everyday speech, they are useful words to learn. Ask the students to group them under the headings. There may be more than one possibility.

Answers
sights to see: Victorian landmark
  quadrangle
museums: Victorian Impressionist collection
shopping: boutique kiosk chain store
nightlife: company premiere comic
  star audience Latin
restaurants: ethnic diner fare

2 Aim: to read for specific information.

● Point out that sometimes we read a text for general interest, and sometimes we read because we are looking for some specific information, perhaps in answer to a question. Ask the students to read and decide where they would recommend for the people described.

Answers
1 Ryle's
2 Fogg Art Museum
3 Cajun Yankee
4 Busch-Reisinger Museum
5 Harvard Co-op
6 Mystery Café
7 Harvard Yard
8 Cajun Yankee, Casa Portugal

3 Aim: to read and evaluate the text.

● Ask students to think about who the passage was written for and where it comes from. In what circumstances would they read or use a passage like this?

Answers
1 a guide book
2 to help them decide what to see there

FUNCTIONS

1 **Aim: to focus on the different uses of the future simple tense.**

● Ask the students to read the information in the functions box and then do the exercises.

> **Answers**
> 1 d 2 f 3 b 4 c 5 a 6 e

2 **Aim: to focus on the different uses of the future simple tense.**

● Ask the students to use the information in the functions box to decide which use of *will* each exchange shows.

> **Answers**
> 1 making an offer
> 2 making a promise
> 3 making a request
> 4 giving an invitation
> 5 making a prediction
> 6 making a threat

SOUNDS

1 **Aim: to focus on polite and friendly intonation.**

● Remind the students that the intonation you use in English can change the meaning of what you say. This activity is designed to help the students recognise polite and friendly intonation.

● 🔲 Play the tape. Ask the students to tick the friendly intonation in the sentences in *Functions* activity 1.

> **Answers**
> 2 I'll arrive as soon as I can.
> 4 Will you sit down with us.
> 5 You'll have a wonderful evening.

2 **Aim: to practise using polite and friendly intonation.**

● Ask the students to repeat the sentences they ticked in 1 using polite and friendly intonation.

SPEAKING AND WRITING

1 **Aim: to practice speaking; to practise note-taking.**

● Ask students to choose a town they know well and to make notes about the aspects mentioned. They may want to read the passage about Cambridge to remind themselves of places and features to include.

● Ask the students to use their notes to write a short tourist guide for the place they have chosen. Each student may like to focus on one particular aspect.

2 **Aim: to practise speaking; to practise using the target structures.**

● Ask the students to plan a day out in the town they have chosen. Make sure they use *going to* and the present continuous for intentions and arrangements. The students can then present their plan and their arrangements for a day out to the rest of the class. You may like to ask the students to write up their guided tour for homework.

VOCABULARY AND READING

1 You're going to read a passage about the city of Cambridge in Massachusetts. Work in pairs. Under which of these headings would you expect to find the words in the box?

– sights to see – restaurants
– museums   – shopping
– nightlife

ethnic diner fare boutique
Victorian Impressionist company
collection kiosk landmark
chain store premiere comic
star audience Latin quadrangle

2 Read the passage. Find out where in Cambridge you would recommend for someone who:

1 likes live music
2 loves 19th-century French art
3 likes cooking from Louisiana
4 is interested in the history of music
5 wants to buy some cheap presents
6 likes eating out and the theatre
7 enjoys historical buildings
8 loves seafood

3 Answer the questions.

1 Where does this passage come from?
 – a guide book   – a letter
 – a history book   – an atlas
2 Why would someone read this text?
 – to guide them round Cambridge.
 – to help them decide what to see there
 – to tell them how to get there
 – to find out about accommodation

FUNCTIONS

Tense review: talking about the future
You can use *will* to:
– **make an offer.** *I'll get the tickets.*
– **make a prediction.** *We'll have a great time together.*
– **make a promise, threat or warning.** *If you won't be quiet, I'll call the waiter.*
– **make a request. Will** *you ask them to be quiet?*
– **to invite someone to do something. Will** *you join us?*
– **refuse something.** *No, I won't be quiet.*

1 Match the sentences on the left with the replies on the right.

1 I'll buy you another drink.
2 I'll arrive as soon as I can.
3 Will you get me something to eat?
4 Will you sit down with us?
5 You'll have a wonderful evening.
6 I'll call the manager if you won't be quiet.

a Yes, they say it's very good.
b Okay, what would you like?
c Thank you. That's very kind of you.
d Thanks. I'll have an orange juice.
e Don't bother. We're leaving.
f Okay, make sure you're not late.

2 Decide which use of *will* each exchange shows.

SOUNDS

1 🔲 Listen to the sentences in *Functions* activity 1. Put a tick (✓) by the ones which sound polite and friendly.

2 Work in pairs. Say aloud the sentences you ticked in 1. Try to sound polite and friendly.

SPEAKING AND WRITING

1 Work in groups of three or four. Choose a town or region that you all know well. Make notes on the following aspects:

– sights to see   – museums   – nightlife   – restaurants   – shopping

Now use the notes to write a short tourist guide to the place you have chosen. Each member of the group could write about one aspect. You can then display your guide for other members of the class to read.

2 Plan a day out in the place you have chosen. Think about what you will do at different times during the day.

We'll start by going to the cathedral.
Okay, and then we'll walk along the city wall.

Present your plan to the rest of the class. Explain where you are going to go and what you are going to do.

VOCABULARY

1 You may find it useful to use a monolingual dictionary. You teacher will help you decide which one would be most suitable. Look at the dictionary extract and answer the questions.

1 How do you find out how to pronounce *reward?*
2 Where does the stress go?
3 How many parts of speech can *reward* be?
4 How many meanings does it have?
5 Are there any prepositions which follow it?

reward /rɪwɔːrd/ **rewards, rewarding, re- ◆◆◆◇◇ warded**

1 A **reward** is something that you are given, for ex- N-COUNT: ample because you have behaved well, worked oft N for n hard, or provided a service to the community. *A bonus of up to 5 per cent can be added to a pupil's final exam marks as a reward for good spelling, punctuation and grammar... He was given the job as a reward for running a successful leadership bid.*

2 A **reward** is a sum of money offered to anyone N-COUNT who can give information about lost or stolen property or about someone who is wanted by the police. *The firm last night offered a £10,000 reward for information leading to the conviction of the killer.*

3 If you do something and **are rewarded** with a VERB particular benefit, you receive that benefit as a re- sult of doing that thing. *Make the extra effort to im-* be V-ed *press the buyer and you will be rewarded with a* Also V n *quicker sale at a better price.*

4 The **rewards** of something are the benefits that N-COUNT: you receive as a result of doing or having that thing. usu pl *The company is only just starting to reap the re-* =benefit *wards of long-term investments... Potentially high financial rewards are attached to senior hospital posts.*

5 If you say that something **rewards** your attention VERB or effort, you mean that it is worth spending some time or effort on it; a fairly formal use. *The com-* V n *pression and density make this a difficult book to read, but it richly rewards the effort.*

Collins Cobuild English Dictionary HarperCollins Publishers Ltd, 1995

2 Here are some words from Lessons 1–4. Choose three and answer the questions for each word. Use a dictionary to help you.

blow   collection   display   point   reservation   stretch   service

1 How do you pronounce it?
2 Where does the stress go?
3 How many parts of speech can it be?
4 How many meanings does it have?
5 Are there any prepositions which follow it?

3 Work in pairs. Discuss which of the following pieces of advice about learning vocabulary would be most useful to you.

1 Write down new words under topics or other features, such as phrasal verbs, words for noises.
2 Write new words in a sentence to show how to use them.
3 Look through your vocabulary notes every few days.
4 Test your vocabulary with a friend.
5 Translate all the new words you record.
6 Write down all the other words formed from a word, and their meanings.
7 Record only words which are useful to you.

GRAMMAR

1 Find the mistakes in these sentences and correct them.

1 ~~When you get up today?~~
2 What did you at the weekend?
3 Where live you?
4 Did she got home late?
5 How long you're learning English?
6 Do you can open the window?

2 Complete these sentences with a suitable question tag, negative question or reply question.

1 Let's go now, ____?
2 '____ it a lovely day!' 'Yes, it is.'
3 'I'm bored.' '____? I'm enjoying myself.'
4 'I don't like the film.' '____ you? I do.'
5 You haven't been here long, ____?
6 '____ she look splendid!' 'Yes, she does!'
7 You don't like learning grammar, ____?
8 There'll be enough time, ____?

Progress check 1–4

GENERAL COMMENTS

You can work through this Progress check in the order shown, or concentrate on areas which may have caused difficulty in Lessons 1 to 4. You can also let the students choose the activities they would like or feel the need to do.

VOCABULARY

1 **Aim: to focus on dictionary techniques.**

● You need to have access to one monolingual dictionary for every three or four students in the class. This activity will remind them that it is not always possible simply to translate words from one language into another.

> **Answers**
> 1 Look at the phonetic information
> 2 The stressed syllable is either preceded by an apostrophe or marked in the phonetic information
> 3 Two
> 4 Four
> 5 **for/with**

2 **Aim: to practise using the dictionary.**

● To do this activity successfully you need to have access to several monolingual or bilingual dictionaries. If you can't get hold of these dictionaries, you can still see if the students know enough about the words to answer the questions.

3 **Aim: to give useful learner training advice.**

● All through the *Reward* series, advice has been given directly and indirectly to the students about how to become effective learners of the language. On this occasion, the advice is a checklist of suggestions to help the student take an active part in the learning process. Ask the students to do this activity in pairs.

GRAMMAR

1 **Aim: to revise the formation of questions.**

> **Answers**
> 1 When **did** you get up today?
> 2 What did you **do** at the weekend?
> 3 Where **do** you live?
> 4 Did she **get** home late?
> 5 How long **have you been** learning English?
> 6 **Can** you open the window?

2 **Aim: to revise question tags, negative questions, imperative questions, reply questions.**

> **Answers**
> 1 Let's go now, **shall we?**
> 2 '**Isn't** it a lovely day!' ' Yes, it is.'
> 3 I'm bored.' '**Are you?** I'm enjoying myself.'
> 4 'I don't like the film.' '**Don't you?** I do.'
> 5 You haven't been here long, **have you?**
> 6 '**Doesn't** she look splendid!' 'Yes, she does!'
> 7 You don't like learning grammar, **do you?**
> 8 There'll be enough time, **won't there?**

3 **Aim: to revise the use of the article.**

> **Answers**
> 1 a
> 2 a
> 3 a
> 4 the
> 5 the
> 6 the
> 7 the
> 8 no article
> 9 no article
> 10 no article

4 Aim: to revise the uses of the present simple and continuous tenses.

Answers
In America, they **play** a different kind of football. Today, some friends **are taking** me to a ballgame between the Redskins and the Cowboys, and I **am looking** forward to it. Before the ballgame, everyone **gets** very excited, and **cheers** their teams. But five minutes after kick-off, the games **stops** and it **keeps** stopping every few minutes while the players and the managers **have** a chat. Fortunately, the Redskins **score** a goal and the game **becomes** more exciting.

5 Aim: to revise use of the future simple.

Possible answers
1 Will you stay and have some lunch?
2 I promise I'll write to you.
3 Will you get me some stamps?
4 I won't pay the bill!
5 I'll pay the bill.

SOUNDS

1 Aim: to focus on different spellings of the sounds /ɔ:/ and /ɜ:/.

● Ask the students to say the words aloud and then write them in two columns.

Answers
/ɔ:/: bored board saw sore four for lawn torn war
/ɜ:/: herd heard bird sir fur learn turn were

● 📼 Play the tape and ask the students to listen and check. Ask the students to say the words aloud and decide which words sound the same but have different spellings.

Answers
/ɔ:/: can be spelt using **or, oar, aw, our, ar**
/ɜ:/: can be spelt using **er, ear, ir, ur, ere**

2 Aim: to focus on the sound /ə/.

● Ask the students to underline the /ə/ sound in these words.

Answers
appointment announcement advertisement grammar mutter acquaintance cousin corner performer spectator department interval

● 📼 Play the tape and ask the students to say the words aloud.

3 Aim: to focus on stressed words in connected speech.

● Ask the students to predict which words the speaker is likely to stress. Remind them if necessary that the words the speaker will stress are those which he or she considers to be important.

Answers
A prisoner in El Paso, Texas, was allowed out of jail to celebrate his twenty-fifth wedding anniversary. When he arrived home, his wife was absent. He then learned that she was in prison after having stolen his anniversary present from a store.

● 📼 Play the tape and ask them to listen and check.

4 Aim: to practise reconstructing a text from stressed words.

● Ask the students to turn to the Communication activity and follow the instructions.

SPEAKING AND WRITING

1 Aim: to practise speaking; to read for specific information; to prepare for writing an informal letter.

● Ask the students to work in groups of three or four and to find out the information listed.

Answers
what he's going to do: get the airport bus to town, bring some things from England
what he needs to know: what to bring, how to greet people, if people are very formal
what he likes doing: going to a football match or other sports and games, going out in the evening

2 Aim: to practise speaking.

● Ask the students to talk about their ideas in response to the prompts. Make sure they imagine that the English friend is coming to stay either with them in their homes or near them, so that the details can be as accurate and realistic as possible.

3 Aim: to practise writing informal letters.

● Make sure the students remember the conventions for writing informal letters. If they're not sure, remind them to look back on page 9 for some help.

● Ask the students to write a letter in reply. They should do this on their own, although they may like to show each other their versions. You may like to ask the students to do this activity for homework.

3 Complete the passage with the indefinite or definite article, or put a – if no article is needed.

In many countries, you need (1) ____ business card if you want to make (2) ____ good impression. To (3) ____ foreigner, it makes it easier to understand your name and (4) ____ job you do. Make sure you include your name, (5) ____ name of (6) ____ company you work for, and (7) ____ position you hold. Use your title, such as (8) ____ vice-president, or (9) ____ doctor, and don't use (10) ____ abbreviations.

4 Choose the correct verb form.

In America, they *play/are playing* a different kind of football. Today, some friends *take/are taking* me to a ballgame between the Redskins and the Cowboys, and I *look /am looking* forward to it. Before the ballgame, everyone *gets/is getting* very excited, and *cheers/is cheering* their teams. But five minutes after kick-off, the games *stops/is stopping* and it *keeps/is keeping* stopping every few minutes while the players and the managers *have/are having* a chat. Fortunately, the Redskins *score/are scoring* a goal and the game *becomes/is becoming* more exciting.

5 Write sentences using *will*.

1 invite someone to stay and have lunch with you.
2 promise to write to someone.
3 ask someone to buy some stamps.
4 refuse to pay the bill.
5 offer to pay the bill.

SOUNDS

1 Say these words aloud. Is the underlined sound /ɜː/ or /ɔː/? Put the words into two columns.

h<u>er</u>d   h<u>ear</u>d   b<u>or</u>ed   b<u>oar</u>d   b<u>ir</u>d   s<u>ir</u>   s<u>aw</u>   s<u>ore</u>
f<u>ur</u>   f<u>our</u>   f<u>or</u>   l<u>ear</u>n   l<u>aw</u>n   t<u>ur</u>n   t<u>or</u>n   w<u>er</u>e   w<u>ar</u>

Listen and check. As you listen, say the words aloud. Which words sound the same but are spelt differently?

2 Underline the /ə/ sound in these words.

appointment   announcement   advertisement grammar   mutter   acquaintance   cousin   corner performer   spectator   department   interval

Listen and check. As you listen, say the words aloud.

3 Predict which words the speaker is likely to stress and underline them.

A prisoner in El Paso, Texas, was allowed out of jail to celebrate his twenty-fifth wedding anniversary. When he arrived home, his wife was absent. He then learned that she was in prison after having stolen his anniversary present from a store.

Listen and check.

4 Write down the words you underlined in 3 on a separate piece of paper. Now turn to Communication activity 9 on page 94.

SPEAKING AND WRITING

1 Work in groups of three or four. Read this letter from your English friend, and find out:

– what he's going to do   – what he needs to know
– what he likes doing

> Thanks very much for your letter. I'm really looking forward to joining you next week. My plane gets in at about four in the afternoon, so I'll get the airport bus to your town. Will you send me directions to your home from the bus station or shall we meet somewhere?
>
> By the way, is there anything I can bring from England which you may like? I don't know, books, food, that sort of thing (nothing too heavy, as my suitcase is likely to be full!).
>
> One important thing, can you tell me how I should greet people, such as your family and friends? Are people very formal? Is there anything I need to know in order to avoid making any major social gaffes?
>
> Is there any chance of going to a football match, or is there any other sports game you think I might enjoy? And I hope there'll be plenty to do in the evenings!
>
> See you!
>
> Paul

2 In your groups, discuss and respond to your friend's letter. Talk about:

– where to meet   – special social customs
– things to do in the evening   – sports games to see
– presents he could bring   – arrangements for his stay

3 Write a letter giving advice and suggestions about the things you talked about in 2.

Achievements and ambitions

Tense review: present perfect simple and continuous

VOCABULARY AND SPEAKING

1 Which of the words in the box can you use to describe important events in your life so far?

marry fall in love job school success fail boring
exciting confident uncertain talent family bring up
optimistic pessimistic travel music painting sport
acting home love hate take an exam pass goal
university degree diploma happy sad target dream
agreement obligation compromise succeed failure

2 Make two lists. In the first list write your achievements – things you have done in your life which you are proud of.
In the second list write your ambitions – things you'd like to do.

3 Now work in pairs, and talk about your achievements and ambitions.

READING

1 The passage comes from *Great Railway Journeys*, in which the English novelist Lisa St Aubin de Terán describes a journey she has always wanted to make in South America. Which of the following words would you expect to see in the passage?

cargo coconut destination drifting frost haze
horizon rhythm sensual steamy transistor tropical

2 Read the passage and find out if she is at the beginning, middle or end of her journey.

3 The writer uses quite a literary style. Find a word or phrase in the passage which means the same as the following (they are in the order in which you'll find them).

on purpose calmed call to mind swollen fighting

I have set out to travel from the Atlantic Ocean to the foothills of the Bolivian Altiplano, from the once famous coffee town of Santos to Santa Cruz de la Sierra. I have made other great railway journeys by chance, but never by design; this is to be a 'proper' journey with a beginning and a prearranged destination. It is early March and I have just left the sharp frosts of a late Italian winter for the steamy heat of the tail end of a tropical rainy season.

Santos is the club Pele, the King of Football, played for. Beyond the heat haze and the pounding rhythm of transistor radios on the beach, and beyond the sinister lines of grey cargo ships on the horizon, there is a halo: Pele's. His fame is the achieved dream of every Brazilian boy and the pride of his nation.

Every few minutes, people come up and ask me my name and if I like Santos. Between assuring strangers how fond I am of their city, I think about it and decide that I really am. I like the sight of so many people enjoying the sun and the sand and their celebration of themselves.

I have bought a guide book and map of Brazil which I study. I am lulled by the general feeling of well-being, of drifting with the tide. I have never had any sense of direction, which is, perhaps, why I feel so safe on a train. Trains move implacably along their own tracks, pausing only at predestined places.

I feel at home in Brazil; I can even evoke my paternal grandfather, a moustachioed Señor Mendonca from Belem, to put me further at ease. Bloated as I am with coconut water and roasting under 100°F (38°C), the sensual hum of warring radio stations is lulling me to sleep. I have a train to catch, though. I have been wanting to make this journey for so many years that I am resolved to make it now, no matter what.

5

GENERAL COMMENTS

Artificial and authentic motivation

Sometimes in the classroom it is difficult to motivate the students all of the time. Motivation can come from using interesting texts. But not every student will find every text interesting, and the teacher or textbook writer needs to supply tasks that offer pedagogic or artificial motivation for activities which one is unlikely to perform in real life. This kind of motivation will come from activities such as jigsaw listening, scrambled texts and other text reconstruction activities.

Tests

Before you begin this lesson, you may want to set the students Progress Test 1 at the back of this book. You may not like setting students tests, but most teachers and students find them useful as a way of evaluating progress and providing motivation.

VOCABULARY AND SPEAKING

1 **Aim: to present the words in the vocabulary box; to present the topic of the lesson.**
   ● The topic of the lesson is achievements and ambitions. Ask the students to look at the words in the box and decide which words describe important events in their lives so far.

   ● Ask two or three students to tell the class which words they have chosen, and then to describe some important events in their lives.

2 **Aim: to organise words in the vocabulary box.**
   ● Ask the students to think about their achievements and ambitions before they list them. You may want to write a few examples of your own on the board, such as *pass my driving test, get married,* and ask them to guess if they are achievements or ambitions for you.

   ● Ask the students to make two lists – in the first list they should write their achievements and in the second, their ambitions.

3 **Aim: to practise speaking.**
   ● Ask the students to discuss their list of achievements and ambitions with a partner.

READING

1 **Aim: to pre-teach some unfamiliar words; to prepare for reading.**
   ● This activity encourages the students to make some predictions about the passage they are going to read, and thus creates the artificial motivation to read. In fact, all the words are in the passage. Help them with the meaning of any words they don't understand.

2 **Aim: to practise reading for main ideas.**
   ● Ask the students to read the passage and to find out if the writer is at the beginning, middle or end of her journey. Try to avoid answering any vocabulary queries at the moment as the task is designed to distract students from reading too closely.

   > **Answer**
   > At the beginning

3 **Aim: to deal with unfamiliar words.**
   ● Now is a suitable moment to take a closer look at the vocabulary. First, ask the students to find words in the passage which are the same as the words in the activity.

   > **Answers**
   > on purpose – by design   calmed – lulled
   > call to mind – evoke   swollen – bloated
   > fighting – warring

   ● Ask the students if there are any other vocabulary difficulties. If there are, see if other students can help to explain the vocabulary.

4 **Aim: to practise reading for specific information.**
- Ask the students to read the sentences 1 – 4 and find the appropriate ending from sentences a – f. There are two extra sentences.

Answers
1 e   2 c   3 b   4 f

5 **Aim: to read and infer; to present the target structures.**
- Ask the students to read between the lines and infer if these statements are true or false or if there is no evidence.

Answers
1 False
2 No evidence
3 True
4 No evidence
5 True
6 True

6 **Aim: to focus on collocation.**
- Once again, ask students to do some collocation work, this time with the words they saw in *Reading* activity 1.

Answers
cargo ship   coconut water   prearranged destination
drifting with the tide   sharp frost   heat haze
ships on the horizon   pounding rhythm
sensual hum   steamy heat   transistor radios
tropical rainy season

SPEAKING AND WRITING

1 **Aim: to practise speaking.**
- This is a jigsaw reading activity in which pairs of students have different information about Lisa St Aubin de Terán's biography. Ask them to follow the instructions in their respective Communication activities.

2 **Aim: to practise writing.**
- A timed writing exercise in which students exchange short written questions and answers. You may like to set a definite time limit and see who has collected the most intriguing information about their partner.

4 Complete the sentences 1 – 4 with a phrase a – f and write the appropriate letter in the box. There are two extra phrases.

1 The other railway journeys she has made were not 'proper' ones… ☐
2 She tells people she likes Santos without really thinking about it… ☐
3 She likes travelling by train… ☐
4 She feels at home in Brazil… ☐

a as she wants them to go away and stop bothering her.
b as trains will take her effortlessly to where she wants to go.
c because she wants to be polite.
d because her grandfather was Brazilian.
e because she didn't plan them.
f because she likes the people and she had a Brazilian grandfather.

5 Decide if these statements about the passage are true, false or if there is no evidence.

1 She has never taken a train before.
2 She has never been to Brazil before.
3 She has just arrived from Italy.
4 She has been staying in Santos for several weeks.
5 She has grown fond of Santos during her stay.
6 She has been writing as she waits for the train.

6 Look at the words in *Reading* activity 1 again and find the words that go with them in the passage.

SPEAKING AND WRITING

1 Work in pairs.

Student A: Turn to Communication activity 4 on page 93.
Student B: Turn to Communication activity 14 on page 95.

2 Work in pairs. You're going to find out as much as possible about your partner, but you can only ask questions in writing. Write a question you would like to ask your partner on a piece of paper.
Where were you born?

Now exchange your questions. Write a short answer to your partner's question.
In Kavala.

Write another question you would like to ask your partner on the same piece of paper.
Where did you go to school?

Then exchange your questions again. Write a short answer to your partner's next question.
In Alexandroupolis.

Continue either until you know everything you want to know about your partner, or until your teacher tells you to stop.

Tense review: present perfect simple and continuous

GRAMMAR

> **Tense review: present perfect simple and continuous**
> **You use the present perfect simple:**
> – to talk about an action which happened at some time in the past. We are not interested in when the action took place. You often use *ever* in questions and *never* in negative statements.
> *I **have made** other great railway journeys.*
>
> – when the action is finished, to say what has been achieved in a period of time, often in reply to *how much/many*.
> *Lisa **has written** several novels.*
>
> – to talk about a past action which has a result in the present, such as a change. You often use *just*.
> *I **have just left** the sharp frost of a late Italian winter.*
>
> **You use the present perfect continuous:**
> – to talk about an action which began in the past, continues up to the present, and may or may not continue into the future, and to say how long something has been in progress.
> *She**'s been writing** for many years.*
>
> – to talk about actions and events which have been in progress up to the recent past and show their present results.
> *She**'s been working** very hard.* (She's stopped work, but she looks tired.)

1 Work in pairs. Choose the best sentence. Explain why the sentence you have chosen is the best.

1 a She's known her second husband since 1990.
　 b She's been knowing her second husband since 1990.
2 a She's been writing her memoirs.
　 b She's written her memoirs.
3 a She's been living in Venezuela.
　 b She's lived in Venezuela.
4 a She's been writing since she was sixteen.
　 b She's written since she was sixteen.
5 a She's been writing her next novel.
　 b She's written her next novel.

2 Work in pairs. Look at the verbs in the sentences in *Reading* activity 5 on page 21. What tense is used and why?

3 Here are the answers to some questions about Lisa St Aubin de Terán. Work in pairs and use the information you have learnt to write the questions.

1 Since 1983.
2 Since 1990.
3 Seven.
4 Seven years.
5 Three, England, Venezuela and Italy.

1 *How long has she been writing novels?*

GRAMMAR

1 Aim: to focus on the difference between the present perfect simple and the present perfect continuous.

● The distinction between these two tenses is a difficult one to grasp, and full explanations tend to be lengthy. The information in the grammar box is necessarily succinct, and may need to be consolidated with the information in the Grammar review.

● Ask the students to read the information and then to do the exercises.

Answers
1a because **know** isn't used in the continuous form
2b because we know she has finished them
3b because she doesn't live there any more
4a because she's still writing
5a because we are focusing on what has been achieved

2 Aim: to focus on the form of the present perfect simple and continuous tenses.

● Ask the students how you form the two tenses.

● Ask the students to say which tense is used in the sentences in *Reading* activity 5.

Answers
Sentences 1, 2: present perfect simple to talk about an action that happened at some time in the past.
Sentences 3, 5: present perfect simple to talk about a past action with a result in the present.
Sentence 4, 6: present perfect continuous to talk about an action which began in the past and continues up to the present.

3 Aim: to practise writing questions.

● Ask the students to use their biography of the writer to write questions about her life.

Answers
1 How long has she been writing novels?
2 How long has she known her husband?
3 How many novels have been published?
4 How long has she been living in England?
5 How many countries has she lived in?

SOUNDS

Aim: to focus on the unstressed auxiliary.

- Remind students that the unstressed words are those which do not carry the main ideas of a sentence.

- 📼 Play the tape. Ask the students to say the sentences aloud.

LISTENING

1 Aim: to prepare for listening.

- Ask the students to read the questions and to think about their answers to them.

2 Aim: to listen for main ideas.

- Explain that the students are going to hear five people talking, and each one will answer a question. Ask the students to listen and put the number of the speaker next to the question they answer.

Answers
Speaker 1: 2
Speaker 2: 4
Speaker 3: 5
Speaker 4: 3
Speaker 5: 1

3 Aim: to check comprehension.

- Ask the students to work together and to try to reconstruct what the speakers said in as much detail as possible. Ask them to take notes.

4 Aim: to provide an opportunity for further listening.

📼 Play the tape again and ask the students to add to their notes.

SPEAKING AND WRITING

1 Aim: to practise speaking; to prepare for writing.

- Ask the students to work with the same student they worked with in *Speaking and writing* activity 2 on page 21 and ask and answer the questions in *Listening* activity 1. They should take notes of their partner's answers.

2 Aim: to expand the notes in 1.

- Explain to the students that they are going to write a biography of their partner. Tell them they must expand the notes they have made in the previous activities to help them write the article.

3 Aim: to practise speaking; to develop writing skills.

- Ask the students to show their partner the biography. They should check it for facts and for mistakes and correct anything that is wrong and then pass it back for rewriting.

4 Aim: to analyse a piece of writing and make corrections.

- Ask the students to read their biography and incorporate any new material or comments from their partner. They should now re-write the article.

SOUNDS

Listen to these sentences. Notice how *been* is pronounced /bɪn/. Now say the sentences aloud.

1 Has she been waiting long?
2 He's been sitting here for ten minutes.
3 She's been living in Italy.
4 I've been reading one of her books.
5 You've been working too hard.

LISTENING

1 You are going to hear a radio programme in which some people talk about their answers to the following questions. First, think about your answers to the questions.

1 What have you achieved in your life which you are most proud of?
2 Who do you particularly admire, and why?
3 Is there anything you have always wanted to do?
4 Where have you always wanted to visit?
5 Where have you been happiest in your life?

2 Listen to five people talking about their answers to the questions. Each speaker will answer one of the questions. Put the number of the speaker by the question they answer.

3 Work in pairs, and make notes about each speaker's answer. Try to include as much detail as possible.

4 Listen again and check your answers to 3.

SPEAKING AND WRITING

1 Work with the same student you worked with in *Speaking and writing* activity 2 on page 21. Ask and answer the questions in *Listening* activity 1. Make notes about your partner's answers.

2 You are going to write a biography of your partner for the local newspaper called *Achievements and ambitions.* Use the short answers your partner gave you in *Speaking and writing* activity 2 on page 21 and the notes you made in *Listening* activity 1 to help you write the article.

3 When you have finished, discuss your article with your partner. Give your partner any suitable further information, and tell him/her about anything which is inaccurate. Now, check the article for vocabulary, spelling and punctuation.

4 Finally, rewrite your first article.

6 | *Trust me – I'm a doctor*

Tense review: past tenses

SPEAKING

1 Work in pairs. This lesson is about truth and deception. Which people do you expect to tell the truth?

politicians   teachers   journalists   police officers
shop assistants   car mechanics   lawyers   doctors

2 Do you think it is ever justified not to tell the truth? Can you think of circumstances when it might be acceptable to deceive someone about:

– reasons for being late?   – their appearance?
– reasons for leaving work early?   – an illness?

3 When was the last time someone told you something which turned out to be untrue? What happened?

LISTENING

1 You're going to listen to *Sister Coxall's revenge*, by Dawn Muscillo, a story about a deception which takes place in a hospital. First, look at the picture and write down any words you think you'll hear.

2 Work in groups of three or four. Look at the events in part 1 of the story. They are in the wrong order. Try and guess the right order.

Sister Coxall was in charge of Violet Ward. ☐
Dr Green was interested in psychiatric medicine. ☐
She met the new doctor. ☐
He got out of his car. ☐
She wondered who the new doctor was. ☐
He nearly ran her over. ☐
She offered him tea. ☐
He gave her a lift to the Nurses' Home. ☐
She listened to his plans for Violet Ward. ☐
He had recently finished his studies. ☐
She walked through the hospital grounds. ☐
He got the new job without an interview. ☐

3 📼 Listen to part 1 of the story. Number the events in the order you hear them.

4 Work in pairs and check your answers to 3. Try to remember as much detail as possible.

📼 Now listen again and check.

5 Work in pairs. What do you think happens next in the story? Answer the questions, then work with another pair and compare your answers.

1 What was Dr Green going to do the next day?
2 How do you think Sister Coxall felt about Doctor Green's plans?
3 How do think she was going to stop him?

📼 Now listen to part 2 of the story and check your answers.

6 Match each question with one of the answers below.

1 Why was Sister Coxall angry?
2 Why did nobody know what Dr Green looked like?
3 Why did she want him to come straight to the ward?
4 How do we know it was a lie that Dr Green was paranoid and confused?
5 Why did she fill the syringe?
6 How do we know this was not the first time she had done this?

a Because the sedative would make Dr Green easy to handle.
b Because she was only pretending to read from a report.
c Because the ward was full of men all insisting they were doctors.
d Because he hadn't been to the General Office yet to get his identity badge.
e Because she didn't want him to suspect that the nurse thought he was a patient.
f Because she wanted to stay in her job.

6

GENERAL COMMENTS

Past tenses

This is the last of the reviews of the tenses. The students will have come across all the past tenses before, but may not have compared their uses. If they seem able to form and use the tenses successfully, you may like to concentrate on other syllabus strands which are practised in this lesson.

Sister Coxall's revenge

It is unusual to find a story which is short enough to be used in a lesson, since most good short stories run over several pages. *Sister Coxall's revenge* is very successful in generating suspense and a sense of mystery in so few words. But although it is of an appropriate length, the activities may take longer to do if the story generates interest among the students.

SPEAKING

1 **Aim: to practise speaking; to introduce the topic.**
- Ask the students to discuss which of the people mentioned they expect to tell the truth. Ask them to rank the people in the order of their trustworthiness. They can then compare their ranking order with others in the class.

2 **Aim: to practise speaking.**
- Ask the students to define the expression *to tell a lie*.

- Ask the students to discuss the circumstances in which it might be acceptable to deceive someone.

3 **Aim: to practise speaking.**
- You may find some students reluctant to talk about occasions when they may have deceived people, so ask them to think whether they have had any recent experiences of people telling a lie. Tell them to think about situations removed from their own personal experiences such as new stories, politics etc.

LISTENING

1 **Aim: to introduce the story.**
- Use the picture to elicit words which are likely to appear in the story. Ask the students to think of other words and write them all on the board. You may want to teach or revise some words to do with hospitals and medical matters.

2 **Aim: to prepare for listening.**
- In case the story is hard to follow while listening, these sentences constitute a summary of the story in simple English. Ask the students to read them and to predict the order of events in the story.

3 **Aim: to listen for main ideas.**
- With the storyline having been explained in 2, the students simply have to listen and number the events as they hear them in the story. Play the tape.

Answers	
Sister Coxall was in charge of Violet Ward.	1
She wondered who the new doctor was.	2
She met the new doctor.	3
She walked through the hospital grounds.	4
He nearly ran her over.	5
He got out of his car.	6
He gave her a lift to the Nurses' Home.	7
She offered him tea.	8
Dr Green was interested in psychiatric medicine.	9
He had recently finished his studies.	10
He got the new job without an interview.	11
She listened to his plans for Violet Ward.	12

[handwritten note: This is all wrong]

4 **Aim: to check comprehension; to practise speaking.**
- Ask the students to work in pairs and to check their answers to 3. You may like to do this with the whole class. If they are using suitable verbs in different past tenses you may be able to spend less time on the grammar work.

- Play the tape again and ask the students to check their answers.

5 **Aim: to prepare for reading; to practise speaking.**
- By now, the students should be interested in knowing what is going to happen next. Make use of this authentic motivation by encouraging them to talk about what happens next. Use the questions to help you.

- Play the tape and ask students to check their answers.

6 **Aim: to check comprehension.**
- Ask students to do this activity on their own and then to check their answers with another student.

Answers
1 f 2 d 3 e 4 b 5 a 6 c

GRAMMAR

1 Aim: to focus on the difference between various past tenses.

● Ask the students to read the information in the grammar box and then to do the exercises.

Answers

1a I left **after** I passed my exams.
1b I left **before** I passed my exams.
2a She moved near the hospital **after** she became a doctor.
2b She moved near the hospital **before** she became a doctor.
3a The ambulance arrived **while** she was reading the patient's notes.
3b The ambulance arrived **after** she had read the patient's notes.
4a Dr Green arrived **while** she was walking home.
4b Dr Green arrived **after** she had walked home.

2 Aim: to focus on the difference between various past tenses.

● To vary these exercises, if you have asked the students to do the last activity in writing, then do this one orally with the whole class.

Answers

1 When she took her driving test, she **had had** about twenty driving lessons.
2 He **was reading** the newspaper when someone knocked at the door.
3 The river **was getting** high. It **had been raining** all week.
4 His face **was** red as he **had forgotten** the sun cream.

3 Aim: to focus on the form of the past perfect continuous.

Answers

1 He had been waiting for an hour.
2 She had been taking a boy home.
3 He had been working too much.
4 He hadn't been sleeping very well.

4 Aim: to practise using the past tenses; to practise writing summaries.

● Summary writing may be a useful skill to develop at this level. This practice activity is tightly controlled, focusing on the past tenses. However, other summary practice activities, such as reading for main ideas, which is the first stage of summary writing, have already been performed. Ask the students to do this activity in pairs.

Answers

Sister Coxall (1) **had been running** Violet Ward for years. One day she (2) **heard** that a new doctor was coming to take over. She (3) **had met** the new doctor when she (4) **was walking** in the grounds of the hospital. He (5) **had** almost (6) **driven** over her. Dr Green (7) **took** Nurse Coxall back to the Nurses' Home and she (8) **offered** him a cup of tea. He told her that when he (9) **had finished** his studies, he (10) **had applied** for the job in the hospital. He (11) **told** Nurse Coxall that he intended to make many changes, including moving the sister on Violet Ward.

The next day Sister Coxall (12) **was sitting** in her office when Dr Green arrived. She (13) **had told** the nurse a few minutes before that a new patient was expected and that he (14) **thought** he was a doctor. Sister Coxall (15) **prepared** a syringe of sedative to make Dr Green easy to handle. Surprisingly, nobody in the hospital seemed to think it odd that Nurse Coxall's ward (16) **was** full of men who (17) **said** they were doctors.

WRITING

Aim: to practise writing; to rewrite a story from another point of view; to practise using the linking words *when, as, while, before* and *after*.

● Ask the students to rewrite the story from Dr Green's point of view. They may like to do this using the first person singular. Encourage them to use the linking words. You may like to ask the students to do this activity for homework.

GRAMMAR

> **Tense review: past tenses**
>
> **You use the past simple to talk about a past state or a past action or event that is finished.**
> *She **looked** around her office.*
>
> **You use the past continuous to talk about something that was in progress at a specific time in the past, or when something else happened. The second action is often in the past simple.**
> *The doctor **was driving** in the hospital grounds when he met Sister Coxall.*
>
> **You use the past perfect to talk about an action in the past which happened before another action in the past. The second action is often in the past simple.**
> *After she **had spoken** to the nurse, she **wrote** the report on Mr Green.*
>
> **You use the past perfect continuous to focus on an action which was in progress up to or near a time in the past rather than a completed action. You often use it with *for* and *since*.**
> *Sister Coxall **had been running** her ward **for** many years.*

1 Look at the tenses used in these sentences. What is the difference in meaning of *a* and *b* in each pair?

1 a I left college when I passed my exams.
  b I had left college when I passed my exams.
2 a When she became a doctor, she moved near the hospital.
  b When she became a doctor, she had moved near the hospital.
3 a She had been reading the patient's notes when the ambulance arrived.
  b She had read the patient's notes when the ambulance arrived.
4 a She was walking home when Dr Green arrived.
  b She had walked home when Dr Green arrived.

2 Look at these sentences and choose the best tense.

1 When she took her driving test, she *had/had had* about twenty driving lessons.
2 He *was reading/read* the newspaper when someone knocked at the door.
3 The river *got/was getting* high. It *rained/had been raining* all week.
4 His face *was/had been red* as he *forgot/had forgotten* the sun cream.

Work with a partner and explain why the tense you have chosen is the best.

3 Answer the questions using the past perfect continuous and the prompts in brackets.

1 Why was the patient so angry? (he/wait/an hour)
2 Why was the doctor late? (she/take/a boy home)
3 Why was the man so stressed? (he/work/too much)
4 Why did the doctor prescribe him some pills? (he/not sleep/very well)

4 Work in pairs and complete these sentences with suitable verbs to give a summary of the story. Use appropriate past tenses.

Sister Coxall (1) ____ Violet Ward for years. One day she (2) ____ that a new doctor was coming to take over. She (3) ____ the new doctor when she (4) ____ in the grounds of the hospital. He (5) ____ almost (6) ____ over her. Dr Green (7) ____ Nurse Coxall back to the Nurses' Home and she (8) ____ him a cup of tea. He told her that when he (9) ____ his studies, he (10) ____ for the job in the hospital. He (11) ____ Nurse Coxall that he intended to make many changes, including moving the sister on Violet Ward.

The next day Sister Coxall (12) ____ in her office when Dr Green arrived. She (13) ____ the nurse a few minutes before that a new patient was expected and that he (14) ____ he was a doctor. Sister Coxall (15) ____ a sedative to make Dr Green easy to handle. Surprisingly, nobody in the hospital seemed to think it odd that Nurse Coxall's ward (16) ____ full of men who (17) ____ they were doctors.

WRITING

Rewrite the story from Dr Green's point of view. Use the linking words, *when, as, while, before* and *after* and suitable tenses.

***When** I finished my studies, I applied for a job in a psychiatric hospital...*

Describing a sequence of events in the past

VOCABULARY AND SOUNDS

1 Put these words under the following headings: *people, places, medicine* and *medical complaints.*

sister dentist pill tablet nurse
hospital wound chemist cut
matron pain ointment ward
disease temperature patient
surgeon surgery injection
blood pressure heart attack
consultant clinic

2 Work in pairs. Here are some more words to do with medical matters. In what circumstances would you use them in English or in your own language?

bandage ambulance appointment
prescription emergency casualty
dizzy shiver outpatients
wheelchair limp plaster stick
crutches disabled sedative

3 Underline the stressed syllables in these words.

hospital chemist injection
patient attack consultant
ointment emergency disabled
disease prescription temperature
ambulance

🔊 Now listen and check. As you listen, say the words aloud.

4 Look at these compound nouns. Underline the stressed word.

hospital ward heart attack
blood pressure outpatients
wheelchair

🔊 Now listen and check.

READING

1 You are going to read a story about another deception involving a doctor which took place in the 19th century. The deception was only discovered when the doctor died. Before you read, look at the picture, and try and guess what the deception was.

In 1812 a young man called James Barry finished his studies in medicine at Edinburgh University. After graduating he moved to London where he studied surgery at Guy's Hospital. After that the popular young doctor joined the army and over the next forty years had a brilliant career as an army medical officer, working in many far-off countries and fighting successfully for improved conditions in hospitals. It was a remarkable career — made even more remarkable by the discovery upon his death that *he* was in fact a *she*. James Barry was a woman.

No one was more surprised at this discovery than her many friends and colleagues. It was true that throughout her life people had remarked upon her small size, slight build and smooth pale face. One officer had even objected to her appointment as a medical assistant because he could not believe that Barry was old enough to have graduated in medicine. But no one had ever seriously suggested that Barry was anything other than a man.

By all accounts Barry was a pleasant and good-humoured person with high cheek bones, reddish hair, a long nose and large eyes. She was well-liked by her patients and had a reputation for great speed in surgery — an important quality at a time when operations were performed without anaesthetic. She was also quick-tempered. When she was working in army hospitals and prisons overseas, the terrible conditions often made her very angry. She fought hard against injustice and cruelty and her temper sometimes got her into trouble with the authorities. After a long career overseas, she returned to London where she died in 1865. While the undertaker's assistant was preparing her body for burial, she discovered that James Barry was a woman.

So why did James Barry deceive people for so long? At that time a woman could not study medicine, work as a doctor or join the army. Perhaps Barry had always wanted to do these things and pretending to be a man was the only way to make it possible. Perhaps she was going to tell the truth one day, but didn't because she was enjoying her life as a man too much. Whatever the reason, Barry's deception was successful. By the time it was discovered that she had been the first woman in Britain to qualify as a doctor, it was too late for the authorities to do anything about it.

VOCABULARY AND SOUNDS

1 **Aim: to present the words in the vocabulary box.**

● Check the students know what all the words mean. Ask other students to answer any questions. Consolidate the learning process by asking the students to put the words under the headings.

> **Answers**
> **people:** sister dentist nurse chemist matron patient surgeon consultant
> **places:** hospital ward surgery clinic
> **medicine:** pill tablet ointment injection
> **medical complaints:** wound cut pain disease temperature blood pressure heart attack

2 **Aim: to present the words in the second vocabulary box.**

● Ask the students to explain the meaning of these words by getting them to describe the circumstances in which they would use the words in English or in their own language.

3 **Aim: to focus on stressed syllables in words.**

● Ask the students to underline the stressed syllables in the words.

> **Answers**
> hospital chemist injection patient attack consultant ointment emergency disabled disease prescription temperature ambulance

● 🔲 Ask the students to listen and check, and then say the words aloud.

4 **Aim: to focus on stressed words in compound nouns.**

● Ask the students to listen to the words *casualty department, dressing gown, Nurses' Home* and to tell you which words are stressed. Now ask them to underline the stressed word in the other compound nouns.

● 🔲 Play the tape and ask the students to listen and check. They should repeat the compound nouns as they hear them.

> **Answers**
> hospital ward heart attack blood pressure outpatients wheelchair

READING

1 **Aim: to prepare for reading.**

● Ask the students to think about life in the 19th century. Ask them how life in hospitals has changed in the last 100 years. Do not give them too much information regarding the roles of men and women doctors at this stage. Elicit ideas as to what they think the deception in the passage is about. Encourage them to look at the picture to help them.

2 **Aim: to read for specific information.**

● Ask the students to read the passage and find one sentence that describes the deception.

> **Answer**
> **First paragraph:** by the discovery upon his death that **he** was in fact a **she**. James Barry was a woman.

3 Aim: to practise reading for specific information.

● Ask the students to read the passage and decide if the statements are true or false.

> **Answers**
> 1 False. James Barry pretended to be a man because women **weren't allowed** to be doctors.
> 2 True.
> 3 False.
> 4 True.
> 5 False. She performed operations at **great speed.**
> 6 False. They discovered she was a woman **after** her death.

4 Aim: to deal with unfamiliar words.

● The words focused on in this activity may be unfamiliar to the students. This activity will help them understand the text even better.

> **Answers**
> 1 popular 2 deceived 3 discovered
> 4 surgery 5 anaesthetic as 6 qualify

5 Aim: to identify reference in a text.

● Ask the students to read the sentences and say what the words in italics refer to.

> **Answers**
> 1 The fact that James Barry was a woman.
> 2 Her speed in surgery.
> 3 James Barry.
> 4 To practise medicine.
> 5 James Barry being a woman and practising medicine.

6 Aim: to focus on a writer's style.

● At this level it is important that students develop an appreciation of a writer's style. Obviously this can be quite subjective and students' opinions may vary.

7 Aim: to check comprehension.

● This activity allows students to demonstrate their understanding of the passage. Ask the students to write true/false statements, similar to those in activity 3. When they have finished, they can exchange statements with their partner and each student should check whether their partner has answered correctly.

FUNCTIONS

1 Aim: to focus on describing a sequence of events in the past.

● Ask the students to look at the passage again and to write down or underline *after, before, when* and *while* constructions.

> **Answers**
> After graduating, ...
> After that, the popular young doctor ...
> When she was working...
> After a long career overseas, ...
> While the undertaker's assistant was preparing her body ...

2 Aim: to focus on describing a sequence of events in the past.

● Ask the students to read the passage again and then to number the events in the order in which they happened.

> **Answers**
> f James Barry wanted to be a doctor.   1
> g James Barry pretended to be a man.   2
> d James Barry graduated in medicine.   3
> h James Barry moved to London.   4
> a James Barry joined the army.   5
> e James Barry gained a reputation as a quick and
>   skilful surgeon.   6
> c James Barry died.   7
> b The undertaker's assistant found out that
>   James Barry was a woman.   8

3 Aim: to practise using *before, after, when* and *while* constructions.

● Ask the students to write the story of James Barry using the structures in the functions box. Go round and check they are using the constructions correctly.

SPEAKING

Aim: to practise speaking.

● Ask the students to discuss their answers to the questions. Start a general discussion of their views concerning working roles of men and women. Do they feel things have changed for the better?

2 Read the passage and find one sentence which describes what the deception was.

3 Decide if these statements are true or false.

1 James Barry pretended to be a man because there were no women doctors.
2 She worked to improve conditions in hospitals.
3 Many people suspected that she was a woman.
4 She was a very good doctor.
5 She performed operations very slowly and carefully.
6 The army authorities discovered that she was a woman while she was working abroad.

4 Find a word or expression in the passage that has a similiar meaning to the words or phrases in italics.

1 James Barry was *liked by a lot of people.*
2 She *tricked* people into thinking she was a man.
3 The undertaker's assistant was very surprised when she *found out* that Barry was a woman.
4 James Barry was skilful at *operating on people.*
5 In the l9th century doctors didn't use *drugs to make people sleep* during operations.
6 To *become* a doctor you have to pass a lot of exams and graduate from university.

5 What do the words in italics refer to?

1 No one was more surprised at *this discovery* than her many friends and colleagues…
2 …*an important quality* at a time when operations were performed…
3 While the undertaker's assistant was preparing *her* body for burial…
4 …and pretending to be a man was the only way to make *it* possible.
5 …it was too late for the authorities to do anything about *it.*

6 Work in pairs. Which of the following words would you use to describe the style of the story?

factual   ironic   persuasive   objective   subjective

Now talk about how the story would change if the deception was revealed in the last paragraph. Would this be better?

7 Write some true and false statements about James Barry. When you're ready, show your statements to another student. Can he/she guess which are true and which are false?

FUNCTIONS

> Describing a sequence of events in the past
>
> You can use *before* and *after* + *-ing* to describe a sequence of two events which both have the same subject.
> *After graduating* he moved to London.
> You can use *when, as* and *while* to describe two events which happen at the same time. The second verb is often in the past simple and is used for the event which interrupts the longer action.
> *When* she was working in hospitals overseas, the terrible conditions *made* her angry.

1 Look back at the passage and find more examples of describing a sequence of events in the past.

2 Number these events in the order in which they happened.

a James Barry joined the army. ☐
b The undertaker's assistant found out that James Barry was a woman. ☐
c James Barry died. ☐
d James Barry graduated in medicine. ☐
e James Barry gained a reputation as a quick and skilful surgeon. ☐
f James Barry wanted to be a doctor. ☐
g James Barry pretended to be a man. ☐
h James Barry returned to London. ☐

3 Write a brief summary of the story of James Barry using the structures in the functions box and the sentences in *Functions* activity 2 to help you.

After graduating from medical school, James Barry moved to London.

SPEAKING

Work in pairs and discuss your answers to these questions.

1 Do you think there was anything wrong in what James Barry did?
2 Are there any jobs today that women are not allowed to do?
3 Are there any jobs that are better done by men?

SPEAKING AND WRITING

1 Put the following features of a holiday in the order of their importance to you.

– beautiful countryside
– peace and quiet   – good food
– sunshine   – swimming
– mountains   – old buildings
– sports facilities   – good nightlife
– sandy beaches   – plenty to read

2 Work in groups of three or four and compare your answers to 1. Now write down statements about holidays which you all agree on.

3 Find out which group in your class has:

– the most statements
– the longest statement

READING

1 Read the passage from *The Lost Continent* by the American writer Bill Bryson and choose the best title.

1   What to see in Arizona.
2   The geography of the Grand Canyon.
3   The beauty of the Grand Canyon.
4   A magical experience.

2 Work in pairs. Look back at the passage and find these words and expressions.

grey soup   a set of theatre curtains
ants   an old shoelace

What is the writer using these words to describe? Do you think the descriptions are good? What other words could you use to describe these things?

I drove through a snow-whitened landscape towards the Grand Canyon. It was hard to believe that this was the last week of April. Mists and fog swirled about the road. I could see nothing at the sides and ahead of me except the occasional white smear of oncoming headlights. By the time I reached the entrance to Grand Canyon National Park, and paid the $5 admission, snow was dropping heavily again, thick white flakes so big that their undersides carried shadows.

The road through the park followed the southern lip of the canyon for thirty miles. Two or three times I stopped in lay-bys and went to the edge to peer hopefully into the silent murk, knowing that the canyon was out there, just beyond my nose, but I couldn't see anything. The fog was everywhere – threaded among the trees, adrift on the roadsides, rising steamily off the pavement.

Afterwards I trudged towards the visitors' centre, perhaps 200 yards away, but before I got there I came across a snow-spattered sign announcing a look-out point half a mile away along a trail through the woods, and impulsively I went down it, mostly just to get some air. The path was slippery and took a long time to traverse, but on the way the snow stopped falling and the air felt clean and refreshing. Eventually I came to a platform of rocks, marking the edge of the canyon. There was no fence to keep you back from the edge, so I shuffled cautiously over and looked down, but could see nothing but grey soup. A middle-aged couple came along and as we stood chatting about what a dispiriting experience this was, a miraculous thing happened. The fog parted. It just silently drew back, like a set of theatre curtains being opened, and suddenly we saw that we were on the edge of a sheer, giddying drop of at least a thousand feet.

The scale of the Grand Canyon is almost beyond comprehension. It is ten miles across, a mile deep, 180 miles long. You could set the Empire State Building down in it and still be thousands of feet above it. Indeed you could set the whole of Manhattan down inside it and you would still be so high above it that the buses would be like ants and people would be invisible, and not a sound would reach you. The thing that gets you – gets everyone – is the silence. The Grand Canyon just swallows sound. The sense of space and emptiness is overwhelming. Nothing happens out there. Down below you on the canyon floor, far, far away, is the thing that carved it: the Colorado River. It is 300 feet wide, but from the canyon's lip it looks thin and insignificant. It looks like an old shoelace. Everything is dwarfed by this mighty hole.

7

GENERAL COMMENTS

Sequence of adjectives and describing position

One of the most common question types in exams, particularly in oral exams, is *Look at the photo and describe what you can see.* To do this successfully, students need to be able to use a variety of prepositions and prepositional phrases and as many adjectives as possible. Many students will already have met and used many prepositions and prepositional phrases, so those selected for this lesson are the more complex ones suitable for this level. If your students have already used *Reward* Intermediate, they will already have covered the sequence of adjectives. In fact, long strings of adjectives are not common in English. In this lesson, the focus is on the position of *fact* and *opinion* adjectives.

Bill Bryson

Bill Bryson is an American author who lives in Britain. He has published several books on travel writing, some of which are *The Lost Continent* and *Neither Here nor There.* He has also written a book about American English called *Mother Tongue.*

SPEAKING AND WRITING

1 Aim: to introduce the theme of the lesson.
● Ask the students to look at the different features of a holiday and put them in order of importance.

2 Aim: to practise speaking.
● Ask the students to work in groups of three or four and compare their order of importance. Ask them to try and write as many statements as possible that they all agree on.

3 Aim: to compare writing.
● Ask the whole class to find out who has the most statements and the longest statement.

READING

1 Aim: to read for main ideas.
● Ask the students to read the passage by Bill Bryson in which he describes a visit to the Grand Canyon in Arizona, USA. They shouldn't worry about unfamiliar words for the moment, but simply focus on the task of choosing the best title.

> **Possible answer**
> A magical experience

● You may like to ask if the students can think of a better title.

2 Aim: to focus on the writer's style.
● Tell the students that Bill Bryson's overall style of writing can best be described as humorous, although this is less evident from this extract. Certainly, Bill Bryson is well known for his descriptive style of writing and his ability to create a 'word picture'. In this activity, the students are focusing on some selected descriptive expressions and asked to find out why the author uses them.

● Ask the students to read the words and expressions taken from the passage and decide what the phrases describe.

> **Answers**
> **grey soup** – the fog over the Grand Canyon ~~heavy/thick/dark~~
> **a set of theatre curtains** – the fog ~~silently draw back~~
> **ants** – the buses ~~far away~~
> **an old shoelace** – the Colorado River

thin + insignificant

snow whitened
white smear
~~the~~ *thick white flakes*
southern lip
silent murk
threaded (fog)
snow-spattered sign
slippery
clean, refreshing
grey soup
dispiriting exp.
miraculous
silently draw back
sheer, giddying drop
overwhelming
thin, insignificant

T 28

3 Aim: to deal with unfamiliar words.

● Ask the students to read the passage again and answer the questions. These questions refer to expressions which might cause the students some difficulty.

Answers

1 He doesn't expect such bad weather.
2 He walked slowly and with difficulty.
3 He thinks it is very big.
4 The silence is impressive.

4 Aim: to focus on the writer's style.

● Encourage the students to look at how the writer uses adjectives to create effective descriptions. Ask them to choose four adjectives which they think Bill Bryson has used well and say why.

● Ask the students to think about how the passage would read if the writer had only reported the facts. Remind them that effective use of adjectives in their own descriptions will contribute greatly to the quality of their spoken and written English.

5 Aim: to focus on facts.

● Ask the students to read the passage again and write down facts about it.

Answers

$5 admission
road through park follows the southern lip for thirty miles, it is ten miles across, a mile deep, 180 miles long
Colorado River is 300 feet wide

GRAMMAR

1 Aim: to focus on the distinction between fact and opinion adjectives.

● Ask the students to read the information in the grammar box and then to do the exercises. Explain that it is sometimes difficult to distinguish between fact and opinion adjectives, but to do so will help them decide on their sequence.
Certain adjectives could be both fact and opinion, *slippery, old, thin* etc, so it doesn't matter where they go in a sequence.

2 Aim: to focus on nouns used as adjectives.

● Ask the students to rewrite the phrases with a noun used as an adjective.

Answers

1 A two-day journey.   2 A twenty-minute walk.
3 A ten-year-old girl.   4 A ten mile-long road.
5 A two-week holiday.   6 A two-storey building.

3 Aim: to focus on the sequence of adjectives and nouns used as adjectives.

● Remind the students that adjectives and adjectival phrases can greatly enrich speech and written work. It's also a way of avoiding abrupt, descriptive sentences.

Answers

1 The Colorado is a slow-moving, very muddy, 300 hundred foot-wide river.
2 The visitors' centre has a collection of interesting, old, black and white photographs.
3 Thousands of excited foreign tourists visit the Grand Canyon every year.
4 The Grand Canyon National Park has a big, new visitors' centre.
5 There is a thirty mile-long, winding road along the southern lip of the canyon.
6 There are strange, huge rock formations in the canyon.

SPEAKING

1 Aim: to practise speaking.

● Ask the students to work in groups of three or four and answer the questions. Go round and encourage them to describe the beautiful regions in detail using adjectives and adjectival phrases.

2 Aim: to practise speaking.

● Extend the activity by asking the students to find out how other people answered the questions. You may like to ask the students to write a report on how other people answered for homework.

3 Look at these sentences from the passage and answer the questions.

1 *It was hard to believe that this was the last week of April.*
   – Does this mean he thinks time is passing very quickly, or that he doesn't expect such bad weather?

2 *Afterwards, I trudged towards the visitors' centre…* – Is it likely that he walked quickly and lightly or slowly and with difficulty?

3 *The scale of the Grand Canyon is almost beyond comprehension.*
   – Does this mean he doesn't believe the facts about it or that he thinks it is very big?

4 *The thing that gets you – gets everyone – is the silence.*
   – Does this mean the silence is impressive or annoying?

4 The writer uses a lot of adjectives to create a 'word picture' of his experience. Underline all the adjectives you can find in the passage. Choose four adjectives which you think have been used well and which give you a clear picture of the scene he is describing or how he feels about it. Work with a partner and say why you have chosen these adjectives.

5 Write down any facts the writer tells us about the Grand Canyon.

GRAMMAR

> **Adjectives**
> **When there is more than one adjective, you usually put *opinion* adjectives before *fact* adjectives.**
> *The **beautiful, silent** Grand Canyon.*
> **You can use a noun as an adjective before another noun.**
> ***canyon** floor   **theatre** curtains*
> **Nouns used as adjectives do not have a plural form. You put a hyphen between the two parts of the noun clause.**
> *The Colorado River is 300 feet wide.*   *It is a 300 **foot-wide** river.*
> *The Grand Canyon is 180 miles long.*   *It is a 180 **mile-long** canyon.*

1 Look at the adjectives you underlined in the passage. Are they *fact* or *opinion* adjectives? If they are *fact* adjectives, what kind are they: size, age, shape etc?

2 What do you call the following?

1 A journey which takes two days.
2 A walk which lasts twenty minutes.
3 A girl who is ten years old.
4 A road which is ten miles long.
5 A holiday which lasts two weeks.
6 A building which has two storeys.

1 A two-day journey.

3 Rewrite these sentences in one sentence.

1 The Colorado is a slow-moving river. It is 300 feet wide and very muddy.
2 The visitors' centre has a collection of photographs of the Canyon. They are black and white. They are old and very interesting.
3 Thousands of tourists visit the Grand Canyon every year. They are foreign. They are excited.
4 The Grand Canyon National Park has a visitors' centre. It is new and big.
5 There is a road along the southern lip of the canyon. It is thirty miles long. It is winding.
6 There are some rock formations in the canyon. They are a strange shape. They are huge.

1 The Colorado is a slow-moving, very muddy, 300 foot-wide river.

SPEAKING

1 Work in groups of three or four and discuss your answers to the questions.

1 Which are the most beautiful regions in your country?
2 What is their special appeal?
3 Is there anywhere which is particularly special which few people have heard of?
4 What kind of threat is there to the environment in these regions?
5 What do you think should be done about the threat?

2 Find out how other groups have answered the questions in 1.

Describing position

LISTENING AND SPEAKING

1 You're going to hear two people, Terry and Kathy talking about holidays. First, think about your answers to the following statements.

– my holiday nightmare is…
– my holiday paradise is…
– my favourite holiday pastime is…
– I never travel without…
– when I'm away I usually miss…

2 🔈 Work in pairs.

Student A: Listen and make notes on Terry's answers to the questions.
Student B: Listen and make notes on Kathy's answers to the questions.

Now work together and tell your partner what you have found out.

3 Complete the sentences below with suitable words or phrases. Use the information in 2 to help you.

1 Terry didn't enjoy his stay in St Ives because _____.
2 Kathy really liked Sark, in the Channel Islands, because _____.
3 Terry first learned to dive when
_____.
4 Terry takes eye shields because
_____.
5 Kathy always takes perfume because _____.
6 Kathy always misses a decent loaf of bread because _____.

🔈 Listen again and check your answers.

4 Look at these extracts from the listening passage. Answer the questions and try and guess the meaning of the phrases in italics.

1 *'There were so many people, all lined up like whales on a beach.'*
– Why does Terry say the people were like whales?
2 *'The shopkeepers have this ritual of greeting you.'*
– Did Terry enjoy the attention he was given in shops?
3 *'I'm ready to read pretty well anything, I abandon all taste when I go away.'* – Does Kathy read only good books when she is on holiday?
4 *'I love to catch up on my reading when I'm on holiday.'* – Does Terry read a lot when he is not on holiday? Does he think he should read more?

VOCABULARY

1 Here are some nouns to describe places. Write down the nouns which go together to make compound nouns.

| bank cathedral centre city country district fishing hall region market mountain seaside square town university village west |

west bank

2 Which words in the box below can you use to talk about the landscape in your country?

| unspoilt plain peak waterfall valley stream wood forest hill meadow river field hedge village footpath quiet jungle desert oasis industrial mountainous low-lying flat tropical vegetation overcrowded picturesque agricultural fertile rugged canyon island range temperate estuary coastline cliff beach |

LISTENING AND SPEAKING

1 Aim: to practise speaking; to prepare for listening.
● Ask the students to work in small groups and to talk about their holiday experiences.

● Ask a student from each group to report back to the rest of the class on what the group talked about. Decide which group talked about the best holiday and which group talked about the worst.

2 Aim: to practise listening for specific information.
● ▭ This is a jigsaw listening activity in which the students listen to the same tape but for different information. Divide the students into pairs and ask them to follow the instructions.

3 Aim: to check comprehension.
● You may like to ask the students to do this activity in pairs.

Answers
1 Terry didn't enjoy his stay in St Ives **because the beaches were full of people.**
2 Kathy really liked Sark, in the Channel Islands, because **there weren't any cars.**
3 Terry first learned to dive when **he was in the Virgin Islands.**
4 Terry takes eye shields because **he can't sleep on the plane without them.**
5 Kathy always takes perfume because **it makes her feel sophisticated.**
6 Kathy always misses a decent loaf of bread **because she gets fresh bread every day at home.**

● ▭ Play the tape again for the students to check their answers.

4 Aim: to focus on some complex expressions.
● The students may find it hard to understand some of the colloquial expressions used by native speakers. Ask them to answer the questions.

Answers
1 All the people were lying in a line on the beach.
2 Yes.
3 No.
4 No. Yes.

VOCABULARY

1 Aim: to focus on compound nouns; to present the words in the vocabulary box.
● Ask the students to use the nouns in the box to make compound nouns. Some words can go in more than one compound.

Answers
west bank   cathedral city   city centre
mountain country   fishing village   town hall
mountain region   market square   seaside town
university district

2 Aim: to present descriptive vocabulary; to practise speaking.
● This activity gives students a further opportunity to explore vocabulary items. Ask the students to work in small groups and to describe their country or a place or region they particularly like, using the words in the vocabulary box.

FUNCTIONS

1 Aim: to focus on the use of expressions for describing location.

- Ask the students to work in pairs and describe the views suggested in this activity.

- You may also like to ask them to close their eyes and to imagine a view which they should then describe.

2 Aim: to focus on the use of expressions for describing position.

- This activity is another variation on the practice provided by 1.

SOUNDS

1 Aim: to focus on linking sounds in connected speech.

- Remind students that in connected speech it is common to join certain phonemes with a linking sound.

- Ask them to say the phrases aloud, and to decide which sound links the words represented with the word link.

- 🔲 Play the tape and ask the students to listen and check.

Answers	
1 on the edge of the oasis	/y/
2 at the end of the estuary	/y/
3 on two or three islands	/w/ /y/
4 empty areas in the east	/y/
5 on the open sea	/y/
6 as far as the eye can see	/y/
7 high above the entrance	/y/
8 down to a river	/w/

- Ask the students to repeat the sentences.

2 Aim: to focus on linking sounds in connected speech.

- The students may have noticed the rule for the sounds which link the words in 1. Ask them to list the link sound which goes with the preceding sounds.

WRITING

1 Aim: to prepare for writing; to practise note-taking; to practise writing a magazine article.

- Explain to the students that they are going to write a magazine article about an attractive region in their country. Ask the students to think about the style of the article and who is likely to be their audience.

- Ask the students to do this note-taking activity alone. Encourage them to think about as many *factual* details as possible.

2 Aim: to practise expanding notes into sentences.

- Ask the students to expand the notes they made in 1 into sentences. Remind them to focus on the facts.

3 Aim: to practise writing a magazine article.

- Explain to the students that they are now going to write the magazine article about the region they have chosen. Ask the students to add opinion adjectives to the sentences they have written and to think about the 'writer's style' as they did when analysing the Bill Bryson passage on page 28. You may like to ask them to do this activity for homework.

FUNCTIONS

> Describing position
> **Here are some useful expressions for describing position.**
> *To the north/south... 70 kms from...*
> *In central (country/region) In the north/south/east/west...*
> *Half-way between... About 200 metres/kilometres from...*
> *On each/either side...*
> *The road leads to... The stream goes/winds/flows past...*
> *At the top/bottom of the hill.*
> *The house is set among trees. It's surrounded by fields. All around...*
> *As far as the eye can see... In the foreground/background/distance...*
> *A little/long way off...*

1 Work in pairs. Take it in turns to describe the photos on these pages. Use the words in the vocabulary boxes and the expressions in the functions box.

2 Work in pairs. Take it in turns to describe two of the following views.

– the view from your classroom   – the view from your house
– a view you particularly like   – a view you particularly dislike

SOUNDS

1 🔲 Listen to the following phrases and decide what sound links the words which are joined.

1 on the edge of the oasis   5 on the open sea
2 at the end of the estuary   6 as far as the eye can see
3 on two or three islands   7 high above the entrance
4 empty areas in the east   8 down to a river

2 Can you work out a rule for the sounds which link the words in 1 in connected speech?

WRITING

1 You've been asked to write a magazine article about an attractive region in your country. Make notes on:

– where it is
– how large it is
– what the landscape is like
– what the buildings are like
– any historical information
– any other special features

For the moment, focus on facts.

Lake Balaton region, in the west of Hungary, 70km south-west of Budapest.

2 Write sentences using the notes you made in 1.

The Lake Balaton region is in the west of Hungary, 70km south-west of Budapest.

3 Think about why the region is attractive or interesting. Rewrite the sentences you wrote in 2 by adding *opinion* adjectives and adjectival phrases.

The picturesque Lake Balaton region is in the west of Hungary...

One night, quite late, I was still awake in the room I shared with my husband. I was lying on my right side and could hear a child crying. Getting up, I went to see if our son was all right. He was sleeping soundly, breathing deeply and gently. So I climbed the stairs to the attic where our daughters were. They too were sleeping very quietly. I stayed a while but nothing changed and I could not hear any sound other than the sea and a slight breeze. I went back to our room and got back into bed.

Laying my head on the pillow, I could hear the crying again. And so, without consciously thinking it out, I sat up, arms around my knees and said clearly but softly, 'Stop crying, darling. You are quite safe. Mother's here.' And the crying stopped.

I used to walk to the bus stop with the elderly gentleman living near us. He became ill and I did not see him until one bright sunny morning a few months later. As I walked down the path, I glanced to the left and I saw the elderly gentleman walking slowly up past the hedge round the front garden.

He turned and looked straight at me, and I was struck by how pale he appeared to be. Not until later did I realise I could not hear the sound of his footsteps, although he appeared to be walking in his usual manner, apart from being slower.

I happened to glance away, and when I looked back there was no one there. There was nowhere he could have disappeared to, and he had not collapsed on the pavement.

In the evening I discovered that he had died about half an hour before I had seen him that morning.

My brother and I were staying with friends. On the second night I just couldn't get to sleep and didn't want to disturb him with a light. Eventually I lay down and placed my hand under the pillow. As I did so, I felt someone grasp my hand, squeezing it in a comforting manner. My eyes were open and I could see the room, but I was paralysed with fear.

I took a deep breath and told myself to relax, then moved my legs. My hand was still being held. I then slowly withdrew my hand and rolled on to my back. I felt no other 'presence' in the room.

Arriving late at Bradshaw Hall, I was shown up to my room immediately and offered a bath before changing for dinner. Tired and travel-stained, I accepted gratefully. On my way along the passage I saw someone enter the bathroom. Thinking this was another guest, I said good evening and returned to my bedroom to wait my turn, leaving the door ajar. A few minutes later I went back, found the bathroom empty and had a bath.

As I came down the stairs, I saw my host waiting for me. I noticed that the table was laid for two people only and to satisfy my curiosity, I made some remark about a fellow-guest going into the bathroom just before me, to which the colonel replied: 'There's no other guest. Just you and me!'

Not wishing to contradict him, I said nothing and we took our seats. Then I became aware of the same figure suddenly appearing directly behind the colonel's chair.

'But there's the gentleman I saw upstairs!' I said.

The colonel turned his head. 'Where? Who?' he asked.

'There!' I said. 'Standing behind the chair, now!'

The colonel turned his head to look and said with some amusement: 'I never can see him. It's our monk, you know! I find it so disappointing. He often appears upstairs and on the staircase, but never for me, I'm sad to say.'

Adapted from *True ghost stories of our time*

8

GENERAL COMMENTS

Vocabulary work

In the *Reward* series there are several types of vocabulary work. The first type is the vocabulary presented in a box, which means it is for productive use and will be easy for the students to revise. These words may be organised in topic areas, such as in this lesson, or may be useful words generated by the reading or listening passage. All the words in the vocabulary box constitute part of the vocabulary syllabus, namely the words which are considered to be suitable to acquire at this level. There is another type of vocabulary work which concerns words which do not need to be learned at upper-intermediate level, but which either need to be pretaught in order to give the student better access to the main idea of a listening or reading passage, or hinder comprehension after students have listened to or read the passage. This kind of vocabulary work constitutes part of the listening or reading syllabus, and is usually signposted in the Teacher's Book as dealing with unfamiliar words. It is important for the students to realise that a passage should not always be exploited for every single new word. While such close attention may increase students' vocabulary bank, this may have a negative effect on their reading and listening ability. They will always be confronted by words they don't understand and it's better to develop the skills of dealing with them rather than treating them as items to acquire productively.

VOCABULARY AND READING

1 Aim: to present the words in the vocabulary box; to introduce the theme of the lesson.

● The theme of the lesson is stories of the supernatural. Much of the discussion about the theme will involve a description of sensations, so the lesson begins with work on words for the senses. Write the five headings on the board, and begin to categorise a few words. Ask one or two students to suggest other words which should go under the headings. Ask the students to finish this activity alone and then check their answers with a partner. Point out that some of the words can go under more than one heading.

Answers
sight: gaze glance glimpse notice observe peer stare
sound: deafening loud noisy silent
smell: fragrant scented smelly sour stinking sweet sweet-smelling
taste: bitter fragrant salty sour spicy sweet
touch: grab grasp pat press punch slap snatch squeeze stroke

2 Aim: to consolidate learning vocabulary.

● Ask the students to answer the questions. You can do this with the whole class. Explain there may be more than one answer.

> **Answers**
> **Sight:** a) glance, glimpse b) stare, gaze c) peer
> **Sound:** a) deafening b) silent
> **A smell to describe:** a) fragrant, scented b) smelly
>   c) stinking d) fragrant, scented
> **A taste to describe:** a) sweet b) salty c) spicy
>   d) sour
> **Touch:** a) grab, snatch b) pat c) squeeze
>   d) punch e) slap

3 Aim: to read for main ideas.

● Ask the students to read the stories and to decide what sense each one features.

● Then ask the students to think of a suitable title for each story. Both of these activities are designed to encourage them to look at the main ideas and not get distracted by difficult items of vocabulary.

> **Answers**
> **Story 1:** sound
> **Story 2:** sight
> **Story 3:** touch
> **Story 4:** sight

4 Aim: to deal with unfamiliar words.

● There may be some words in the stories which get in the way of overall understanding of the general sense. Ask them to find words which mean the same as the simplified explanations.

> **Answers**
> **Story 1:** top rooms in the house – attic
> light wind – breeze
> **Story 2:** quite old – elderly very aware – struck
> fallen down – collapsed
> **Story 3:** wake up – disturb unable to move – paralysed
> took away – withdrew
> **Story 4:** open – ajar interest – curiosity

5 Aim: to react to the text.

● Ask the whole class if they liked the stories, and if so, which one they liked best. Don't spend too long on this as they will discuss the issue further in *Speaking*.

GRAMMAR

1 Aim: to focus on participle clauses.

● Ask the students to read the information in the grammar box and then to do the exercises.

> **Answers**
> 1 **Going** back to our room, I got back into bed.
> 2 Our son was in the room **backing** on to the wall immediately behind our bed.
> 3 **Lying** down, I placed my hand under the pillow.
> 4 **Taking** a deep breath, I told myself to relax.
> 5 **Walking** down the path, I glanced to the left…
> 6 **Finding** the bathroom empty, I had a bath.
> 7 **Coming** down the stairs, I saw my host…
> 8 **Turning** his head to look, the colonel said…

2 Aim: to focus on participle clauses.

● This may be a difficult activity for some students. For others, it may help consolidate the function of participle clauses.

> **Answers**
> 1 when one action happens after another
> 2 reduced relative clause
> 3 when two actions happen at the same time
> 4 when two actions happen at the same time
> 5 when an action happens in the middle of a longer action
> 6 to say why something happens
> 7 when an action happens in the middle of a longer action
> 8 when one action happens after another

SPEAKING

1 Aim: to practise speaking.

● Ask the students to discuss their answers to the questions in small groups.

2 Aim: to practise speaking.

● Ask a student to say what his/her group's answer to the first question was.

● Ask a second student to paraphrase what the first student said and to add an opinion.

● Ask a third student to paraphrase what the second student said and to add an opinion.

● Do the same for all the questions. This procedure will not only encourage speaking skills but also encourage careful listening.

VOCABULARY AND READING

1 Put the words in the box under these headings: *sight, sound, smell, taste, touch.*

bitter scented sweet-smelling deafening
fragrant gaze glance glimpse grab grasp
loud pat noisy notice observe sweet
peer press punch salty silent slap
smelly snatch sour spicy squeeze
stinking stroke stare

2 Look at the words you wrote under each heading in 1. Find a word to describe the following:

Sight
a) look at quickly   *glance*
b) look at fixedly
c) look at in a confused way

Sound
a) very loud   b) very quiet

A smell to describe:
a) petals   b) strong cheese
c) drains   d) perfume

A taste to describe:
a) sugar   b) bacon
c) curry   d) vinegar

Touch
a) to take roughly
b) to touch kindly with the hand
c) to hold tightly then loosely
d) to hit with your fist
e) to hit with open hand

3 Read the four stories and decide which of the senses each one features. Think of a suitable title for each story.

4 Look back at the stories and find a word which means the same as:

– *top rooms in the house   light wind* (story 1)
– *quite old   very aware   fallen down* (story 2)
– *wake up   unable to move*
  took away (story 3)
– *open   interest* (story 4)

5 Work in pairs. Which story did you enjoy most, or find most strange? Can you explain why?

GRAMMAR

Participle *-ing* clauses
Participle clauses are often used in stories to describe background information. They focus on the action by leaving out nouns, pronouns, auxiliary verbs and conjunctions. This often creates a more dramatic effect. You can use a participle clause:
– when two actions happen at the same time. You use it for one of the actions.
Laying my head on the pillow, I could hear the crying again.
– as a 'reduced' relative clause.
I used to walk to the bus stop with the elderly gentleman living near us.
(= who lived near us)
– when one action happens immediately after another action. You use it for the first action.
Getting up, I went to see if our son was all right.
– when an action happens in the middle of a longer action. You use it for the longer action.
Thinking this was another guest, I returned to my room.
– to say why something happens.
Not wanting to contradict him, I said nothing.

1 Rewrite these extracts from the stories as participle clauses.

1 I went back to our room and got back into bed.
2 Our son was in the room which backed on to the wall immediately behind our bed.
3 I lay down and placed my hand under the pillow.
4 I took a deep breath and told myself to relax.
5 As I walked down the path, I glanced to the left...
6 Because I found the bathroom empty, I had a bath.
7 As I came down the stairs, I saw my host...
8 The colonel turned his head to look and said...

1 Going back to our room, I got back into bed.

2 Look at the sentences in *Grammar* activity 1. Use the information in the grammar box to decide which type of participle clause each one of your answers is.

SPEAKING

1 Work in groups of three or four and discuss your answers to the questions.

1 Are there stories of ghosts or spirits in your country?
2 Where do the best-known ghost stories come from?
3 Do you believe in ghosts? Do you like ghost stories?
4 The stories in this lesson are supposed to be true. Do you believe they really happened?
5 Can you think of an explanation for what happened?

2 Find out what the rest of the class thinks.

Verbs of sensation

SOUNDS AND VOCABULARY

1 🔊 Listen to someone reading the first story on page 32 in a dramatic way. Note how the speaker uses pauses, word stress, intonation, pitch of voice (loud or soft).

2 Work in pairs. Choose one of the other stories and decide which effects in 1 you would use and where, to make the story sound dramatic.

Now read the story aloud in a dramatic way.

3 These words all describe sounds. Say who or what makes these sounds.

> hum creak groan sigh whistle clatter
> buzz cry bark whisper hiss sniff sob
> roar gasp crash bang rustle thud clang
> rumble rattle bleep screech cough
> hiccup snore

4 🔊 Listen and tick (✓) the sounds in 3 which you hear.

GRAMMAR

> **Verbs of sensation**
> *See, hear, feel, watch, listen to* and *notice* are verbs of sensation. You can put an object + *-ing* when you only see or hear part of an action and the action continues over a period of time.
> *I heard **a child crying.***
> *I felt **someone squeezing** my hand.*
> You can put an object + infinitive when you see or hear the whole action and the action is now finished.
> *I felt **someone grasp** my hand.*
> *I saw **someone enter** the bathroom.*

1 Work in pairs and say what you heard happen or happening in *Sounds and vocabulary* activity 4. Use the infinitive if you heard the whole sound.

I heard a bee buzzing.

2 Complete the sentences with a verb from below in its infinitive or *-ing* form.

sing bark walk nod wave .

I had a strange dream last night. I dreamt I was in bed when suddenly I heard a dog ____, then scratching at the front door. I went to the door and opened it, but there was nothing there. Then I heard someone ____ in the distance. It went on for a minute or so. I stood there and suddenly I saw a man ____ slowly towards me, singing and dancing along the path. Behind him was a dog. I asked him who he was. He called out that he used to live in the house. I knew the previous owner was dead, so I asked him if he was a ghost. I saw him ____ his head and say 'yes'. Then I saw him ____ once and he was gone.

3 Think back to the ghost stories you read on page 32.

Write sentences using verbs of sensation and object + *-ing* or infinitive.

In the first story, the woman heard a child crying.

LISTENING

1 Work in pairs. You're going to hear Louise telling some friends a story about something strange which happened to her. Here are some words and phrases from part 1 of her story. Discuss what you think the strange event was.

school Scotland castle spooky share bedroom cookery music piano imagine Chopin visit same date

SOUNDS AND VOCABULARY

1 Aim: to practise recognising tones of voice for dramatic effect.

● ▭ Ask the students to listen to someone reading the first story in a dramatic way. Draw their attention to the pauses, the word stress, the intonation and the pitch of voice.

2 Aim: to practise using different tones of voice for dramatic effect.

● Ask the students to work in pairs and choose a story. Ask the students to consider how they could use intonation, word stress, pauses, pitch of the voice etc to make the story they have chosen sound more dramatic. Ask the students to read the story aloud in pairs.

3 Aim: to present the words in the vocabulary box.

● Ask the students to look at the words for sounds in the box and decide who or what might make them.

4 Aim: to practise using the words in the vocabulary box; to prepare for the presentation of the target structure.

● ▭ Play the tape and ask the students to say what each noise is.

> **Answers**
> a bee buzzing, a man snoring, a dog barking,
> a lion roaring, a car crashing, a tree creaking

GRAMMAR

1 Aim: to present verbs of sensation.

● Ask the students to read the information in the grammar box and then to do the exercises.

> **Answers**
> I heard a bee buzzing, a man snoring, a dog barking,
> a lion roaring, a car crash, a tree creaking.

2 Aim: to practise using the new vocabulary; to practise using verbs of sensation.

> **Answers**
> I had a strange dream last night. I dreamt I was in bed when suddenly I heard a dog **barking** then scratching at the front door. I went to the door and opened it, but there was nothing there. Then I heard someone **singing** in the distance. It went on for a minute or so. I stood there and suddenly I saw a man **walking** slowly towards me, singing and dancing along the garden path. Behind him was a dog. I asked him who he was. He called out in a ghostly voice that he used to live in the house. I knew the previous owner was dead, so I asked him if he was a ghost. I saw him **nod** his head and say 'yes'. Then I saw him **wave** once and he was gone.

3 Aim: to practise using verbs of sensation.

● Ask the students to work in pairs and to remember what happened in the ghost stories on page 32. Go round and make sure they are using verbs of sensation.

LISTENING

1 Aim: to prepare for listening; to pre-teach some useful vocabulary.

● Ask the students to work in pairs and to predict what the story is likely to be about.

● Ask two or three pairs for their predictions.

2 Aim: to practise listening for main ideas.

● 📼 Play the tape and ask the students to tick the sentences which are true and put a cross by those which are false.

Answers
1 True
2 False
3 False
4 True
5 False
6 True
7 False
8 True

3 Aim: to check comprehension.

● 📼 Ask the students to check their answers to 2. When they have finished, play the tape again and ask them to check.

4 Aim: to check comprehension.

● Ask the students to read the sentences and then listen to part 2 of the tape. When they have finished, ask them to complete the sentences based on what they remember of the story.

Answers
1 One night after they had been asleep for sometime, Melissa and Louise **suddenly woke up.**
2 There was a smell of gas in **the house.**
3 The same thing happened **twice more in the night.**
4 The next morning the teacher **was just laughing at them.**
5 The old cook asked them **which room they were sleeping in.**
6 She told them that the bedroom they were sleeping in had belonged to **the son and heir who had been killed in the war.**
7 He had been killed **during the First World War.**
8 They smelt the gas on the anniversary of **his death.**

5 Aim: to check comprehension; to practise speaking.

● Ask the students to work in pairs and check their answers to 4.

● 📼 Play the tape again.

6 Aim: to focus on colloquial language.

● Explain that the speaker uses some colloquial language used in everyday speech which makes the story a bit more difficult to understand.

● Ask the students to say what they think the speaker means by the expressions. Do this activity orally with the whole class.

Answers
1 The castle looked frightening.
2 She was very nice.
3 She thought Melissa was mad.
4 It was very smelly.
5 The teacher was making fun of us.
6 It made us very cross.
7 She sat there laughing.
8 She looked very frightened.

7 Aim: to encourage a reaction to the story.

● Ask the students to choose one or more of the words to describe Louise's friends' reactions to the story.

● Ask the students to talk about their reactions to the story.

SPEAKING AND WRITING

1 Aim: to practise speaking; to prepare for writing.

● Encourage the students to be as creative as possible for this activity. Their stories can be an amalgam of well-known stories. You may like to suggest to any group which is having difficulty in getting started to set the story in the school or classroom where you are now, and to use the other students as their characters. Ask the students to follow the rest of the instructions.

2 Aim: to practise writing; to practise using the linking words for story telling *meanwhile, eventually, finally.*

● Make sure everyone understands what the linking words mean, particularly *eventually* which has a 'false friend' in many languages. In English, *eventually* refers to something that has finally been accomplished.

● You may like to ask the students to do this activity for homework. However, make sure you create an opportunity for everybody to read or hear all the stories. If they read them aloud, ask them to do so in as dramatic a way as possible.

2 🔈 Listen to part 1 and decide which of the following statements are true.

1 Louise shared a bedroom with Melissa.
2 They had cookery lessons every evening.
3 They kept hearing someone playing music.
4 Melissa heard someone playing the piano.
5 The teacher believed Melissa's story.
6 Chopin had once stayed in the castle.
7 Melissa didn't recognise the music.
8 She heard the music on the anniversary of Chopin's visit.

Did you guess correctly in 1?

3 Work in pairs and check your answers to 2.
🔈 Now listen again and check.

4 🔈 Listen to part 2 and complete these sentences.

1 One night after they had been asleep for some time, Melissa and Louise _____.
2 There was a smell of gas in _____.
3 The same thing happened _____.
4 The next morning the teacher _____.
5 The old cook asked them _____.
6 She told us that the bedroom that they were sleeping in had belonged to _____.
7 He had been killed _____.
8 They smelt the gas on the anniversary of _____.

5 Work in pairs and check your answers.
🔈 Now listen again and check.

6 What do you think Louise means by the following expressions? Say them in a simpler way.

1 'It reminded me of something out of a horror film.'
2 'The old Scottish cook, she was an absolute darling.'
3 'She thought Melissa was completely out to lunch.'
4 'It was a real stench.'
5 'She was taking the mickey out of us.'
6 'It made us really mad.'
7 'She just sat there splitting her sides.'
8 'She looked as if she'd seen a ghost.'

1 The castle looked frightening.

7 Which of these words would you use to describe her friends' reactions to Louise's story?

amused   incredulous   frightened   mocking
unbelieving   sarcastic   sympathetic   astonished

What is your reaction to the story?

SPEAKING AND WRITING

1 A national newspaper is running a series called *Ghost stories from around the world*.

Work in groups of two or three. You're going to write a ghost story together. First decide where your story will take place. Choose from one of these places or think of a place of your own.

– a castle   – an old house   – a school   – a cemetery

Now decide who the characters are. Did the story happen to you or someone you know?
Next, decide what happened. Did the person *see, feel, hear* or *smell* something strange? What did they do?
Finally, decide what happened at the end of the story. Did the person escape from the ghost or not?

2 In your groups, write the story. Use linking words to join each event.

You can use *meanwhile* for something that was happening at the same time.
I tried to fix my car. **Meanwhile**, *it was getting dark.*

You can use *eventually* for the last in a long sequence of events.
Eventually, *he found a door that led to the room.*

You can use *finally* for the last event of all.
Finally, *he locked the front door and drove away.*

When you have finished, display your story for the rest of the class to read. Which group wrote the most frightening story? Were any of the stories amusing?

VOCABULARY

1 *Connotation* refers to the feeling or image an adjective creates rather than its meaning. There are many adjectives which usually have either positive or negative connotations.

Positive   *practical, hard-working, romantic*
Negative   *mean, nosy, careless*

In different contexts the same adjectives can have the opposite connotation.

He was very dull and serious. He didn't laugh a lot.
I am serious about my work and passed my exams.
She was proud of her children.
She was rather proud and unfriendly.
His piano playing was very sensitive.
She was very sensitive and kept bursting into tears.

Now decide if the adjectives in these sentences have a positive or a negative connotation.

1 She was wearing a very curious hat.
2 He was very ambitious and was prepared to do anything to succeed.
3 He was very talkative and interesting.
4 She has a naïve charm.
5 He's very extravagant when he throws a party and we all enjoy ourselves.
6 It was a simple idea and everyone liked it.

2 Write sentences using the same adjectives in the sentences above with the opposite connotation.

3 You can often make an adjective from nouns or verbs by using the following suffixes:

-able -al -ant -ar -ual -atic -ific -ative -erial
-ish -ive -ful -y

comfort – comfortable

Now use the suffixes to make adjectives from the following words. You may have to change the noun or verb by leaving off the last one or two letters.

talk innovate fruit child smell create fun
manage boss pain haze tropic fragrance
notice

GRAMMAR

1 Choose the best tense.

1 I've never *learned/been learning* Spanish.
2 She *has* just *left/been leaving* for work.
3 For the last year he *has written/been writing* his autobiography.
4 I *have* always *wanted/been wanting* a Mercedes.
5 They *have* just *gone/been going* to the shops.
6 He's *lived/been living* in France for a long time and he's going to stay.

2 Look at these sentences and explain the difference between them. Which sentences mean the same?

1 a I had left the office when I heard the explosion.
    b I left the office when I heard the explosion.
2 a She changed her mind when she saw him.
    b She changed her mind when she had seen him.
3 a I felt better when I heard the news.
    b I felt better when I had heard the news.
4 a She ran away when he arrived.
    b She had run away when he arrived.
5 a When he became a pilot, he earned a lot of money.
    b When he became a pilot, he had earned a lot of money.
6 a She bought a flat when she moved to Turin.
    b She bought a flat when she had moved to Turin.

3 Answer the questions using the prompts in brackets and the past perfect continuous.

1 How long had you been at the bus stop? (I/wait/for twenty minutes)
2 How many years had he had the same job? (He/work/there/since 1967)
3 Why did you look so tired? (I/revise/my vocabulary/all evening)
4 Why hadn't you spoken to your parents? (I/work/too much)
5 Why was the river so high? (It/rain/for two weeks)
6 What had you been doing before the accident? (I/drive/from Oxford to London)

Progress check 5–8

GENERAL COMMENTS

You can work through this Progress check in the order shown, or concentrate on areas which may have caused difficulty in Lessons 5 to 8. You can also let the students choose the activities they would like or feel the need to do.

VOCABULARY

1 Aim: to focus on positive and negative connotation.

● Ask the students to read the explanation about connotation and then find out if something similar exists in their own language. Students should decide if the adjectives in the sentences have a positive or negative connotation.

> **Answers**
> 1 negative   2 negative   3 positive
> 4 positive   5 positive   6 positive

2 Aim: to practise using adjectives with positive or negative connotation.

● Ask the students to write sentences using the same adjectives as in 1 but with the opposite connotation. Can the students think of other adjectives with both positive and negative connotations?

3 Aim: to focus on adjective suffixes.

The students will have already come across these adjectives and their suffixes, but this activity is designed to encourage their creativity in language by explaining a generative rule. Find out if they can do this in their own language.

> **Answers**
> talkative innovative fruitful childish smelly
> creative funny manageable bossy painful
> hazy tropical fragrant noticeable

GRAMMAR

1 Aim: to revise present perfect tenses.

> **Answers**
> 1 I**'ve never learned** Spanish.
> 2 She **has** just **left** for work.
> 3 For the last year he **has been writing** his autobiography.
> 4 I **have** always **wanted** a Mercedes.
> 5 They **have** just **gone** to the shops.
> 6 He**'s been living** in France for a long time and he's going to stay.

2 Aim: to revise the past tenses.

> **Answers**
> 1 a I heard the explosion **after** I had left the office.
> 1 b I heard an explosion. **Then** I left the office.
> 2 a and b mean the same.
> 3 a and b mean the same.
> 4 a He arrived. **Then** she ran away.
> 4 b He arrived **after** she had run away.
> 5 a He became a pilot. **Then** he earned a lot of money.
> 5 b He became a pilot **after** he had earned a lot of money.
> 6 a and b mean the same.

3 Aim: to revise the past perfect continuous.

> **Answers**
> 1 I'd been waiting for a bus for twenty minutes.
> 2 He'd been working there since 1967.
> 3 I'd been revising my vocabulary all evening.
> 4 I'd been working too much.
> 5 It had been raining for two weeks.
> 6 I'd been driving from Oxford to London.

4 Aim: to revise *after + -ing*.

Answers
2 **After getting** married, she had a baby.
5 **After going to** the cinema, we had dinner.
6 **After getting** to the hotel, he rang home.

5 Aim: to revise fact and opinion adjectives.

Answers
fact: tropical, dizzy, bald, agricultural, west, frosty
opinion: sensual, plump, smelly

6 Aim: to revise participle clauses.

Answers
1 **Lying** down on the bed, I went to sleep.
2 **Telling** everyone to be quiet, I sat down.
3 **Feeling** relaxed at the party, I talked to most people.
4 **Sitting** in the garden, I could hear birds singing.
5 The man **standing** by me was wearing a hat.
6 **Seeing** the accident, I called an ambulance.

7 Aim: to revise verbs of sensation.

Answers
1 She saw him working in a shop.
2 He heard something fall to the ground.
3 I noticed her look quickly at him.
4 I felt her touch my hand for a moment.
5 They watched the children playing all day.
6 I saw him crash the car.

SOUNDS

1 Aim: to focus on the /ɔɪ/ and /əʊ/ sounds.
• Ask the students to do this activity on their own. You may like to say the words aloud once.

• Ask the students to put the words in two columns.

• Play the tape and ask the students to repeat the words.

Answers
/əʊ/: nose toe bow sew bowl chose loan cone
/ɔɪ/: noise toy boy soil boil choice loin coin
/əʊ/: ose oe ow oan one
/ɔɪ/: oi oy

2 Aim: to focus on word stress in connected speech.
• Ask the students to listen and underline the words which are stressed.

• Play the tape.

Answers
I used to walk to the bus stop with the elderly gentleman living near us. He became ill and I didn't see him until one bright sunny morning a few months later. As I walked down the path, I glanced to the left and I saw the elderly gentleman walking slowly up past the hedge round the front garden.

3 Aim: to focus on word stress in connected speech.
• Ask the students to predict which words are likely to be stressed, and to underline them.

• Play the tape and ask the students to listen and check their answers.

Answers
He turned and looked straight at me, and I was struck by how pale he appeared to be. Not until later did I realise I could not hear the sound of his footsteps, although he appeared to be walking in his usual manner, apart from being slower.

LISTENING AND SPEAKING

1 Aim: to practise listening and note-taking.
• Listening and writing is a difficult skill to develop, so you may need to play the tape a couple of times for this activity.

2 Aim: to practise speaking.
• Ask the students to work in pairs and to compare and expand their notes.

3 Aim: to practise speaking and listening.
• This activity will encourage the students to listen very carefully to what the others say. Ask the students to follow the instructions. Go round and check everyone is telling the story in as much detail as possible.

4 Which pairs of sentences have the same subject? Rewrite them as one sentence using *after + -ing*.

1 I had lunch. Then the boss called me.
2 She got married. Then she had a baby.
3 They bought a car. Then he lost his job.
4 They went on holiday. Then she fell ill.
5 We went to the cinema. Then we had dinner.
6 He got to the hotel. Then he rang home.

5 Decide if these are usually *opinion* or *fact* adjectives.

tropical sensual dizzy plump bald agricultural west smelly frosty

6 Rewrite these sentences with participle clauses.

1 I lay down on the bed. I went to sleep.
2 She told everyone to be quiet and listen.
3 I felt relaxed at the party. I talked to most people.
4 I sat in the garden. I could hear birds singing.
5 The man who was standing by me was wearing a hat.
6 I saw the accident, and called an ambulance.

7 Complete the sentences with the verb in brackets in its infinitive or *-ing* form.

1 She saw him (work) in a shop.
2 He heard something (fall) to the ground.
3 I noticed her (look) quickly at him.
4 I felt her (touch) my hand for a moment.
5 They watched the children (play) all day.
6 I saw him (crash) the car.

SOUNDS

1 Underline the /ɔɪ/ sound and circle the /əʊ/ sound. Put the words in two columns.

nose noise toe toy bow boy sew soil boil choice chose loin loan cone coin

[cassette] Now listen and say the words aloud. How many different spellings are there for each sound? What letters follow the letter(s) you have underlined or circled?

2 [cassette] Listen and underline the words which the speaker stresses.

I used to walk to the bus stop with the elderly gentleman living near us. He became ill and I didn't see him until one bright sunny morning a few months later. As I walked down the path, I glanced to the left and I saw the elderly gentleman walking slowly up past the hedge round the front garden.

3 Underline the words you think the speaker will stress.

He turned and looked straight at me, and I was struck by how pale he appeared to be. Not until later did I realise I could not hear the sound of his footsteps, although he appeared to be walking in his usual manner, apart from being slower.

[cassette] Listen and check. As you listen, say the passage aloud.

LISTENING AND SPEAKING

1 [cassette] Work in pairs. You're going to hear a story about a chauffeur in a hospital. Listen and make notes about what happened.

2 Work together and check you remember the story. Make sure you get the sequence of events correct. Expand your notes with as much detail as possible.

The husband had died before his wife.

3 Work with another partner.

Student A: Start telling the story and try to include as much detail as possible. Answer Student B's questions. If you cannot answer a question, Student B will continue telling the story and you must ask questions.
Student B: Listen to Student A telling the story. Ask questions about any details he or she leaves out. If he/she cannot answer your questions, continue telling the story.

Keep asking and answering questions. The person telling the story at the end is the winner.

Impressions of school

9

Talking about memories: *remember* + noun/-*ing*

SPEAKING

1 This lesson is about school and your impressions.
Can you remember:

– how old you were when you first went to school?
– the names of the friends you made?
– the name of your first teacher?
– how you felt about going to school?

2 Work in groups of two or three and take turns to tell
each other about the things you remembered in 1.

3 It is often said that your schooldays are the best days
of your life. Decide in your groups if you agree with
this. Tell the class whether you agree or disagree
and why.

READING

1 The passage is taken from the novel *Jane Eyre* by
Charlotte Brontë, which was first published in 1847.
Jane's parents are dead, and she has been brought up
by relatives. At the age of ten, she is sent away from
home to her first school. The passage describes her
first day at school. Work in pairs. The following words
are in the order in which they appear in the passage.
Check that you know what they mean.

bell   dawn   shiver   basin   stairs   school room
prayers   Bible   exercise   breakfast

Can you use the words to guess what the answers to
these questions might be?

At what time of day does the passage take place?
Is the school likely to be a day school or a
boarding school?
What does Jane do at the start of the passage?
What is the main activity for the schoolchildren?
What happens at the end of the passage?

2 Read the passage and check your answers to 1.
Did you guess correctly?

The night passed rapidly: I was too tired even to dream; I only once
awoke to hear the wind rave in furious gusts, and the rain fall in
torrents, and to be sensible that Miss Miller had taken her place by
my side. When I again unclosed my eyes, a loud bell was ringing;
the girls were up and dressing; day had not yet begun to dawn, and
a rushlight or two burnt in the room. I too rose reluctantly; it was
bitter cold, and I dressed as well as I could for shivering, and
washed when there was a basin at liberty, which did not occur soon,
as there was but one basin to six girls, on the stands down the
middle of the room. Again the bell rang: all formed in file, two and
two, and in that order descended the stairs and entered the cold and
dimly-lit schoolroom: here prayers were read by Miss Miller;
afterwards she called out –

'Form classes!'

A great tumult succeeded for some minutes, during which Miss
Miller repeatedly exclaimed, 'Silence!' and 'Order!' When it
subsided, I saw them all drawn up in four semi-circles, before four
chairs, placed at the four tables: all held books in their hands, and
a great book, like a Bible, lay on each table, before the vacant seat.
A pause of some seconds succeeded, filled up by the low, vague hum
of numbers; Miss Miller walked from class to class, hushing this
indefinite sound.

A distant bell tinkled: immediately three ladies entered the room,
each walked to a table and took her seat; Miss Miller assumed the
fourth vacant chair, which was nearest the door, and around which
the smallest of the children were assembled: to this inferior class I
was called, and placed at the bottom of it.

Business now began: the day's Collect was repeated, then certain
texts of Scripture were said, and to these succeeded a protracted
reading of chapters in the Bible, which lasted an hour. By the time
that exercise was terminated, day had fully dawned. The
indefatigable bell now sounded for the fourth time: the classes were
marshalled and marched into another room to breakfast. How glad
I was to behold a prospect of getting something to eat! I was now
nearly sick from hunger, having taken so little the day before.

9

GENERAL COMMENTS

Jane Eyre by Charlotte Brontë is one of the most widely read English novels. The novel describes how Jane refused to accept her appointed place in society and became a governess in the household of Mr Rochester, with whom she fell in love. Charlotte Brontë had two sisters, both of whom were novelists at a time when female novelists were very rare: Emily, who wrote *Wuthering Heights,* another classic of English literature, and Anne, who wrote *The Tenant of Wildfell Hall.* They lived in a beautiful rural region of Yorkshire, which is now commonly known as Brontë country.

SPEAKING

1 Aim: to introduce the theme of the lesson.
● The theme of this lesson is school. If your students are still in full-time education, they will still have impressions of their early days at their first school. Ask the students to work alone and think about their answers to the questions. Ask one or two students to talk about their first impressions of school.

2 Aim: to practise speaking.
● Ask the students to work together in groups of two or three and discuss their memories. Do they have any particularly interesting, amusing or frightening memories?

3 Aim: to practise speaking.
● Ask the students first to tell each other in pairs what they think of the opinion that schooldays are the best days of your life. Can they think of arguments either in favour or against, or both? Students should report back to the rest of the class on their arguments in favour or against.

READING

1 Aim: to prepare for reading; to practise speaking; to pre-teach some useful words; to predict before reading.
● You may like to tell the students a little about the background of *Jane Eyre* and Charlotte Brontë, which you can find in the general comments. Draw attention to the fact that neither Charlotte nor her fictitious character, Jane, was prepared to be subjected to the usual place of women in society.

● Ask the students to predict what the passage is likely to be about by explaining, if necessary, what the words mean, and by asking the students to use the words in answer to the questions. Ask several pairs to describe their predictions to the rest of the class.

2 Aim: to read for main ideas.
● Ask the students to read the passage and to check their answers to 1.

3 Aim: to deal with unfamiliar words.

● Sometimes it's easier to deal with an unfamiliar word when you're not distracted by its appearance. This activity focuses on some words with which students may have difficulty. Ask them to think of a word which can go in each gap.

4 Aim: to deal with unfamiliar words.

● Tell the students that the words here are simpler forms of the words from the passage. Are they similar to the words they thought of in 3?

● Ask the students to check what the word is in the passage.

> **Answers**
> rave – blow
> tinkled – rang
> assumed – sat down in
> protracted – lengthy
> at liberty – available

5 Aim: to check comprehension; to present the target structures.

● Ask the students to read the passage again and to decide which of the statements are true.

> **Answers**
> 2 True 3 True 5 True
> 8 True 9 True

6 Aim: to practise speaking.

● Ask the students to compare their first day at school with Jane's. Was it better or worse?

GRAMMAR

1 Aim: to focus on the form of *remember* + noun/*-ing*.

● Ask the students to read the information in the grammar box.

● Students should look at the sentences in *Reading* activity 5 and decide which *remember* construction they show.

> **Answers**
> remember + *-ing*: 1, 5, 8, 9, 10
> remember + noun: 2, 4, 6
> remember + noun + *-ing*: 3, 7

2 Aim: to practise using the target structures.

● Ask the students to rewrite the false sentences in *Reading* activity 5.

> **Answers**
> 1 She **remembers sleeping** but not dreaming.
> 4 She **remembers getting up** before dawn.
> 6 She **remembers waiting** a long time for breakfast.
> 7 She **remembers the children** having the classes all in one room.
> 10 She **remembers feeling** very hungry.

3 Aim: to practise using the target structures.

● Ask the students to use the structure to describe things they did as children.

VOCABULARY AND SPEAKING

1 Aim: to present the words in the vocabulary box.

● Ask the students to put the words under the three headings.

> **Answers**
> **people:** headteacher caretaker dinner lady staff
> **places:** canteen classroom playground gym
>   playing field   assembly hall
> **equipment:** blackboard chalk pen
>   exercise book register desk bench

2 Aim: to practise using the words in the vocabulary box.

● This activity is designed to find out if the words in the box trigger special memories of school. Ask the students to think of memories they have which are prompted by the words, and to talk about them.

● Ask the students to report back on their partner's memories. Which are the most interesting?

3 Here are some sentences from the passage which contain some difficult words. The words are missing.
Think of a word to go in each gap.

1 I only once awoke to hear the wind ____.
2 ...and washed when there was a basin ____.
3 A distant bell ____.
4 Miss Miller ____ the fourth vacant chair.
5 ...and to these succeeded a ____ reading of chapters in the Bible.

4 Here are some words and expressions which have a similar meaning to the ones missing in the sentences in 3. Are any of these words the same as the ones you thought of?

blow rang sat down in lengthy available

5 Which of these statements about the passage are true?

Jane remembers...

1 dreaming in her sleep.
2 the wind and the rain.
3 her teacher sleeping in the same bed.
4 the sunrise as she lay in bed.
5 waiting her turn to get washed.
6 the excellent breakfast.
7 the children going into separate classrooms.
8 saying prayers.
9 studying the Bible for an hour.
10 not feeling very hungry.

6 Work in pairs. Talk about Jane Eyre's experience of her first day at school.
Was it similar to yours?

GRAMMAR

> **Talking about memories:** *remember* + **noun/-ing**
>
> You can use *remember* + noun or *-ing* to talk about a memory.
> She **remembers sleeping** *deeply*.
> She **remembers the wind** *and the rain*.
>
> When the subject of the memory is different from the subject of the sentence, you put a noun or a pronoun subject between *remember* and the *-ing* form.
> She **remembers Miss Miller reading** *the prayers*.
> She **remembers her calling** *out, 'Form classes!'*
>
> **For other uses of** *remember*, **see the Grammar review at the back of the book.**

1 Look at the sentences in *Reading* activity 5.
Do they show examples of *remember* + *-ing*, *remember* + noun, or *remember* + noun + *-ing*?

2 Correct the false statements in *Reading* activity 5.

She remembers sleeping but not dreaming.

3 Write down five things you remember doing as a child. Talk about them to a partner.

I remember arriving at the school gates with my mother.

VOCABULARY AND SPEAKING

1 Here are some words to do with school.
Put them under these headings: *people, places, equipment*.

> canteen headteacher caretaker blackboard
> classroom playground gym chalk pen
> exercise book register dinner lady desk
> bench playing field assembly hall staff

2 Work in pairs. Are there any words in the box which bring back particular memories of school for you? Tell your partner about them.

Used to and *would* + infinitive, *be/get used to* +
noun/-*ing*

LISTENING

1 Work in pairs. You're going to hear Matthew
Sherrington, an Englishman, talking about his
experience of teaching in a school in Sudan.
Before you listen, write down some questions which
you'd like to find out the answers to.

Why did he go to Africa?

2 Look at the chart below. Try to guess what Matthew
Sherrington will say about each point.

School subjects	
Pupils	
Classroom	
Equipment	
Length of lessons	
Exams	
Amusing or embarrassing incidents	

3 Work in pairs:

Student A: Turn to Communication activity 5 on
page 93.
Student B: Turn to Communication activity 15 on
page 95.

4 Work together and complete the chart. Were your
predictions in 2 right?

5 Complete these sentences with suitable phrases.

1 Matthew used to work in _____.
2 He used to teach _____.
3 Every day he would _____.
4 At first he wasn't used to _____.
5 After a while, he got used to _____.
6 There didn't use to be _____ in the classroom.
7 The number of pupils in a class would be
about _____.

🔲 Now listen again and check.

6 Work in pairs. What can you guess about Matthew's
life when he left Africa?

GRAMMAR

Used to and *would* + infinitive
Remember that you use *used to* and *would* + infinitive
to talk about past habits and routines which are now
finished. You often use them to contrast past routine
with present state.
You can also use *used to* to talk about past states, but
not *would*.
Be/get used to + noun/-*ing*
You use *be used to* + noun/-*ing* to mean *be
accustomed to.*
You can use *get used to* to mean *become used to.*

1 Look at the sentences in *Listening* activity 5 and find
examples for each of the rules in the grammar box.

2 In which of these sentences can you rewrite the
underlined verbs using *used to* or *would*?

When I was a child I went to a school which <u>was</u> about
fifty miles away from home, so I <u>stayed</u> there the whole
term, and only <u>returned</u> home for holidays. At first I
<u>missed</u> my parents, but I got used to it. In fact, during
the long summer holidays, I <u>got</u> bored and <u>wanted</u> to
see my friends. My parents <u>were</u> delighted that I
enjoyed school, but I think they <u>regretted</u> encouraging
me to be so independent at such a young age.

LISTENING

1 Aim: to prepare for listening.
- Ask the students to prepare for listening by making a list of questions they'd like to ask Matthew Sherrington, who is illustrated in the photo. Ask them to think about the difficulties there might be teaching in the conditions you can see in the photo.

2 Aim: to prepare for listening.
- Ask the students to predict what Matthew might say about the points in the chart.

3 Aim: to listen for specific information.
- ▭ This is another jigaw listening activity, so ask the students to turn to their Communication activities and follow their instructions.

4 Aim: to practise speaking.
- Having listened to the same tape but for different information, it is now time for the students to work together and complete the chart. Ask them to include as much detail as possible.

> **Answers**
> **Subjects:** English and a little literature
> **Pupils:** From 45 – 70 in a class
> **Classroom:** Very primitive, no glass in windows, no electricity
> **Equipment:** Only blackboard and chalk, no OHP, insufficient books
> **Length of lessons:** 40 minutes
> **Exams:** End of year exams
> **Amusing or embarrassing incidents:** He remembers washing his hands in the drinking water

5 Aim: to check comprehension; to provide a second opportunity for listening.
- Ask the students to complete the sentences. They can do this activity in pairs or orally.

> **Answers**
> 1 Matthew used to work in Sudan.
> 2 He used to teach English.
> 3 Every day he would have breakfast in a cafe.
> 4 At first he wasn't used to the primitive working conditions.
> 5 After a while, he got used to the lack of equipment.
> 6 There didn't use to be any electricity or equipment in the classroom.
> 7 The number of pupils in a class would be about forty-five to seventy.

- ▭ Play the tape again and ask the students to check their answers to 4 and 5.

6 Aim: to predict future events.
- Ask students to think about Matthew's comments in *Listening* activity 3. What do they think Matthew is doing now? If your students are interested, you can tell them that Matthew left Sudan and went back to university to study Development. He now works for a well-known Development Agency in the UK.

GRAMMAR

1 Aim: to present the target structures.
- Ask the students to read the information in the grammar box and then to do the exercises.

- These are all structures which often get confused.

> **Answers**
> **used to:** 1, 2, 6
> **would:** 3, 7
> **be/get used to:** 4, 5

2 Aim: to focus on the difference between *used to* and *would*.
- Make sure the students understand that you can only use *used to* to talk about past states.

> **Answers**
> When I was be a child, I went to a school which **was** about fifty miles from home, so I **used to/would** stay there the whole term, and **would** only return/only **used to** return home for holidays. At first, I **used to** miss my parents, but I got used to it. In fact, during the long summer holidays, I **used to/would** get bored and **used to** want to see my friends. My parents **used to** be delighted that I enjoyed school, but I think they **used to** regret encouraging me to be so independent at such a young age.

3 Aim: to practise using *get used to + -ing.*

● Make sure the students understand the difference between *used to* + infinitive, which refers to a past state or habit, and *be/get used to + -ing*, which means to become accustomed to doing something. Ask the students to write sentences about things they have to or had to get used to doing using the prompts.

SOUNDS

1 Aim: to focus on differences in pronunciation between British and American English.

● Explain that the /j/ combined with another consonant is more common in British English than in American English.

> **Answers**
> The underlined words contain the sound /j/
> New York you used tune
> clues few duke drew blue

● 🔲 Play the tape and ask the students to say the words aloud.

2 Aim: to focus on differences in pronunciation between British and American English.

● 🔲 Play the tape and ask the students to compare the American English pronunciation with the British English in 1.

> **Answers**
> The underlined words contain the sound /j/
> New York you used tune
> clues few duke drew blue

Ask the students to say the words aloud.

WRITING

1 Aim: to practise reading and inferring; to practise using the target structures.

● This is meant to be a lighthearted look at school reports. Explain that teachers are generally very nice people who like to encourage rather than discourage their pupils. In the school reports they try to be positive about negative aspects of each school child. Ask the students to read the report and then match the five interpretations with the subjects.

> **Answers**
> a French b maths c chemistry
> d English e geography

2 Aim: to practise using the target structures.

● Ask the students to write realistic interpretations of the other subjects. Ask them to do this in pairs.

● Ask each pair to read out their interpretation to the rest of the class, who must match it with the subject.

3 Aim: to practise writing.

● Encourage the students to be lighthearted about their fictitious school reports.

● Ask the students to exchange reports, and to write a realistic interpretation of the report they have received. You may like to ask them do part or all of this activity for homework.

3 Write sentences describing things which you have to *get used to* doing:

– when you learn a foreign language
– when you live in a foreign country
– when you leave school
– when you buy a house

When you learn a foreign language, you have to get used to learning lots of vocabulary.

SOUNDS

1 Which words contain the /j/ sound in British English?

New York   you   used   tune
clue   few   duke   drew   blue

🔊 Listen and check. As you listen, say the words aloud.

2 Which words in 1 contain the /j/ sound in American English?

🔊 Listen and check. As you listen, say the words aloud.

WRITING

1 Here's an old school report about a pupil's progress in different subjects. It was written in a very positive way. An old school friend has interpreted the report in a much more realistic way. Read it and match the interpretations below with five of the subjects.

a She never used to open her mouth.

b She didn't use to be able to count from one to ten.

c She used to like making bombs.

d She used to send the boys love letters.

e The teachers didn't use to know where she was most of the time.

ST AGNES SCHOOL FOR GIRLS

SCHOOL REPORT FORM

NAME: *Karen Leary*   **FORM** *5B*

Subjects

Mathematics
Karen has a growing understanding of numbers.

French *She must realise that language learning involves an element of interaction..*

Physics *She likes exploring the unknown.*

Chemistry *Enjoys innovative experimentation*

English *Has taken a personal interest in the Romantic poets*

Geography *Karen usually loses herself completely in the study of maps.*

History *Has a very individual understanding of important dates*

Art *Has an individual sense of form.*

Music *Could become a useful member of our large choir.*

Physical Education *Likes to take physical risks.*

Form Teacher *Gillian Bridges*

---

2 Write realistic interpretations about the other five subjects.

3 Think about how good you were in different subjects in a school report. Write a positive report about yourself.

Now show it to another student. Can he or she interpret it in a more realistic way?

10 Rules of law

Modal verbs: *must, have to, have got to, can't, mustn't*

VOCABULARY AND SOUNDS

1 Look at the sentences below. Match the definitions of crimes to words from the box.

> blackmail kidnapping arson trespass hijacking
> manslaughter murder smuggling drug dealing
> forgery fraud mugging spying shoplifting libel
> bribery burglary speeding

1 When someone kills someone else deliberately.
2 When someone offers you money to do something.
3 When someone steals something from your home.
4 When someone captures you and demands money for your release.
5 When someone attacks you in the street and takes your money.
6 When someone writes something false and offensive about someone.

Find out what the other words in the box mean.

2 Underline the stressed syllable in these words.

illegal blackmail forbidden compulsory
manslaughter forgery libel obligatory

Put the words in two columns according to the stressed syllable.

[cassette icon] Now listen and check.

3 Work in pairs. Decide on punishments for some of the crimes in the vocabulary box in 1.

prison sentence fine caution life sentence
damages community service disqualification

READING

1 Read *Rules of law* and decide which laws the cartoons illustrate. Now work in pairs and discuss which law you find most amusing or strange.

Rules of law

◆ In Lancashire, it is against the law to hang male and female underwear on the same line.
◆ **In Saskatchewan, Canada, you must not drink water in a beer house.**
◆ A transportation law in Texas, USA: when two trains approach each other at a crossing, they should both stop, and neither shall start up until the other has gone.
◆ **In Waterloo, Nebraska, USA, it is illegal for a barber to eat onions between 7am and 7pm.**
◆ The town council of Widnes, Lancashire, England introduced a fine of £5 for those who made a habit of falling asleep in the reading rooms of libraries.
◆ **Duelling in Paraguay is legal as long as both participants are registered blood donors.**
◆ In New York City there is still a law which makes it illegal for women to smoke in public.
◆ **The citizens of Kentucky, USA, are required by law to take a bath once a year.**
◆ In 1659 it became illegal to celebrate Christmas in Massachusetts.
◆ **In New York State you are not allowed to shoot at a rabbit from a moving trolley car. You have to get off the car, or wait for it to come to a complete stop, then fire away.**
◆ In Malaysia it is against the law to dance on the backs of turtles.
◆ **In Madagascar it is illegal for pregnant women to wear hats or eat eels.**
◆ In Alaska, USA, it is illegal to look at a moose from the window of an airplane or any other flying vehicle.
◆ **It is illegal to hunt camels in the state of Arizona, USA.**
◆ In Indiana, USA, it is against the law to travel on a bus within four hours of eating garlic.
◆ **During the reign of Elizabeth 1, the wearing of hats was made compulsory in England.**
◆ In 1937 in Hungary spring cleaning became compulsory. All lofts and cellars had to be cleaned.

10

GENERAL COMMENTS

Learner training

Although the learner training syllabus has not been overtly specified, there have been many activities which encourage the students to take personal responsibility for their learning. There are several main types of activities. **Communication strategies** encourage students to realise that they can make themselves understood even if they do not know specific words. This can be done with mime, gesture, description and paraphrase. Organising learning for **personal requirements** covers many of the vocabulary acquisition activities which focus on noting words most relevant to the students. Activities to explore **English outside the classroom** remind the student that even in non-native English speaking contexts, some English can be found, either in writing or in speech. Activities for **study skills** encourage the use of dictionaries and other reference books by students in order to counterbalance reliance on the teacher.

VOCABULARY AND SOUNDS

1 Aim: to present the words in the vocabulary box; to present the theme of the lesson.

● The theme of the lesson is law and order. Some students may have come across some of these words for crimes already. All relevant to the current level, they are now presented in the box as productive items. Ask the students to match the words with their definitions.

Answers
1 murder 2 bribery 3 burglary
4 kidnapping 5 mugging 6 libel

● Ask the students to discuss what the other words for crimes mean. Ask them to write simple definitions for each one.

2 Aim: to focus on stressed syllables in words.

● Ask the students to underline the stressed syllable in each word.

● 🔲 Play the tape and ask the students to listen and check. Ask the students to say the words aloud.

Answers
First syllable: blackmail manslaughter
forgery libel
Second syllable: illegal forbidden
compulsory obligatory

3 Aim: to practise speaking.

● Ask the students to work in pairs and to talk about suitable punishments for the various crimes in 1.

● Ask the class to put the crimes on a scale of
1 = minor crime to 10 = very serious crime.
Try to reach an agreement with the whole class.

● Ask the students to work with another pair and to discuss their idea of suitable punishments for the crimes in 1.

● Ask groups to report on their discussion to the rest of the class.

READING

1 Aim: to read for main ideas.

● Explain that all the laws in the passage are or were real ones, but were chosen because they are particularly strange. Ask the students to read the passage and to decide which laws the cartoons illustrate.

Answers
1 A fine of £5 for those who made a habit of falling asleep in libraries.
2 In Malaysia it is against the law to dance on the backs of turtles.

2 Aim: to read for specific information.
- Ask the students to find the answers to these questions as quickly as possible. You may like to see who does this activity the quickest.

Answers
1 Waterloo, Nebraska
2 During the reign of Elizabeth 1 in England
3 In 1937 in Hungary
4 Stop and wait until the other one has left
5 Travel by bus in Indiana
6 Look at a moose in Alaska

3 Aim: to read for specific information.
- Ask the students to match the strange laws and the reason for introducing them.

Answers
1 Onion-eating barbers
2 Dancing on turtles in Malaysia
3 Shooting rabbits from a trolley car in New York State
4 Christmas in Massachusetts
5 Women smoking in public
6 Falling asleep in libraries

- Ask the students to work in pairs and to think of reasons why the other laws were introduced.

- Find out which pair has thought of the most creative reasons.

GRAMMAR

1 Aim: to focus on present and past modals.
- Ask the students to read the information in the grammar box and then to do the exercises.

- Students should look at the various modal verbs in the passage and decide if they show obligation (*must, have to*) or prohibition (*mustn't, can't*).

2 Aim: to practise using present and past modals.
- Ask the students to rewrite the sentences using present or past modals.

Answers
1 In Malaysia you **mustn't** dance on the backs of turtles.
2 During the reign of Elizabeth I, you **had to** wear a hat.
3 From 1659 you **weren't allowed to** celebrate Christmas in Massachusetts.
4 You **mustn't** hunt camels in Arizona.
5 From 1937 in Hungary, you **had to** spring clean all lofts and cellars.

3 Aim: to practise using suitable expressions for obligation and prohibition.
- Ask the students to rewrite six more laws using present or past modals.

SPEAKING AND WRITING

1 Aim: to practise speaking.
- Ask the students to work in groups of two or three and to discuss laws they would like to introduce in their country using the prompts in the Student's Book. These laws can be as inventive or as humorous as they like.

2 Aim: to practise writing.
- Ask the students to write down the laws they thought of in 1 or think of some other laws.

- If possible, put the laws on the walls for everyone to read. Which are the most inventive or humorous laws?

2 Answer the questions. Try to do this in one minute.

1 Where can't barbers eat onions during the day?
2 Where and when did you have to wear a hat?
3 Where and when did you have to clean out your lofts and cellars?
4 What must two trains do at a crossing in Texas?
5 What mustn't you do if you've just eaten some garlic?
6 What mustn't you do from an airplane window?

3 Work in pairs. Here are some possible reasons why some of the laws were introduced. Match the reason and the law.

1 Because it makes their breath smell.
2 Maybe they're an endangered species.
3 It doesn't give the animal a sporting chance.
4 Because it distracted people from the true meaning of their religion.
5 Maybe because it was considered unsuitable behaviour for a lady.
6 In case people snored.

Can you think of reasons why the other laws were introduced?

GRAMMAR

Modal verbs: *must, have to, have got to, can't, mustn't*
You usually use *must* when the obligation comes from the speaker.
You often use it for strong advice or safety instructions.
*You **must** ring me as soon as you arrive.   You **must** drive carefully.*
You usually use *have to* when the obligation comes from someone else.
You often use it for rules.
*I **have to** buy a television licence.*
*You **have to** drive on the left in Britain.*
But you use *have to* for things which happen regularly, especially with an adverb or adverbial phrases of frequency.
*We **have to** buy a television licence **every year**.*
You can often use *have got* to instead of *have to*, especially for a specific instance.
*We've **got to** buy a television licence this week.*
You use *can't* and *mustn't* to talk about what you're not allowed to do or what it is not possible to do.
*You **can't** hunt camels in Arizona.*
*Women **mustn't** smoke in public in New York.*
You can only use *must, mustn't* and *have got to* to talk about the present and future. This is how you talk about obligation and prohibition in the past.

Present	*must*	*have to*	*have got to*	*mustn't*
Past	*had to*	*had to*	*had to*	*couldn't* or *wasn't/weren't allowed to*

1 Look back at the passage and find sentences using the present or the past form of a modal verb. Are they examples of obligation or prohibition?

2 Rewrite these rules using the present or the past form of a modal verb.

1 In Malaysia, it is against the law to dance on the backs of turtles.
2 During the reign of Elizabeth I the wearing of hats was made compulsory.
3 In 1659 it became illegal to celebrate Christmas in Massachusetts.
4 It is illegal to hunt camels in Arizona.
5 In 1937 in Hungary the spring cleaning of all lofts and cellars became compulsory.

3 Choose six other laws in *Rules of law* and rewrite them using the present or the past form of a modal verb.

SPEAKING AND WRITING

1 Work in groups of two or three. Are there any laws you would like to introduce in your country? Think about:

– use of mobile phones   – smoking in public places   – use of cars
– pollution   – healthcare   – housing   – pets   – language learning
– school leaving age

2 Write some new laws for your country. They can be as amusing or strange as you like.

Modal verbs:
don't need to/needn't,
needn't have/didn't need to,
should/shouldn't

VOCABULARY AND LISTENING

1 Work in groups of two or three. Look at the words in the box and use them to complete the gaps in the questions.

innocent guilty prison offence
weapon arrest lawyer suspect
crime legal charged with
confess custody magistrate
trial sentence executed for
jury judge bail

1 Are you innocent until you're proved to be ____, or the other way round?
2 If you're convicted of drug dealing, are you always sent to ____ or is there sometimes a fine?
3 Is it an offence to carry a ____, such as a gun or a knife?
4 If the police arrest you, are you allowed to call a ____?
5 If the police ____ you for a crime, is it legal to remain silent when they question you?
6 If you're ____ a crime, are you always kept in custody while you wait for a trial?
7 If you ____ to a crime, do you always get a lighter sentence?
8 Are there any crimes which you can be ____?
9 Is there always trial by ____ for serious crimes?
10 Who decides on a sentence? Is it the ____ or the jury?

Now answer the questions in 1 for your country.

2 Check you know what the other words in the box mean.

3 🔲 Listen to a radio programme about law and order in Britain. What are the speaker's answers to the questions in 1?

4 Work in pairs. Complete these sentences about law and order in Britain.

1 In Britain you are innocent until _____.
2 The law is different _____.
3 It is an offence to carry a _____.
4 When you are arrested, they allow you _____.
5 You have the right to _____.
6 When you are charged with a crime, you don't always go _____.
7 Even if you confess to a crime, the sentence still depends on _____.
8 Treason is the only crime for which you can _____.
9 There is always trial by jury for _____.
10 The jury decides whether they're _____.

🔲 Now listen again and check.

GRAMMAR

Don't need to/needn't, needn't have/didn't need to, should/shouldn't

You can use *don't need to* + infinitive or *needn't* + infinitive to say what isn't necessary or what you don't have to do.
*You **don't need to/needn't** call a lawyer, but it's a good idea.*
You use *needn't have* + past participle to say what someone did, although it was unnecessary or they didn't have to do it.
*He **needn't have taken** a gun. (= It wasn't necessary to take a gun, but he did.)*
You use *didn't need to* + infinitive to say that something was unnecessary. We don't know if the person did it or not.
*He **didn't need to take** a gun.*
(= It wasn't necessary to take a gun; we don't know if he did or not.)
You can use *should/shouldn't* to say what is right or wrong.
*It **should be** the judge who decides on the sentence. It **shouldn't be** the jury.*
You use *should have/shouldn't have* to say that someone did something wrong in the past.
*He **should have stayed** in bed, but he didn't.*
*He **shouldn't have got up**, but he did.*

1 Write sentences saying what you *needn't/don't need to* do in your country.

– carry an ID card at all times
– have a work permit
– be 21 before you can marry

– be 21 before you can drive
– call a police officer sir or madam
– have a licence to own a gun

VOCABULARY AND LISTENING

1 Aim: to present some of the words in the vocabulary box; to prepare for listening.

● The theme of this part of the lesson is the legal system in England and Wales (Scotland's laws are slightly different). Ask the students to read the questions and complete them with suitable words from the vocabulary box.

> **Answers**
> 1 guilty 2 prison 3 weapon 4 lawyer
> 5 arrest 6 charged with 7 confess 8 executed for
> 9 jury 10 judge

● Many of these questions are at the heart of the legal system and of the rights of the individual, so it would be helpful if you were sure of the answers in respect of your own country.

● Ask the students to try and decide what the answers to the questions are in their countries. It doesn't matter if they don't know, as long as they are aware of what the questions and the vocabulary items mean.

2 Aim: to present the other words in the vocabulary box; to prepare for listening.

● Ask various students in turn what the other words mean. They may like to do this activity in pairs and then explain them to the rest of the class.

3 Aim: to listen for specific information.

● Explain that you're going to play a recording of someone talking about the legal system in Britain. Ask the students to write down the speaker's answers to the questions in 1.

● 📼 Play the tape.

● Ask the students to work in pairs and talk about the answers to the questions.

> **Answers**
> 1 yes 2 quite often a fine 3 yes 4 yes 5 yes
> 6 no 7 no 8 no, only possibly treason 9 yes
> 10 usually the judge

4 Aim: to check comprehension.

● Ask the students to complete the sentences.

> **Answers**
> 1 In Britain you are innocent until **proved guilty**.
> 2 The law is different **in Scotland**.
> 3 It is an offence to carry a **weapon**.
> 4 When you are arrested, they allow you **to call a lawyer**.
> 5 You have the right to **remain silent, although the law has changed.**
> 6 When you are charged with a crime, you don't always go **to prison**.
> 7 Even if you confess to a crime, the sentence still depends on **the seriousness of the crime**.
> 8 Treason is the only crime for which you can **be executed.**
> 9 There is always trial by jury for **serious crimes**.
> 10 The jury decides whether they're **guilty or not.**

● 📼 Play the tape again and ask the students to listen and check.

GRAMMAR

1 Aim: to focus on *needn't* and *don't need to.*

● Ask the students to read the information in the grammar box and then to do the exercises.

● Make sure that the students write sentences which are true for their country.

2 Aim: to focus on the difference between *needn't have* and *didn't need to.*

● The difference between these two structures is a difficult one for many students to grasp so you may like to do this activity orally with the whole class.

> **Answers**
> 1 we don't know 2 yes 3 yes 4 we don't know
> 5 yes

3 Aim: to practise using *should have* and *shouldn't have.*

● This may not be a new structure for the students, so they may have few problems with this exercise. Ask them to make sentences using the structure.

> **Answers**
> 1 He **should have gone** to prison.
> 2 It **shouldn't have been** so high.
> 3 He **shouldn't have had** the gun.
> 4 He **should have driven** more slowly.
> 5 She **should have shown** it to the police.
> 6 They **shouldn't have employed** him.

READING AND WRITING

1 Aim: to practise reading and writing; to react to a text.

● The newspaper article describes a particularly difficult but common legal dilemma. Ask the students to read the article.

● Ask the students to discuss who they agree with.

2 Aim: to practise using *didn't need to*, *should have* and *shouldn't have.*

● Ask the students to discuss Jack Lewis's actions using the structures shown.

● Find out what various students around the class think.

3 Aim: to practise writing a discursive letter to a newspaper; to practise using linking words and expressions.

● A discursive piece of writing usually puts one or both sides of an argument. If the students need some help with arguments for and against, ask them to turn to the Communication activity in the Student's Book. However, encourage students who have opinions of their own to use them as the basis of their letter.

● Ask the students to work in pairs to plan a letter to a newspaper setting out their position on the judgement.

● Ask the students to write the letter to the newspaper. Make sure they use some or all of the linking words and expressions to set out both sides of the argument, and follow the model suggested. You may like to ask the students to do this activity for homework.

2 Read the sentences and answer the questions.

1 She didn't need to show her driving licence.
  – *Did she show it or not?*
2 He needn't have driven so fast because he's now in a traffic jam. – *Did he drive fast or not?*
3 I think the sentence needn't have been so severe. After all, it was a first conviction.
  – *Was the sentence severe or not?*
4 He pleaded guilty to the crime so there didn't need to be a trial. – *Was there a trial or not?*
5 He could prove he was out of the country so in my opinion, they needn't have arrested him.
  – *Did they arrest him or not?*

3 Make sentences using *should have* and *shouldn't have* and the words in brackets.

1 I'm sure he was guilty. (He/go/to prison)
2 The fine was very high. (It/be/so high)
3 He didn't have a licence. (He/have/the gun)
4 There was a lot of traffic. (He/drive/more slowly)
5 She didn't have her ID. (She/show/it/to the police)
6 He didn't have a work permit. (They/employ/him)

READING AND WRITING

1 Read the newspaper article and the letter in reply to it. Who do you agree with – the judge or the writer of the letter?

2 Work in pairs and talk about what Jack Lewis *didn't need to* do, *should have* or *shouldn't have* done.

He shouldn't have shot him.
He didn't need to use his gun.

3 Write a letter to a newspaper giving your opinion about the judgement. If you need some arguments for and against it, turn to Communication activity 10 on page 94. Use the linking words and expressions to help you write the letter.

Explain why you're writing.
I am writing to you because...
Give your opinion. *In my opinion,...*
Give the opposite opinion.
It may be true that..., however...
Many people believe that...
Give your opinion again, more strongly.
But as far as I am concerned,...
But in practice,...

A judge ordered an 82-year-old man to pay £4,000 damages to a burglar who was trying to break into his house. Jack Lewis was asleep in his house in Maidstone, Kent when he heard noises. He picked up his shotgun and went downstairs where he found Michael Phillips in the hall with a bag full of electrical equipment. Phillips claimed that because he was unarmed, he put the goods down and raised his hands when he saw the shotgun. Lewis said Phillips had turned to run out of the open front door, so he shot him. Phillips suffered minor wounds to the legs. In the trial, the judge said despite the fact that Lewis was defending his own property, the shotgun was unlicenced and in any case, it was not acceptable for people to take the law into their own hands.

Sir, I am writing in disbelief at the judgement passed on Jack Lewis yesterday. In my opinion, it is absolutely unfair to make him pay for his act of self-defence. In theory he has committed an offence by firing an unlicenced shotgun, and he should be prosecuted for this. But in practice the law should be more flexible. As far as I'm concerned, for a criminal to receive compensation for an injury sustained while carrying out a crime is quite outrageous.

Yours faithfully
Brian Forbes
Brian Forbes

11 | *Discoveries and inventions*

Clauses of purpose

SPEAKING AND READING

1 Work in groups of three or four. Discuss which of the following inventions have made the most important contribution to improving people's lives. Number them in order of their importance.

television radio telephone
gunpowder penicillin
light bulb computer
petrol engine

2 Read the passage about Francis Galton and choose the best title.

1 A practical man
2 A curious life
3 An inventor and traveller
4 The eccentric inventor

3 Find a word in the passage which means the same as:

1 something which makes an explosion
2 a painful swelling on the skin
3 a sharp pain caused by an insect
4 wipe a sticky substance
5 stomach
6 unwilling
7 with holes to let air in
8 long and difficult
9 disadvantage
10 a small mechanical device

4 Read the passage again and find out how many inventions or tips are mentioned.

If you ever feel ill when travelling in remote foreign parts, just drop some gunpowder into a glass of warm, soapy water, and swallow it. That was the advice of Francis Galton in a book called *The Art of Travel*.

Sore feet? Blisters? Simply put soap suds inside your socks and break a raw egg into each boot to soften the leather. Wasp stings? Well, the tar scraped out of a tobacco pipe and smeared on the skin relieves the pain as well as anything.

Galton's book proved a best-seller. It covered every situation, from constructing boats, huts, and tents in a hurry to catching fish without a line. It told readers how to find firewood in a rainstorm (under the roots of a tree) and where to put your clothes when it's raining so that they don't get wet (just take them off and sit on them).

The horse, he found, was a very useful animal to have around when travelling. If you want to protect yourself from the wind, you can always shelter behind it and to light your pipe in a hurricane, creep under its belly and stay there. If you wanted to cross a river and the horse was a reluctant swimmer, the best solution, said Galton, was to lead it along a steep bank so you could take it by surprise and push it in when its mind was on other things.

Francis Galton, born in 1822, was a remarkable man. He was one of the first men to discover that every human being has a different set of fingerprints. He also invented the word association test and wrote a book on heredity that changed the ideas of a generation. But it is his genius for solving life's everyday problems that makes him endearing.

For example, when he was at university, he studied so hard that he was worried about the possible overheating of his brain, so he invented a ventilated hat in order to let the fresh air circulate around his head.

Tired after his studies and longing for the wide open spaces, he left for Syria, Egypt and the Sudan. After two years and an arduous journey of 1,700 miles, he returned home to write *The Art of Travel*.

In 1857 he bought a house in South Kensington, London. In order not to attract dust, there were no carpets, curtains and wallpaper. Visitors had to slide over the floor so that it shone like glass, and sit upright in plain wooden chairs which offered no comfort. The house was full of his inventions, including a signal that warned people that the lavatory was engaged so that they didn't have to climb the stairs.

Galton was not tall, and this was a drawback when it came to watching processions and ceremonies, which he loved. As usual, he had a practical solution. He would arrive on the scene with a large wooden brick, lower it to the ground with a piece of rope and stand on it. Then he would take from his pocket a gadget he had invented called a *hyperscope* – like a miniature periscope – to give him a splendid view over hats and heads.

For many years he had gone abroad for the winter, but in the autumn of 1910 the effort was too much for him. He died peacefully in his bed in January 1911.

11

GENERAL COMMENTS

Reading

The principal aim of the reading practice in *Reward* is to encourage students to read as fluently and with as much enjoyment as they would read in their own language. However, it is never certain that a passage will motivate everybody, and so the accompanying exercises provide the artificial motivation to read for pedagogical purposes. The main idea of the initial exercises in an activity sequence is to encourage students to read the passage as they would read a similar passage in their own language. Certain activities have been specifically designed to help the students gain access to the passage's main ideas. Subsequent exercises focus on apects of style, unfamiliar vocabulary and other features.

SPEAKING AND READING

**1 Aim: to introduce the theme of the lesson;
to practise speaking.**

● This activity is not a test of language skill, but is designed to encourage the students to start thinking about inventions. Ask the students to work in groups of three or four and to decide which of the inventions in 1 have made the greatest contribution to people's lives. They should rate the inventions according to their importance. What would it be like without them?

● Do students know who invented/discovered the items in 1?

> **Answers**
> **Television:** John Logie Baird
> **Radio:** Marconi
> **Telephone:** Alexander Graham Bell
> **Gunpowder:** the Chinese
> **Penicillin:** Alexander Fleming
> **Light bulb:** Thomas Edison
> **Computer:** Professor Max Newman

● Ask the students to think of other inventions and discoveries, especially from their own countries, and say who invented/discovered them and when.

2 Aim: to read for main ideas.

● Explain to the students that they are going to read about Francis Galton, an Englishman who lived in the 19th century, which was a particularly rich period in Britain's history for discoveries and inventions, science and travel. Ask the students to read the passage and to choose the best title.

> **Probable answer**
> A curious life

● You may like to explain that *curious* means both *strange* and *enquiring*.

3 Aim: to deal with unfamiliar vocabulary.

● The words under scrutiny in this activity are those which may cause the students some difficulty. Ask them to match the unfamiliar words with their simpler explanations in this activity.

> **Answers**
> 1 gunpowder 2 blister 3 sting 4 smear 5 belly
> 6 reluctant 7 ventilated 8 arduous 9 drawback
> 10 gadget

4 Aim: to practise reading for main ideas.

● Ask the students to read the passage again and to find out how many things Galton invented.

> **Answer**
> About 14 inventions are mentioned, although there were many more.

5 Aim: to read and link ideas.

● It's sometimes difficult for students to understand referents, ie, what is being referred to by a pronoun or synonym of an idea that has been presented earlier in a sentence or a passage. Ask them to find these sentences in the passage and to decide what the italicised word refers to.

Answers
1 the drink 2 your clothes 3 the horse 4 the horse
5 the book on heredity 6 the brick

6 Aim: to react to the passage.

● Ask the students to decide which were Galton's most and least useful inventions or discoveries. Discuss Galton's inventions and discoveries with the whole class. How would he be regarded in your students' countries?

GRAMMAR

1 Aim: to present clauses of purpose.

● Ask the students to read the information in the grammar box and then to do the exercises.

Answers
1 Galton wrote *The Art of Travel* **in order to** share his travel advice.
2 He said that **in order to** protect yourself from the wind, you should shelter behind your horse.
3 He invented a special hat **so that** air circulated around his head.
4 When watching processions, he used to stand on a brick **so** he could see over people's heads.
5 He also used a hyperscope **to** get a better view.

2 Aim: to practise using clauses of purpose.

● Ask the students to continue using clauses of purpose to discuss the answers to the questions.
You may like to discuss the answers with the whole class.

Possible answers
1 In order to lose weight.
2 To speak with people from other countries.
3 To get a suntan, to relax and enjoy themselves.
4 In order to stay healthy.

● If you have time, you can extend this activity by asking students to think of as many answers to each question as possible. Encourage them to be as inventive or humorous as possible.

SPEAKING AND WRITING

1 Aim: to practise speaking.

● Ask the students to give practical advice for the everyday situations mentioned. Make sure they use clauses of purpose. Go round and check each group is discussing the situations using the clauses of purpose.

2 Aim: to practise writing.

● Ask the students to write down their advice.

● When everyone has finished, put the pieces of advice in a place, such as on the wall, where everyone can see them.

5 Look at these sentences from the passage. What do the words in italics refer to?

1 ...just drop some gunpowder into a glass of warm, soapy water and swallow *it*.
2 ...just take *them* off and sit on *them*.
3 ...and push *it* in when its mind was on other things.
4 If you want to protect yourself from the wind, you can always shelter behind *it*...
5 ...and wrote a book on heredity *that* changed the ideas of a generation.
6 ...with a piece of rope and stand on *it*.

6 Work in groups of three. Decide which of Francis Galton's inventions or discoveries was the most useful for people and which the least useful. Tell the rest of the class what you have decided.

GRAMMAR

> **Clauses of purpose**
> **You use *to/in order to* to describe the purpose of an action when the subject of the main clause and the purpose clause are the same.**
> *Break a raw egg into each boot **to** soften the leather.*
> **In order to makes a clause of purpose sound formal.**
> *Break a raw egg into each boot **in order to** soften the leather.*
> **In negative sentences, you have to say *in order not to*.**
> ***In order not to** attract dust, there were no carpets.*
> **You use *so (that)*:**
> **– when the subjects of the main clause and the purpose clause are different.**
> *Visitors had to slide over the floor **so that** it shone like glass.*
> **– when the purpose is negative.**
> *Sit on your clothes when it's raining **so that** they **don't** get wet.*
> **– with *can* and *could*.**
> *Galton invented a gadget so he **could** watch processions.*

1 Rewrite these sentences with *in order to, to* or *so (that)*.

1 Galton wrote *The Art of Travel* because he wanted to share his travel advice.
2 He said that if you wanted to protect yourself from the wind you should shelter behind your horse.
3 He invented a special hat which let fresh air circulate around his head.
4 When watching processions, he used to stand on a brick as he couldn't see over people's heads.
5 He also used a hyperscope which allowed him to get a splendid view.

2 Work in pairs. Discuss the answers to these questions using *to, so (that)* or *in order to*.

1 Why do people go on diets?
2 Why do people learn English?
3 Why do people go on holiday?
4 Why do you need to eat good food?

Compare your answers with another pair.

SPEAKING AND WRITING

1 Work in groups of three. Think of practical advice for these situations. Use the structures in the grammar box.

– how to work less   – how to save money
– how to avoid being burgled   – how to get guests to leave

2 Write down your advice for the situations in 1 and show it to other groups. Use the structures in the grammar box.

Noun/adjective + *to* + infinitive

VOCABULARY

1 Work in pairs. Look at these words for tools and household equipment. Which do you think are the most and least useful? Are there any that you never use?

> hammer fork spade mop broom screwdriver spanner chisel scissors
> corkscrew tin opener strainer grater breadboard peeler carving knife
> tweezers ladle ironing board lawnmower saw drill toaster coffee grinder
> nail saucepan dustbin watering can sieve brush chopping board

Work with another pair and compare your ideas.

2 Work in pairs. Take turns to choose a tool or piece of household equipment. Tell your partner what you use it to do. Your partner must guess what it is.

You use it to bang nails into wood.   Is it a hammer?

SPEAKING AND LISTENING

1 Work in pairs. You're going to hear someone talking about the inventions in the illustrations. Look at the illustrations below and discuss what you think their purpose is.

I think you use it to...   I think it's for...

Work with another pair and compare your answers.

2 🔲 Listen and number the inventions in the order you hear them described.

3 Work in pairs and make notes on the following aspects of each invention.

name of invention   purpose   advantages   possible disadvantages

4 Complete the sentences with a few words about each invention.

1 In the night, it's difficult for the parents to ____ and to ____ fall asleep.
2 But it's careless of the inventor to ____.
3 When your hands are full, it's not always easy to ____.
4 But it's rare for men to ____.
5 When you're boiling something, it's sometimes difficult to ____.
6 But it's essential for you to ____.
7 After a meal, we're often surprised to ____.
8 But it would be unusual for you to ____.
9 When eating grapefruit, it's essential for you to ____.
10 But it might be easier for you to ____.

🔲 Listen again and check.

5 Which do you think is the best invention? Can you think of any more advantages and disadvantages of them?

6 Which of these inventions do you think were really invented?

Turn to Communication activity 22 on page 96 to find out.

VOCABULARY

1 Aim: to present the words in the vocabulary box.

● Ask the students to look at the words in the box and to check they understand them all.

● Ask the students to decide which tools and household equipment they use most and least often. You may like to ask the students to rank them according to their usefulness.

2 Aim: to practise using the words in the vocabulary box; to practise using clauses of purpose.

● This activity will involve revising some of the constructions covered on the preceding pages. Ask the students to work in pairs. In turn, they should choose a tool or piece of household equipment and say what you use it for, but without saying the name of the item. The other student must guess what it is. You may like to suggest a score of one point if the student describes usage correctly; if the other student does not guess the name of the item the first student can gain an additional point. The other student gains a point if he/she does guess correctly.

SPEAKING AND LISTENING

1 Aim: to practise speaking; to prepare for listening.

● Ask the students to look at the illustrations and to discuss what they think the purpose of the invention is. Explain that they will hear someone talking about the inventions on the tape.

2 Aim: to practise listening for main ideas.

● 📼 Play the tape and ask the students to tick the inventions in the order in which they are mentioned.

> **Answers**
> 1 baby patting device   2 saluting device
> 3 fork hook   4 knife mirror   5 grapefruit shield

3 Aim: to practise speaking.

● Ask the students to make notes about the different aspects of each invention.

4 Aim: to check comprehension; to present the target structures.

● This activity focuses on the structures which are explained in the grammar box. It will also check that students have understood many of the details in the listening passage.

> **Answers**
> 1 In the night, it's difficult for the parents **to stay awake** and to **help the baby to** fall asleep.
> 2 But it's careless of the inventor to **use electricity.**
> 3 When you hands are full it's not always easy to **raise your hat.**
> 4 But it's rare for men to **wear a hat these days.**
> 5 When you're boiling something, it's sometimes difficult to **lift it without burning your hands.**
> 6 But it's essential for you to **be careful when you use it as a fork.**
> 7 After a meal, we're often surprised to **find a bit of food stuck on our teeth.**
> 8 But it would be unusual for you to **clean it off at the table.**
> 9 When eating grapefruit, it's essential for you to **avoid getting the juice in your eyes.**
> 10 But it might be easier for you to **cut the grapefruit into pieces.**

5 Aim: to practise speaking.

● Ask the students to give their opinions on the usefulness of the inventions. Ask them to think of other advantages and disadvantages about the inventions.

6 Aim: to practise speaking.

● Ask the students to decide which of the inventions really were invented. Then ask them to turn to the Communication activity on page 96 to find out.

> **Answer**
> They were all invented and patented.

Answers					
Name of invention	Baby patting device	Saluting device	Fork hook	Knife mirror	Grapefruit shield
Purpose	Puts the baby to sleep	Raises your hat when you have your hands full	Allows you to pick up hot buckets	Allows you to check for food on your teeth	Protects you when you cut a grapefruit
Advantages	Allows parents to do something else while the baby gets to sleep	Allows you to remain polite on all occasions	Avoids burning your fingers	Avoids social embarrassment	Avoids painful juice in the eye
Possible disadvantages	Might harm the baby. Electricity could be dangerous	No one wears a hat these days	No use as a fork	If you spot food, it will be embarrassing	Shield on the wrong side

GRAMMAR

1 Aim: to present the constructions in the grammar box.

● Ask the students to read the information in the grammar box.

● Write on the board *It's a device to put fires out.* Ask the students to guess which tool or piece of equipment the sentence describes (a fire extinguisher).

● Ask the students to write similar sentences to describe the purpose of the various tools or pieces of equipment 1 – 6 in this activity.

> **Answers**
> 1 It's thing to keep keys on.
> 2 It's a device to cut things with.
> 3 It's a thing to keep you cool.
> 4 It's a thing to boil water in.
> 5 It's a thing to clean your teeth.
> 6 It's a thing to send documents by telephone.

● You may need to explain that the prepositions usually go at the end of the sentence.

2 Aim: to present adjective + infinitive constructions.

● Ask the students to rewrite the sentences using adjective + infinitive constructions.

> **Answers**
> 1 It was careless of you to spill the milk.
> 2 It's normal for bread to go stale after a few days.
> 3 It was wrong of him to use all the hot water.
> 4 It wasn't necessary for you to turn on the lights.
> 5 It was unusual for him to do all the housework.
> 6 It was stupid of her to leave the oven on.

SOUNDS

Aim: to focus on assimilation of sounds.

● ▭ Ask the students to listen and say the words aloud. Play the tape. Make sure the last /t/ and /d/ sound disappears as the students repeat the words.

WRITING

1 Aim: to practise speaking; to prepare for writing.

● Ask the students to work in their groups and choose an invention. If they are a particularly creative class, encourage them to think of their own invention.

2 Aim: to practise writing.

● Ask the students to use the aspects listed in *Speaking and listening* activity 3 as a framework for making notes about their invention. Ask them to prepare a product description and choose a name for their invention.

3 Aim: to practise writing.

● Ask the students to think of an advertising poster which demonstrates all the features of their invention. Suggest that they plan the poster first and then decide what information they are going to include on it.

GRAMMAR

> Noun/adjective + *to* + infinitive
>
> **You can put *to* + infinitive after certain nouns and pronouns, usually to describe purpose.**
> *It's a thing **to pat** the baby.   Where are the keys **to lock** this door?*
>
> **You can put *to* + infinitive after a number of adjectives, such as *pleased, disappointed, surprised, difficult, easy.***
> *It's **difficult to raise** your hat when your hands are full.*
>
> **You can put *of* (someone) + *to* + infinitive after certain adjectives, such as *nice, kind, silly, careless, good, wrong, clever, stupid, generous.***
> *It's **stupid of the inventor to use** electricity.*
>
> **You can put *for* + object + *to* + infinitive after certain adjectives, such as *easy, common, important, essential, (un)usual, (un)necessary, normal, rare.***
> *It's **rare for men to wear** a hat these days.*
>
> **You can put *for* + -*ing* to describe the purpose of something.**
> *It's a thing **for patting** a baby.*
> *It's a device **for shaving**.*

1 Use *to* + infinitive to describe the purpose of the following tools and pieces of equipment.

1 a key-ring	3 a fan	5 a toothbrush
2 a knife	4 a kettle	6 a fax machine

2 Make sentences beginning with the words in brackets and *of* (someone) or *for* + object + *to*.

1 You spilt the milk. (It was careless)
2 After a few days, bread goes stale. (It's normal)
3 He used all the hot water. (It was wrong)
4 You turned the lights on. (It wasn't necessary)
5 He did all the housework. (It was unusual)
6 She left the oven on. (It was stupid)

1 It was careless of you to spill the milk.

SOUNDS

In connected speech, the last /t/ or /d/ sound in some words disappears before the first consonant of the next word. Listen and repeat these phrases.

dustbin   difficult time   cardboard
different table   household task
bread toaster   hand drill   felt tip

WRITING

1 Work in groups of three or four. You are going to persuade the company you work for to manufacture *either* one of the inventions in the illustrations, *or* an invention of your own choice. First, choose an invention. Make sure that you choose something which will make a great contribution to improving people's lives.

2 Prepare a description of the invention. Use the notes in *Speaking and listening* activity 3 to help you. Think of a name for your invention.

3 Design a poster for your invention to display in the classroom. Make sure that it says clearly the name of the invention, what it does and what its advantages are.

Food, glorious food!

Conditionals (1): zero, first and second conditionals; *if* and *when*

VOCABULARY AND SPEAKING

1 Look at the words in the box and put them under these headings: *breakfast, lunch, dinner, preparation* and *cooking*. Some may go in more than one category.

apple	aubergine	bake	boil
butter	cake	carrot	chop
coffee	cut	dice	fry	grate
grill	grind	milk	oil	onion
peel	pepper	potato	pour
roast	spread	steam	stew
tomato	trout	water	

2 Work in pairs. Look at the words in the box for food and drink and answer these questions.

– how do you usually cook them?
– how do you prepare them?

READING AND LISTENING

1 Read and answer the questionnaire. Now turn to Communication activity 2 on page 92 to find your score.

2 Work in groups of two or three and talk about your answers to the questionnaire. Do you all have similar answers or different attitudes and tastes?

3 Listen to Philip and Josie having a conversation in a restaurant. Decide which one of them lives to eat.

Do you eat to live or live to eat?

1 When you buy food, which is most important?
a appearance **b** price **c** quality

2 If you buy apples, which kind do you choose?
a red **b** green **c** the cheapest

3 When you have a meal, what do you enjoy it most for?
a the food **b** the company **c** the relaxation **d** the television

4 If you were stranded on a desert island what food would you miss most?
a chocolate **b** steak **c** bread

5 If a waiter suggests water, which do you ask for?
a sparkling **b** still **c** tap

6 When you look at the menu in a restaurant, what do you usually choose?
a a dish you know **b** a dish you don't know

7 If you're having dinner in a restaurant, will you always have a dessert?
a yes **b** no

8 If someone offered the following unusual food, which would you try?
a cheese-flavoured ice cream **b** strawberry flavoured crisps **c** neither

9 If someone suggested a quick meal, what would you choose?
a fast food **b** a sandwich **c** a picnic **d** something more substantial

10 What would you be happiest to leave out of your present diet?
a meat **b** vegetables and fruit **c** desserts **d** wine

11 If you could put a flavour on stamps, what would you choose?
a chilli **b** cheese **c** banana **d** another **e** none

12 If someone said 'Never eat anything you can't pronounce' what would you say?
a I couldn't agree more. **b** Nonsense!

12

GENERAL COMMENTS

Socio-cultural training

In the *Reward* series, there are many opportunities to explore customs, traditions, attitudes and behaviour of other cultures. There are a number of reasons for doing this. Firstly, information about other cultures is usually very interesting for the students. Secondly, it serves to remind them why they're studying English, as a means of communication with people who don't speak their own language. Socio-cultural training should not encourage them to adopt the customs, traditions, attitudes and behaviour of other cultures, particularly not those of native English speakers. It should encourage the students to become aware that their own culturally guided behaviour is not always automatically transferable to other cultural contexts, and that if this does happen, at worst, offence may be caused or perceived where none was intended. Thus, another aim of socio-cultural training is for the students to become aware of aspects of their own culture.

VOCABULARY AND SPEAKING

1 Aim: to present or practise using the words in the vocabulary box.

● Students will have come across most, if not all, of these words before. They are presented here as items for revision. Ask them to put the words in the categories.

> **Answers**
> Categorising the words according to **breakfast, lunch** and **dinner** will reflect the cultural origins and/or the personal preferences of the students.
> **preparation:** chop cut dice grate grind peel pour spread
> **cooking:** bake boil fry grill roast steam stew

2 Aim: to practise using the words in the vocabulary box.

● Ask the students to use the words in the box to talk about how they cook and prepare food and drink.

READING AND LISTENING

1 Aim: to read and answer a questionnaire.

● Explain that the questionnaire focuses on people's attitudes to food. Your students are likely to give very different answers to the questionnaire, depending on their personal preferences.

● Ask the students to turn to the Communication activity on page 92 to find their score and the interpretation of their answers.

2 Aim: to check comprehension; to practise speaking.

● Ask the students to talk in groups about their answers to the questionnaire. Ask them to compare their preferences, attitudes and tastes.

● Check the answers to the questionnaire with the whole class.

3 Aim: to listen for main ideas.

● Ask the students to decide how someone who 'lives to eat' might answer the questionnaire.

● 🔊 Play the tape and ask the students to decide which person lives to eat.

Conditionals (2): *unless, even if, as long as, provided (that), or/otherwise*

READING AND SPEAKING

1 Work in groups of three. You are going to read a passage called *Meals on wheels*. Before you read the passage try to predict what it might be about. Try to think of at least five ideas.

2 Read *Meals on wheels* and write a sentence saying what the passage is about. Were any of your ideas correct? (For the moment, ignore the gaps in the text.)

3 Find a word in the text that means the same as the words and phrases below:

1 not cooked
2 a kind of seat you put on a horse
3 soft or easy to cut and eat
4 a break in a journey for rest or food
5 something which is wrapped
6 to tie something to something else
7 to make a hole in something

Meals on wheels

It is perfectly possible to use the engine in your car to cook food. It's not a new idea. After all, Genghis Khan is believed to have put raw meat under the saddle of his horse to make it tender as he rode. This is said to be the origin of *steak tartare*. (1) _____ the food should be ready when you arrive or at some convenient stopover. It allows you to eat good, freshly-cooked, hot food anywhere on the way even if you find yourself in a remote place. Anyone can try car-engine cooking (2) _____. Driving conditions can vary the cooking process considerably. Most of the recipes are based on cooking times generated by empty freeways in America and its 55 mile an hour speed limit. But if you ignore the speed limit (3) _____, this will affect the process. It's probably not a good idea to use your engine for cooking in Central London (4) _____. The classic cooking method is *en paupiette*, or wrapped in foil. There's usually room to do six small foil-wrapped parcels at a time (5) _____. Here are a few tips for car engine cooking:

1 Do not expect to boil anything; if your engine is boiling, you'll have to stop anyway. But you can still bake, roast, poach and stew, even if you have a cool-running diesel engine.

2 Don't choose dishes which need careful timing.

3 On long journeys, provided that you choose dishes which cook slowly, your cooking will be very successful. For short journeys, only fish, diced vegetables and sliced meat will be ready in time.

4 Always wrap everything in three layers of foil, otherwise it will smell or get dirty. If you use baking paper it burns. As long as you wrap everything carefully, the food will be all right.

5 Make sure you don't pierce the package when you put it in place or there will be a serious loss of sauce, which only smells nice at first.

6 Try using the foil trays in which you get ready prepared supermarket meals.

7 Wrap sweet peppers, tomatoes, potatoes (which can take some time), bits of aubergine, apples and hamburgers in small round parcels. Long, thin parcels are better for pieces of meat, mackerel, trout and sausages.

8 Strap sausages, lamb chops and fillets of fish to the exhaust pipe to brown them on one side.

9 Take care not to let the cookery parcels get in the way of the accelerator cable or any other moving part of the engine.

10 Make sure you pierce any cans you intend to heat with two holes. Unless you do this, they will explode.

11 Never use the car engine fan as a food processor for slicing carrots.

Adapted from *Meals on wheels* by Robin Young, *The Times*

12

GENERAL COMMENTS

Socio-cultural training

In the *Reward* series, there are many opportunities to explore customs, traditions, attitudes and behaviour of other cultures. There are a number of reasons for doing this. Firstly, information about other cultures is usually very interesting for the students. Secondly, it serves to remind them why they're studying English, as a means of communication with people who don't speak their own language. Socio-cultural training should not encourage them to adopt the customs, traditions, attitudes and behaviour of other cultures, particularly not those of native English speakers. It should encourage the students to become aware that their own culturally guided behaviour is not always automatically transferable to other cultural contexts, and that if this does happen, at worst, offence may be caused or perceived where none was intended. Thus, another aim of socio-cultural training is for the students to become aware of aspects of their own culture.

VOCABULARY AND SPEAKING

1 Aim: to present or practise using the words in the vocabulary box.

● Students will have come across most, if not all, of these words before. They are presented here as items for revision. Ask them to put the words in the categories.

> **Answers**
> Categorising the words according to **breakfast, lunch** and **dinner** will reflect the cultural origins and/or the personal preferences of the students.
> **preparation:** chop cut dice grate grind peel
>   pour spread
> **cooking:** bake boil fry grill roast steam stew

2 Aim: to practise using the words in the vocabulary box.

● Ask the students to use the words in the box to talk about how they cook and prepare food and drink.

READING AND LISTENING

1 Aim: to read and answer a questionnaire.

● Explain that the questionnaire focuses on people's attitudes to food. Your students are likely to give very different answers to the questionnaire, depending on their personal preferences.

● Ask the students to turn to the Communication activity on page 92 to find their score and the interpretation of their answers.

2 Aim: to check comprehension; to practise speaking.

● Ask the students to talk in groups about their answers to the questionnaire. Ask them to compare their preferences, attitudes and tastes.

● Check the answers to the questionnaire with the whole class.

3 Aim: to listen for main ideas.

● Ask the students to decide how someone who 'lives to eat' might answer the questionnaire.

● 🔲 Play the tape and ask the students to decide which person lives to eat.

4 Aim: to practise inferring.
● Ask the students to think about what they know about Philip and Josie from what they heard on the tape. Ask the students to decide which questions they can answer for Philip and Josie.

5 Aim: to check comprehension.
● Ask the students to complete the sentences with a few words.

● Check the answers with the whole class.

> **Answers**
> 1 Philip doesn't mind paying a high price if the food **is good quality**.
> 2 For Josie what's important when she goes out for a meal is **the company.**
> 3 Philip always tries dishes he **can't pronounce**.
> 4 For Josie a sandwich is **lunch.**
> 5 Philip would find it difficult to give up fruit because he likes **the taste and the texture.**
> 6 Josie likes to finish a meal with an apple because **it makes her mouth feel fresh.**

6 Aim: to listen for specific information.
● ▭ Play the tape again and ask the students to listen and check their answers to activities 3 and 5.

GRAMMAR

1 Aim: to present the difference between the first, second and zero conditionals.
● Ask the students to read the information in the grammar box and then to do the exercises.

> **Answers**
> 1a This is a likely situation and a likely result.
> 1b This is an unlikely situation and its result.
> 2a I'm not sure that you'll be here at 9am.
> 2b I'm sure you'll get here at 9am.

2 Aim: to practise using conditional sentences.
● You may like to do this activity with the whole class.

> **Answers**
> 1 If you **go** to the new restaurant, I'm sure you **will enjoy** yourself.
> 2 If I **have** too much to eat, I **get/will get** sleepy.
> 3 If I **were** you, I **would choose** the chef's speciality.
> 4 If I **had** a lot of money, I **would go** out more often.
> 5 If you **chop** the vegetables, they **cook** more quickly.

3 Aim: to focus on the distinction between *if* and *when*.
● Ask the students to do this activity alone, and then to check their answers with another student.

> **Answers**
> 1 She's coming with us tonight. **When** you see her, you can ask her.
> 2 **If** we're late, start without us.
> 3 I'm going to the restaurant now. **When** I get there, I'll ring her.
> 4 **If** it's a nice day tomorrow, we'll have a barbecue.
> 5 They may not be at home, but **if** they are, I'll invite them round.

SOUNDS

1 Aim: to focus on word stress in sentences.
● Remind students that a speaker will stress the words he or she thinks are important. If the students use similar word stress in sentences, they will sound much more fluent speakers of the language.

● Ask the students to predict the words the speaker will stress in *Grammar* activity 3.

2 Aim: to focus on word stress in sentences.
● ▭ Play the tape and ask the students to check their answers to 1.

> **Answers**
> 1 She's <u>coming</u> with us <u>tonight</u>. When you <u>see</u> her, you can <u>ask</u> her.
> 2 If we're <u>late</u>, start <u>without</u> us.
> 3 I'm going to the <u>restaurant now</u>. When I <u>get</u> there, I'll <u>ring</u> her.
> 4 If it's a <u>nice day</u> tomorrow, we'll have a <u>barbecue</u>.
> 5 They <u>may</u> not be at <u>home</u>, but if they <u>are</u>, I'll <u>invite</u> them <u>round</u>.

SPEAKING

Aim: to practise speaking.
● Ask the students to talk about and make notes on food and drink in their country. They should use the prompts in the Student's Book to help them.

● Ask the students to work with another pair and to compare the notes they have made.

4 Which questions in the questionnaire can you answer for Josie and Philip?

5 Complete the sentences with a few words or phrases.

1 Philip doesn't mind paying a high price if the food ____.
2 For Josie, what's important when she goes out for a meal is ____.
3 Philip always tries dishes he ____.
4 For Josie, a sandwich is ____.
5 Philip would find it difficult to give up fruit because he likes ____.
6 Josie likes to finish a meal with an apple because ____.

6 🔲 Listen again and check your answers to 3 and 5.

GRAMMAR

> **Conditionals (1): zero conditional**
> You use *if/when* + present simple or continuous when you talk about general truths, habits or routines. *If* has the same meaning as *whenever*.
> *If Josie* **goes** *to a restaurant, she* **orders** *something she knows she likes.*
>
> **First conditional**
> You use *if* + present simple or continuous, + *will* when you talk about a likely situation and its result.
> *If I'm working late tonight, I'll go out and buy a sandwich.*
>
> **Second conditional**
> You use *if* + past simple, + *would* + infinitive when you talk about an imaginary or unlikely situation in the present or future and its result. You often use the contraction *'d* .
> *If I* **had to** *give up something, I think I'd give up meat.*
>
> **If and when**
> You use *if* in zero and first conditional sentences for actions and events which are not certain to happen.
> *If a waiter* **suggests** *water, I* **ask** *for sparkling.*
> *If I go out tonight, I'll have dinner early.*
> You use *when* in zero and first conditional sentences for actions and events which are more certain.
> *When I'm really enjoying myself, I sometimes don't know what I'm eating.*
> *When I go out tonight, I'll have dinner in a restaurant.*

1 Look at these sentences and explain the difference between them.

1 a If you give me £1, I'll spend it all.
   b If you gave me £25,000, I'd spend it all.

2 a I'll give it to you if you get here at 9am.
   b I'll give it to you when you get here at 9am.

2 Complete the sentences using a suitable conditional form. There may be more than one possibility.

1 If you ____ to the new restaurant, I'm sure you ____ yourself.
2 If I ____ too much to eat, I ____ sleepy.
3 If I ____ you, I ____ the chef's speciality.
4 If I ____ a lot of money, I ____ out more often.
5 If you ____ the vegetables, they ____ more quickly.

3 Complete the sentences with *if* or *when*.

1 She's coming with us tonight. ____ you see her, you can ask her.
2 ____ we're late, start without us.
3 I'm going to the restaurant now. ____ I get there, I'll ring her.
4 ____ it's a nice day tomorrow, we'll have a barbecue.
5 They may not be at home, but ____ they are, I'll invite them round.

SOUNDS

1 Underline the words you think the speaker will stress in *Grammar* activity 3.

2 🔲 Listen and check your answers to 1. As you listen, say the sentences aloud.

SPEAKING

Work in pairs. Talk about food and drink in your country. Discuss the following:

– most typical dish   – typical drinks
– typical produce   – typical snacks
– eating out   – family meals

The most typical dish for us in Tunisia is couscous.

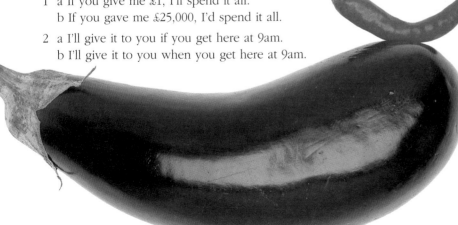

Conditionals (2): *unless, even if, as long as, provided (that), or/otherwise*

READING AND SPEAKING

1 Work in groups of three. You are going to read a passage called *Meals on wheels*. Before you read the passage try to predict what it might be about. Try to think of at least five ideas.

2 Read *Meals on wheels* and write a sentence saying what the passage is about. Were any of your ideas correct? (For the moment, ignore the gaps in the text.)

3 Find a word in the text that means the same as the words and phrases below:

1 not cooked
2 a kind of seat you put on a horse
3 soft or easy to cut and eat
4 a break in a journey for rest or food
5 something which is wrapped
6 to tie something to something else
7 to make a hole in something

Meals on wheels

It is perfectly possible to use the engine in your car to cook food. It's not a new idea. After all, Genghis Khan is believed to have put raw meat under the saddle of his horse to make it tender as he rode. This is said to be the origin of *steak tartare*. (1) _____ the food should be ready when you arrive or at some convenient stopover. It allows you to eat good, freshly-cooked, hot food anywhere on the way even if you find yourself in a remote place. Anyone can try car-engine cooking (2) _____. Driving conditions can vary the cooking process considerably. Most of the recipes are based on cooking times generated by empty freeways in America and its 55 mile an hour speed limit. But if you ignore the speed limit (3) _____, this will affect the process. It's probably not a good idea to use your engine for cooking in Central London (4) _____. The classic cooking method is *en paupiette*, or wrapped in foil. There's usually room to do six small foil-wrapped parcels at a time (5) _____. Here are a few tips for car engine cooking:

1 Do not expect to boil anything; if your engine is boiling, you'll have to stop anyway. But you can still bake, roast, poach and stew, even if you have a cool-running diesel engine.

2 Don't choose dishes which need careful timing.

3 On long journeys, provided that you choose dishes which cook slowly, your cooking will be very successful. For short journeys, only fish, diced vegetables and sliced meat will be ready in time.

4 Always wrap everything in three layers of foil, otherwise it will smell or get dirty. If you use baking paper it burns. As long as you wrap everything carefully, the food will be all right.

5 Make sure you don't pierce the package when you put it in place or there will be a serious loss of sauce, which only smells nice at first.

6 Try using the foil trays in which you get ready prepared supermarket meals.

7 Wrap sweet peppers, tomatoes, potatoes (which can take some time), bits of aubergine, apples and hamburgers in small round parcels. Long, thin parcels are better for pieces of meat, mackerel, trout and sausages.

8 Strap sausages, lamb chops and fillets of fish to the exhaust pipe to brown them on one side.

9 Take care not to let the cookery parcels get in the way of the accelerator cable or any other moving part of the engine.

10 Make sure you pierce any cans you intend to heat with two holes. Unless you do this, they will explode.

11 Never use the car engine fan as a food processor for slicing carrots.

Adapted from *Meals on wheels* by Robin Young, *The Times*

READING AND SPEAKING

1 Aim: to prepare for reading.

● Ask the students to look at the photo and the title of the passage, and to predict what the passage is likely to be about. Ask the students to predict a few words which they expect to see in the passage.

2 Aim: to read for main ideas.

● Ask the students to read the passage and then to write a sentence saying what the passage is about. This is a very simple summary writing activity.

● Ask the students to work in pairs and see if they can improve their one-sentence summaries. Find out who has written the shortest and most accurate summary.

> **Possible answer**
> The passage is about using your car engine to cook food.

● You may like to point out to the students that although the passage comes from an authentic text, it is inadvisable to try any of the cooking methods mentioned.

3 Aim: to deal with unfamiliar vocabulary.

● This activity focuses on words the students may not be familiar with. Ask them to match the word in the passage with the simplified explanation in the activity.

> **Answers**
> 1 raw 2 saddle 3 tender 4 stopover
> 5 parcel 6 strap 7 pierce

4 Aim: to check comprehension; to read for specific information.

● Ask the students to read the passage again and to find the answers to the questions. You may like to ask them to do this in pairs.

Answers
1 To make it tender.
2 Because it will cook too quickly.
3 Because the heavy traffic means the car is stationary most of the time and the food won't get cooked.
4 Because the engine does not have to be hot/boiling to cook the food.
5 Because you never know how long your journey is going to take or if you are going to be delayed.
6 Because the parcels may cause the cable to jam.

X 7 Y/N.

5 Aim: to read for text organisation; to present the target structures.

● This is a difficult activity but it presents the structures in the grammar box and encourages the students to read very carefully. Ask them to decide where the sentences go in the passage.

Answers
1 c 2 b 3 d 4 e 5 a

6 Aim: to check comprehension.

● Ask the students to decide which of the points you should follow, and which ones you shouldn't follow.

Answers
1 ✗ 2 ✗ 3 ✓ 4 ✓ 5 ✗ 6 ✓
7 ✓ 8 ✓ 9 ✗ 10 ✓ 11 ✗

7 Aim: to practise speaking; to react to the passage.

● Ask the students what they think about the idea of car engine cooking. Ask them how much time it took them before they realised the passage was a serious one and not a joke.

GRAMMAR

1 Aim: to present conditional sentences.

● Ask the students to read the information in the grammar box and then to do the exercises.

Answers
4: zero conditional: If you use baking paper it burns.
All other sentences are first conditional sentences.

2 Aim: to practise using *if, even if* and *as long as*.

● Ask the students to complete the sentences. You can do this with the whole class.

Answers
1 I wouldn't use my car engine for cooking **even if** I was starving.
2 I'd try car engine cooking **as long as** the food stayed clean.
3 **If** there were no restaurants on a long journey, I think I'd try it.
4 **As long as** there was no risk of the food falling off, I'd try cooking some steak.
5 **Even if** it was easier to take a picnic, I'd still want to try it out.

3 Aim: to practise using *if, unless, even if, as long as/provided that* and *or/otherwise*.

● Ask the students to choose four or five sentences and to rewrite them using one of the words in conditional clauses.

4 Aim: to practise using *or/otherwise*.

● Ask the students to rewrite the sentences in 3 using *or/otherwise* + clause.

WRITING

Aim: to practise speaking; to practise writing.

● Ask the students to choose one of the topics in the list and to write tips. Make sure they include some or all of the words used in conditional clauses. Suggest that they look at the tips in *Meals on wheels* as a model. You may like to ask students to do this activity for homework.

4 Answer the questions.

1 Why did Genghis Khan put raw meat under his saddle?

2 Why will ignoring the speed limit affect the cooking process?

3 Why isn't it a good idea to use your engine for cooking in central London?

4 Why will you still be able to cook with a cool-running diesel engine?

5 Why shouldn't you choose dishes which need careful timing?

6 Why should you take care not to let cookery parcels get in the way of the accelerator cable?

7 Would it have occurred to you to use the car engine fan to slice carrots?

5 Work in pairs. Look back at the passage and decide where these conditional clauses go in the gaps.

a even if you have an average car

b if the driving conditions are suitable

c As long as you plan your journey and your cooking carefully

d or if you come up against heavy traffic jams

e unless you like raw food

6 Look back at the passage and put a tick (✓) by the tips which say what you *should* do and a cross (✗) by the ones which say what you *shouldn't* do.

7 Work in pairs and answer the questions.

1 What do you think of the idea of car engine cooking?

2 Would you like to try it?

3 If so, where would you try it?

4 What would you cook?

5 How would you cook it?

6 How long would it take?

Now work with another pair and compare your answers.

GRAMMAR

> Conditionals (2): *unless, even if, as long as, provided (that), or/otherwise*
>
> **You can use *unless, even if, as long as, provided (that)* with zero and first conditionals to talk about likely situations and their results.**
> **You can use *unless* to mean *if... not*.**
> *Unless you pierce the tins, they will explode.*
> (= If you don't pierce the tins, they will explode.)
> **You use *even if* to express a contrast or to give some surprising information.**
> *You can cook food **even if** you have a cool-running diesel engine.*
> **You use *as long as* or *provided (that)* to mean *on condition that*.**
> *The food will be ready **as long as**, **(provided that)** you plan your journey carefully.*
> **You can also use the expressions with second conditional sentences, when you talk about an unlikely situation and its result.**
> **You can follow an instruction with *or* or *otherwise* + a clause describing the result if you don't follow the instruction.**
> *Always wrap everything in three layers of foil, **otherwise** it will smell or get dirty.*
> (= If you don't wrap everything in three layers of foil it will smell or get dirty.)

1 Look back at *Meals on wheels* and find some examples of conditional sentences. Say which type of conditional (zero, first or second) they are and why they are used. You can use the grammar box to help you.

2 Complete these sentences with *if, even if* or *as long as*.

1 I wouldn't use my car engine for cooking ____ I was starving.

2 I'd try car engine cooking ____ the food stayed clean.

3 ____ there were no restaurants on a long journey, I think I'd try it.

4 ____ there was no risk of the food falling off, I'd try cooking some steak.

5 ____ it was easier to take a picnic, I'd still want to try it out.

3 Choose four or five tips for car engine cooking, and rewrite them using *if, unless, even if, as long as, provided that* and *or/otherwise*.

As long as you choose dishes which cook slowly, you can use your engine to cook food.

4 Rewrite the sentences in 3 using *or/otherwise* + a clause describing the result.

WRITING

Choose one of the following topics and write a list of ten tips for it.

– having a picnic   – eating a meal out in your country
– having a barbecue   – an unusual method of cooking

Give your tips.   *Always take a rug...*
Explain your reasons.   *...as the ground may be damp...*
Explain the consequences describing the result if you don't follow the instructions.   *...otherwise, you might catch a cold.*

Progress check 9–12

VOCABULARY

1 After the following verbs you can use the *-ing* form and *to* + infinitive but the meaning changes: *remember, forget, try, stop, regret*

I remembered him saying he felt ill.
(= He said he felt ill and I remember this.)
I remembered to call him.
(= I remembered, then I called.)
You've forgotten asking for my help.
(= You asked for my help, then you forgot.)
I forgot to tell you what I'd done.
(= I didn't tell you because I forgot.)
He had even tried working at weekends.
(= as an experiment.)
He had tried to revise for about eight hours a day.
(= He made an effort to do so.)
I stopped feeling so generous.
(= I was feeling generous, then I stopped.)
He stopped his studies to get a job.
(= He stopped his studies in order to get a job.)
I now regret being so mean.
(= I regret something I have already done.)
I regret to tell you that I can't come.
(= I'm sorry to have to tell you that I can't come now.)

For more information, turn to the Grammar review at the back of the book.

Now complete these sentences with the verb in brackets in the correct form.

1 I remember ____ her at a party a year ago. (meet)
2 During the journey we stopped ____ something to eat. (have)
3 She regretted not ____ an earlier train. (take)
4 Please try ____ very carefully. (drive)
5 Don't forget ____ me some money. (give)
6 Remember ____ a newspaper when you're shopping. (buy)

2 You often use a prefix to give a word an opposite or negative meaning. Here are some common prefixes:

dis- il- im- in- ir- over- re- un- under-

Use your dictionary to find out which prefixes the following words take. Some words may take more than one prefix.

able   agree   approve   charge   convenient   edible
fair   legible   literate   load   patient   place
probable   read   replaceable   reversible   use   work

GRAMMAR

1 Write down five things you remember doing last year.

2 Put a tick (✓) by the sentences where you can use *used to* or *would* and a cross (✗) where you can only use *used to*.

1 When I was young, I *used to/would* be very shy.
2 We *used to/would* spend our holidays in Scotland.
3 There *used to/would* be a shop on the corner.
4 In the summer, they *used to/would* go out every day.
5 Years ago he *used to/would* have a moustache.
6 I *used to/would* be afraid of the dark.

3 Complete the sentences with *must* or a form of *have to*. Sometimes both are possible.

1 You ____ have a passport when you go abroad.
2 I'll ____ do some shopping tomorrow.
3 I'm tired. I ____ leave before I fall asleep.
4 She ____ go home because she felt sick.
5 I ____ go by bus this morning because my car broke down.
6 She doesn't enjoy ____ cook every day.

Progress check 9 – 12

GENERAL COMMENTS

You can work through this Progress check in the order shown, or concentrate on areas which may have caused difficulty in Lessons 9 to 12. You can also let the students choose the activities they would like or feel the need to do.

VOCABULARY

1 Aim: to present the *-ing* form or *to* + infinitive after *remember, forget, try, stop, regret.*

● Explain that *remember, forget, try, stop, regret* can have an *-ing* form or an infinitive afterwards, depending on the meaning. Ask students to read the example sentences and read the Grammar review for more information.

● Ask the students to do the exercise. Check the answers with the whole class.

> **Answers**
> 1 I remember **meeting** her at a party a year ago.
> 2 During the journey we stopped **to have** something to eat.
> 3 She regretted not **taking** an earlier train.
> 4 Please try **to drive** very carefully.
> 5 Don't forget **to give** me some money.
> 6 Remember **to buy** a newspaper when you're shopping.

2 Aim: to present negative or opposite prefixes.

● Ask the students to make opposite or negative words using the prefixes. Do this with the whole class.

> **Answers**
> unable disable disagree disapprove discharge undercharge overcharge inconvenient inedible unfair illegible illiterate unload impatient displace replace improbable reread irreplaceable irreversible overuse underuse overwork underwork

GRAMMAR

1 Aim: to revise the use of *remember.*

● Encourage the students to write about their own memories of things they did last year.

2 Aim: to revise the use of *used to* and *would.*

> **Answers**
> 1 ✗ 2 ✓ 3 ✗ 4 ✓ 5 ✗ 6 ✗

3 Aim: to revise *must* and *have to.*

> **Answers**
> 1 You **have to** have a passport when you go abroad.
> 2 I'll **have to** do some shopping tomorrow.
> 3 I'm tired. I **must** leave before I fall asleep.
> 4 She **had to** go home because she felt sick.
> 5 I **had to** go by bus this morning because my car broke down.
> 6 She doesn't enjoy **having to** cook every day.

4 Aim: to revise *mustn't, don't need to, needn't have, didn't need to.*

> **Answers**
> 1 You **don't need to** get up early as it's Sunday.
> 2 He **didn't need to** pay so he didn't get out his wallet.
> 3 We **mustn't** annoy him as he gets very angry.
> 4 You **don't need to** call a taxi. I'll drive you home.
> 5 I **didn't need to** ring her because she called round to see me.
> 6 You **needn't** drive so fast. We've got plenty of time.
> 7 You **mustn't** drive on the right in Britain.
> 8 I didn't go shopping yesterday. I **didn't need to** because I still had plenty of food.

5 Aim: to revise *in order to, to* and *so that.*

● Ask the students to write their own answers to the questions.

6 Aim: to revise adjective + infinitive constructions.

> **Answers**
> 1 It was **nice of** you to ring me.
> 2 It wasn't **necessary for** her to bring some flowers.
> 3 It's **important to** speak clearly.
> 4 It was **unusual for** him to refuse a second helping.
> 5 It was **careless of** her to leave her bag in the taxi.
> 6 It was **generous of** her to buy me lunch.

7 Aim: to revise *if, when, even if* and *as long as.*

> **Answers**
> 1 even if   2 If   3 When   4 if
> 5 Even if   6 As long as

SOUNDS

1 Aim: to focus on the spelling of /ɑʊə/, /ɔː/ or /əʊ/.

● Remind the students that some sounds can be spelt in different ways. Ask them to put the words in three columns.

● 🔲 Play the tape and ask them to say the words aloud.

> **Answers**
> /ɔː/: shore tore floor sore
> /ɑʊə/: shower tower flower sour
> /əʊ/: show toe flow sew

2 Aim: to focus on different pronunciations of *-ough.*

● There are several ways of pronouncing the ending *-ough*. Ask the students to say the words aloud and decide in which two words is *-ough* pronounced the same.

● 🔲 Play the tape and ask the students to say the words aloud.

> **Answer**
> *-ough* is pronounced the same in *rough* and *enough*.

3 Aim: to focus on contrastive stress.

● Remind the students that you change the meaning of a sentence by changing the stress on words. Ask them to underline the words the speakers will stress in the dialogue.

● 🔲 Play the tape and ask the students to listen and check.

> **Answers**
> A How are you?
> B Fine. How are you?
> A OK. Did you have a good weekend?
> B Yes, I did. Did you?
> A Very nice. What did you do?
> B I played tennis. What did you do?
> A I went to the cinema. I saw the latest Woody Allen film. Have you seen it?
> B Yes, I have. Did you like it?
> A Yes, I did. Did you?
> B Yes, I did.

● Ask the students to act out the dialogue in pairs.

LISTENING AND WRITING

1 Aim: to practise listening and note-taking.

● 🔲 Explain to the students that they are going to hear three news stories. Ask them to listen and take notes.

2 Aim: to practise speaking.

● Ask the students to work in groups and compare their notes and expand them if necessary. Encourage them to collect as much detail as possible.

3 Aim: to practise writing.

● Ask the students to write down the news stories as accurately as possible. They can either remain in their groups or do this activity individually.

4 Aim: to provide an opportunity for a second listening; to check the answers to activity 3.

● 🔲 Play the tape again and ask the students to check their versions. Did any group reconstruct the news stories exactly?

4 Choose the best verb.

1 You *mustn't/don't need to* get up early as it's Sunday.

2 He *needn't have* paid/*didn't need to* pay so he didn't get out his wallet.

3 We *mustn't/haven't got to* annoy him as he gets very angry.

4 You *mustn't/don't need to* call a taxi. I'll drive you home.

5 I *needn't have* rung/*didn't need to* ring her because she called round to see me.

6 You *needn't/mustn't* drive so fast. We've got plenty of time.

7 You *mustn't/don't have to* drive on the right in Britain.

8 I didn't go shopping yesterday. I *didn't need to/needn't have* because I still had plenty of food.

5 Answer the questions with *in order to, to* or *so that.*

1 Why do some people spend their holidays in sunny countries?

2 Why does the government make us pay taxes?

3 Why do some people wear hats?

4 Why do some people keep guard dogs?

5 Why do you carry an umbrella?

6 Why should you take exercise?

6 Rewrite these sentences using the words in brackets and *of* or *for.*

1 You rang me. (It was nice)

2 She brought some flowers. (It wasn't necessary)

3 Speak clearly. (It's important)

4 He refused a second helping. (It was unusual)

5 She left her bag in the taxi. (It was careless)

6 She bought me lunch. (It was generous)

7 Complete the sentences with *if, when, even if* or *as long as.* There may be more than one possibility.

1 I wouldn't go ____ you paid me.

2 ____ you help wash up, I'll help you with your homework.

3 I'm going to work now. ____ I get there I'll speak to my boss.

4 She may not be there, but ____ she is, I'll tell her.

5 ____ it was well-cooked, I wouldn't eat meat.

6 ____ it's not illegal, I'll try anything.

SOUNDS

1 Say these words aloud. Is the underlined sound /əʊə/, /əu/ or /ɔː/. Put them into three columns.

sh<u>ore</u>   sh<u>ow</u>   sh<u>ow</u>er   t<u>ore</u>   t<u>oe</u>   t<u>ow</u>er
fl<u>oor</u>   fl<u>ow</u>   fl<u>ow</u>er   s<u>ore</u>   s<u>ew</u>   s<u>our</u>

Listen and check. As you listen, say the words aloud.

2 Say these words aloud. In which two words is *ough* pronounced the same?

through   though   bough   rough   cough   thorough   enough

Now listen and check.

3 Underline the words you think the speaker will stress in this dialogue.

A   How are you?

B   Fine. How are you?

A   Okay. Did you have a good weekend?

B   Yes, I did. Did you?

A   Very nice. What did you do?

B   I played tennis. What did you do?

A   I went to the cinema. I saw the latest Woody Allen film. Have you seen it?

B   Yes, I have. Did you like it?

A   Yes, I did. Did you?

B   Yes, I did.

Listen and check. Then work in pairs and act out the dialogue.

LISTENING AND WRITING

1   Listen to three news stories and take notes.

2 Work in groups of three, and compare notes. Check you have noted down as much detail as possible.

3 In your groups, write out the news stories in full. Try to reconstruct them as accurately as you can.

4   Listen again and check your stories in 3. Did you remember everything?

13 | *High-tech dreams or nightmares?*

The passive

VOCABULARY AND READING

1 Look at the words for items of technology in the box. Which ones would you find at work, which at home and which at work and at home?

> computer   video recorder   microwave   CD player
> food processor   camcorder   camera   photocopier
> washing machine   telephone   refrigerator   stereo
> security system

2 Work in groups of three or four. Discuss if you are happy with or afraid of technology. Which items in the box do you most or least like using? What can go wrong with technology?

3 Read the passage about a computerised home. Is the writer's home a high-tech dream or a high-tech nightmare?

4 Read the passage again and find out six things which went wrong in the writer's home.
Now work in pairs and check your answers.

5 Which of these statements are true?

1 On December 3, the computer damaged all the electrical appliances. T
2 The software company tested the system from a distance. T
3 Vibrations on the window set off the security alarm and call the police. T
4 The universal remote usually changes the TV channels. won't let me T
5 On December 12, the computer caught a virus from inside the home system. T
6 Usually, you could raise or lower the garage doors automatically. T
7 On December 21, the programmers upgraded the system. T

Nov 28: Moved in at last. Finally, we live in the smartest house in the neighborhood. Everything is networked. The cable TV is connected to our phone, which is connected to my personal computer, which is connected to the power lines, all the appliances and the security system. Everything runs off a universal remote.

Nov 30: Hot Stuff! Programmed my video recorder from the office, turned up the thermostat and switched on the lights with the car phone. Everything nice and cozy when I arrived.

Dec 3: Yesterday the kitchen CRASHED. As I opened the refrigerator door, the light bulb blew. Immediately, all the electrical appliances were shut down by the computer. So the software company runs some remote telediagnostic tests via my house processor. Turns out the problem was that the network had never seen a refrigerator bulb failure while the door was open. The burned out bulb was interpreted as a power surge and THE ENTIRE KITCHEN WAS SHUT DOWN.

Dec 7: The police are not happy. Our house keeps calling them for help. We discover that whenever we play the TV or stereo above 25 decibels, it creates vibrations which are amplified when they hit the window. The police computer concludes that someone is trying to break in.

Another glitch: the universal remote won't let me change the channels on my TV. That means I actually have to get up off the couch and change the channels by hand. The software and the utility people say this flaw will be fixed in the next upgrade – SmartHouse 2.1.

Dec 12: This is a nightmare. There's a virus in the house. My personal computer caught it while browsing on the public access network. I come home and the living room is a sauna, the bedroom windows are covered with ice, the refrigerator has been defrosted, the basement has been flooded by the washing machine, the garage door is going up and down and the TV is stuck on the home shopping channel.

Dec 18: They think they've disinfected the house, but the place is a shambles. Pipes have burst and we're not completely sure we've got the part of the virus that attacks the toilets.

Dec 19: Apparently our house isn't insured for viruses.
We call our lawyer. He laughs. He's excited!

Dec 21: I get a call from a SmartHouse sales rep. As a special holiday offer, we get the free opportunity to become a site for the company's new SmartHouse 2.1 upgrade. He says I'll be able to meet the programmers personally. 'Sure,' I tell him.

13

GENERAL COMMENTS

The passive

Not every language has a passive form, and some students may have difficulty in understanding why a passive is more appropriate than the active form of the verb. It should also be remembered that when we use the passive form the focus of the sentence is different from the active equivalent. For example, in the active sentence *The software company tested the system,* we are learning about *the software company*, whereas, in the passive equivalent, *The system was tested by the software company,* we are more interested in *the system*. By now, most students will be familiar with active versus passive sentences in the actual formation, but the subtleties of use can be difficult.

High technology

High technology or high-tech is a term used to describe the technology of computers, the Internet and CD Roms etc. Many students may not be interested in high technology, but it constitutes an important topic and vocabulary area, particularly as English is probably the most significant language for computer users.

VOCABULARY AND READING

1 Aim: to present the words in the vocabulary box.

● Ask the students to look at the words, and to check they understand what they mean. If anyone has any difficulties, ask other students to explain the words. You may find it useful to bring a shopping catalogue with photos of all the items to help you explain.

2 Aim: to practise speaking; to practise using the words in the vocabulary box.

● Ask the students to talk about their attitudes and feelings towards technology. Write the following attitude words on the board, and ask students to choose two or three to describe their responses.
fascination interest boredom apathy fear confidence curiosity clumsiness control

3 Aim: to read for main ideas.

● Explain that the passage is about a house which is fully computerised. Ask the students what they think a fully computerised house might be. What features in a home might be computerised? What would be the possible advantages and disadvantages of a computerised house?

● Make sure everyone understands the meaning of the word *nightmare* (bad dream).

● Ask the students to read the passage and decide if the writer's home is a high-tech dream or nightmare.

> **Answer**
> High-tech nightmare

4 Aim: to read for specific information.

● This activity involves a closer reading of the passage. Ask the students to find at least six things which went wrong.

> **Answers**
> Kitchen crashed, alarm system goes off when the TV or stereo is too loud, TV remote control doesn't work, living room is a sauna, bedroom windows covered with ice, refrigerator defrosted, basement flooded, garage door going up and down, TV channel stuck, burst pipes, toilets not working

● Ask the students to check their answers in pairs.

5 Aim: to check comprehension.

● Ask the students to check which statements are true.

> **Answers**
> Sentences: 1, 2, 3, 4, 5, 6 are all true.

6 Aim: to check comprehension; to read and infer.

- This activity involves some careful reading between the lines. Ask the students to do it in pairs.

Answers

1 Enthusiastic. **Hot stuff** is an expression of enthusiasm.
2 Because the sound waves are picked up by the windows which have alarm sensors.
3 The lawyer is looking forward to having a lawsuit against someone.
4 He probably wants to tell them what he thinks of their software.

GRAMMAR

1 Aim: to focus on the use of the passive.

- There is no correct answer to this exercise as it concerns a matter of focus rather than one of fact. Explain to the students that when choosing the most appropriate sentence they should think about the focus of the sentence and the context in which they imagine they would see it. The passive form is used in reports or official documents to give a more official or impersonal tone.

2 Aim: to present *by* and *with*.

- Ask the students to complete the sentences.

Answers

1 The TV is connected to the computer **by** a cable.
2 The floor was flooded **with** water **by** the washing machine.
3 Nothing was detected **by** the security sensors.
4 He was told **by** the claims adjuster that the house wasn't insured.
5 The system was attacked **by** a virus.
6 The computer was tested **with** special software **by** the software company.

WRITING

Aim: to practise writing a letter of complaint.

- Ask the students to suggest three pieces of electrical equipment or an item of high technology, such as a computer. Write their suggestions on the board.

- Ask the students to think of three things which can go wrong with the items you have written on the board.

- Ask the students to imagine that you're writing a letter of complaint about the piece of equipment you have just bought and write a model letter of complaint on the board, following the steps described in this activity.

- Now ask the students to choose either a piece of electrical equipment or an item of high technology and write a letter of complaint using the model on the board to help them.

- Go round and make sure they are using the expressions suggested, and are following the steps described. You may like to ask the students to do this activity for homework.

6 Work in pairs and talk about your answers to the questions.

1 Is the writer enthusiastic or indifferent about his home at first?
2 Why does the system keep calling the police?
3 Why do you think the lawyer is excited?
4 How does the writer feel about meeting the programmers?

GRAMMAR

The passive

You use the passive:

– when you do not know *who* or *what* does something.
*The cable TV **is connected** to our phone.*

– when you are not interested in *who* or *what* does something.
*All the electrical appliances **were shut** down.*

– when you want to take away the focus on the personal responsibility.
*This flaw **will be fixed** in the next upgrade.*

You use *by* to say *who* or *what* is responsible for an action.
*The basement **has been flooded by** the washing machine.*

You use *with* to talk about the instrument which is used to perform the action.
*The lights **were switched** on by the writer **with** his car phone.*

You also use *with* to talk about materials or ingredients.
*The bedroom windows **are covered with** ice.*

The passive is often used in sales brochures and product information to give an 'official' tone.

---

1 Look at these pairs of active and passive sentences.
In each pair, which do you think is the better sentence? Explain why.

1 a My computer is checked for viruses every six months.
  b A company checks my computer for viruses every six months.
2 a As the refrigerator door was opened the light bulb blew.
  b As I opened the refrigerator door, the light bulb blew.
3 a Many children are being shown how to use computers in schools.
  b Teachers are showing many children how to use computers in schools.
4 a You can change channels by using the remote control.
  b Channels can be changed by using the remote control.
5 a We will install a security system free of charge.
  b A security system will be installed free of charge.

2 Complete these sentences with *by* or *with*.

1 The TV is connected to the computer ____ a cable.
2 The floor was flooded ____ water ____ the washing machine.
3 Nothing was detected ____ the security sensors.
4 He was told ____ the claims adjuster that the house wasn't insured.
5 The system was attacked ____ a virus.
6 The computer was tested ____ special software ____ the software company.

WRITING

Think of a piece of electrical equipment, for example, a computer or a video recorder, and write down three things that could go wrong with it. Imagine that you bought one last weekend and now you are writing to the manufacturers to explain what went wrong and to demand a replacement or your money back.

Begin your letter by saying what you bought and where you bought it.

Next, explain what the problems were and when they happened.

Finally, tell them that you would like a replacement or your money back.

Use these expressions to help you.

Dear Sir/Madam
I am writing to inform you that...
Firstly, the box was damaged when the video was delivered...
I would be grateful if you would...
Yours faithfully

Passive infinitive, passive gerund

VOCABULARY AND LISTENING

1 Match the definitions below with the means of communication in the box.

> CD-ROM e-mail fax
> the Internet satellite TV cable TV

a a system which allows messages to be sent and received by a group of computer users

b a means of storing information on a disk to be read by a computer.

c a system of broadcasting television using a satellite in space.

d a means of sending or receiving printed material in electronic form along a phone line.

e a network which allows computer users around the world to communicate with each other.

f a system of broadcasting television by cable, giving viewers access to more channels.

Which of these means of communication do you use?

2 🔈 Listen to Anna describing the words in the box to Richard, and check your answers to 1.

3 Work in pairs. Which of the following uses for the new technology might Anna mention?

- shopping
- making travel arrangements
- booking concert tickets
- having access to research
- playing games
- having access to the latest news
- visiting museums and galleries
- communicating with people around the world

4 Look at the chart and decide who is likely to hold these opinions, Anna or Richard. Put a tick (✓)in the appropriate column.

	Richard	Anna
CD-ROMS are much better than books because more information can be stored on them.		
Being connected to an e-mail system is very useful.		
Most people like being contacted by e-mail.		
To be contacted by e-mail is not very sociable.		
The Internet should be controlled by the government.		
Some people are now afraid of being censored by the government.		
There's no point in being connected to TV stations around the world if you don't speak the language.		

5 🔈 Listen and check your answers to 4.

6 Complete the sentences summarising what Anna says. Use the information in *Vocabulary and listening* 5 to help you.

1 It's good to be connected to e-mail because it is _____.
2 A fax is a good way of sending _____.
3 Being connected to foreign TV stations helps you to _____.
4 Watching cable and satellite TV isn't _____.

🔈 Listen again and check your answers.

VOCABULARY AND LISTENING

1 Aim: to present the words in the vocabulary box; to prepare for listening.

● These words may not be ones which the students need to use at the moment, but they are likely to become increasingly common in the future. Ask them to match the words and their definitions. Don't check the students' answers at this stage as they will do this in the next activity. The answers given below are merely for the teacher's information in case the students need more help at this stage.

> **Answers**
> a e-mail b CD-ROM c satellite TV
> d fax e the Internet f cable TV

● Ask the students which means of communication they use, if any.

2 Aim: to listen for main ideas.

● Explain to the students that they're going to hear Anna describing and defining the words in the vocabulary box to Richard. She won't use exactly the same words as in the definitions in 1, only the main ideas.

● 🔲 Play the tape and ask the students to check their answers to 1.

3 Aim: to infer; to prepare for listening.

● Ask the students to work in pairs, and to try and predict the uses for technology Anna will mention in the next activity.

4 Aim: to prepare for listening.

● Ask the students to read the statements and to decide if they agree or disagree with them.

● Ask the students who is more enthusiastic about new technology, and who is more sceptical, Anna or Richard?

● Ask the students to predict who is likely to agree with the statements, Anna or Richard.

5 Aim: to listen for main ideas.

● 🔲 Explain that the statements represent the main ideas of what Anna and Richard are going to say. Play the tape and ask the students to tick the statements the two speakers would agree with.

● You can now ask the students to look back at *Vocabulary and listening* activity 3 and see which of the uses of new technology Richard or Anna mentioned.

Answers	Richard	Anna
Being connected to an e-mail system is very useful.		✓
Most people like being contacted by e-mail.		✓
CD-ROMS are much better than books because more information can be stored on them.		✓
To be contacted by e-mail is not very sociable.	✓	
The Internet should be controlled by the government.	✓	
Some people are now afraid of being censored by the government.		✓
There's no point in being connected to TV stations around the world if you don't speak the language.	✓	

6 Aim: to check comprehension.

● Ask the students to read the sentences and complete them with their own opinions. They could discuss their completed sentences with their partner, if you wish.

● Now ask the students to complete the sentences using the information in the listening passage.

> **Answers**
> 1 It's good to be connected to e-mail because it is **much faster.**
> 2 A fax is a good way of sending **documents using a telephone line.**
> 3 Being connected to foreign TV stations helps you to **learn foreign languages.**
> 4 Watching cable and satellite TV isn't **very expensive.**

● 🔲 Play the recording again and ask the students to check their answers.

7 Aim: to focus on spoken style.

● The students may find it hard to understand some of the colloquial expressions used by native speakers. Ask them to guess the meaning.

> **Answers**
> 1 Nothing is better than authentic art.
> 2 ... that LPs and tapes were no longer fashionable.
> 3 It doesn't sound very friendly.

8 Aim: to practise speaking.

● Ask the students to work in pairs and discuss their reactions to the statements in 4.

● One person from each pair should present their reactions and opinions. Ask another person to paraphrase what they've just heard, and to add an opinion of their own. Continue in this way until each opinion, paraphrase and further opinion has been exchanged four or five times.

GRAMMAR

1 Aim: to practise forming passives.

● Ask the students to read the information in the grammar box and then to do the exercises.

> **Answers**
> 1 I won't come to the party without **being invited**.
> 2 She's concerned about **being sent** unwanted mail.
> 3 **Being lost** in the snow is very frightening.
> 4 You **should be paid** for the work you do.
> 5 He mustn't **be given** more time to finish the test.
> 6 The tablets must **be taken** twice a day.

2 Aim: to practise forming passives.

> **Answers**
> 1 He doesn't like **being phoned** after 10 pm.
> 2 She's nervous about **being charged** too much.
> 3 He's interested in **being connected** to cable TV.
> 4 She's looking forward to **being invited** over for a chat.
> 5 He wants to communicate with friends without **being overheard**.
> 6 She needs **to be told** what to do.

SOUNDS

1 Aim: to focus on stressed words in compound nouns.

● Ask the students to underline the stressed words.

● ▭ Play the tape and ask the students to listen and check.

> **Answers**
> <u>computer</u> screen <u>travel</u> arrangements
> <u>concert</u> tickets <u>satellite</u> dish <u>TV</u> channel

2 Aim: to focus on stressed words in compound nouns.

● These words are stressed differently to the compound nouns in 1. Ask the students to say the words aloud and to underline the stressed word.

● ▭ Play the tape and ask the students to listen and check.

> **Answers**
> mobile <u>phone</u> late-night <u>phone</u> call electronic <u>mail</u>
> cable <u>TV</u>

SPEAKING AND WRITING

1 Aim: to practise speaking.

● Ask the students to work in two groups. Tell them which is group A and which is group B. If you have a large class, there can be two or three groups of A and B, but each group must be small enough for everyone to be able to join in the discussion.

● Explain that the discussion is about the opinions expressed in this lesson, and that each group will either agree or disagree with the statement *More technology means less communication.*

● Ask each group to go back over the lesson and look for arguments in favour of or against the statement. They should also add some of their own opinions.

● Explain that each group will give three opinions in favour of or against the statement. Check that every group will be able to do this.

2 Aim: to practise speaking.

● Read the statement again and invite someone from group A to give the first of their opinions in favour of it.

● Ask someone from group B to respond if possible to group A's opinion and to give the first of their opinions against the statement.

● Continue with a response from group A and the second of their opinions.

● Continue in this way until each group has given its three opinions.

● With a large class, this stage must be done with the groups A and B paired off and exchanging opinions with each other.

3 Aim: to practise using linking expressions *on the one hand, however, moreover,* and *in conclusion.*

● Ask the students to write a report of the discussion, but adding a conclusion of their own. Make sure they use the linking expressions suggested, and include the arguments for and against the statement which they heard in the discussion. You may like to ask the students to do this activity for homework.

7 What do you think the speaker means by the following sentences? Say them in a simpler way.

1 'When it comes to art there's no substitute for the real thing.'
2 'A friend convinced me that LPs and tapes were out.'
3 'It sounds horribly cold to me.'

8 Work in pairs. Discuss your own reactions to the opinions in 4.

GRAMMAR

> **Passive infinitive, passive gerund**
> **You often use the passive to begin a sentence with known information and to end a sentence with new information.**
> **You can use the passive infinitive as the subject of a sentence for emphasis.**
> *To be contacted by e-mail is not very sociable.*
> **You can use the passive infinitive without *to* after modal verbs.**
> *The Internet should be controlled by the government.*
> **You can use the passive gerund:**
> **– as the subject of a sentence.**
> *Being connected to an e-mail system is very useful.*
> **– as the object of a sentence.**
> *Most people like being contacted by e-mail.*
> **– with a preposition.**
> *People are afraid of being censored by the government.*

1 Rewrite the sentences using the words in brackets and a suitable passive.

1 I won't come to the party without (invite).
2 She's concerned about (send) unwanted mail.
3 (Lose) in the snow is very frightening.
4 You should (pay) for the work you do.
5 He mustn't (give) more time to finish the test.
6 The tablets must (take) twice a day.

1 *I won't come to the party without being invited.*

2 Rewrite these sentences in the passive.

1 He doesn't like people phoning him after 10pm.
2 She's nervous about people charging too much.
3 He's interested in someone connecting him to cable TV.
4 She's looking forward to people inviting her over for a chat.
5 He wants to communicate with friends without other people overhearing.
6 She needs someone to tell her what to do.

1 *He doesn't like being phoned after 10pm.*

SOUNDS

1 Say these compound nouns aloud. Underline the stressed word.

computer screen   travel arrangements
concert tickets   satellite dish   TV channel

Listen and say the words aloud.

2 Say these compound nouns aloud. Underline the stressed word.

mobile phone   late-night phone call
electronic mail   cable TV

Listen and say the words aloud.

SPEAKING AND WRITING

1 Work in groups. You're going to take part in a discussion about the statement: *More technology means less communication.*

Group A: You agree with the statement.
Make a list of Richard's opinions and add some of your own.
Group B: You disagree with the statement.
Make a list of Anna's opinions and add some of your own.

2 Start the discussion. Your teacher will explain the procedure.

3 Write a summary of the discussion using the statement as a title.

Introduce the subject and explain what it's about.
There has been much discussion recently about the communications revolution. More people are using e-mail, cable TV and the Internet...

Present the arguments in favour.
On the one hand, using the new technology means faster communication...
The advantages are ...
The disadvantages are...
However,...
Moreover...

Present the arguments against.
However, many people think it makes it more difficult to communicate.

Present your conclusion.
In conclusion, I think that...

Now, America is as modern a place as you will find in all the world, I imagine, but when you travel a few miles into Pennsylvania from Philadelphia and enter a place called Lancaster County, you could believe you had travelled back in time to the last century and even beyond. For that is where the Amish established themselves and held fast to their customs and beliefs. They are farming people who are immediately recognisable by their unusual dress – severe black suits for the men, long skirts and bob caps for the women, since it seems the heads must be covered at all times, even the children's. The men wear broad-brimmed black hats for best, and straw ones for working. They will not use electricity or motor-propelled vehicles of any kind; they work the land with horses and light their homes with kerosene lamps and candles. I have to confess that I lived something of an Amish life for many years in Baldersdale, but not through choice.

Lancaster County was very rural. And down every narrow lane you could see half a dozen of those strange, black, horse-drawn buggies, totally enclosed and usually driven by an old, white-bearded man. The Amish are people whose ancestors came from Switzerland in the sixteenth century. The community living in Lancaster County came from Germany, and still spoke a Rhine dialect. Indeed, the children do not begin to learn English until they start their education, and even then they go to one-room Amish schools. And from a very young age they are all given jobs to do in the home or on the farm, which gives them even less time to mix with non-Amish children. After baptism, you cannot marry outside the faith. Owning motorised transport is banned because cars would give youngsters a chance to travel and experience other ways. You could not go far in a horse and buggy.

Sunday worship is held in one of their homes, and the location is known only to the Amish, week by week. Apparently, the services start at 11am and last for three hours.

On my last day, I was invited by the Meyer family to go for a buggy ride and then join them for dinner. I sat beside Mr Jack Meyer, a large, bearded man, who was dressed in the traditional manner. He told me the time when the standard Amish day starts is 4.30am and the milking goes on until breakfast at seven. Half an hour later the children are sent off to school, which starts at eight, and then the men start work until lunch is served by the women at eleven. Around three in the afternoon the final milking of the day begins. That is followed by supper, and by seven-thirty most farmers are in bed.

Dinner with the Meyers was a remarkable experience. They do take in paying guests, but you are not to use alcohol prior to your arrival, and not to smoke on their property. Most importantly, you are specifically requested not to bring a camera with you. But for my benefit, they allowed us to film them at their table.

Lancaster Amish are famous for their food, and justifiably so. Jugs of water washed down the feast, but midway we were offered tea made from herbs which grow wild.

There was clearly a lot of love and laughter in the Meyer household, and the children were exceedingly well behaved. They all returned obediently to the dining room when the final ritual of the evening was to begin. They formed a group with their mother and father and sang a hymn in a manner I had not heard before, all harmonising beautifully.

All in all, a vivid and memorable occasion.

14
GENERAL COMMENTS

The Amish

The passage in the first part of the lesson describes the lifestyle of the Amish community. The Amish are a group of people who follow the Christian religion in a very strict and old fashioned way. They live mostly in Pennsylvania and Ohio, USA. They originally came from Europe in the sixteenth century and they wear clothes dating from that time. They aren't allowed to use any machinery, so the most common form of transport is a horse and buggy. Their lifestyle was recently portrayed in the police thriller film *Witness,* starring Harrison Ford.

Hannah Hauxwell

Hannah Hauxwell spent most of her life in a cottage on the Yorkshire Moors, where she was completely isolated from twentieth-century life. She had no running water, no electricity and no access to television and radio. In her sixties, she was obliged to abandon this existence, and a television programme was made of her first impressions of modern-day life in Britain today. The programme was very popular because of the freshness of her reactions to things which we take for granted. She was invited to do two more series of programmes describing her impressions as she was taken on a tour of Europe and of the USA. The passage is taken from the book based on the second series of programmes. In the passage, Hannah mentions how her life in Baldersdale, Yorkshire was similar to the Amish way of life.

SPEAKING AND READING

1 **Aim: to practise speaking.**

● The theme of the lesson is lifestyles, and this opening activity is designed to encourage the students to start thinking about their own lifestyles. Ask the students to think about various aspects of their lifestyles and rank things in order of importance. Students should work in pairs to compare their lists.

● You may like to write the aspects on the board, and find out how many students chose which aspect as the most and least important.

● Encourage the students to think about places in the world where people may have different priorities in their lifestyles. Find out if anyone has been to any countries where the lifestyle is very different.

2 **Aim: to read for specific ideas.**

● Ask the students if they know who the Amish are, where they live and what is special about their lifestyle.

● Ask the students to read the passage and to make notes on the aspects mentioned.

> **Answers**
> **clothing:** black suits, black or straw hats for men, long skirts and bob caps for women
> **work:** farming
> **transport:** horse-drawn buggies
> **education:** one-room Amish schools
> **meals:** no alcohol, no smoking, water, herb tea
> **other customs and beliefs:** no electricity, children have little time to mix with non-Amish, Sunday worship is held in someone's home, early start to the day, no photographs to be taken

3 **Aim: to focus on the writer's style.**

● Ask the students to work together and discuss their answers to these questions.

GRAMMAR

1 **Aim: to present and revise relative clauses.**

● Ask the students to read the information in the grammar box and then to do the exercises.

> **Answers**
> 1 They are farming people **who** are immediately recognisable by their unusual dress. **(Defining)**
> 2 The Amish are people **whose** ancestors came from Switzerland. **(Defining)**
> 3 …Mr Jack Meyer, a large, bearded man, **who** was dressed in the traditional manner. **(Non-defining)**
> 4 …the children are sent off to school, **which** starts at eight… **(Non-defining)**

2 **Aim: to focus on defining relative clauses.**

● Ask the students to use the information in the passage to complete the sentences.

> **Answers**
> 1 The Amish are people **who** have held fast to their customs and traditions.
> 2 Lancaster County is the place **where** you can see an Amish community.
> 3 Eight o'clock is the time **when** school starts.
> 4 Food is one of the things **which** the Amish are famous for.
> 5 Smoking and drinking are things **which** are forbidden.

3 **Aim: to focus on non-defining relative clauses.**

● Ask the students to rewrite the sentences and include the information in brackets. Make sure they do so by using a non-defining relative clause. You may like to do this activity orally with the whole class.

> **Answers**
> 1 The Amish, whose ancestors came from Switzerland, live in Lancaster County.
> 2 Men and women, whose heads must be covered all the time, wear black hats or caps.
> 3 The buggies, which are horse-drawn, are usually driven by old, white-bearded men.
> 4 The children, who are not allowed to mix with the non-Amish, are given work to do.
> 5 Worship is held at someone's home, where they meet every Sunday at 11am.

SPEAKING AND VOCABULARY

1 **Aim: to practise speaking.**

● Ask the students to talk about how different their lives would be without the aspects mentioned. Are they aspects which anyone could live without?

● Ask the students if there are other aspects of modern life which they could live without. Suggest *telephone, television, CD player* etc.

2 **Aim: to present the words in the vocabulary box.**

● The words in the box all come from the passage, and are suitable to be learnt at this level. First, check everyone understands what they mean. Then ask the students to work in pairs and to follow the instructions.

● If you have time, you may like to continue this activity with words you need to revise from earlier lessons.

SPEAKING AND READING

1 Make a list of important things in your life. Number them in order of their importance with 5 being the most important and 1 being the least important.

family, good health, money...

Now work in pairs and compare your list.

2 Read the passage, which is about a woman who is visiting the Amish people of Pennsylvania. Make notes about these aspects of their lifestyle.

– clothing   – work   – transport   – education
– meals   – customs and beliefs

Compare your notes with a partner.

3 Work in groups of three or four. Discuss your answers to these questions.

1 Was the writer sympathetic to the Amish way of life?
2 What aspects of the Amish life was she impressed by?
3 What things did she find strange?
4 What do you think about the lifestyle of the Amish?
5 What are the good and bad points about the Amish lifestyle?

Work with another group and compare your answers.

GRAMMAR

> **Relative clauses**
> You use a defining relative clause (without commas) to give essential information about the subject or object of the sentence. You use:
> – *who* or *that* for people, and *which* or *that* for things.
> – *whose* to talk about possession.
> – *where* for places.
> – *when* for times. You can usually leave out *when*.
> You use a non-defining relative clause (with commas) to give more information about the subject or object of the sentence. It is more common in formal English, especially writing. You use:
> – *who* for people.
> – *which* for things. You cannot use *that*.
> You can use *which* to refer back to a whole clause.

1 Look at the passage and find sentences with *who, whose, which, where* and *when*. Use the information in the grammar box to decide if they are defining or non-defining relative clauses. Are there any sentences with *which* referring to the whole clause?

2 Use the information in the passage to complete these sentences about the Amish with defining relative clauses.

1 The Amish are people ____.
2 Lancaster County is the place ____.
3 Eight o'clock is the time ____.
4 Food is one of the things ____.
5 Smoking and drinking are things ____.

3 Rewrite these sentences adding the extra information in brackets, using a non-defining relative clause.

1 The Amish live in Lancaster County.
   (Their ancestors came from Switzerland.)
2 Men and women wear black hats or caps.
   (Their heads must be covered all the time.)
3 The buggies are usually driven by old, white-bearded men. (The buggies are horse-drawn.)
4 The children are given work to do.
   (They are not allowed to mix with the non-Amish.)
5 Worship is held at someone's home.
   (They meet there every Sunday at 11am.)

SPEAKING AND VOCABULARY

1 Work in pairs. Talk about how your lifestyle would change if you had to live without:

– electricity   – central heating
– motor vehicles   – plumbing

If there was no electricity, there wouldn't be any television and I couldn't live without that.

Is there any other aspect of your modern lifestyle which you couldn't live without?

2 Work in pairs.

Student A: Choose a word in the box and ask Student B to define it.
Student B: Define the word Student A chooses.
You can use the passage to help you.

Change round when you're ready.

> custom   horse   lamp   candle   buggy   ancestor
> dialect   baptism   home   farmer   guest   alcohol
> jug   herb   hymn

Relative and participle clauses

VOCABULARY AND LISTENING

1 Work in groups of three. Use the information you have learnt about the Amish people's way of life to answer the lifestyle questionnaire below. Give a score of I – 5 with 5 being the most important and 1 being the least important. Write the score in the appropriate column.

Lifestyle Questionnaire

1 How important are these things in your life?	Amish	California	Your country
Possessions			
Leisure interests			
Physical fitness			
Mental and spiritual development			
Work			
Attitude towards visitors			
2 Give the pace of life a score from 1–5 with 5 being fast and 1 being slow.			

2 You are going to listen to Don Wright talking about the lifestyle in California. In your groups, try to predict what the answers to the lifestyle questionnaire will be for California. Write the score in the appropriate column.

3 [cassette] Listen and check if your predictions in 2 were correct.

4 Tick the words in the box that you heard.

anti-conformist   materialistic   limousine   laid-back   tense   jogging   fortune
vineyard   racist   mild   diverse   stress   calm   elegant   wealthy   cosmopolitan

5 Complete these statements with a few words or phrases from the interview.
1 The man the interviewer spoke to is a ____.
2 The house Don lives in is ____.
3 The family living next door have ____.
4 The beach, situated close to the town, is used ____.
5 The lifestyle he leads is quite ____.
6 The work he does is important for ____.

6 [cassette] Listen again and check your answers to 4 and 5. Can you add any extra information?

7 Now complete the questionnaire for your own country.

SOUNDS

[cassette] Listen to these sentences. Mark where the speaker pauses.

1 The Californians are people who are famous for their relaxed lifestyle.
2 They are generally very friendly people, whose pace of life is fast.
3 It has an economy which is one of the richest in the world.
4 The climate, which is mild, is very pleasant.
5 It has wonderful beaches, which make it attractive to tourists.

Can you work out a rule for pauses in defining and non-defining relative clauses?

VOCABULARY AND LISTENING

1 Aim: to prepare for listening; to practise speaking.
● Ask the students to predict how the Amish might answer the Lifestyle Questionnaire and to put a score in the appropriate column.

2 Aim: to prepare for listening; to practise speaking.
● Ask the students to suggest aspects of lifestyle in California. What images do they have of the people who live there and the facilities or possessions they have? Encourage them to think of stereotypical images of Californians. How different would their lifestyle be to that of the Amish and to the students' own lifestyles?

● Ask the students to put a score in the appropriate column.

3 Aim: to listen for main ideas.
● 📼 The questionnaire is a framework for the questions which Don Wright answers. Ask the students to listen to him talking and to check if their predictions in 2 were correct. The score the students actually give for the pace of life will probably be subjective. You can use the students' answers as the basis for a discussion about pace of life, if you wish.

> **Answers**
> **Possessions:** Quite important
> **Leisure interests:** Very important, surfing, rock-climbing, roller-blading, camping, jogging
> **Physical fitness:** Very important for all Californians
> **Mental and spiritual development:** Important, lived in a hippy commune when younger, now looking towards Buddhism and the east
> **Work:** Very important – both for self-esteem and enjoyment of work
> **Attitude towards visitors:** Very friendly – people come from many different backgrounds

4 Aim: to present the words in the vocabulary box.
● Ask the students to check they understand the meaning of the words in the box. Ask other students to explain the meanings if anyone has difficulty with any of the words.

● Ask the students to tick the words they heard in the interview.

● Check the answers with the whole class.

> **Answers**
> elegant, limousine, materialistic, tense, jogging, vineyard, diverse, wealthy, laid-back, cosmopolitan, racist

5 Aim: to check comprehension.
● Ask the students to complete the statements. They may like to do this in pairs.

> **Answers**
> 1 The man the interviewer spoke to is a **computer engineer.**
> 2 The house Don lives in is **an elegant ranch-style house.**
> 3 The family living next door have **vineyards**.
> 4 The beach, situated close to the town, is used **by everyone.**
> 5 The lifestyle he leads is quite **expensive.**
> 6 The work he does is important for **his self-esteem.**

6 Aim: to provide an opportunity for a second listening.
● 📼 Play the tape again and ask the students to check their answers to 4 and 5.

7 Aim: to encourage the students to reflect on their own culture.
● This activity can be done in pairs, even if the students come from different countries. It is designed to create an opportunity to use the information about the Amish and Californian lifestyles as a mirror to reflect their own lifestyles.

● Lead a group discussion about the lifestyles of the people in your students' countries. Would anyone like a different lifestyle?

SOUNDS

1 Aim: to focus on pauses in relative clauses.
● Remind students that a comma in written English usually corresponds to a brief pause in spoken English.

● 📼 Ask the students to listen to the tape, and to notice how the speaker pauses when there is a comma in the written sentence.

GRAMMAR

1 Aim: to focus on relative clauses where you can leave out the relative pronoun.

● Ask the students to read the information in the grammar box and then to do the exercises.

Answers

Last year we visited my cousin who lives in Los Angeles, which was very exciting. We stayed with him in his huge house in Pasadena, which is in the north of the city. The people **who** we met were very friendly and made us feel at home. There is no real downtown area in Los Angeles, which we found strange. We drove everywhere on the freeways, which are excellent, in a car **which** we borrowed from my cousin, who has several. The place **which** we liked best was Santa Barbara, which is about sixty miles away.

2 Aim: to focus on participle clauses.

● A certain amount of work on present participle clauses was done in Lesson 8. This activity revises past participle clauses. Ask the students to rewrite the sentences.

Answers

1 The houses **built** in the thirties are the largest.
2 There are freeways **leading** to most cities in the state.
3 The mountain range, **called** the Sierra Nevada, has good ski resorts.
4 The beaches, **cleaned** every day, are very popular.
5 Disneyland, **attracting** millions of people a year, is the number-one tourist attraction.
6 There are guided tours of the studios for anyone **interested** in television and the movies.

WRITING

1 Aim: to practise speaking; to prepare for writing.

● Ask the students to work in pairs and to choose one of the lifestyles presented to them in this lesson. Ask them to make notes about what they like or dislike about it.

2 Aim: to practise writing.

● Ask the students to imagine they are spending a day in the lifestyle of an Amish person or a Californian. Ask them to write a diary entry of their day, and to include information about things that happened during the day, and things they particularly liked or disliked.

GRAMMAR

Relative and participle clauses

In a defining relative clause you can leave out the relative pronoun if the clause is defining an object.

*The man **(who)** the interviewer spoke to was Don Wright.*
*The county **(which)** she visited was Marin County.*

If you leave out *where*, you have to add a preposition.

*The house **where** Don lives is near the beach.*
*The house Don lives **in** is near the beach.*

Participle clauses

You can use a participle clause instead of a relative clause if the noun or pronoun is the subject of the clause. You use:

– a present participle to replace the relative pronoun + a present or past tense in a defining relative clause.

*The family **who** lives next door are very friendly.*
(= The family living next door are very friendly.)

– a past participle to replace the relative pronoun + *be* in passive sentences in a defining relative clause.

*Any house **(which is)** situated on the beach is in danger from storms.*

It is also possible, but less common, to do this with a non-defining relative clause.

*The people, **who** were working hard...*
(= the people, working so hard...)
*The beach, **(which is)** situated close to the town, is used by everybody.*

---

1 Read the passage below. Underline any relative pronouns which can be left out.

Last year we visited my cousin who lives in Los Angeles, which was very exciting. We stayed with him in his huge house in Pasadena, which is in the north of the city. The people who we met were very friendly and made us feel at home. There is no real downtown area in Los Angeles, which we found strange. We drove everywhere on the freeways, which are excellent, in a car which we borrowed from my cousin, who has several. The place which we liked best was Santa Barbara, which is about sixty miles away.

2 Rewrite these sentences using participle clauses.

1 The houses which were built in the thirties are the largest.
2 There are freeways which lead to most cities in the state.
3 The mountain range, which is called the Sierra Nevada, has good ski resorts.
4 The beaches, which are cleaned every day, are very popular.
5 Disneyland, which attracts millions of people a year, is the number-one tourist attraction.
6 There are guided tours of the studios for anyone who is interested in television and the movies.

1 The houses built in the thirties are the largest.

WRITING

1 Think about the two different lifestyles of the Amish people and people in California. Choose one of them and make notes about aspects of the lifestyle that you like or dislike.
Work with a partner who has chosen the same lifestyle, if you wish.

2 Imagine you have spent a day either as part of an Amish family or in a Californian home. Write your diary for the day. Begin by saying what time you got up and what you had for breakfast.

I woke up at six o'clock and went for a run on the beach. Then I had a light breakfast of toast and coffee.

Then describe what you did during the day.

First of all, we went to the mall.

Use your notes from 1 to describe anything you enjoyed or didn't enjoy about the lifestyle.

15 Lucky escapes

Third conditional

VOCABULARY AND SPEAKING

1 This lesson is about occasions when people have been lucky or unlucky. Look at the adjectives in the box and put a + by the positive feelings and a – by the negative feelings.

ecstatic +   disappointed –

> ecstatic disappointed devastated grateful fed-up
> frustrated frantic happy confused excited inspired
> enthusiastic thrilled furious anxious tired nervous
> upset worried depressed

Which adjectives can you use to describe mild feelings, and which ones extreme feelings?

2 Think of situations you have experienced when you could use some of the adjectives to describe how you felt.

Now work in pairs and talk about these situations.

LISTENING

1 🔲 You're going to hear Janet, Paul and Fiona talking about three situations in which they had a lucky escape. Listen and put the name of the speaker by the situation below which he or she is talking about.

– a plane crash   – a traffic accident   – a fight

2 Choose the best answer.

Janet says that:
a) If she hadn't been delayed in Zanzibar she would have caught the plane that crashed.
b) If her plane hadn't crashed, she would have been in Nairobi on time.
c) If she had arrived in Nairobi on time, the plane wouldn't have crashed.

Paul says that:
a) If he had known the youth had a knife he wouldn't have tried to stop the fight.
b) If the youth had attacked him with a knife his injuries would have been more serious.
c) If the police hadn't arrived, the youth wouldn't have attacked him.

Fiona says that:
a) She would have been killed if the lorry had been driving faster.
b) She would have worn her seat belt if she had known that there would be an accident.
c) She might have been killed if she hadn't been wearing her seat belt.

15

GENERAL COMMENTS

Progress

By now, you are three-quarters of the way through *Reward* Upper-intermediate, and it may be a suitable time to review your students' progress. It is easy to evaluate progress in terms of marks scored in tests, and the tests in this Teacher's Book are designed to help you do this. But it is equally useful to see it in terms of attitude and confidence. Here are some questions you may like to discuss with your students, and the answers will help you guide the course to a successful conclusion.

Do you feel more confident about your English now than you did at the beginning of the course?
In what areas or skills do you feel more or less confident?
Which aspects of the course do you enjoy the most?
Is there any aspect of the teaching and learning of English which you would like more of, such as grammar, writing, pronunciation?
Are you more able to understand native English speakers?
Are you more easily understood by native English speakers?
Do you do more work on your English outside the classroom than you used to?

VOCABULARY AND SPEAKING

1 Aim: to present the theme of the lesson; to present the words in the vocabulary box.

● Many students will already know some or all of the words in the box, but may need to be reminded of them. Check everyone understands the words, and, as usual, if there are any questions, see if another student can answer them.

● Ask the students to decide if the words can be used to describe positive or negative feelings.

Answers	
+	–
grateful	devastated
happy	fed-up
excited	frustrated
inspired	frantic
enthusiastic	confused
thrilled	furious
	anxious
	tired
	nervous
	upset
	worried
	depressed

● Ask the students to decide which ones can be used to describe extreme and mild feelings.

2 Aim: to practise using the words in the vocabulary box.

● Ask the students to talk about situations they have experienced and to use the words to describe their feelings.

LISTENING

1 Aim: to prepare for listening; to listen for main ideas.

● Explain that you are going to play a recording in which three people talk about a situation in which they had a lucky escape. Ask the students to predict words which they expect to hear in each situation.

● Ask the students to compare their list of words in pairs.

● 🔲 Ask the students to listen and to put the name of the speaker by the situation.

Answers	
Janet: a plane crash	
Paul: a fight	
Fiona: a traffic accident	

● Ask the students to check if they heard the words they predicted in 1.

2 Aim: to check comprehension.

● Answering these questions will ensure that everyone has understood the main ideas of the recordings. You may like to do this orally with the whole class.

Answers	
Janet: a	
Paul: b	
Fiona: c	

3 **Aim: to check detailed comprehension; to provide an opportunity for a second listening.**

● 📼 Ask the students to answer the questions. They may like to do this in pairs.

● Rewind the cassette and ask students to check their answers.

Answers
1 Paul   2 Janet   3 Paul   4 Fiona   5 Janet

GRAMMAR

1 **Aim: to focus on how to form the third conditional.**

● Ask the students to read the information in the grammar box and then to do the exercises.

● Your students will already have come across the third conditional in *Reward* Intermediate Lesson 40, so it is hoped that the grammar box and this activity will serve as revision.

Answer
You form the third conditional by using *if* + past perfect for the condition and *would have* + past participle for the result.

2 **Aim: to practise using the third conditional.**

● Ask the students to complete the sentences with information they heard in the recordings.

Answers
1 If Janet hadn't been delayed, she would have been on the plane that crashed.
2 If she had got to Nairobi on time, she would have caught the plane.
3 If Paul hadn't tried to stop the fight he wouldn't have got a black eye.
4 If he had known the man had a knife, he might not have stopped the fight.
5 If Fiona had not been so close to the lorry, she might not have been in an accident.
6 If she hadn't been wearing her seat belt she would have been killed.

READING AND WRITING

1 **Aim: to read for main ideas.**

● Tell the students that they are going to read a passage about another lucky escape.

● Explain that each of the three options describe the events in the story, but only one describes the lucky escape.

● Ask the students to read the passage and to decide what the lucky escape was.

Answer
1

2 **Aim: to practise using the third conditional; to check comprehension.**

● Ask the students to practise using the third conditional in answer to these questions. You may like to do this orally.

Answers
1 If she hadn't gone to meet her husband, she wouldn't have been in the car when the brakes failed.
2 If the writer had not had a vision, her daughter would have gone to the wrong airport.
3 If Genevieve had not managed to stop the car, she might have been killed.
4 If Alan hadn't called, Genevieve would have gone to Birmingham.
5 If Genevieve hadn't called her mother, she would have travelled to the wrong airport.
6 If the taxi driver hadn't stopped for cigarettes, Genevieve wouldn't have telephoned her mother.

3 **Aim: to practise writing summaries.**

● Ask the students to write a summary of the story in about 100 words. The sentences in 2 will help them do this. You may like to ask the students to do this activity for homework.

3 Which speaker did the following things? Put the name of the speaker in the box.

1 Who intends to complain? ☐
2 Who became very anxious? ☐
3 Who was furious at the end? ☐
4 Who thinks he/she was extremely lucky? ☐
5 Who managed to stay calm at the start? ☐

🔊 Now listen again and check.

GRAMMAR

> **Third conditional**
> **You use the third conditional to talk about an imaginary or unlikely situation in the past and to describe its result. You separate the two clauses with a comma.**
> *If she **hadn't been delayed**, she **would have caught** the plane that crashed.*
> **You can also use *may have*, *might have* or *could have* if the result is not certain.**
> *If he **had pulled** out his knife, I **could have been** seriously injured.*

1 Complete this sentence saying how you form the third conditional.

You form the third conditional by using *if* + ____ for the condition and ____ for the result.

2 Complete these sentences using suitable words or phrases.

1 If Janet hadn't ____, she would have ____.
2 If she had ____.
3 If Paul hadn't ____.
4 If he had ____.
5 If Fiona had ____.
6 If she hadn't ____.

READING AND WRITING

1 Read this story about a lucky escape. Decide what the lucky escape was.

1 Genevieve nearly had an accident.
2 Alan's plane was diverted from Heathrow.
3 The taxi driver stopped for cigarettes.

My daughter, Genevieve, had decided to fetch her husband from Heathrow airport when he was flying in from Frankfurt. As I was busy in the kitchen, I had a sudden vision. A freezing fog had come down and my daughter was involved in an accident on the motorway into Heathrow.

My daughter arrived at my house before leaving for the airport and I tried to persuade her not to go, without telling her why. The sun was still shining brightly after lunch when she left for Heathrow. About two and half hours later the thick freezing fog came down. I tried to ring the airport but there was no reply.

The next four hours were the longest of my life – then the telephone rang. A man spoke and told me what had happened. 'The young lady was pulling off the motorway to go to the airport and braked behind the lorry in front of her. Her brakes failed. Somehow she managed to pull up, stopping with the car bonnet just under the tail of the lorry. I promise you she isn't hurt,' he added quickly. 'I have the car here at my garage for repair, and she was told by the airport that her husband's plane has been diverted to Birmingham. She's on her way there now by taxi.'

Soon, the telephone rang again. It was Genevieve's husband, Alan. 'My plane's been diverted to Stanstead (another airport near London),' he said. 'I've been trying to get through to Heathrow to tell Genevieve to wait for me at the information desk as I am arranging to travel on the airport coach.'

I explained that she was on her way to Birmingham. I put the phone down, closed my eyes and tried to imagine Genevieve on the motorway, thinking desperately, 'Please, wherever you are, telephone me.' Five minutes later the phone rang, I heard Genevieve's voice say, 'What's the matter? I felt I had to phone you.'

Later, I learned that on the way up to Birmingham, the taxi driver said he must stop at the motorway service station for cigarettes and as he pulled up Genevieve said, 'I have to telephone my mother at once.' It was only later that he found his wife had put cigarettes for him in the glove compartment. They returned safely to Heathrow and Genevieve made her way to the information desk, arriving at the same time as Alan.   *Adapted from the Fortean Times*

2 Work in pairs and say what would have happened *if*:

1 Genevieve had not gone to meet her husband.
2 The writer had not had a vision.
3 Genevieve had not managed to stop the car.
4 Alan had not called.
5 Genevieve had not called.
6 The taxi driver had not stopped for cigarettes.

3 Write a summary of the woman's story in about 100 words. You may like to use the sentences in 2 to help you, although you will have to adapt them slightly. Begin like this:

A woman described how her daughter, Genevieve, was going to fetch...

Expressing wishes and regrets

READING AND WRITING

1 You are going to read some stories about people who had some bad luck. The first story is about a young man taking his driving test. Guess what kind of bad luck he might have had.

2 Read the story. Did you guess correctly in 1?

A young man was taking his driving test and was looking forward to passing it and buying himself a new car. He began very attentively and successfully until the examiner slightly raised his clipboard. The driver had heard about this sort of test of reactions, and interpreting this as the sign for an emergency stop, he put his foot sharply on the brakes.

To his horror, his passenger had forgotten to fasten his seatbelt, and taken completely by surprise, hurtled forward and hit his head against the windscreen, then fell back bloody and unconscious. The distraught man immediately drove him to a hospital then went home in a miserable mood.

The very next day he received official notice that he had failed his test for driving without due care and attention. Attached to the form was a note from the examiner himself. On it he explained that…

3 Try to guess what the missing line is. Now turn to Communication activity 11 on page 94.

4 Work in pairs. You're going to read a story about a couple having a meal in a restaurant. Put the parts of the story in the right order.

a) Feeling good about themselves, the couple asked for their bill. But after checking it, they called the manager demanding to have the massive total explained.

b) They smiled back politely and the old lady made her way to their table. 'I'm sorry to trouble you,' she began. 'But you look so like my daughter. She was killed last year and I do miss her terribly. I wonder if you'd do me an enormous favour?'

c) 'That includes the charge for the lady's meal, the manager explained. 'She said her daughter would pay.'

d) 'Certainly,' the couple replied. How could they possibly refuse? A few minutes, later the old lady gathered her belongings and stood up to leave, and the two diners cheerily waved and said goodbye as 'mum' left the restaurant.

e) The couple nodded compassionately. 'It would give me such a thrill if, just as I am leaving, you would say, "Goodbye mum", and wave me off,' the old lady said.

f) Our sister's friend and her new husband were enjoying a meal at a good restaurant. As they were eating they noticed sitting next to them an elderly lady, alone and gazing in their direction.

READING AND WRITING

1 Aim: to predict before reading.
- The stories in this lesson are all to do with bad luck. Ask the students to look at the cartoon of the two men in the car. Ask them to predict what the story will be about.

2 Aim: to read and complete a story.
- Ask the students to read the story and see if they guessed correctly in 1.

3 Aim: to practise reading and speaking.
- Ask the students to try and guess what the missing last line is. Ask the students to turn to the Communication activity on page 94 to see if they were correct.

4 Aim: to focus on text organisation.
- Ask the students to read the next story and put the paragraphs in the right order.

Answers
f b e d a c

5 Aim: to practise writing and speaking.
- This is a mutual dictation activity where one student reads one part of the story and their partner reads the other part. Together they have to reconstruct the story.
- Ask the students to turn to their respective communication activities.

6 Aim: to practise speaking.
- Ask the students to write a sentence saying what would have happened in the three stories in this lesson if someone had done something differently.

FUNCTIONS

1 Aim: to focus on regrets about a present/past state.

● Ask the students to read the information in the functions box and then to do the exercises.

● This exercise draws attention to the different tenses used in expressing regret.

> **Answers**
> a I don't know what is going to happen.
>   (present regret)
> b I didn't know what was going to happen, and I
>   wish I had known. (past regret)

2 Aim: to practise expressing regret.

● Ask the students to look back at the stories and to say what they think the people wished had been different or regretted about what happened.

3 Aim: to practise using *should have* and *shouldn't have*.

● The students will have come across this construction in *Reward* Intermediate Lesson 37. Ask them to think about what the people in the stories *should have/shouldn't have* done.

4 Aim: to practise expressing wishes and regrets.

● Ask the students to talk about wishes they have for the present and regrets for the past. It may be better to avoid this activity becoming too personal, so keep it fairly light-hearted.

SOUNDS

1 Aim: to focus on /s/ and /ʃ/.

● Some students may have difficulty in distinguishing between /s/ and /ʃ/. The spelling of the word doesn't always help as sometimes, similar letters are pronounced differently. Ask them to look at the words and decide if they contain /s/ or /ʃ/.

> **Answers**
> /s/: send sun depressed guess school
> /ʃ/: should English anxious frustration
> depression affectionate

● ▭ Ask the students to listen and check. As they listen, ask them to say the words aloud.

2 Aim: to focus on the intonation of strong wishes and regrets.

● Ask the students to listen and underline the words they think the speaker will stress.

> **Answers**
> 1 If only I could speak to her.
> 2 I wish you'd be quiet.
> 3 If only you'd listened to me.
> 4 I wish I'd kept quiet.
> 5 If only I understood Chinese.
> 6 I wish he wouldn't do that.

VOCABULARY AND SPEAKING

1 Aim: to present the words in the vocabulary box.

● The words in the box can all be used to describe stories. Ask the students to decide which ones are similar in meaning.

> **Answers**
> peculiar far-fetched bizarre eccentric
> sad gloomy pathetic
> amusing hilarious
> boring uneventful
> exciting profound fascinating stimulating
> charming delightful touching

2 Aim: to practise using the words in the box; to react to the texts.

● Ask the students to reflect on the stories they have heard or read in this lesson and to choose words from the box to describe them.

● Ask the students to choose words to describe the stories mentioned in the questions.

3 Aim: to practise speaking.

● Ask the students to carry on talking about the stories in the lesson.

● Can the students tell any stories of their own about lucky escapes or bad luck?

5 Work in pairs. You're going to recreate a story about a woman who goes on a shopping trip.

Student A: Turn to Communication activity 6 on page 93.

Student B: Turn to Communication activity 16 on page 95.

6 Write a sentence saying what would have happened in the three stories if someone had done something different.

FUNCTIONS

> **Expressing wishes and regrets**
>
> **You can express:**
>
> – regret about a present state with *wish* + past simple or continuous.
> *I wish I knew what I was going to do.*
>
> – regret about the past with *wish* + past perfect.
> *I wish I hadn't acted so badly.*
>
> – a wish with *could*.
> *I wish I could travel more.*
>
> **You can use *if only* if the feeling is stronger.**
> *If only I had phoned the department store to check the call was genuine!*
>
> **You use *should have* or *shouldn't have* to express regret or criticism about actions in the past.**
> *I should have phoned the department store to check the call was genuine.*

1 Explain the difference between these two sentences.

  a I wish I knew what was going to happen.
  b I wish I had known what was going to happen.

2 Work in pairs. Talk about what each person in the stories wished or regretted about what happened.

3 Write sentences saying what the people in the stories *should* or *shouldn't have* done.

4 Work in pairs. Talk about three wishes and regrets you have for the present and three for the past.

SOUNDS

1 Say these words aloud. Is the underlined sound /s/ or /ʃ/? Put the words into two columns.

<u>s</u>hould <u>s</u>end <u>s</u>un Engli<u>s</u>h depre<u>ss</u>ed anx<u>i</u>ous frustra<u>tion</u> depre<u>ssion</u> affec<u>tio</u>nate gue<u>ss</u> <u>s</u>chool

Listen and check. As you listen, say the words aloud.

2 Look at these sentences. Underline the words you think the speaker will stress.

  1 If only I could speak to her.
  2 I wish you'd be quiet.
  3 If only you'd listened to me.
  4 I wish I'd kept quiet.
  5 If only I understood Chinese.
  6 I wish he wouldn't do that.

Now listen and check.

VOCABULARY AND SPEAKING

1 Work in pairs. Which words in the box are similar in meaning?

> peculiar sad amusing far-fetched boring
> uneventful exciting gloomy profound pathetic
> fascinating charming delightful stimulating bizarre
> eccentric touching hilarious

2 Which words could you use to describe the stories you read in this lesson? Which of the words would you use to describe the following stories?

  1 A story about a woman who looks after injured animals.
  2 A story about a couple who take a holiday where everything goes wrong.
  3 A story about a person who discovers a cure for cancer.
  4 A story about a child with a serious illness who finds ways to help other children who are in trouble.

3 Did you like the stories in this lesson? Which story did you like best? Tell a partner and give your reasons.

16 All-time greats

Phrasal verbs

SPEAKING

1 Work in groups of three. Look at the list of types of music below. Add as many more kinds as you can.

classical   jazz   opera   rock   folk   reggae   blues

2 Now choose one of the types of music in your list. Think about what instruments it is played on, what country it comes from and any famous musicians who play it.

3 Work with another group and guess what type of music they have chosen. They must try to guess the type of music you have chosen. Take turns asking questions. You can only answer *yes* or *no*. You cannot guess the type of music until you have received a *yes* answer.

Can you dance to it?   No.
Is it played by an orchestra?   Yes.
Is it classical music?   Yes.

4 Go round the class and find someone who shares your taste in music. Are there many people who share your taste or are you on your own?

VOCABULARY AND READING

1 Look at the words in the box. Find:

– four words for *types of music.*
– two adjectives to *describe* music.
– three words for *musicians.*
– three words for a *form of recording.*
– one word for a *song.*
– one word for a *great success.*

> lyrics bossa nova melody samba cool mellow chord tenor guitarist LP album feature number hit chart guitar single disc composer jazz saxophonist rock

Find out what the remaining words mean.

2 Work in pairs. Write down five more words for musical instruments and five words for the musicians who play them.

piano – pianist

Compare your list with another pair.

3 Read the passage, which comes from a magazine, and decide what it is about.

– Stan Getz   – Astrud and Joao Gilberto   – Tom Jobim
– The *bossa nova*   – *The Girl from Ipanema*

16

GENERAL COMMENTS

Phrasal verbs

Verbs with two or more parts are often called phrasal verbs. In fact, phrasal verbs are only those followed by an adverb particle, eg *turn on, put off*. The noun object can go either before or after the particle but the pronoun object must go before the particle. If the verb is followed by a preposition, it is called a prepositional verb, eg *fall off, look at,* and the object, noun or pronoun must go after the particle. For most students, the distinction is difficult to grasp, and in many ways it is not really important as the meaning is often idiomatic. In *Reward* Intermediate, multi-part verbs were treated as vocabulary items, so the meaning and word order of each verb was taught. The students are now at a suitable level to be exposed to a more grammatical explanation. For the sake of simplicity, the verbs are still all referred to as phrasal verbs. For more information than the grammar box within this lesson allows, ask the students to look at the Grammar review at the back of the book.

SPEAKING

1 Aim: to present the theme of the lesson; to practise speaking.

● Ask the students to tell you what kind of music they like.

● Write the types of music on the board and ask the students to suggest some more. How many types of music can you write on the board?

2 Aim: to practise speaking.

● Ask the students to choose one of the types of music and to list the instruments which are typically used to play it. Ask the students to make a list of any famous musicians who are associated with the music.

3 Aim: to practise speaking.

● Ask the students to work with another group and to follow the instructions.

4 Aim: to practise speaking.

● Ask the students to find people who share the same taste in both music and performers. What is the most popular type of music? Who is the most popular performer?

VOCABULARY AND READING

1 Aim: to present the words in the vocabulary box.

● Ask the students to look at the words in the box and answer the questions. They are all words which come from the passage the students are going to read.

> **Answers**
> **types of music:** bossa nova samba jazz rock
> **adjectives to describe music:** cool mellow
> **words for musicians:** guitarist composer saxophonist
> **words for a form of recording:** album disc LP
> **word for a song:** number
> **word for a great success:** hit

● Ask the students what the remaining words mean. The words are likely to be ones which the students have already come across.

2 Aim: to extend vocabulary.

● Ask the students to work in pairs and to write down five more words for musical instruments and five words for the musicians who play them.

> **Possible answers**
> piano – pianist, violin – violinist, drum – drummer cello – cellist, trumpet – trumpeter, percussion – percussionist

3 Aim: to read for main ideas.

● Ask the students to read the passage and to decide which phrase describes the main idea.

> **Answer**
> *The Girl from Ipanema*

4 Aim: to check comprehension.
- Ask the students to decide if the statements are true or false.

> **Answers**
> 1 False 2 True 3 True 4 False 5 False
> 6 False 7 True

5 Aim: to focus on difficult expressions.
- Ask the students to find the expressions in the passage and answer the questions.

> **Answers**
> 1 The song was popular with both singers and jazz musicians.
> 2 Rock 'n' roll
> 3 Less popular
> 4 Made his name famous
> 5 Nothing

6 Aim: to present some phrasal verbs.
- Ask the students to read the passage again and to find phrasal verbs which have a similar meaning to the words and phrases given.

> **Answers**
> put on paper – wrote down
> watched – looked at
> caused to happen – brought about
> composed – came up with
> became popular – caught on
> evolved – came about
> played with – got together with
> participated – joined in
> was released – came out
> got rid of – did away with
> continued its progress – went on
> call to mind – think of
> requested – asked for
> refused – turned down

SPEAKING

Aim: to practise speaking.
- Ask how many of your students know the song *The Girl from Ipanema.* Is it very popular in their country? Why do they think some songs become popular worldwide? Ask the students to look at the questions in the Student's Book and discuss their answers.

Tall, and tan and young and lovely,
The girl from Ipanema goes walking,
And when she passes
Each one she passes goes Ah!

These are the lyrics Antonio 'Tom' Jobim wrote down on the back of a cocktail napkin as he looked at a beautiful sixteen-year-old girl on a beach in Rio de Janeiro in 1964. And with these opening lines he not only brought about a musical revolution but also came up with one of the best known songs in the world. The 1960s craze for the *bossa nova* caught on and made Tom Jobim's name, and today many years later his melodies remain highly popular with singers and jazz musicians alike, and none more so than *The Girl from Ipanema.*

The musical revolution of *bossa nova* 'new flair' came about in the early sixties. It was a mixture of jazz and samba and, in those days, came second in importance only to rock 'n' roll. With its cool, mellow chords, it captured the upbeat mood of a generation of Brazilians whose country was beginning to emerge as a great industrial power. Brasilia, its futuristic capital – built from scratch on an arid stretch of land in the country's interior – was nearing completion and the world was looking at the Latin American giant as a great example of modernity. Brazil became known to the rest of the world as 'the country of the future'.

'Jobim took the traditional street samba and combined it with our North American cool school,' the jazz tenor saxophonist Stan Getz said. 'And that's what came out – the *bossa nova.*' In 1962, after a tour of Brazil, Getz and the guitarist Charlie Byrd made an LP called *Jazz Samba.* The album featured two Jobim songs: *Samba de una nota so* 'One note samba' and *Desafinado* 'Slightly out of tune'. Both numbers became hits and *Jazz Samba* was in the best seller chart in the United States for over a year.

In 1964 Getz got together with the Brazilian singers Joao and Astrud Gilberto. On the *Garota de Ipanema* 'The Girl from Ipanema' track, Joao sang in Portuguese and Astrud joined in in English, with Getz on saxophone and Jobim on guitar. When the song came out as a single they did away with Joao Gilberto's vocal and the only voice heard on the disc was his wife Astrud's. The song went on to be an international hit, selling more than a million copies, staying at Number 5 in the US charts for two weeks and winning a Grammy.

Soon such Jobim songs as *Corcovado* 'Quiet Nights', Quiet Stars achieved similar fame, and were sung by such celebrities as Ella Fitzgerald, Dionne Warwick, Nat King Cole and Frank Sinatra. But when people think of *bossa nova,* it's still *The Girl from Ipanema,* which nearly everyone remembers and loves.

How did Tom Jobim feel about being the composer of one of the world's greatest songs? He admitted it had helped make him Brazil's foremost composer for thirty years. But towards the end of his life (he died in 1994), when audiences at concerts asked for the song he often turned them down. 'A guy writes 400 songs in his life and they only remember him for one. There's no justice.'

4 Decide if these statements are true or false.

1 Stan Getz was the creator of *bossa nova.*
2 *Bossa nova* was relaxing but optimistic music.
3 Tom Jobim had two successful songs in 1962.
4 The international version of *The Girl from Ipanema* was sung in Portuguese.
5 Tom Jobim's other songs were more successful.
6 He never liked playing it.
7 He didn't want to be known just for one song.

5 Look at the phrases from the passage. Answer the questions and try to guess the meaning of the phrases in italics.

1 *with singers and jazz musicians alike…*
   – Why are they alike?
2 *…came second in importance only to rock 'n' roll.* – Which was first?
3 *…and none more so than The Girl from Ipanema.* – Are Jobim's other songs more or less popular than *The Girl from Ipanema?*
4 *…made Tom Jobim's name…* – Made his name what?
5 *…built from scratch …* – What was there before they started building?

6 Find phrasal verbs in the passage which are similar in meaning to the following words and phrases:

put on paper   watched   caused to happen
composed   became popular   evolved
played with   participated   was released
got rid of   continued its progress
call to mind   requested   refused

SPEAKING

Work in pairs and discuss your answers to the questions.

1 Can you think of a song from your country which is known around the world?
2 Are there musicians in the past or the present which are internationally famous?
3 What is the most popular style of music in your country?
4 Has rock ever been the most popular style of music in your country?

Phrasal verbs

GRAMMAR

Phrasal verbs

1 Phrasal verbs are verbs with a particle which have a different meaning from the verb when it is on its own. Sometimes the meaning is obvious because it is a combination of the meanings of verb and particle.
*Tom Jobim **wrote down** the lyrics on the back of a cocktail napkin.*
*He **looked at** a beautiful girl on a beach.*

Sometimes the meaning is not obvious because it has a different meaning from the meaning of the verb and particle.
*He **brought about** a musical revolution.*

2 There are four types of phrasal verbs.

Type 1 These do not take an object. *The craze for bossa nova **caught on**.*

Type 2 These take an object. The noun object goes before or after the particle. *He **wrote down** the lyrics.* or *He **wrote** the lyrics **down**.*
The pronoun object must go before the particle.
*He wrote **them** down.*

Type 3 These also take an object. The noun and the pronoun object go after the particle.
*He looked at **a beautiful girl** on a beach.*
*He looked at **her**.*

Type 4 These have two particles and take an object. The noun and the pronoun object go after the particle.
*He came up with **one of the best known songs**. He came up with **it**.*

3 It is usual to use phrasal verbs, especially in spoken English. But it's usually possible to replace them with another verb or verbal phrase.
*When audiences **asked for** the song, he often **turned them down**.*
*When audiences **requested** the song he often **refused**.*

---

1 Look back at the passage and decide if the meaning of the phrasal verbs in the passage is obvious from the meaning of the verb + particle, or not.

2 Decide what types the phrasal verbs in the passage are.

3 Look at the phrasal verbs which have a similar meaning to the words and phrases in *Vocabulary and reading* activity 6 on page 69. Which do you think is better, the phrasal verb or the alternative?

SOUNDS

Underline the words you think the speaker will stress in these sentences.

1 Turn it up.   4 He put it on.   7 Don't tear it up.
2 I'll look into it. 5 I'll let it out.   8 Will you sit down?
3 Please stand up.   6 Please carry on.

🔲 Listen and check. As you listen, say the words aloud.

VOCABULARY AND LISTENING

1 You're going to hear Steve and Francesca talking about their favourite pieces of music and favourite books. Which are they likely to use the following words to talk about?

symphony   choir   volume
biography   novel   literary   plot
fiction   diary   paperback
soprano   rhythm   lead singer
key   bass   concerto   band
portrayal

2 Write a definition of six words from the box.

A symphony is a piece of music for a full orchestra.

3 Work in pairs.

Student A: Tell Student B one of the words you have defined.
Student B: Give a definition of Student A's word.

Decide which is the better definition. Change round when you're ready.

GRAMMAR

1 Aim: to focus on the phrasal verbs.

● Ask the students to read the information in the grammar box and then to look back at the passage to decide whether the meaning is obvious from the verb + particle or not.

> **Answers**
> **Obvious meaning verb + particle:** wrote down looked at got together with joined in came out think of asked for turned down

2 Aim: to focus on phrasal verbs.

● Ask the students to look at the phrasal verbs in the passage and decide which type they are. Refer the students to the grammar box or the Grammar review if you feel they will need more help with this activity.

> **Answers**
> **Type 1:** caught on came about went on joined in came out
> **Type 2:** wrote down brought about turned them down
> **Type 3:** looked at
> **Type 4:** did away with came up with got together with

3 Aim: to focus on phrasal verbs and their alternatives.

● Generally speaking, native speakers use phrasal verbs. The alternative phrases are acceptable, but tend to sound less fluent.

SOUNDS

Aim: to focus on stress in phrasal verbs.

● Point out that the two parts of a phrasal verb are usually stressed and the pronoun object is not. Ask the students to underline the words they think the speaker will stress.

● 🔊 Play the tape and ask the student to repeat the sentences.

> **Answers**
> 1 <u>Turn</u> it <u>up</u>.
> 2 I'll <u>look into it</u>.
> 3 Please <u>stand up</u>.
> 4 He <u>put</u> it <u>on</u>.
> 5 I'll <u>let</u> it <u>out</u>.
> 6 Please <u>carry on</u>.
> 7 <u>Don't tear</u> it <u>up</u>.
> 8 Will you <u>sit down</u>?

VOCABULARY AND LISTENING

1 Aim: to present the words in the vocabulary box; to prepare for listening.

● Ask the students to predict which of the words Steve and Francesca are likely to use to talk about their favourite pieces of music and favourite books.

2 Aim: to practise using the words in the vocabulary box.

● Ask the students to write definitions for six of the words in the vocabulary box.

3 Aim: to practise using the words in the vocabulary box; to practise speaking.

● Ask one or two students in the class for a definition of one of the words they have chosen and ask the other students to try and guess what the word is.

● Ask the students to work in pairs of Student A and Student B. Student A should tell Student B one of the words he/she has chosen to define. Student B must then give *their* definition of that word. Together the students should decide whose definition is the best. When they are ready, ask the students to change round.

4 Aim: to listen for specific information.

● 🔲 This is a jigsaw listening activity. Ask the students to turn to the Communication activities and to follow the instructions.

5 Aim: to check comprehension; to practise speaking.

● Ask the students to work together and to complete the chart with as much information as possible.

> **Answers**
> Francesca
> **Favourite music:** Pie Jesu by Andrew Lloyd Webber
> First heard it five years ago
> She thinks it is very beautiful
> **Favourite book:** Wuthering Heights
> First read it when she was doing her A'levels
> She likes it because there is a lot of passion
> Steve
> **Favourite music:** Mahler's Second Symphony
> First heard it in 1978 when he was eighteen
> He likes it because it is amazing music
> **Favourite book:** A History of the World in Ten and a Half Chapters
> It contains ten stories
> He has read it many times

6 Aim: to provide an opportunity for second listening.

● 🔲 Ask the students to listen again and check their answers.

WRITING AND SPEAKING

1 Aim: to present some attitude words.

● Ask the students to read through the attitude words and phrases and check that they know how they are used. In pairs, ask the students to complete the book review, using attitude words. There may be more than one answer in some instances.

> **Possible answers**
> (1) **As far I'm concerned** my favourite book is *The House of the Spirits* by Isabelle Allende.
> (2) **Clearly** it's her best book, although
> (3) **amazingly**, I only read it for the first time a couple of months ago; I'd already read most of her other novels. (4) **Generally**, I read a lot of novels by South American writers, but what I (5) **really** like about this book is the atmosphere, which is
> (6) **quite** superb, and the plot, which is wonderful.
> (7) **In fact**, after reading the book I felt that I would like to live in the world that she describes.
> (8) **To my mind** it's the most magical book I've read.

2 Aim: to practise speaking.

● Ask the students to talk about their favourite pieces of music and favourite books. Encourage them to use the attitude words in 1.

3 Aim: to write a review of a favourite book or piece of music.

● Ask the students to use the words and expressions in 1 and the text to help them to write a review of their favourite pieces of music and favourite books. You may like to ask them to do this activity for homework.

4 Listen to Steve and Francesca talking about their favourite pieces of music and their favourite books. Work in pairs.

Student A: Turn to Communication activity 20 on page 96.
Student B: Turn to Communication activity 17 on page 95.

5 Work together and complete the chart with as much detail as possible.

	Favourite music	Favourite book
Francesca		
Steve		

6 Listen again to Steve and Francesca, and check your answers to 5.

WRITING AND SPEAKING

1 Look at some attitude words and their uses.

To express an opinion.   *I suppose, as far as I'm concerned, to my mind, personally*
To emphasise.   *really, definitely, clearly, obviously, in fact, actually*
To express surprise.   *amazingly, curiously, strangely*
To express a generality.   *in general, broadly speaking*

Now complete this review of a favourite book with a suitable attitude word or phrase.

(1) ____, my favourite book is *The House of the Spirits* by Isabelle Allende. (2) ____ it's her best book, although (3) ____, I only read it for the first time a couple of months ago; I'd already read most of her other novels. (4) ____, I read a lot of novels by South American writers, but what I (5) ____ like about this book is the atmosphere, which is (6) ____ superb, and the plot, which is wonderful. (7) ____, after reading the book I felt that I would like to live in the world that she describes. (8) ____, it's the most magical book I've read.

2 Work in groups of three or four. Talk about your favourite pieces of music and favourite books. Can you explain why you like them?

3 Use the words and expressions in activity 1 to write a review of your favourite pieces of music or your favourite books. You can use the text in activity 1 to help you.

Say what it is.
My favourite pieces of music/books are...
Say who wrote/played it.
...by (writer/composer), with (musicians)
Say when you read/heard it.
The first time I read/heard it...
Say why you like it in general.
The reason I like it is...
Say what you particularly like.
In particular, I like...

Progress check **13–16**

VOCABULARY

1 There are many phrasal verbs which are based on the following verbs:

break bring come do get go let look make put run see set take turn

Make twenty phrasal verbs with the verbs above and the following particles.

about at away with by down down to for forward to in into of off on out out of over round to through up up for up to up with with without

2 Rewrite these sentences replacing the words in italics with a suitable phrasal verb and particle in 1.

1 They couldn't *tolerate* their noisy neighbours any longer so they called the police.
2 She has always *greatly respected* her teacher.
3 We must *deal with* the arrangements for our holiday.
4 She *met unexpectedly* an old friend yesterday.
5 He *refused* the invitation to the party.
6 I've *postponed* the meeting until next week.
7 We should *begin our journey* before seven o'clock.
8 The travel agency paid us some money to *compensate us* for the unsuccessful holiday.
9 The police are *investigating* the crime.

3 There are many other expressions based on the verbs in 1.

break	the news, your heart, a record
bring	into force, to light, out the best in someone
come	to an end, to a decision, to your senses
do	the housework, homework, your best, business with
get	rid of, your own back
go	far, to great lengths, bankrupt
let	someone down, it slip
look	small, someone in the eye, down your nose at something
make	a mistake, arrangements, a suggestion, an excuse
put	your foot down, someone's back up, your mind to something
run	a business, you off your feet
see	your way to, the wood for the trees
set	your heart on something, fire to, a good example
take	care of, for granted, advantage of, pride in
turn	over a new leaf

Which verbs go with these phrases? What do the expressions mean?

on the bright side   without saying   into contact with   your sights on   two and two together   off to a good start   your breath away   into the open   a fuss of someone

GRAMMAR

1 Complete these sentences with *by* or *with*.

1 The principle of radio broadcasting was invented ____ Marconi.
2 The computer is covered ____ a plastic wrapper.
3 We receive our television programmes ____ cable.
4 The system was sold to us ____ a computer specialist.
5 It was checked ____ the engineer ____ a circuit tester.
6 The camera was supplied ____ the shop ____ films.

2 Rewrite these sentences in the passive.

1 He likes people calling him by his first name.
2 She doesn't want people to exploit her.
3 He's hoping his boss will give him a pay rise.
4 I want someone to tell me how it works.
5 They were looking forward to their neighbours inviting them to dinner.
6 He wants people to elect him as chairman of the club.

Progress check 13 – 16

GENERAL COMMENTS

You can work through this Progress check in the order shown, or concentrate on areas which may have caused difficulty in Lessons 13 to 16. You can also let the students choose the activities they would like or feel the need to do.

VOCABULARY

1 Aim: to practise making phrasal verbs.

● Ask the students to make as many phrasal (two or three part) as possible.

> **Suggested answers**
> **break** down, in, into, off, out, out of, through, up
> **bring** about, down, in, into, off, on, out over, up
> **come** about, down, down to, in, into, off, on, out, out of, round to, through, up, up with
> **do** away with, in, out of, up, without
> **get** at, away with, down to, in, into, off, on, out, out of, over, through
> **go** at, down, down to, for, in, into, off, on, out, over, through, up to, without
> **let** down, in, into, off, on, out, out of, through, up
> **look** at, down, for, forward to, in, into, on, out, out of, over, through, up, up to
> **make** away with, for, off, out, up for
> **put** down, in, into, off, on, out, up with
> **run** away with, down, in, into, off, out of, over, through, up to
> **see** about, into, off, out, out of, over, to, through
> **set** about, down, in, off, out, to
> **take** down, in, off, on, out, out of, round, to, up
> **turn** down, into, off, on, out, out of, over, round, to, up, up with

● You may need to prepare some sentences which show their meanings.

2 Aim: to practise using phrasal verbs.

● Ask the students to use the phrasal verbs in 1 to rewrite these sentences.

> **Answers**
> 1 put up with   2 looked up to   3 see to   4 ran into
> 5 turned down   6 put off   7 set out   8 make up
> 9 looking into

3 Aim: to practise using phrasal verbs.

● Explain to the students that there are many expressions and idiomatic phrases based on the phrasal verbs in 1. Ask them to read through the list in this activity. Discuss with the students whether they have similar expressions in their own language.

● Ask the students to match one of the verbs in this activity with one of the phrases below.

> **Answers**
> look on the bright side
> go without saying
> come into contact with
> set your sights on
> put two and two together
> get off to a good start
> take your breath away
> bring into the open
> make a fuss of someone

GRAMMAR

1 Aim: to revise *by* and *with* in passives.

> **Answers**
> 1 The principle of radio broadcasting was invented **by** Marconi.
> 2 The computer is covered **with** a plastic wrapper.
> 3 We receive our television programmes **by** cable.
> 4 The system was sold to us **by** a computer specialist.
> 5 It was checked **by** the engineer **with** a circuit tester.
> 6 The camera was supplied **with** films **by** the shop.

2 Aim: to revise the passive.

> **Answers**
> 1 He likes **to be called** by his first name.
> 2 She doesn't want **to be exploited**.
> 3 He's hoping **to be given** a pay rise.
> 4 I want **to be told** how it works.
> 5 They were looking forward to **being invited** to dinner by their neighbours.
> 6 He wants **to be elected** as chairman of the club.

3 Aim: to revise non-defining relative clauses.

Answers
1 The city which is growing at the fastest rate is Mexico City. The population, which has been estimated at 16 million, will grow to over 31 million by the year 2000. This is five times more than all the people who live in Switzerland at present.
2 Mount Isa, Queensland, which is in Australia, spreads over 41,000 square kilometres, which makes it the largest town in the world. It covers an area 26 times greater than that of London, which means that it is about the same size as Switzerland.
3 The city which has the greatest amount of traffic is Los Angeles. At one interchange almost 500,000 vehicles were counted in 24 hours, which is an average of 20,000 cars and trucks an hour.

4 Aim: to practise writing participle clauses.

Answers
1 The capital **lying** furthest to the north is Reykjavik.
2 Twenty-one huts **discovered** in France in 1960 are believed to date from 400,000 BC, **making** them the oldest buildings in the world.
3 Concorde, **travelling** between London and New York, flies at over twice the speed of sound.
4 The language **spoken** by the greatest number of people is Chinese.

5 Aim: to revise the third conditional.
● Ask the students to write sentences about their own personal experiences.

SOUNDS

1 Aim: to revise the sounds /θ/ and /ð/.
● 🎞 Ask the students to say the words and check they can pronounce the two sounds correctly. Some students may try to replace these sounds with /z/.

● Ask the students to put the words in two columns.

Answers
/θ/: think thin theatre thank tooth bath thread three thick
/ð/: this that the they then with

2 Aim: to focus on silent letters.
● Remind the students that there are many letters in English which are not pronounced. Ask them to cross out the silent consonants in the words.

Answers
comb dumb lamb doubt subtle debt
could calm half honour honest hour
knee know knife psychiatry receipt pneumatic
card burn work mother sister teacher
whistle fasten soften

● 🎞 Play the tape and ask them to listen and check. Ask them to say the words aloud.

3 Aim: to focus on voice pitch and intonation.
● Check everyone understands the words *factual, mysterious, excited* and *vague.*
● 🎞 Play the tape and ask the students to listen to someone saying the sentences in four different ways. Ask the students to repeat the sentences.

4 Aim: to focus on voice pitch and intonation.
● Ask the students to listen and decide how the speaker says the sentences – *factual, excited, mysterious, vague.*

Answers
excited: This is a photo of Mount Etna.
vague: I'll mention it when I see him.
mysterious: Maybe I'll go along later.
factual: I've missed my bus.
vague: I haven't got any film for my camera.
mysterious: I get home some time tomorrow night.

● Ask the students to say the sentences in the same ways. Alternatively, ask the students to work in pairs and choose different ways of saying the sentences. Their partner must guess in which way they have chosen to say the sentence – *factual, excited, mysterious, vague.*

WRITING AND SPEAKING

Aim: to practise writing and speaking.
● This activity is a way of revising the formation of third conditional sentences in a game format. Ask the students to read the instructions and to form pairs. They should write some sentences.

● Ask them to work with another pair and each one should say their sentences in turn.

● Ask the students to play the game. Go round and check that everyone is following the rules. Find out who has scored the highest number of points.

3 Put commas in these sentences, if necessary.

1 The city which is growing at the fastest rate is Mexico City. The population which has been estimated at 16 million will grow to over 31 million by the year 2000. This is 5 times more than all the people who live in Switzerland at present.

2 Mount Isa, Queensland which is in Australia spreads over 41,000 square kilometres which makes it the largest town in the world. It covers an area 26 times greater than that of London which means that it is about the same size as Switzerland.

3 The city which has the greatest amount of traffic is Los Angeles. At one interchange almost 500,000 vehicles were counted in 24 hours which is an average of 20,000 cars and trucks an hour.

4 Rewrite these sentences using participle clauses.

1 The capital which lies furthest to the north is Reykjavik.

2 Twenty-one huts which were discovered in France in 1960 are believed to date from 400,000 BC, which makes them the oldest buildings in the world.

3 Concorde, which travels between London and New York, flies at over twice the speed of sound.

4 The language which is spoken by the greatest number of people is Chinese.

5 Write down five or six important events which have happened in your life.

I moved to Paris.

Now write sentences saying what *would have* or *might have* happened if these events hadn't happened.

If I hadn't moved to Paris, I wouldn't have met Pierre.

SOUNDS

1 Say these words aloud. Is the underlined sound /ə/ or /ð/. Put them in two columns.

think   thin   this   that   theatre   the   thank   tooth   bath   thread   three thick   they   then   with

[cassette] Listen and check. As you listen, say the words aloud.

2 Underline the silent consonant in these words.

comb   dumb   lamb   doubt   subtle   debt   could   calm   half   honour honest   hour   knee   know   knife   psychiatry   receipt   pneumatic   card burn   work   mother   sister   teacher   whistle   fasten   soften

[cassette] Listen and check. As you listen, say the words aloud.

3 [cassette] Listen to someone saying these sentences in four different ways. As you listen, repeat the sentences in the same way.

I arrive at nine o'clock. – *factual*   He finally called me! – *excited*
Let's meet tomorrow. – *mysterious*   See you next week, perhaps. – *vague*

4 [cassette] Look at the sentences below. Decide in which of the four ways in 3 the speaker says these sentences.

1 This is a photo of Mount Etna.

2 I'll mention it when I see him.

3 Maybe I'll go along later.

4 I've missed my bus.

5 I haven't got any film for my camera.

6 I get home sometime tomorrow night.

Now say the sentences in the same ways.

WRITING AND SPEAKING

Work in pairs. You're going to play a game called *If things had been different.*

How to play

1 Look back over the texts in Lessons 13 –16, and think about some of the events and situations described. Write as many sentences as possible saying what might or would have happened if they had not happened.
If the Amish had stayed in Europe, their way of life might not have survived.

2 Work with another pair. Each pair should say one of their sentences in turn.

3 You score one point for each correct sentence.

4 You cannot repeat a sentence which is similar to or the same as one which the other pair has already said.

5 Continue until one pair has no more sentences.

6 The pair which has the largest number of points is the winner.

17 Spending money

Countable and uncountable nouns

> loaf of bread
> pair of shoes
> hat
> tube of toothpaste
> silk scarf
> handkerchief
> fresh coffee
> newspaper
> cushion
> necklace
> 3 silk flowers

SPEAKING

This lesson is about spending money. Look at this shopping list. Which of these things have you bought recently? Which do you buy more than once a month?

Discuss your answers with a partner.

READING

1 The passage is taken from the novel *Tender is the Night* by the American writer, F Scott Fitzgerald, which was first published in 1934. Nicole is doing some shopping. Listed below are some of the items she buys. Do you think Nicole is rich or poor? Is she a young person or an old person?

dress   hat   coloured beads   beach cushion
artificial flowers   love bird   bathing suit
leather jacket

Which items would you like to buy?

2 Read the passage. Were you right about Nicole?

With Nicole's help Rosemary bought two dresses and two hats and four pairs of shoes with her money. Nicole bought from a great list that ran two pages, and bought the things in the windows besides. Everything she liked that she couldn't possibly use herself, she bought as a present for a friend. She bought coloured beads, folding beach cushions, artificial flowers, honey, a guest bed, bags, scarves, love birds, miniatures for a doll's house, and three yards of some new cloth the colour of prawns. She bought a dozen bathing suits, a rubber alligator, a travelling chess set of gold and ivory, big linen handkerchiefs for Abe, two chamois leather jackets of kingfisher blue and burning bush from Hermès. Nicole was the product of much hard work. For her sake trains began their run at Chicago and crossed the continent to California; in factories men mixed toothpaste in vats and girls canned tomatoes quickly in August or worked hard at the local store on Christmas Eve; Indians worked on Brazilian coffee plantations – these were some of the people who contributed to Nicole's wealth and, as the whole system swayed and thundered onward, it gave a rosy colour to such processes of hers as wholesale buying.

3 Work in pairs and discuss your answers to the questions.

1 What impression of Nicole does the author want to give in his description of her shopping list?

2 What type of person do you think Nicole is? Would you say that she is selfish or generous, serious or frivolous? Find words and phrases in the passage to support your opinion.

3 Do you think Nicole has worked hard to earn her wealth?

4 Who has worked hard to make Nicole wealthy?

17

GENERAL COMMENTS

Countable and uncountable nouns

The students will certainly have come across countable and uncountable nouns before. They will also have learnt that nouns can be both countable and uncountable depending on how they are used. This lesson focuses on this aspect. The students may also have noticed that not all languages treat countables and uncountables in a similar way. For example, *hair* may be a plural countable in many languages but is uncountable in English.

SPEAKING

Aim: to introduce the theme of the lesson; to practise speaking.

● Ask the students to look at the shopping list and to discuss which items they have bought recently. Ask them to say which items they buy more than once a week or a month. Check the answers with the whole class.

READING

1 Aim: to prepare for reading; to pre-teach some unfamiliar words.

● Ask the students if they have ever heard of F Scott Fitzgerald. You may like to tell them that he lived from 1896 to 1940 and was a well-known American writer who wrote many novels about rich and privileged people. Probably his most famous book was *The Great Gatsby.* Another of his famous books was *Tender is the Night* and it is from this book that the reading passage is taken. Explain to the students that one of the main characters in the story is a woman called Nicole.

● Ask the students to look at the words and decide if Nicole is rich or poor. Is she is a young or an old person?

2 Aim: to read and check the answer to 1.

● Ask the students to read the passage and check their answers to 1. The impression the writer wants to give is a satirical one, describing Nicole's passion for shopping as making an important contribution to the economy.

Answer
Nicole is young and wealthy.

3 Aim: to check comprehension; to practise speaking; to evaluate the passage.

● Ask the students to discuss their answers to the questions.

Answers
1 That she is extravagant and generous.
2 Generous.
3 No – other people have worked hard.
4 Men in factories, girls, people at the local store, Indians on coffee plantations.

4 Aim: to check comprehension.

● It may be difficult for the students to understand what the passage is about, and this activity is designed to help them see the main ideas.

> **Answer**
> a

5 Aim: to react to the passage.

● Ask the students to think if they would like Nicole if they met her. Does anyone know anyone like her? Are there people like her in your students' countries or do you think this could only happen in America?

GRAMMAR

1 Aim: to focus on expressions of quantity.

● Ask the students to read the information in the grammar box and then to do the exercises.

> **Answers**
> **countable:** dress hat shoe bead bag
> **uncountable:** money honey cloth gold
>   ivory linen rubber

2 Aim: to focus on countable and uncountable nouns.

● Ask the students to choose the correct word.

> **Answers**
> I'm off on a **trip** to Paris tomorrow by car as I'm looking for **work**. I saw an **advertisement** for a job in a company there which does scientific research. I'm only taking one **bag** and a briefcase because I'm only staying for two nights. I hope there isn't too much **traffic** on the motorway as I don't like traffic jams. I must buy a **paper** to find what **information** there is about roadworks. I believe that **accommodation** for me has been booked in a hotel close to the centre. I hope I get a **view** of the Eiffel Tower. They say it's not expensive, but I must go to the bank as I haven't got any **money.** The last time I was there I bought a lot of **wine** and some **cheese**.

SPEAKING AND SOUNDS

1 Aim: to focus on humorous sayings.

● Ask the students to match the two sides of the sayings.

> **Answers**
> 1 e 2 b 3 d 4 c 5 a

2 Aim: to practise speaking.

● Ask the students to say if they found the jokes amusing. Ask them which one they liked best.

3 Aim: to focus on intonation and timing in jokes.

● Ask the students to listen to someone telling the jokes. Explain that intonation and timing are very important. Tell the students that each humorous saying will be said twice and they should decide which version is best. Encourage them to listen for the rise and fall of the speaker's voice when the joke is said in a lively way.

● ▭ Play the tape.

● Now ask the students to tell the jokes to each other. Make sure they think about intonation and timing.

4 Decide which of the following summaries of the passage is the most accurate.

a The first part of the passage is a list of what Nicole buys, and the second is a list of the people who have been exploited and who have contributed to her wealth.

b The passage describes Nicole and Rosemary on a shopping trip in which they spend a great deal of money on some expensive and frivolous things.

c The passage describes how Nicole and Rosemary exploited the capitalist system and became rich.

5 Read the passage again and decide if Nicole is the sort of person you would like to know.

GRAMMAR

Countable and uncountable nouns

Many nouns can be both countable and uncountable depending on the way they are used. Uncountable nouns can often be countable if you use them to describe different types.

Would you like some **wine**? *Burgundy and claret are* **wines** *from France.*

Words for materials are usually uncountable but we can often use the same word as a countable noun to describe something made of that material.

made of cloth   several tea cloths

Some countable nouns are seen more as a mass than a collection of separate elements.

bean(s), spice(s)

Sometimes a word is uncountable in English and countable in other foreign languages. For example, *accommodation* **is uncountable in English but countable in many European languages.**

Uncountable: *accommodation, advice, baggage, information, money, news, travel, work*

Countable: *somewhere to live, a piece of advice, a case/bag, a piece of information, a sum of money, an item of news, a journey, a job*

---

1 Here are some words from the passage about Nicole's shopping trip. Which are countable and which are uncountable?

dress   hat   shoe   money   bead   honey   bag   cloth   gold   ivory
linen   rubber

2 Choose the correct word.

I'm off on a *travel/trip* to Paris tomorrow by car as I'm looking for *work/job*. I saw an *advertisement/publicity* for a job in a company there which does scientific *research/experiment*. I'm only taking one *bag/baggage* and a briefcase because I'm only staying for two nights. I hope there isn't too much *traffic/cars* on the motorway as I don't like traffic jams. I must buy a *paper/some paper* to find what *information/piece of information* there is about roadworks. I believe that *place to stay/accommodation* for me has been booked in a hotel close to the centre. I hope I get *scenery/a view* of the Eiffel Tower. They say it's not expensive, but I must go to the bank as I haven't got any *money/coins*. The last time I was there I bought a lot of *wine/wines* and some *cheese/cheeses*.

SPEAKING AND SOUNDS

1 Here are some humorous sayings about money. Match the two parts of these sentences.

1 I've got all the money I need...
2 Money can't buy you love...
3 Money isn't everything,
4 Money can't buy you friends,...
5 Money doesn't go as far as it used to,...

a ...but it certainly goes faster.
b ...but it certainly puts you in a wonderful bargaining position.
c ...but you can get a better class of enemy.
d ...but it's certainly handy if you don't have a credit card.
e ...if I die by four o'clock.

2 Work in pairs and compare your answers to 1. Which saying did you like best? Which was the funniest?

3 When people say funny things or tell jokes, timing and intonation are very important. The amusing part usually comes at the end after a slight pause.

Listen to the two versions of each saying. Which do you think is better the first version or the second? Now say the sayings aloud in a lively way.

Ways of expressing quantity

VOCABULARY AND SPEAKING

1 Match the statements below with a word(s) from the box.

building society   cash   cheque   credit card   currency deposit   fee   grant   income tax   in credit   interest loan   mortgage   overdrawn   pension   rate of exchange receipt   rent   salary   statement   unemployment benefit (VAT) value added tax   wages   withdrawal

1 A word for a document you receive when you buy something.
2 A word for an organisation which lends you money to buy a house or flat.
3 A word for a document your bank sends you telling you what you have in your account.
4 A word for money you earn from a larger amount of money or pay on money you borrow.
5 Two words for money which is lent to you.
6 Two words for the action of taking out or putting money into a bank account.
7 Three words for methods of paying for things you buy.
8 Two words to describe the status of your account.
9 Two words for money the government takes away from you.
10 Three words to do with money from a foreign country.
11 Three words to describe the payment you receive for work you do.
12 Three words or expressions to describe money which the government may pay you.

2 Think about your answers to the statements 5–12. What's the difference between the words?

3 Work in pairs. Discuss the answers to these questions.
1 Which of the words in the box have an equivalent in your language?
2 Do people borrow money to buy houses in your country?
3 What money do you have to pay to the government?
4 What does the government pay you?

GRAMMAR

Ways of expressing quantity
You can use the following expressions of quantity: **– with countable nouns.** *a(n), few, a few, many, both (of), several, neither (of),* ***a couple*** *(of) cheques*   ***a few*** *dollars*   ***several*** *pounds* **– with uncountable nouns.** *very little, not much, a little, less, much, a great deal of,* ***very little*** *money*   ***less*** *tax* **– with both countable and uncountable nouns.** *some, any, no, none, hardly any, half, all, a lot of, lots of, (not) enough, more, most* ***some*** *money*   ***hardly any*** *cash* ***Some*** **is common in affirmative clauses, and *any* is common in questions and negatives. But you use *some* in questions if you expect, or want to encourage, the answer *yes*.** *Would you like to borrow* ***some*** *more money?* **You can use *any* when you mean *it doesn't matter which*.** *You can get a loan from* ***any*** *high street bank.*

1 Complete the sentences with suitable expressions of quantity from the list below.

a few   some   some more   a couple   hardly any   a lot
any   at least three

A: Can you lend me ____ money? I forgot to go to the bank.

B: Well, I've only got ____ pounds left.

A: Oh, dear. I need quite ____ . Don't worry. I'll go to the bank when I go shopping.

B: If you're going shopping, can you get me ____ of bottles of water? You can get bottled water at ____ shop on the high street.

A: Yes, and we need ____ tins of tomatoes. I'm making spaghetti bolognese tonight. We've got ____ beans. Shall I get ____ beans as well?

B: All right.

🔊 Now listen and check your answers.

2 Work in pairs. Imagine that you are planning to invite some friends to a barbecue. You have already got the items listed below. Make a list of the things that you will need to buy.

– a small piece of cheese
– five bottles of water
– one sausage
– two tomatoes
– half a bottle of milk
– one bread roll

Now prepare a conversation about the things you need to buy using the dialogue in 1 to help you. Act out your dialogue for the class.

VOCABULARY AND SPEAKING

1 Aim: to present the words in the vocabulary box.

● The words in the box are used to describe financial matters. Ask the students to read them and to check they understand them all. You may like to explain that in Britain a building society is mainly used to lend people money to buy a house. This kind of loan is called a mortgage. However, it can also be used as a kind of savings bank.

> **Answers**
> 1 receipt 2 building society 3 statement 4 interest
> 5 loan, mortgage 6 withdrawal, deposit
> 7 cash, cheque, credit card 8 in credit, overdrawn
> 9 income tax, VAT 10 currency, rate of exchange
> 11 fee, salary, wages 12 grant, pension, unemployment benefit

2 Aim: to focus on the words in the vocabulary box.

● Ask the students to use a dictionary to find out the difference between the words 5 – 12.

3 Aim: to practise speaking.

● You may like to do this activity with the whole class.

GRAMMAR

1 Aim: to focus on ways of expressing quantity.

● Ask the students to read the information in the grammar box and then to do the exercises.

● Do this activity with the class as a whole.

> **Answers**
> A: Can you lend me **some** money? I forgot to go to the bank.
> B: Well, I've only got **a few** pounds left.
> A: Oh, dear. I need quite **a lot**. Don't worry, I'll go to the bank when I go shopping.
> B: If you're going shopping, can you get me **a couple** of bottles of water? You can get bottled water at **any** shop on the high street.
> A: Yes, and we need **some** tins of tomatoes. I'm making spaghetti bolognese tonight. We've got **hardly any** beans. Shall I get **some more** beans as well?
> B: All right.

● Ask the students to listen to the tape to check their answers.

2 Aim: to practise using expressions of quantity.

● Ask the students to work in pairs and to make a shopping list of things to buy for a barbecue. The list in the exercise shows what they already have.

● Ask the students to prepare a dialogue about things they already have and need to buy for the barbecue.

● Ask two or three pairs to act out their dialogues for the rest of the class.

LISTENING AND SPEAKING

1 Aim: to complete a questionnaire; to prepare for listening.
● Ask the students to work in pairs and to look at the questionnaire. Ask them what they think the title means. Explain that someone who is born to shop is someone who likes shopping very much.

2 Aim: to listen for specific information.
● This is another jigsaw listening activity. Ask the students to turn to the relevant Communication activity.

3 Aim: to check comprehension; to practise speaking.
● Ask the students to work together and to complete the chart with as much detail as possible.

Answers

Mehmet

How often do you go shopping?	About once a week.
What do you spend most money on?	Food, clothes, CDs
How often do you buy clothes?	Every week
How often do you buy things for the home?	Every few months
Which items you buy are necessities?	Food, clothes, a newspaper
How often do you buy presents for other people?	Only on special occasions
Which do you prefer to use, cash, credit cards or cheques?	Cash and credit cards for large items
Do you ever borrow money from friends or from a bank?	Only a little from friends
Do you try to save money?	Usually spends money straightaway

Nanthapa

How often do you go shopping?	Every day
What do you spend most money on?	Food, clothes
How often do you buy clothes?	Occasionally
How often do you buy things for the home?	Not often
Which items you buy are necessities?	Only food
How often do you buy presents for other people?	Quite often
Which do you prefer to use, cash, credit cards or cheques?	Cash
Do you ever borrow money from friends or from a bank?	No
Do you try to save money?	Yes, but it's difficult

4 Aim: to check detailed comprehension; to provide an opportunity for a second listening.
● Ask the students to complete these sentences in pairs.

Answers
1 Nanthapa buys food every day at the market because **you know that it is really fresh**.
2 Mehmet thinks clothes are a necessity if **you buy them because you need them**.
3 Nanthapa buys presents if **she is going to someone's house**.
4 Mehmet would never ask a friend **to lend him a lot of money**.
5 Nanthapa thinks saving money is **very difficult**.
6 Mehmet usually spends money **as soon as he's earned it**.

SPEAKING AND WRITING

1 Aim: to practise writing.
● Ask the students to work in groups of three or four, and to write a questionnaire about people's shopping habits. They can use the questionnaire in this lesson as the basis for their own, but they should try and add at least five more questions.

2 Aim: to practise speaking.
● The students should use their questionnaire to interview each other about their shopping habits.

3 Aim: to practise writing a report.
● Ask the students to give their feedback to the whole class.

● Ask the students to write a report about the other students' shopping habits. Find out if anyone enjoys shopping very much. You may like to ask the students to do this writing activity for homework.

LISTENING AND SPEAKING

1 You are going to hear two people talking about shopping. First, look at this questionnaire, which is about shopping habits. What do you think the title *Were you born to shop?* means?

Were you born to shop?	Mehmet	Nanthapa
How often do you go shopping?		
What do you spend most money on?		
How often do you buy clothes?		
How often do you buy things for the home?		
Which items you buy are necessities?		
How often do you buy presents for other people?		
Which do you prefer to use, cash, credit cards or cheques?		
Do you ever borrow money from friends or from a bank?		
Do you try to save any money?		

2 🔲 Work in pairs.
Student A: Turn to Communication activity 3 on page 93.
Student B: Turn to Communication activity 7 on page 94.

3 Work together and complete the chart.

4 🔲 Listen again and complete these sentences with suitable words or phrases.

1 Nanthapa buys food every day at the market because _____.
2 Mehmet thinks clothes are a necessity if _____.
3 Nanthapa buys presents if _____.
4 Mehmet would never ask a friend _____.
5 Nanthapa thinks saving money is _____.
6 Mehmet usually spends money _____.

SPEAKING AND WRITING

1 Work in groups of three. Write a questionnaire to find out about other people's shopping habits. You can use some of the questions in *Listening and speaking* activity 1 but try to add at least five more questions.

2 Each member of the group should go around the class and interview different people using your questionnaire. Make notes of their replies.

3 In your groups, share the answers you have got and use the information to write a report on other students' shopping habits.

Do you think anyone you interviewed was 'born to shop'?

18 | *Trends*

Future continuous and future perfect

READING AND SPEAKING

1 Work in pairs. You're going to read an article called *Growing trends* which is about life in the future. Here are the topic sentences taken from four of the paragraphs. Discuss what you think each paragraph will say.

1 In the 21st century we will almost certainly be living in a warmer world.

2 In the 21st century most families will be using computers in the home to do a wide variety of tasks.

3 By the 21st century a population explosion will have taken place in the developing world.

4 Statistics show that society is becoming more violent.

Now read the passage and check if you were correct.

2 Answer these questions and try and guess the meanings of the words and phrases in italic.

1 *…sketched in outline…* – Does this mean *described in detail* or *in general terms*?

2 *The vast bulk of the technology…* – Is this likely to mean the *majority* or the *minority*?

3 *A population explosion…* – Is this likely to mean an *increase* or a *decrease*?

4 *…will have stabilised…* – Does this mean *will have continued to change* or *will have stopped changing*?

3 Here are some suggestions to help you survive the 21st century. Match each suggestion with one of the predictions in the text.

1 Don't fear technology or become a slave to it. It's more important to learn what technology can do for you than to understand how it is done.

2 Do your best to conserve energy.

3 Buy sun-hats and sun-cream and teach children to keep out of the sun.

4 Start talks with neighbours about hiring private security guards.

5 Take out a private pension plan so that you are not dependent on the government when you are older.

6 Travel as much as you can now. With decreasing fuel supplies it may not be possible when you are older.

4 Work in pairs and discuss what you think about these suggestions. Are there any that you don't agree with? Now work with another pair and compare your ideas.

Growing trends

What will our world be like in the next century? Scientists today are analysing statistics that show how the world has changed in previous years and using them to try to predict the future. They want to know what sort of jobs we will be doing, what technology we will be using in our daily lives, what kind of homes we will be living in and what our world will look like in the 21st century.

  We have sketched in outline some of the growing trends and the scientists' predictions below.

The environment In the 21st century we will almost certainly be living in a warmer world. The world will continue to use fossil fuels which release carbon dioxide, the main cause of global warming.

  Damage done to the ozone layer by man-made chemicals will mean that our children will have an increased risk of developing skin cancer.

  We will be living in a world with less energy available and we will be forced to reduce our energy consumption.

Technology In the 21st century most families will be using computers in the home to do a wide variety of tasks. The vast bulk of the technology we will be using a generation from now already exists in some form. Over 3 million British households have personal computers today and a further 650,000 are expected to acquire them in the next year. In 25 years' time computers will be a million times faster than they are today and will work in a way that resembles the human brain. They will have become easier to use, but anyone who has not learnt how to use the new technology will be seriously disadvantaged, particularly in the field of employment.

18
GENERAL COMMENTS

Future perfect and continuous

Apart from those presented in the grammar box, there are some other uses of these two tenses. Both can be used to make predictions or deductions about present activities, for example, *It's after five so he'll have left work and he'll be driving home right now.* Like other progressive forms, the future continuous can also be used to distance the speaker. For example, *Will you be going to Britain for your holidays?* sounds more casual and polite than *Are you going to Britain for you holidays?* which may sound rather direct or inquisitive.

Mother tongue

Fifteen or twenty years ago, the 'direct method' of language teaching suggested that the mother tongue should never be used. However, these days there is a feeling that the mother tongue has an important role to play in the language class and as long as the students are dissuaded from the notion that every word has a direct translation, they should not be discouraged from using it. If you are also able to speak the mother tongue of some or all of the students, there is no reason not to do so in the interests of helping them to understand certain points, particularly grammar, quickly and efficiently.

READING AND SPEAKING

1 Aim: to focus on topic sentences; to prepare for reading.

● Remind the students that they first saw topic sentences in Lesson 3. Ask them to say what a topic sentence is. Remind them that topic sentences not only will help them to understand a passage, but also will help them to structure their compositions effectively.

● Ask the students to read the topic sentences and to discuss what they think the rest of the paragraph is about.

● Ask the students to read the passage and to see if they guessed correctly.

2 Aim: to deal with unfamiliar phrases.

● These phrases may get in the way of the students' overall comprehension of the passage. Ask them to try and guess what the phrases mean. Encourage them to look at the phrases in context.

Answers
1 in general terms
2 majority
3 increase
4 will have stopped changing

3 Aim: to read for specific information.

● Ask the students to match the suggestions with a prediction or issue in the passage.

Answers
1 Technology
2 The environment
3 The environment
4 Society
5 Population
6 The environment

4 Aim: to practise speaking.

● Ask the students to discuss the suggestions in pairs. Find out if there are any suggestions the students don't agree with.

GRAMMAR

1 **Aim: to focus on the formation of the future perfect and future continuous tense.**

● Ask the students to look at the examples of these tenses and to say how they are formed.

> **Answers**
> **future perfect:** *will have* + past participle
> **future continuous:** *will be* + present participle

2 **Aim: to focus on the difference between the future perfect and future continuous tense.**

● Ask the students to complete the sentences with a suitable tense. You may like to do this orally with the whole class.

> **Answers**
> 1 **Will you be going** to the energy conference next week?
> 2 This time next week **I'll be flying** to Switzerland.
> 3 I can't give you the report on Sunday because I **won't have finished** it by then.
> 4 It's after six o'clock so he **will have finished** work by now.
> 5 He didn't sleep last night. If he doesn't sleep tonight, he **won't have slept** for two nights.
> 6 When I am going to bed in London, they **will be getting** up in Australia.

3 **Aim: to focus on the uses of the future perfect and future continuous tense.**

● This inductive work is designed to encourage the students to look back at the grammar box and use the information there to explain why a particular tense has been chosen.

> **Answers**
> 1 polite enquiry
> 2 something in progress at a particular time
> 3 something which won't be completed by a specific time
> 4 something which will be completed
> 5 something which won't have happened by a specific time
> 6 something which is part of routine

4 **Aim: to practise using the future perfect and future continuous tense.**

● Ask the students to use the information about growing trends to make predictions about the future in 10 years' time. Go round and check everyone is using a suitable tense.

WRITING AND SPEAKING

Aim: to practise writing predictions.

● Ask the students to compare the trends in Britain in *Grammar* activity 4 with those in their own countries. Are there trends in Britain which have not occurred at all in their countries?

● Ask the students to write some predictions about trends in their own country.

● In groups, ask the students to write ten pieces of advice to help people survive the 21st century.

GRAMMAR

> **Future continuous and future perfect**
>
> **You use the future continuous:**
> – to talk about something which will be in progress at a particular time in the future.
> *We **will** almost certainly **be living** in a warmer world.*
> – to talk about something which is already planned or is part of a routine.
> *In the 21st century most families **will be using** computers in the home.*
> – to ask politely about someone's plans.
> ***Will you be taking** care of the older members of your family?*
> **You use the future perfect to talk about something which will be completed by a specific time in the future.**
> *The proportion of older people **will have increased** dramatically.*

1 Look at the examples of the future continuous and future perfect in the text. How do you form these tenses?

2 Complete these sentences with a future continuous or future perfect form of the verb in brackets.

1 ____ (go) you to the energy conference next week?
2 This time next week I ____ (fly) to Switzerland.
3 I can't give you the report on Sunday because I ____ (not finish) it by then.
4 It's after six o'clock so he ____ (finish) work by now.
5 He didn't sleep last night. If he doesn't sleep tonight, he ____ (not sleep) for two nights.
6 When I am going to bed in London, they ____ (get) up in Australia.

1 Will you be going to the energy conference next week?

3 Use the information in the grammar box to describe the uses of the future continuous or future perfect in the sentences in 2.

4 Here are some growing trends in Britain.
Work in pairs and make predictions.

1 In 1995 one person in three uses a mobile telephone.
2 Two million people in Britain now use telephone banking services.
3 Forty-eight per cent of householders own the house they are living in.
4 People today live on average two years longer than they did 20 years ago.
5 People are spending 80% more money than they did in 1971.

1 In the future more and more people will be using mobile telephones.

WRITING AND SPEAKING

Work in groups of three or four. Are the trends in *Grammar* activity 4 similar in your country? Write some predictions about life in the future in your country. Try to use the future continuous and future perfect forms.

Now write ten pieces of advice to help you survive the 21st century.

Population By the 21st century a population explosion will have taken place in the developing world. In developed countries, the size of the population will have stabilised but the proportion of older people will have increased dramatically and there will be problems associated with care of the elderly and increasing pressure on the medical services. It may no longer be possible for the government to provide pensions for everybody.

Society Statistics show that society is becoming more violent. 95% of Britons think that it is unsafe to walk the streets at night; 85% believe that it used to be safe 30 years ago. The average person's risk of becoming a victim of violent crime has trebled since 1979.

This trend will almost certainly continue. Rising crime will be one of the main problems that people in the 21st century will have to deal with.

Future in the past

VOCABULARY

1 Work in pairs. Complete the sentences below with words from the box. There may be more than one answer.

> parliament   general election
> the opposition   candidate
> constituency   policy   referendum
> senate   vote for   politician   mayor
> president   prime minister   minister
> ministry   deputy   councillor
> Member of Parliament (MP)
> assembly   elect   government

1 The main party in power forms the ____.
2 A ____ is an election about a specific policy of the government.
3 A ____ is an opportunity for voters to elect a new government.
4 The ____ is the district or region which an MP represents.
5 The ____ is the head of government.
6 A ____ is someone who is elected to the city or local government.
7 The ____ is the group of people elected to make or change laws.
8 A ____ is the head of the city or local government.
9 In an election you ____ the person you want to represent your constituency.
10 In a country's parliament, the ____ refers to the politicians who are not in government.

2 Which words in the box can you use to talk about the political system in your country?

We don't have a prime minister but we have a president.

LISTENING

1 🔲 You're going to hear a radio interview with Geraldine Faulkes, a politician. She is talking about future trends and her party's policies if it wins the general election. Listen and tick (✓) the points below which she mentions.

falling unemployment ☐	rising trade surplus ☐
greater provision for healthcare ☐	more money for foreign aid ☐
lower interest rates ☐	closer links with Europe ☐
reduction in income tax ☐	more action on global warming ☐
lower rate of inflation ☐	more action on poverty ☐
reduction in mortgage relief ☐	more money for medical research ☐

2 Work in pairs. Can you remember what Geraldine Faulkes actually said about the points you ticked?

3 🔲 Listen again and check your answers to 1 and 2.

4 Complete the sentences with suitable words or phrases from the interview.

1 Five years ago Geraldine Faulkes said she was going to spend more money on ____.
2 The hospitals are understaffed because ____.
3 The Conservative Party has reduced government spending on ____.
4 Part of the government's increased spending on healthcare would go towards ____.
5 Geraldine Faulkes thinks people are happier if they ____.

VOCABULARY

1 Aim: to present the words in the vocabulary box.
The words in the vocabulary box belong to the vocabulary field of politics. Ask the students to use them to complete the sentences.

Answers
1 The main party in power forms the **government**.
2 A **referendum** is an election about a specific policy of the government.
3 A **general election** is an opportunity for voters to elect a new government.
4 The **constituency** is the district or region which an MP represents.
5 The **prime minister** is the head of government.
6 A **councillor** is someone who is elected to the city or local government.
7 The **assembly/senate** is the group of people elected to make or change laws.
8 A **mayor** is the head of the city or local government.
9 In an election you **elect** the person you want to represent your constituency.
10 In a country's parliament, the **opposition** refers to the politicians who are not in government.

2 Aim: to practise using the words in the vocabulary box.
● Ask the students to talk about the political system in their own countries. Which words can they use to describe it?

LISTENING

1 Aim: to listen for main ideas.
● Ask the students to read through the trends. They represent a simplification of what the politician says.

● 🔲 Play the tape and ask the students to tick the trends the politician mentions.

Answers
falling unemployment ✓
greater provision for healthcare ✓
lower interest rates ✓
reduction in income tax ✓
closer links with Europe ✓
more action on poverty ✓
more money for medical research ✓

2 Aim: to check comprehension; to prepare for presenting the target structures.
● Ask the students to work in pairs and try and remember what the politician actually said.

3 Aim: to check comprehension; to provide an opportunity for a second listening.
● 🔲 Play the tape again and ask the students to check their answers to 1 and 2. You may like to stop the tape every so often to check everyone has understood.

4 Aim: to check comprehension.
● Ask the students to complete the sentences with a few words from the interview.

Answers
1 Five years ago Geraldine Faulkes said she was going to spend more money on **healthcare**.
2 The hospitals are understaffed because **there isn't enough money to pay the doctors and nurses**.
3 The Conservative Party has reduced government spending on **healthcare**.
4 Part of the government's increased spending on healthcare would go towards **medical research**.
5 Geraldine Faulkes thinks people are happier if they **earn their own money**.

GRAMMAR

1 Aim: to present the future in the past.
- Ask the students to look at the information in the grammar box and then to do the exercises.

- Refer the students back to *Listening* activity 2 when they talked about what Geraldine Faulkes actually said. Ask them to write sentences using a future in the past structure of the politician's broken promises.

2 Aim: to practise using the future in the past.
- Ask the students to match the beginnings and endings of the sentences.

> **Answers**
> 1 e 2 c 3 a 4 b 5 d

3 Aim: to practise using the future in the past.
- Think of something you were going to do in the past, but didn't. Write what you were going to do on the board, and then ask the students to guess what you did instead, and why.

- Ask the students to write sentences describing things they were going to do, but didn't. Make sure they include the reasons why they didn't do them.

SOUNDS

1 Aim: to focus on shifting word stress.
- The words in this exercise are common nouns and verbs, which are spelt the same, but have a different word stress depending on the part of speech. Ask the students to predict where the stress goes in each word. Do this orally with the whole class.

2 Aim: to focus on shifting word stress.
- Play the tape and ask the students to listen and check.

> **Answers**
> to pre<u>side</u> – the <u>pres</u>ident
> to op<u>pose</u> – the oppo<u>sit</u>ion
> to re<u>cord</u> – the <u>rec</u>ord
> to <u>anal</u>yse – the ana<u>lys</u>is
> to <u>constitute</u> – the consti<u>tu</u>ency
> to ex<u>plain</u> – the expla<u>na</u>tion
> to e<u>xam</u>ine – the exami<u>na</u>tion
> to e<u>con</u>omise – econo<u>mic</u>

WRITING

1 Aim: to focus on attitude words and phrases.
- Ask the students to look at the attitude words and phrases often used in discussions. Make sure that they understand them all. Draw attention to any 'false friends' such as *eventually, actually*.

- Ask the students to complete the sentences using the words and phrases. There may be more than one possibility.

> **Answers**
> 1 It took many years but **eventually** they got to the moon.
> 2 He had a white coat on so **presumably** he was a scientist.
> 3 **Personally**, I think the next century will be very interesting.
> 4 **Hopefully**, in the future life will be better for everyone.
> 5 He said class sizes would get smaller. **On the contrary**, I said, they'll get bigger.
> 6 He lost his job, but **fortunately**, found another one immediately.

2 Aim: to practise writing.
- Ask the students to write a composition with the title *The 21st century: for better or for worse.* Ask the students to look back at the passage on page 78 if they need help with this activity. You may like to ask the students to do this activity for homework.

GRAMMAR

> **Future in the past**
> **You can use** *was/were going to* **+ infinitive to talk about something that was planned or promised for the future at some point in the past but which didn't happen.**
> *You* **were going to lower** *taxes five years ago but you didn't.*

1 Look at your answers to *Listening* activity 2 and write sentences describing the government's broken promises. Use a future in the past structure.

2 Match the two parts of these sentences.

1 The prime minister was going to call an election in two years' time...
2 The government was going to reduce taxes in 1995...
3 Parliament was going to take three months' holiday...
4 The council was going to ban all traffic in the city...
5 The referendum was going to be a vote on economic policy...

a but the government recalled it because of the war.
b so why did they let the buses go through the centre?
c but it spent too much during 1994.
d so why did the government ignore the result?
e but he lost his majority, so he had to hold it sooner.

3 Think of things you had planned to do last month but didn't. Explain why you didn't do them.

SOUNDS

1 Some words change their stress when they change their part of speech. Underline the stressed syllable in these words.

to preside	the president
to oppose	the opposition
to record	the record
to analyse	the analysis
to constitute	the constituency
to explain	the explanation
to examine	the examination
to economise	economic

2 🔲 Listen and check. As you listen, say the words aloud.

WRITING

1 Look at these words and phrases often used in discussions and use them to complete the sentences below.

To express an opinion.	*personally, in my opinion*
To contradict someone.	*on the contrary*
To express something obvious.	*obviously, actually*
To make an assumption.	*presumably, I suppose*
To express a wish for the future.	*hopefully*
To describe an outcome.	*eventually, as a result*
To sum up (very formal).	*in conclusion, to sum up*
To say how it appears.	*apparently, evidently*
To express a happy outcome.	*luckily, fortunately*

1 It took many years but ____ they got to the moon.
2 He had a white coat on so ____ he was a scientist.
3 ____, I think the next century will be very interesting.
4 ____, in the future life will be better for everyone.
5 He said class sizes would get smaller ____, I said, they'll get bigger.
6 He lost his job, but ____, found another one immediately.

2 Work in pairs. Write a composition with the title *The 21st century: for better or worse.*

Start by saying if people are optimistic or pessimistic about the future.
Many people are looking forward to the 21st century.

Continue the paragraph with extra information and examples.
They think the world will be a better place than it was at the beginning of the 20th century.

Begin a new paragraph with a topic sentence presenting an opposite view.
However, there are many who are nervous about their future.

Continue the paragraph with extra information.
They expect a drop in standards of living, greater unemployment and generally have little confidence in the government.

Finish the composition with a new paragraph, starting with a topic sentence which states your conclusion.
But in my opinion, the future looks good.

State your reasons.
We'll be enjoying greater security and we will also have found the cure for many unpleasant diseases.

Passive constructions with *say*, *believe*

The legend of King Arthur and the Knights of the Round Table is well-known. It is said that the young Arthur pulled out the sword Excalibur from a stone, which no one except the next king could do. It was thought that Camelot was the ideal court, famous for bravery, chivalry, romantic love and magic, which was practised by Merlin, the wizard. Here, at a round table – round so that no one could be said to be above anyone else – sat the bravest and most noble Knights in the land, Sir Galahad, Sir Lancelot, Sir Bedivere and others.

But England and Arthur began to lose power when Arthur learned about the love affair between his wife, Guinevere, and his best friend, Sir Lancelot. Then Arthur began the search for the Holy Grail (the wine cup used at Christ's last meal), which Sir Galahad finally found and brought back. Arthur grew strong again and he went into battle to save England from his evil cousin Mordred, whom he killed. But Arthur himself was seriously wounded in the great battle. Knowing that he was dying, he ordered Sir Bedivere to throw his sword Excalibur into a lake. The hand of the Lady of the Lake came out of the water, caught the sword, and took it under. Then three mysterious women arrived on a boat and took Arthur to his final resting place at Avalon. It is believed that Arthur and his Knights are not dead but merely sleeping and that they will return if England is ever in danger again.

Did Arthur really exist? It is said by some people that he may have been a Celtic leader of the 6th or 7th century. It is claimed by some that many of the stories of the Arthurian legend were invented by Geoffrey of Monmouth. But it is believed by others that Arthur really existed, and there are many places in Britain which claim to have connections with the story or to be the actual site of Camelot. Perhaps we will never know – unless England is in trouble and Arthur reappears with his Knights to rescue it from danger.

19

GENERAL COMMENTS

English outside the classroom

This might be a good occasion to make a list of all the places in your town or city where your students can read or hear English. It's surprising that examples of English can be found even in places which are far from English-speaking countries. Ask your students if they can see or hear English in the following places or through the following means of communication:

local airport, local railway station, radio, television, tourist information office, tourist sites, video films, newspapers, books, cinemas, magazines, supermarkets.

You can find English in many surprising places, such as on T-shirts or on clothes labels (*made in France, wool* etc). Encourage your students to go out and find examples of English around them.

READING

1 **Aim: to introduce the theme of the lesson; to prepare for reading.**

● Tell the students that the theme of the lesson is famous legends in Britain. Check that everyone understands that a legend is a story about some person or event in the past. Very often a legend is part of a tradition of storytelling. Ask students to suggest legends from their own countries, but don't spend too much time on this, as they will have more opportunity to talk about these later in the lesson.

Ask the students if they have ever heard of the Legend of King Arthur. Ask them to write down four or five questions they would like the passage to answer. Encourage them to look at the illustration to help them.

2 Aim: to read for main ideas.
- Ask the students to read the passage and to choose the best title for it.

> **Possible answer**
> King Arthur: fact or myth

- Did the passage answer any of the questions they wrote in 1?

3 Aim: to read for specific information.
- Ask the students to reread the passage and to write down who or what the people, places and things are in the legends.

> **Answers**
> 1 Excalibur was Arthur's sword.
> 2 Camelot was where his court was.
> 3 Merlin was the magician.
> 4 Sir Lancelot was Arthur's best friend.
> 5 Mordred was Arthur's cousin.
> 6 Avalon was where Arthur was buried.

4 Aim: to practise speaking; to read for specific information.
- This is a jigsaw reading and information exchange activity. Ask the students to turn to the relevant Communication activities. When they are ready, they should tell their partner what they have read.

5 Aim: to check comprehension.
- Ask the students to discuss the questions in pairs.

- Check the answers to these questions with the whole class.

> **Answers**
> 1 Because it wasn't built until later.
> 2 Because it brings good luck – and tourists.
> 3 Because Merlin's Oak was cut down, but Carmarthen remains.

GRAMMAR

1 Aim: to present passive constructions.
- Ask the students to read the information in the grammar box and then to do the exercises.

- Ask the students to explain the difference between the two sentences.

> **Answers**
> Sentences 1a and 2a are presented factually.
> Sentences 1b and 2b suggest the speaker is not sure of the truth of the statements.

2 Aim: to focus on more passive constructions.
- Ask the students to read both passages in the Communication activities and underline the words which can be used with passive constructions.

3 Aim: to focus on passive constuctions.
- Ask the students to rewrite the sentences, or to rephrase them orally.

> **Answers**
> 1 **It is said** that Arthur was born in Tintagel.
> 2 **It is believed** that Arthur pulled a sword out of a stone and became king.
> 3 **It is reported** that monks found Arthur and Guinevere's remains.
> 4 **It is understood** that Arthur is buried at Glastonbury.
> 5 **It was expected** that Carmarthen would be destroyed if they cut down Merlin's Oak.
> 6 **It is said** that Arthur will return if England is in danger again.

SPEAKING

1 Aim: to practise speaking.
- Ask the students to talk about legends from their countries. They will have the opportunity to write about them at the end of this lesson.

2 Aim: to practise speaking.
- Hold a class discussion about legends. Do people believe that these legends actually took place? Has anyone heard of them before?

READING

1 Work in pairs. This lesson is about *Legendary Britain.* You are going to read a passage about the legend of King Arthur and the Knights of the Round Table. Have you ever heard of this legend? If so, what do you know about it? Write four or five questions which you would like the passage to answer. Use the illustration to help you.

2 Read the passage and choose the best title.

1 Camelot
2 King Arthur: fact or myth
3 Celtic leaders of the Middle Ages
4 Arthur and Guinevere: a love story

3 Work in pairs. Explain what part the following people, places or things play in the legend.

– Excalibur   – Camelot   – Merlin
– Sir Lancelot – Mordred   – Avalon

4 Work in pairs. You are going to read some more about the Arthurian legend.

Student A: Turn to Communication activity 12 on page 94.
Student B: Turn to Communication activity 18 on page 96.

Now tell each other about the passage you've just read.

5 Work with the same partner and answer these questions.

1 Why is it unlikely that Arthur was born in Tintagel Castle?
2 Why are so many places in England keen to be connected to the legend of King Arthur?
3 Was it true that Carmarthen would be destroyed if Merlin's Oak was cut down? How do you know?

GRAMMAR

> **Passive constructions with *say, believe***
> **You can use the following passive constructions with *say, believe* etc. to show that you're not sure of the truth of the statement or that you want to distance yourself from it.**
> ***It* + passive + *that* clause**
> ***It is said that** Arthur pulled out Excalibur from a stone.*
> ***It is believed that** the Holy Grail was the wine cup at Christ's last meal.*

1 Look at the sentences below. In which sentence is the speaker distanced from the information?

1 a Arthur was a Celtic leader of the 6th or 7th century.
 b It is said that Arthur was to have been a Celtic leader of the 6th or 7th century.
2 a Arthur will reappear when England is in trouble.
 b It is believed that Arthur will reappear when England is in trouble.

2 Underline the passive constructions in the passage in the Communication activities. Add to the list of verbs in the grammar box that you can use these passive constructions with.

3 Rewrite the following sentences using *it* and a suitable passive construction.

1 Arthur was born in Tintagel.
2 Arthur pulled a sword out of a stone and became king.
3 Monks found Arthur and Guinevere's remains.
4 Arthur was buried at Glastonbury.
5 Carmarthen will be destroyed if they cut down Merlin's Oak.
6 Arthur will return if England is in danger again.

1 It is said that Arthur was born in Tintagel.

SPEAKING

1 Work in pairs. Can you think of any well-known legends about people or places in your country? Talk about:

– who the person was
– if he or she really lived
– what he or she is famous for
– where the legend takes place
– what happened

2 Tell your legends to the rest of the class. Has anyone heard of them before? Are any of the legends similar?

**Speculating about the past: *may have,
might have, must have, can't have***

VOCABULARY AND LISTENING

1 You're going to hear Stephen talking about the following legendary places in Britain.

1 Stonehenge   2 Sherwood Forest
3 Lyonesse   4 Holy Island

Each place is famous for one of the following features or characters.

a monastery   standing stones
drowned land   Robin Hood

Match the places with the feature or character.
Look at the pictures to help you.

2 Look at the pictures and decide which of the legendary places in 1 you think these words could be used to describe.

drowned tide stone Christianity float mainland
alien outlaw knight raider earthquake saint
sunworshipping tidal wave rock bell spire band
outer space raft drag log windswept castle

3 🔊 Listen and find out what the legend about each place is. Write a sentence describing the place and the legend.

4 🔊 Work in pairs. Listen again and take notes on the legends. Find the answers to the following questions.

1 What caused Lyonesse to sink under the sea?
2 What can you hear on certain days?
3 Why was Robin Hood popular with local people?
4 Why is it not certain that Robin Hood existed?
5 Why do some people think aliens from outer space helped to build Stonehenge?
6 Why is it thought that Stonehenge was built as a temple for worshipping the sun?
7 Why did St Aidan build a monastery on Holy Island?
8 Why was Lindisfarne Castle built?

5 Work in pairs. Decide which of the following statements are true.

1 The Scilly Isles can't always have been islands because Lyonesse joined them to the mainland.
2 Robin Hood must have lived in Sherwood Forest at some time.
3 Stonehenge can't have been built from local stone.
4 Christianity must have arrived in England many years before St Aidan.

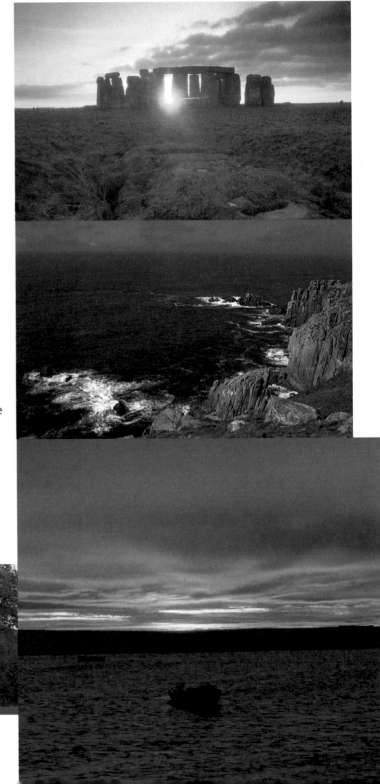

VOCABULARY AND LISTENING

1 Aim: to prepare for listening.

● Ask the students if the photos show places which look like places in their own countries. Ask them why or why not.

● Ask the students to look at the photos and match each of the four places with one of the features or characters listed.

Answers
1 Stonehenge – standing stones
2 Sherwood Forest – Robin Hood
3 Lyonesse – drowned land
4 Holy Island –a monastery

2 Aim: to present the words in the vocabulary box.

● Ask the students to match the words with the legendary places in 1.

Answers
Stonehenge: stone, outer space, rafts, alien, logs, drag, sunworshipping, float
Sherwood Forest: outlaw, band
Holy Island: Christianity, tide, mainland, raider, saint, castle, windswept
Lyonesse: drowned, mainland, knight, earthquake, tidal wave, bell, rock, spire

3 Aim: to listen for main ideas.

● 🔲 The work on describing the photos in 1 will have prepared the students for this activity.

● Ask the students to find out what the legend about each place is. When they have finished, ask them to write a sentence describing each legend. They can do this activity in pairs.

4 Aim: to provide an opportunity for a second listening; to practise note-taking.

● 🔲 Ask the students to read the questions. Remind students that note-taking while listening is a difficult skill, but one which will be useful at higher levels.

Answers
1 An earthquake and a tidal wave.
2 The bells of the churches ringing from under the sea.
3 Robin Hood stole money from the rich to give to the poor.
4 The character of Robin Hood may have come from a number of different people.
5 Because the stones had to be carried so far.
6 Because on 21st June each year the sun rises directly above a line drawn by the most important stones.
7 To establish a base for his mission to introduce Christianity.
8 To protect the island from the Scots.

5 Aim: to check comprehension; to present the target structures.

● Ask the students whether the statements are true or false.

Answers
1 True   2 True   3 True   4 False

GRAMMAR AND FUNCTIONS

1 Aim: to present ways of speculating about the past; to focus on the difference between *may have, must have, might have* **and** *can't have.*

● Ask students to read the information in the grammar and function box and then to do the exercises.

> **Answers**
> a It's possible that he lived there.
> b It's probable or certain that he lived there.
> c It's possible that he lived there.
> d It's probable or certain that he didn't live there.
>
> Sentences a and c mean the same.

2 Aim: to practise using *may have, must have, might have* **and** *can't have.*

● Ask the students to write sentences drawing conclusions.

> **Answers**
> 1 He **must have** had an accident.
> 2 She **may have** heard some bad news.
> 3 He **must have** seen something frightening.
> 4 It **might have** been the wind.
> 5 She **can't have** slept at all last night.
> 6 He **must have** enjoyed it.

SOUNDS

1 Aim: to focus on word stress in sentences.

● Ask the students to underline the words which are likely to be stressed.

● 🔲 Play the tape and ask the students to listen and check.

> **Answers**
> A It <u>must</u> have been the <u>monster</u>. It was <u>only</u> a few <u>metres away</u>.
> B No, it <u>can't</u> have been. You <u>must</u> have <u>imagined</u> it.
> A It <u>might</u> have <u>crossed</u> the <u>lake</u>. <u>Where's</u> your <u>camera?</u>
> B I <u>don't</u> have any <u>film</u>. It <u>could</u> have been a big <u>fish</u>.
> A But it <u>must</u> have been at <u>least</u> four metres <u>long</u>.

2 Aim: to focus on word stress; to practise speaking.

● Ask students to act out the dialogue paying particular attention to the weak pronunciation of /həv/.

WRITING

1 Aim: to practise writing.

● Explain that the students are going to prepare a regional, national or international guide to legendary people or places. Ask the students to work on their own and to think of a legendary person or place from their own country. If there are others from their own country, ask them to check they have not chosen the same legend. Ask the students to write notes about the legend they have chosen.

2 Aim: to practise writing.

● Ask the students to turn the notes they have written in 1 into a paragraph.

3 Aim: to practise writing.

● Ask the students to exchange paragraphs and to read their partner's legend. They should write questions about the legend they have just read.

4 Aim: to practise writing.

● Ask the students to think of answers to the questions their partners have just written about their legend. They should rewrite the legend incorporating the answers to the questions. You may like to ask the students to do this activity for homework.

5 Aim: to practise speaking.

● If you have a map of the world or of the country where you're working, it would be nice to put the legends on or near the places to which they refer.

GRAMMAR AND FUNCTIONS

> Speculating about the past: *may have*, *might have*, *must have*, *can't have*
>
> You can use past modal verbs to speculate about the past and draw logical conclusions based on known facts.
>
> You can use *may have* or *might have* to talk about something which possibly happened or was true in the past.
>
> You use *must have* to talk about something which probably/certainly happened or was true in the past.
>
> You use *can't have* to talk about something which probably/certainly didn't happen or was not true in the past.
>
> You can also use the main verb in its continuous form with past modals.

1 Look at these sentences and explain the difference between them. Which mean the same?

a Robin Hood may have lived in Sherwood Forest.
b Robin Hood must have lived in Sherwood Forest.
c Robin Hood might have lived in Sherwood Forest.
d Robin Hood can't have lived in Sherwood Forest.

2 Write sentences drawing conclusions about what *must have*, *might have* or *can't have* happened.

1 His car is wrecked.
2 She's crying.
3 He looks terrified.
4 I'm sure I heard a strange noise outside.
5 She seems tired.
6 He's still laughing about the film last night.

1 His car is wrecked. He must have had an accident.

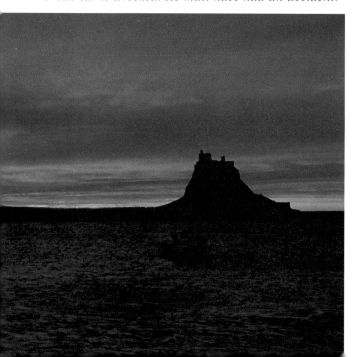

SOUNDS

1 Underline the words which are likely to be stressed in this dialogue.

A It must have been the Loch Ness monster. It was only a few metres away.
B No, it can't have been. You must have imagined it.
A It might have crossed the lake. Where's your camera?
B I don't have any film. It could have been a big fish.
A But it must have been at least four metres long.

Now listen and check.

2 Work in pairs and act out the dialogue.

WRITING

1 You are going to prepare a guide to legendary people or places in your country, or around the world. Working on your own, choose a legend and write notes about it. Make sure you all choose different legends.

The Lorelei maiden – sings on the Lorelei Rock to attract sailors...

2 Use your notes to write a paragraph about the legend.

It is said that the Lorelei maiden sings on the Lorelei Rock to attract sailors...

3 Work in pairs. Give your partner the paragraph you wrote in 2 and read the paragraph he/she gives you. Read it and write questions concerning details which you would like to know more about.

Where's the Lorelei Rock?

Then pass the notes and your questions back to your partner.

4 Rewrite your paragraph including the answers to the questions your partner asked in 3, if possible.

It is said that the Lorelei maiden sings on the Lorelei Rock, which is on the River Rhine in Germany, to attract sailors.

5 With the whole class, draw a rough map of the world or the country where your legend takes place. Put your paragraph by the town or country where the legend took place.

20 | *The real thing?*

Reported speech

SPEAKING AND LISTENING

1 This lesson is about advertising. First, check that you know what the word *brand* means.

2 Look at the well-known brand names. Which ones do you recognise?

What type of product do you associate each brand with?

3 Think about brand names you know from your own and other countries. What values and qualities do they suggest?

4 You are going to hear someone talking about some brands and the image they present. First, look at the list of international brands. Which country do you associate them with?

- ☐ Peugeot
- ☐ Mercedes
- ☐ Heinz
- ☐ Volvo
- ☐ Braun
- ☐ Benetton
- ☐ Chanel
- ☐ Swatch
- ☐ Fiat
- ☐ Kellogg's
- ☐ Gillette
- ☐ Bata
- ☐ Phillips
- ☐ Apple
- ☐ American Express

What type of product do you associate these brands with? Choose from the following.

drinks   food   personal care and pharmaceuticals   cosmetics   fashion
household products   high tech products   motor vehicles
leisure and cultural   credit and retail

5 🔲 Listen to someone talking about three brands. Put a number 1–3 by the brand name and the product in activity 4.

6 Work in pairs. Make notes on what the speaker mentioned about the following aspects of each brand:

– brand name   – product
– image   – appeal

7 Which of the following sentences did the speaker say?

1 'You shouldn't buy a Mercedes because it'll let you down.'
2 'In the past, drivers of Mercedes Benz belonged to all social classes.'
3 'Mercedes now only appeals to rich people.'
4 'Benetton began their advertising campaign by wanting to shock people.'
5 'Benetton appeals to the young consumers who feel they have accepted the world as it is.'
6 'You could only buy Gillette products in America.'
7 'Gillette is a luxury product.'
8 'Gillette has always had the same image.'

8 🔲 Listen again and check your answers to 5, 6 and 7. Are there any details you can add to your notes?

20

GENERAL COMMENTS

Review of *Reward* Upper-intermediate

This may be a good opportunity to ask the students to look back over the 20 lessons in *Reward* Upper-intermediate and ask them to think about what they've learned during their course. Ask them to write a review of their course.

Reported speech

The students will already have come across reported speech in *Reward* Intermediate Lessons 23, 24 and 25, so this lesson's work should be seen as revision for them.

SPEAKING AND LISTENING

1 Aim: to present the theme of the lesson.
- The word *brand* is used a lot in this lesson, so it seems suitable to begin by checking students understand it.

2 Aim: to practise speaking.
- Ask the students if they recognise the famous brand names.
- Ask the students which products they associate each brand with and which country.

3 Aim: to practise speaking.
- Ask the students to think of brands from their own country. Do they know how well these brands are exported around the world? What products are the brands associated with?
- Ask the students to think of values and qualities which the brands suggest. For example, Mercedes Benz – reliability, safety, style, speed. You may want to distinguish between values and qualities which the brands attempt to suggest and the reality.

4 Aim: to practise speaking.
- Most famous brands are associated with the country where they are produced, and indeed, may even add indirectly to the image of the country itself. Ask the students to think of countries associated with the brands.

Answers

Peugeot – France	Benetton – Italy
Gillette – USA	Mercedes – Germany
Chanel – France	Bata – Czechoslovakia
Heinz – USA	Swatch – Switzerland
Phillips – Holland	Volvo – Sweden
Fiat – Italy	Apple – USA
Braun – Germany	Kellogg's – USA
American Express – USA	

- Ask the students which products they associate with the brands.

Answers
Peugeot – motor vehicles Benetton – fashion
Gillette – personal care Mercedes – motor vehicles
Chanel – cosmetics Bata – fashion
Swatch – household products Heinz – food
Phillips – high tech products Volvo – motor vehicles
Fiat – motor vehicles Apple – high tech products
Braun – household products Kellogg's – food
American Express – credit and retail

5 Aim: to listen for main ideas.
- Ask the students to listen and put the number 1 – 3 of each brand by the brand name and product in activity 4.

Answers
1   Mercedes – cars
2   Benetton – fashion products
3   Gillette – personal care

6 Aim: to check comprehension.
- Ask the students to work in pairs and make notes about what the speaker said about the different aspects of each brand.

Answers
Brand name: Mercedes
Product: cars
Image: reliability/safety
Appeal: everyone

Brand name: Benetton
Product: fashion garments
Image: well- made/inexpensive/stylish
Appeal: young people

Brand name: Gillette
Product: personal care
Image: freshness/a love of life
Appeal: the modern man

7 Aim: to check comprehension; to prepare for the presentation of the target structures.
- Ask the students to decide which of the sentences the speaker said.
- Do not correct the students' answers at this stage as they will do this as a writing activity in *Grammar* activity 1.

8 Aim: to listen and take notes; to provide an opportunity for a second listening.
- Ask the students to listen and add to their notes. They should then work together and expand their notes.

GRAMMAR

1 Aim: to focus on reported speech.

● Ask the students to look at the information in the grammar box and then to do the exercises.

● Ask the students to correct the statements in *Speaking and listening* activity 7.

Answers

1 She said that Mercedes was well known for its reliability.
2 She said in the past Mercedes Benz appealed to only the very rich.
3 She said that now Mercedes appeals to people of all incomes and backgrounds.
4 She said that Benetton began their advertising campaign with an international appeal.
5 She said that Benetton appeals to young consumers who feel different and special.
6 She said that Gillette could be bought all over the world.
7 She said that Gillette is an essential product.
8 She said that Gillette has changed its image.

2 Aim: to practise using reported speech.

● Make sure the students make the necessary changes to the times as well as the tenses.

Answers

Last week a woman went into town to do some shopping. A man was standing outside the supermarket handing out small cups of a new soft drink. **He said it would be the best thing she'd ever tasted.** She tried it. **She said it tasted horrible. He said that he didn't like it much either.** She laughed and went into the supermarket. At the cheese counter the woman couldn't decide whether to buy Cheddar or Brie. **She asked the shop assistant which cheese she liked best. The assistant said she thought she should buy some Brie. She said she had had some the week before and it had been delicious.** Next the woman went to get some juice. She wanted orange and they only had pineapple left. **She asked another assistant where she would find the orange juice. But the assistant replied that they had just sold out. She said they would be getting some more the following day but that she had better come early as they were selling out quickly in this hot weather. She suggested that she tried some of the refreshing new soft drink they were advertising outside the store.**

SOUNDS

Aim: to focus on voice pitch and attitude.

● Explain that the words are all to do with voice pitch which can suggest the speaker's mood. Ask the students to see which words they recognise. For the ones they don't recognise, explain what the word means in a way which illustrates its meaning.

● 🔲 Play the tape and ask the students to listen and choose a word which describes how the speaker spoke. Ask them to describe the speaker's attitude.

Answers

1 I want to go home. (groan)
2 I think this is a lovely country. (stammer)
3 I can't go on like this. (shout)
4 What an amazing place! (whisper)
5 What a beautiful morning! (sing)
6 I said I agree with you! (laugh)

● Ask the students to check their answers in pairs. If necessary play the tape again.

VOCABULARY AND LISTENING

1 Aim: to prepare for listening.

● Ask the students if they listen to adverts on the radio. What kind of products or services do they advertise?

● Ask the students what words might be used to advertise the products or services they have just mentioned.

● Ask the students to look at the radio adverts listed. Ask them to predict which words they think will be used to advertise each product.

2 Aim: to listen for main ideas.

● 🔲 Ask the students to listen to the four radio adverts and find out which products are being advertised.

Answers

a concert a car a music CD a film

3 Aim: to present the words in the vocabulary box; to practise speaking.

● Ask the students to look at the words in the vocabulary box. Which words did they hear mentioned in the radio adverts?

● 🔲 Play the tape again and ask the students to listen again and check.

4 Aim: to practise speaking.

● Ask the students to decide for which products they are likely to hear the words in the box not mentioned in the radio adverts.

5 Aim: to extend vocabulary; to practise speaking.

● Ask the students to think of words they might hear for the products listed in the Student's Book.

GRAMMAR

> **Reported speech**
>
> When you put direct speech into reported speech, you usually change:
> – the tense of the verb.
> – adverbs of time and place.
> – the pronouns, unless the speaker is talking about him/herself.
>
> You don't usually make these changes:
> – when the tense of the main reporting verb is in the present tense.
> – if the statement is still true at the time of reporting.
> – if the direct speech contains the modals *may, might, could, should, ought to.*

1 Correct the statements in *Speaking and listening*, activity 7.

She said that Mercedes was well known for its reliability.

2 Rewrite this passage changing the direct speech to reported speech.

Last week a woman went into town to do some shopping. A man was standing outside the supermarket handing out small cups of a new soft drink. He said, 'It'll be the best thing you've ever tasted.' She tried it. 'It tastes horrible,' she said. 'I don't like it much either,' he said. She laughed and went into the supermarket. At the cheese counter the woman couldn't decide whether to buy Cheddar or Brie. 'Which cheese do you like best?' she asked the shop assistant. 'I think you should buy the Brie,' the assistant said. 'I had some last week and it was delicious.' Next the woman went to get some juice. She wanted orange but they only had pineapple left. She asked another assistant, 'Where will I find the orange juice?' But the assistant replied, 'We've just sold out. We'll be getting some more tomorrow, but you'd better come early as we're selling out quickly in this hot weather. You should try some of that refreshing new soft drink they are advertising outside the store.'

SOUNDS

Do these verbs suggest a loud, soft or neutral voice? What would the speaker's mood be?

stammer   laugh   whisper   groan   sing   shout

[cassette] Now listen to the following sentences. Which words can you use to describe the way the speaker speaks?

1 I want to go home.
2 I think this is a lovely country.
3 I can't go on like this.
4 What an amazing place!
5 What a beautiful morning!
6 I said I agree with you!

VOCABULARY AND LISTENING

1 Work in pairs. You're going to hear radio adverts for four of the following products:

– a car   – health insurance
– soap powder   – a music CD
– a concert   – a film

Think of words which you may hear in each advert.

2 [cassette] Listen and number the products in 1 as you hear the advert.

3 Which of the following words did you hear in each advert?

> amazing bright classic colossal essential excellent
> finest gem mad magical miraculous mysterious
> new quiet raving reliable romantic sparkle
> standard surprise star tasty tricky wild wonderful

[cassette] Listen again and check.

4 In which adverts for products are you likely to hear the other words in 3?

5 Think of words you might use in adverts for:

– an airline   – shampoo   – a camera
– a computer   – washing-up liquid

Reporting verbs

SPEAKING

Work in groups of three or four and discuss your answers to these questions.

1 What are the best and the worst adverts in your country at the moment?
2 Where do you see or hear them?
3 Are there any restraints on claims in advertisements in your country?
4 What do you think advertisers should or shouldn't do?

READING

1 You're going to read a passage about global advertising. First, here are some key sentences from the passage. Write the questions which these sentences answer.

1 The idea behind the advertising is that we really are part of some global village.
2 Corporations such as Coca Cola and BA want to be seen as worldly, altruistic giants.
3 Coca Cola's advertising agencies have been able to promote the drink with messages so simple that they can be posted around the world.
4 Simplicity is the key; they are easy to understand, easy to translate.

2 Read the passage and choose the best summary.

1 Coca Cola is one of a number of companies which are involved in global advertising.
2 The main advantage of global advertising is that you spend more money on a single advertisement.
3 Global advertising is about creating a single, simple message which can be used to promote a product around the world.

I'd like to teach the world to sell

Telephone Coca Cola and, while you wait to be put through, the corporation's 'It's the Real Thing' jingle crackles down the line. 'It's the Real Thing' is a global message first used by Coca Cola in the 1940s; its meaning is clear (do not be fooled by lesser imitators) and it is inescapable. It translates perfectly well into Roman, Arabic, Cyrillic script and most other languages and stands for an instantly recognisable product in Brussels, Birmingham, Bali or Bangkok.

This is the advertising technique now being taken up by more and more companies and advertising agencies from British Airways to Benetton as their products reach out around the world. Huge resources are being poured into single advertising campaigns: the recent wave of BA advertisements features a cast of thousands – literally.

The idea behind the advertising is that we really are part of some global village: we all want the same things, we all have access to them and we all respond to the same imagery. Coca Cola sells itself as democratic, international and liberating; no wonder it's good for you.

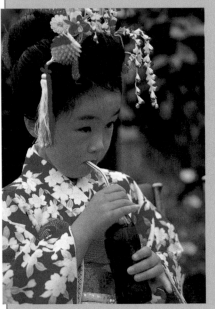

The sub-text might be that corporations such as Coca Cola and BA want to be seen as worldly, altruistic giants, linking the people of the world in one warm and smiling embrace – all the better to sell them things. An added bonus for the company is that they only need their advertising agencies to produce one idea, rather than one for every country. This means the advertisement itself can be more spectacular, without the campaign being more expensive.

The latest BA adverts read exactly this way, as did the 'United Colours of Benetton' ads in their less controversial days – when, rather than seabirds smothered in oil, or scenes of war, their striking images depicted children of different colours wearing different coloured jumpers.

Coca Cola was the first company to break into global advertising. The most memorable of these early international adverts was 'I'd like to teach the world to sing... Coca Cola... the real thing', made in 1971 and reshot in 1989. The ad featured a crowd of young people, ostensibly from all corners of the world, learning to sing the words 'Coca Cola' in perfect harmony while smiling through even more perfect white teeth.

By making just one key, desirable and homogeneous product, Coca Cola's advertising agencies have been able to promote the drink with messages so simple that they can be posted around the world without causing confusion, upset or censure.

Simplicity is the key; they are easy to understand, easy to translate and, after being repeated enough times, become synonymous with the product.　　　Adapted from an article by Jonathan Glancey from *The Independent*

SPEAKING

Aim: to practise speaking.

● The discussion in this section has moved from products and brands to advertising in general. Ask the students to discuss the questions in groups. Ask one student from each group to give feedback on his/her group's discussion to the rest of the class.

READING

1 Aim: to prepare for reading.

● Ask the students what they understand by the term *Global advertising*. Ask them if there are any adverts which could be used in different countries with very few changes apart from translation.

● Ask the students to write questions to which these sentences are the answers.

> **Possible answers**
> 1 What's the idea behind global advertising?
> 2 How do corporations such as Coca Cola and BA want to be seen?
> 3 How have Coca Cola's agencies been able to promote the drink?
> 4 What is the key to effective advertising?

2 Aim: to read for main ideas.

● The passage is quite a difficult one. Ask them to read the passage and to choose the best summary.

> **Answer**
> 3

3 Aim: to read and link ideas.

● Ask the students to check they have understood what the words in italics refer to. The referent is much longer and more complex than is usually the case in this type of activity.

> **Answers**
> 1 Coca Cola's message *It's the real thing.*
> 2 A global message which is clear and inescapable.
> 3 Thousands of people.
> 4 The same products.
> 5 The company's.
> 6 The one idea.
> 7 The advertising message.

4 Aim: to distinguish between main ideas and examples.

● Ask the students to look at the first and last sentences of the paragraphs in the passage and ask them to say if the sentences are main ideas or examples. Ask them to do this alone and then check with another student. Correct this activity with the whole class.

> **Answers**
> 1 example, main idea   2 main idea, example
> 3 main idea, example   4 main idea, main idea
> 5 example   6 example, example   7 main idea
> 8 main idea

LISTENING AND VOCABULARY

1 Aim: to prepare for listening.
● Explain that the sentences come from a dialogue between a customer and a shop assistant. Ask the students to decide who says which. Do not check their answers at this stage.

2 Aim: to present the reporting verbs in the vocabulary box.
● Ask the students to match the reporting verbs with the sentences in 1. There may be more than one possibility. You may like to do this with the whole class.

Answers	
Can I help you sir? **(offer)**	1
Would you like me to replace it with a similar model? **(offer)**	6
What seems to be the trouble? **(ask)**	3
Well, the salesperson said it was waterproof, but it just filled with water. **(explain)**	4
Let me see. Oh, yes, we have had some problems with this model. **(explain/admit)**	5
Do you have your receipt? **(ask)**	9
Yes, I bought this watch from you last week and I've been having a few problems with it. **(explain/complain)**	2
Thank you. **(thank)**	11
Of course we can do that for you. **(offer)**	8
I think I'd rather have my money back, actually. **(point out/explain)**	7
Yes, here it is. **(offer)**	10
I'm very sorry this has happened. **(apologise)**	13
By the way, I think you should check what you sell more carefully. **(warn)**	12

3 Aim: to listen for specific information.
● ▭ Play the tape and ask the students to listen and number the sentences in the order in which they hear them.

● Ask the students to act out the dialogue paying attention to stress and intonation.

GRAMMAR

1 Aim: to focus on reporting verbs.
● Ask the students to read the information in the grammar box and then to do the exercises.

● Ask the students to write sentences showing what pattern the verbs in the vocabulary box follow.

2 Aim: to practise using reporting verbs.
● Ask the students to write the dialogue in *Listening and vocabulary* 1 using reporting verbs.

Answers
The sales assistant offered to help the customer. The customer explained that he had bought a watch the week before and that he'd been having a few problems.
The sales assistant asked what the trouble seemed to be. The customer complained that the salesperson said the watch was waterproof, but that when he wore it at the swimming pool it had just filled with water.
The sales assistant admitted there had been some problems with that brand. She offered to replace it with a similar model.
The customer asked for his money back. The sales assistant agreed to do that for him, asked him for his receipt and thanked him. The customer suggested that they should check what they sold more carefully. The sales assistant apologised.

3 Aim: to practise using reporting verbs.
● Ask the students to choose four or five of the reporting verbs. Tell them that they should write a sentence on a piece of paper, leaving out the reporting verb. When they have written four or five sentences they should exchange papers with their partner. Their partner must try and guess what the missing reporting verbs should be.

WRITING AND SPEAKING

1 Aim: to practise speaking and writing.
● Ask the students to look at the adverts and decide what they think the products are.

● Ask the students to choose one of the adverts and write a dialogue of complaint between the customer and the sales assistant. The students can use the model dialogue in this lesson to help them.

2 Aim: to practise speaking.
● Ask the students to act out the dialogues they have written in 1. Which dialogue is the most amusing?

3 Look at these sentences from the passage. Decide who or what the word in italics refers to.

1 ...*its* meaning is clear...

2 *This* is the advertising technique now being taken up...

3 ...the recent wave of BA advertisements features a cast of *thousands*...

4 ...we all have access to *them*.

5 An added bonus for the company is that they only need *their* advertising agencies...

6 *This* means the advertisement itself can be more spectacular...

7 ...*they* are easy to understand, easy to translate.

4 The passage contains a mixture of main ideas and examples. Look at the first and last sentences of each paragraph. Do they express a main idea or an example?

LISTENING AND VOCABULARY

1 Here are some sentences from a dialogue between a customer and a shop assistant. Decide who says each sentence. Write C or SA after each sentence.

- [ ] Can I help you, sir?
- [ ] Would you like me to replace it with a similar model?
- [ ] By the way, I think you should check what you sell more carefully.
- [ ] What seems to be the trouble?
- [ ] Well, the salesperson said it was waterproof, but when I wore it at the swimming pool it just filled with water.
- [ ] Let me see. Oh yes, we have had some problems with this brand.
- [ ] Do you have your receipt?
- [ ] Yes, I bought this watch from you last week and I've been having a few problems with it.
- [ ] Thank you.
- [ ] Of course we can do that for you.
- [ ] I think I'd rather have my money back, actually.
- [ ] Yes, here it is.
- [ ] I'm very sorry this has happened.

2 Match the sentences above with a suitable reporting verb from the list below.

explain complain thank apologise warn offer insist
promise suggest argue point out suggest admit

3 🔊 Listen and number the sentences in the order you hear them.

Now work in pairs and act out the dialogue.

GRAMMAR

> **Reporting verbs**
>
> **You can often use a reporting verb to describe the general sense of what someone thinks or says. The main patterns for these verbs are:**
>
> – **verb + *to* + infinitive**
> *He decided to ask for his money back.*
>
> – **verb + object + *to* + infinitive**
> *He asked her to replace it.*
>
> – **verb + (*that*) + clause**
> *She agreed that there had been some problems.*
>
> – **verb + object + (*that*) + clause**
> *He told her that he'd got the receipt.*
>
> – **verb + object(s)**
> *He thanked her. She offered to give him his money back.*

1 Look at the reporting verbs in the vocabulary box in *Listening and vocabulary* 2. What pattern does each verb follow? Write sentences showing how they are used.

2 Rewrite the sentences in *Listening and vocabulary* 1 using suitable reporting verbs.

3 Choose four or five verbs from the vocabulary box and write similar sentences, leaving out the verb. When you're ready, show your sentences to another student. Can he/she decide which verbs you left out?

WRITING AND SPEAKING

1 Work in pairs. Look at the advertising claims below. What do you think the products are? Choose one (or write your own) and use it to write a dialogue between a customer and the person who sold him/her the product.

LEARN WHILE YOU SLEEP

LOSE TEN KILOS IN A WEEK

TEACH YOUR DOG TO SPEAK

ENGLISH BY MICROWAVE

SPEAK A LANGUAGE OF YOUR CHOICE FLUENTLY IN THREE WEEKS

2 Perform your dialogue for the rest of the class.

Progress check **17–20**

VOCABULARY

1 Remember that it's more important to recognise what idioms mean than to use them yourself. People use them in informal situations, often to create a personal and sometimes exaggerated impression of what they are describing.

There are many ways of categorising idioms. Here are some idioms:

– to describe personal qualities or behaviour.
to have a heart of gold   to be as hard as nails   to go over the top
to be quick off the mark

– to describe feelings.
to be on cloud nine   to be down in the dumps   to be all in
to be at death's door

– to describe problems or reactions to situations.
to be in a fix   to sweep things under the carpet
to see the light at the end of the tunnel

– to talk about communication.
to talk down to someone   to get to the point   to speak your mind

Look at these sentences and decide which of the above categories each idiom belongs to.

1 He never remembers anything.
   He has a head like a sieve.
2 She crept behind him and said Boo!
   She frightened the life out of him.
3 Your children are well-behaved.
   They were as good as gold.
4 He was very irritable. He was like a bear with a sore head.
5 I think I'll take a back seat and let him do all the work.
6 You must get your act together and organise your work better.
7 I won't beat about the bush. I'll tell you what I really think.
8 She's very long-winded. She always uses ten words where two will do.

You may like to use these categories when you note down new idioms.

2 There are many words which have very informal or slang equivalents.

children – kids   advertisement – ad   television – telly   pound – quid

It may be useful to note down if a word is informal or slang. Use your dictionary to find out what these words mean:

Ta!   pal   Cheerio!   spud   fridge

GRAMMAR

1 What are the countable equivalents of the following words?

grass   furniture   luggage   information   advice   luck   clothing   smoke   sugar   news   lightning

a blade of grass

2 Choose the correct word.

A Can I draw *some/several* cash, please.
B Yes sir, how *much/many* do you need?
A Thirty pounds.
B There you are, sir. Are you interested in our new saving account? It offers *much/many* more interest than usual.
A At the end of the month, I've only got *a few/a little* money left. How *much/many* do I need to open the account?
B Five hundred pounds. And you can take it out at *any/some* time.
A Five hundred pounds! I don't have five hundred pence!

Progress check 17 – 20

GENERAL COMMENTS

You can work through this Progress check in the order shown, or concentrate on areas which may have caused difficulty in Lessons 17 – 20 You can also let the students choose the activities they would like or feel the need to do.

VOCABULARY

1 Aim: to focus on idioms.

● Ask the students to look at the different ways of categorising idioms.

● Ask the students to look at the sentences and put them in similar categories.

> **Answers**
> 1 – to describe behaviour
> 2 – to describe feelings
> 3 – to describe behaviour
> 4 – to describe feelings
> 5 – to describe reactions to situations
> 6 – to describe problems
> 7 – to talk about communication
> 8 – to talk about communication

2 Aim: to focus on slang.

● You may need to point out to your students that slang expressions go out of date quite quickly and that unless a slang expression is used in exactly the right way and by the right people, it can sound strange. However, it may be useful to know what a slang expression means.

> **Answers**
> Ta! – thank you   pal – friend   Cheerio! – goodbye
> spud – potato   fridge – refrigerator

GRAMMAR

1 Aim: to revise countable and uncountable nouns.

> **Answers**
> a blade of grass   a piece/an item of furniture
> a piece of luggage   a piece of information
> a piece of advice   a stroke of luck
> an item of clothing   a cloud of smoke
> a lump of sugar   a piece of news
> a streak of lightning

2 Aim: to revise expressions of quantity.

> **Answers**
> A: Can I draw **some** cash, please.
> B: Yes sir, how **much** do you need?
> A: Thirty pounds.
> B: There you are , sir. Are you interested in our new savings account? It offers **much** more interest than usual.
> A: At the end of the month, I've only got **a little** money left. How **much** do I need to open the account?
> B: Five hundred pounds. And you can take it out at **any** time.
> A: Five hundred pounds! I don't have five hundred pence!

3 Aim: to revise future continuous and future perfect.

Answers
1 This time tomorrow, I **will be attending** a meeting in New York.
2 I can't give you back your book when I see you because I **won't have finished** it by then.
3 **Will you be taking** the train or the plane tomorrow?
4 It's after eight o'clock, so he **will have left** for work by now.
5 While we're having our lunch here, they **will be having** breakfast in Washington.
6 In two hours' time I **will have worked** on this report for three days.

4 Aim: to revise *must have* and *can't have*.

Answers
1 She **must have** been crying.
2 She **can't have** gone out tonight.
3 They **must have** gone out.
4 He **must have** been telling lies.
5 He **must have** been sunbathing.
6 The film **can't have** been very good.

5 Aim: to focus on passive constructions.

Answers
1 **It is said** that carrots make you see in the dark.
2 **It is thought** that Queen Elizabeth is the richest woman in the world.
3 **It is believed** that smoking is bad for you.
4 **It is claimed** that computers will run our lives in the future.
5 **It is known** that certain people have more bad luck than others.
6 **It is expected** that a cure for cancer will be discovered.

6 Aim: to focus on subject + passive constructions.

Answers
1 Carrots **are said** to make you see in the dark.
2 Queen Elizabeth **is thought** to be the richest woman in the world.
3 Smoking **is believed** to be bad for you.
4 Computers **are claimed** to run our lives in the future.
5 Certain people **are known** to have more bad luck than others.
6 A cure for cancer **is expected** to be discovered.

7 Aim: to focus on reporting verbs.

Answers
1 **He threatened** to call the police if they didn't go away.
2 **She suggested** that he went home early.
3 **She begged** him to come with her.
4 **He promised** to be there on time.
5 **She complained** that he never bought her flowers.
6 **He admitted** that he had been thoughtless.

SOUNDS

1 Aim: to focus on homophones.
● Ask the students to find the words which do not sound the same.

● 🔲 Play the tape and ask them to listen and check.

2 Aim: to focus on homographs.
● Ask the students how the words in italics are pronounced.

● 🔲 Play the tape and ask the students to say the sentences aloud.

● Encourage the students to keep a separate record of homophones and homographs.

SPEAKING

1 Aim: to practise speaking.
● Ask the students to work in groups of three or four. Find out if anyone has lived in a foreign country for any length of time. Ask them what they missed while they were away.

● Ask the students to imagine they are going to live in a foreign country for a long period of time. Ask them to look at the prompts in the Student's Book and make joint decisions. They can make notes if they find it helpful.

2 Aim: to practise speaking; to listen and take notes.
● Ask the students to work with students from another group and find out the decisions they made in 1. They should take notes and use the appropriate reporting verbs.

3 Aim: to practise writing; to practise using reported speech and reporting verbs.
● Ask the students to write a brief report of what they learned in activity 2. Remind them to use reported speech and reporting verbs. You may like to ask them to do this activity for homework.

3 Complete the sentences with a future continuous or future perfect form of the verb in brackets.

1 This time tomorrow, I ____ (be) in a meeting in New York.
2 I can't give you back your book when I see you because I ____ (finish) it by then.
3 ____ (take) the train or the plane tomorrow?
4 It's after eight o'clock, so he ____ (leave) for work by now.
5 While we're having our lunch here, they ____ (have) breakfast in Washington.
6 In two hours' time, I ____ (work) on this report for three days.

4 Complete the sentences with *must have* or *can't have* and a suitable form of the verb in brackets.

1 Her eyes are red. She ____ (cry).
2 She's never out. She ____ (go out) tonight.
3 There's no answer. They ____ (go out).
4 It wasn't true. He ____ (tell) lies.
5 He looks brown. He ____ (sunbathe).
6 They looked bored. The film ____ (be) very good.

5 Rewrite these sentences with *It* and a suitable passive construction.

1 People say that carrots make you see in the dark.
2 People think that Queen Elizabeth is the richest woman in the world.
3 People believe that smoking is bad for you.
4 People claim that computers will run our lives in the future.
5 People know that certain people have more bad luck than others.
6 People expect that a cure for cancer will be discovered.

It is said that carrots make you see in the dark.

6 Rewrite the sentences in 5 with a subject + passive construction.

Carrots are said to make you see in the dark.

7 Rewrite the main idea of these sentences in reported speech, using one of these reporting verbs.

admit   beg   complain   promise   suggest   threaten

1 'Go away, or I'll call the police,' he said.
2 'Why don't you go home early?' she said.
3 'Oh, John, please come with me.' she said.
4 'I'll be there on time, I really will,' he said.
5 'You never buy me flowers,' she said.
6 'Well yes, I suppose I have been rather thoughtless,' he said.

SOUNDS

1 Homophones are words which sound the same but have different meanings and spellings. Which of the following words are NOT homophones?

1 right   write   5 where   were
2 weather whether   6 raise   rays
3 aloud   allowed   7 team   tame
4 waist   waste   8 bean   been

Listen and check. As you listen, say the words aloud.

2 Homographs are words which have the same spelling but a different sound. How do you pronounce the words in italics in these sentences?

1 I *read* a newspaper every day
  I *read* The Guardian yesterday.
2 We *live* in London.
  There's *live* music at the pub tonight.
3 There's a north *wind* today.
  I must *wind* up the clock.
4 I like to wear a *bow* tie.
  The Japanese usually *bow* when they greet each other.

Listen and check. As you listen, say the sentences aloud. You may need to keep a special record of homophones and homographs.

SPEAKING

1 Work in groups of three or four. Imagine you're going to live in a foreign country for a long period of time. Decide:

– which country you're going to
– how long you'll be staying there
– what you'll take with you
– what you'll do there
– what you'll enjoy most
– what you'll find most difficult

2 Work with someone from another group, and make notes about what their group decided. Tell them what your group decided. Try to use reported speech and reporting verbs.

3 Write a brief description of what your partner in 2 told you about his/her group.

Communication activities

1 *Lesson 3*
Functions, activity 4

Student A: Criticise the following behaviour and habits and listen to Student B's response. If Student B disagrees, add another criticism to justify your viewpoint. Use the expressions in the *functions box*.

1 Pete spends all his time reading detective novels. He never talks to people at home because he's always reading. He never goes out and has very few friends.

2 Lydia starts work at seven o'clock in the morning. She usually finishes at around eight o'clock at night. Sometimes, she doesn't come home until ten o'clock. She often brings work home and works at the weekends as well.

3 Joan never throws anything away. Her kitchen is full of old newspapers, empty bottles, plastic containers and old paperbags. Joan says they will come in useful one day.

Now listen to Student B criticising someone. If you think the person's behaviour is unreasonable, agree with them. If not, disagree and justify your viewpoint.

Use the expressions in the *functions box*.

Now turn back to page 13.

2 *Lesson 12*
Reading and listening, activity 1

Add up your scores using the following table. Then look at the profiles below.

1	a 2	b 1	c 3		
2	a 2	b 2	c 1		
3	a 3	b 2	c 1	d 0	
4	a 1	b 2	c 3		
5	a 2	b 2	c 1		
6	a 0	b 2			
7	a 1	b 2			
8	a 3	b 2	c 1		
9	a 0	b 1	c 2	d 3	
10	a 2	b 3	c 1	d 3	
11	a 1	b 1	c 1	d 0	e 0
12	a 0	b 3			

25 – 30 points.

You are a true gourmet. You are adventurous in your eating habits and not afraid to try something new. You appreciate good food and if you opened your own restaurant you would probably be successful.

15 – 25 points.

You are quite conservative in your eating habits, but you know what you like and you enjoy your food. If you tried eating a few different things you might be pleasantly surprised.

0 – 15 points.

You don't much mind what you eat as long as there is plenty of it. However, you feel safest with foods you know. Why not try something different for a change? If you try something new, you may find that you like it.

Now turn back to page 50.

3 *Lesson 17*

Listening and speaking, activity 2

Student A: 🔊 Listen to Mehmet talking about his shopping habits.

Make notes on what he says.
Turn back to page 77 and fill in the chart as you listen.

4 *Lesson 5*

Speaking and writing, activity 1

Student A: Read this biography of Lisa St Aubin de Terán. There is some information missing. Ask Student B questions to find the missing information and fill in the gaps.

Lisa St Aubin de Terán was born in (1) _____ in 1953. She left school at the age of sixteen and got married to a Venezuelan. They travelled in Italy for (3) _____ and then returned to his family home in the Andes. During her seven years in South America she managed her husband's sugar plantation, and she based her first novel, *Keepers of the House* (1983), on this experience. During this period she had a daughter. She is the author of (5) _____ novels, and has also written a volume of poetry, a collection of short stories and a book of memoirs. She left Venezuela and returned to live in England with her daughter. She then married her second husband in (7) _____, bought a house in Italy and lived there for three years. She returned from Italy in 1993 to live in (9) _____ again. She's working on her next novel.

Now turn back to page 21.

5 *Lesson 9*

Listening, activity 3

Student A: 🔊 Listen to Matthew Sherrington talking about his experiences of teaching in Sudan.
Make notes on what he says about:

– school subjects
– the classroom
– length of lessons
– amusing incidents

Now turn back to page 40.

6 *Lesson 15*

Reading and writing, activity 5

Student A: Dictate these sentences to Student B in turn. Write down the sentences Student B dictates.

1 A woman was doing her Christmas shopping and after buying the last present she went to have a cup of tea in a department store café.

2 _____
_____
_____
_____

3 She told the department store security what had happened, but she didn't really expect to see her possessions again.

4 _____
_____
_____
_____

5 She was delighted by the news and hurried to the store.

6 _____
_____
_____
_____

7 The disappointed shopper went home and as she opened her front door, she suddenly realised that it was the handbag thief who had spoken to her on the phone.

8 _____
_____
_____
_____

Now turn back to page 67.

7 *Lesson 17*

Listening and speaking, activity 2

Student B: 📼 Listen to Nanthapa talking about her shopping habits.

Make notes on what she says.
Turn back to page 77 and fill in the chart as you listen.

8 *Lesson 2*

Listening, activity 2

Student A: 📼 Listen to Mary and Peter talking about social customs.

Find out:

– what Mary thinks about children's behaviour in the past
– what Peter says about family decision-making today
– what Mary thinks about manners today

Now turn back to page 8.

9 *Progress check 1–4*

Sounds, activity 4

Rewrite the story using the key words on your piece of paper to help you.

Now turn back to page 19.

10 *Lesson 10*

Reading and writing, activity 3

Write a letter to a newspaper giving your opinion about the judgement. Here are some arguments for and against the judgement.

In favour of the judgement: Phillips was unarmed; the shotgun was unlicenced; Lewis committed a crime by shooting at Phillips; if you can shoot burglars, you can shoot anyone, even young boys stealing from an apple tree.

In protest of the judgement: Lewis acted in self-defence; he is an elderly man, who may have been very frightened; people who are injured while they are committing crimes deserve all they get; the law treats criminals too leniently.

Now turn back to page 45.

11 *Lesson 15*

Reading and writing, activity 3

...the reason he had raised his clipboard was to take a pen from the sideclip.

Now turn back to page 66.

12 *Lesson 19*

Reading, activity 4

Student A: Read the passage below and find out:

– where Arthur was born
– where Camelot was
– where Arthur and his Knights lie sleeping

Arthur is said to have been born at Tintagel Castle in Cornwall, although it is known that the castle which stands there now was not built until the 12th century. If Arthur was born in Tintagel, it can't have been in the present castle. From a cove down on the shore, Merlin's Cave can be entered. The ghost of the wizard Merlin is alleged to wander in the cave.

The site of King Arthur's Camelot is thought to be South Cadbury Castle in Somerset. At midsummer, Arthur and his Knights are said to ride over the hill and down to a spring beside the church.

In Cadbury Camp, near Nailsea, Avon, there is said to be a cavern where King Arthur and his Knights lie sleeping, waiting to be called out to help England face her enemies.

Now turn back to page 83.

13 *Lesson 2*

Listening, activity 2

Student B: 📼 Listen to Mary and Peter talking about social customs.

Find out:

– what Peter thinks about discipline today
– at what age girls got married
– what Peter thinks about relations between friends and neighbours today

Now turn back to page 8.

14 *Lesson 5*

Speaking and writing, activity 1

Student B: Read this biography of Lisa St Aubin de Terán. There is some information missing. Ask Student A the questions to find the missing information and fill in the gaps.

Lisa St Aubin de Terán was born in London in (2) _____. She left school at the age of sixteen and got married to a Venezuelan. They travelled in Italy for two years and then returned to his family home in the Andes. During her (4) _____ years in South America she managed her husband's sugar plantation, and she based her first novel, *Keepers of the House* (1983), on this experience. During this period she had a daughter. She is the author of seven novels, and has written a volume of poetry, a (6) _____ and a book of memoirs. She left Venezuela and returned to live in England with her daughter. She then married her second husband in 1990, bought a house in (8) _____ and lived there for three years. She returned from Italy in 1993 to live in England again. She's now working on (10) _____.

Now turn back to page 21.

15 *Lesson 9*

Listening, activity 3

Student B: 📼 Listen to Matthew Sherrington talking about his experiences in Sudan.
Makes notes on what he says about:

– pupils
– equipment
– examinations
– embarrassing incidents

Now turn back to page 40.

16 *Lesson 15*

Reading and writing, activity 5

Student B: Dictate these sentences to Student A in turn. Write down the sentences Student A dictates to you.

1 _____
_____
_____
_____

2 Minutes later, she suddenly realised that someone had taken her bag, with her purse, cheque book, front door keys, everything.

3 _____
_____
_____
_____

4 So, she was pleased when the department store rang her later that day and told her they had found her bag and she could collect it immediately.

5 _____
_____
_____
_____

6 But no one knew what the lady was talking about.

7 _____
_____
_____
_____

8 While she was out, he had burgled her house and had taken everything.

Now turn back to page 67.

17 *Lesson 16*

Vocabulary and listening, activity 4

Student B: 📼 Listen and find the answers to these questions.

– when did Francesca first hear *Pie Jesu*?
– why does Steve like his favourite piece of music?
– why does Francesca like her favourite book?
– how many stories are there in *A History of the World in Ten and a Half Chapters*?

Now turn back to page 71.

18 *Lesson 19*

Reading, activity 4

Student B: Read the passage below and find out:
  – where Merlin was born
  – where Sir Bedivere threw Exalibur
  – where Arthur and Guinevere were buried

Merlin, the wizard, is said to have been born in Carmarthen in Wales. An old oak tree in the town was known as Merlin's Oak and it was believed that it could never be cut down because if it was, Carmarthen would also be destroyed. However, in 1978 the dead tree's stump was removed because it was a traffic hazard, and fortunately Carmarthen is still there.

The pool in Trent in Dorset is thought to be the lake where Excalibur was thrown, and was caught by the Lady of the Lake. It is only a few miles from South Cadbury Castle, which may have been the site of Camelot.

It has been claimed that Glastonbury in Somerset is the Isle of Avalon where King Arthur and Queen Guinevere were buried. It is reported that monks in the abbey discovered their remains and reburied them in the church. Historians doubt that the monks really did find Arthur's grave, but no one can be certain.

Now turn back to page 83.

19 *Lesson 3*

Functions, activity 4

Student B: Listen to Student A criticising someone. If you think the person's behaviour is unreasonable, agree with them. If not, disagree and justify your viewpoint.

Use the expressions in the *functions box.*

Now criticise the following behaviour and habits and listen to Student A's response. If Student A disagrees, add another criticism to justify your viewpoint.

1 When Martin gets the bill in a restaurant, he always demands a menu and then checks the bill item by item with a pocket calculator. If there is anything wrong, he questions the waiter in a loud voice. His friends find this very embarrassing.

2 Bill is obsessively tidy and spends his time cleaning, tidying and washing up. As soon as you put down your coffee cup, he takes it to the kitchen to wash it. His friends feel very uncomfortable in his home and would like him to be more relaxed.

3 Anna keeps rabbits. She has about fifty of them. Some live in the house and some in the garden. The neighbours are often angry because the rabbits in the garden escape and eat all the vegetables in their gardens. Anna has plans to buy at least twenty more rabbits.

Now turn back to page 13.

20 *Lesson 16*

Vocabulary and listening, activity 4

Student A: Listen and find the answers to these questions.
  – when did Steve first hear Mahler's First Symphony?
  – why does Francesca like her favourite music?
  – when did Francesca first read *Wuthering Heights*?
  – how many times has Steve read his favourite book?

Now turn back to page 71.

21 *Lesson 2*

Listening, activity 2

Student C: Listen to Mary and Peter talking about social customs.

Find out:

  – who was served first at meals in Mary's household
  – at what age Peter thinks people should get married
  – what Mary says about where young people lived before they got married

Now turn back to page 8.

22 *Lesson 11*

Speaking and listening, activity 6

All the inventions were invented and patents applied for.

Now turn back to page 48.

Grammar review

CONTENTS

Present simple

Use

You use the present simple:

- to talk about a general truth, such as a fact or a state. (See Lesson 3)
  On Sunday afternoons, a million Italians go to watch football.

- to talk about something that is regular, such as routines, customs and habits.
  In Milan, the women sit in the expensive seats, and wear their fur coats.
  Every Saturday we go to the stadium to watch the football match.

- to talk about events in a story or a commentary on a game.
  .... after 10 minutes, Parma scores a beautifully simple goal.

- to criticise behaviour with *just*.
  He just watches movies all day.

Present continuous

Use

You use the present continuous:

- to talk about an action which is happening at the moment or an action or state which is temporary. (See Lesson 3)
  Today, Inter is playing at home to Parma.
  I am living in Italy at the moment.

- to give background information.
  Before kick off, the Parma fans are shouting at the Inter fans.
  As we walk into the stadium the band is playing and the crowd is cheering.

- to criticise behaviour with *always*.
  He's always watching the football on TV.

You don't usually use these verbs in the continuous form.
believe feel hate hear know like love smell sound taste understand want

Past simple

Use

You use the past simple:

- to talk about a past action or event that is finished. (See Lesson 6)
  I went to London yesterday.

Irregular verbs

There are many verbs which have an irregular past simple. For a list of the irregular verbs which appear in **Reward Upper-intermediate**, see page 109.

Pronunciation of past simple endings

/t/ *finished liked walked*
/d/ *continued lived stayed*
/ɪd/ *decided started visited*

Future simple *(will)*

Use
You use the future simple:

- to talk about decisions you make at the moment of speaking. (See Lesson 4)
  I'll give you the money right now.

- to make an offer. (See Lesson 4)
  I'll get the tickets.

- to make a prediction about the future. (See Lesson 4)
  We'll have a great time together.

- to make a promise, threat or warning. (See Lesson 4)
  If you won't be quiet, I'll call the waiter.

- to make a request. (See Lesson 4)
  Will you ask them to be quiet?

- to make an invitation. (See Lesson 4)
  Will you join us?

- to refuse something. (See Lesson 4)
  No, I won't be quiet.

Remember that you can also use the future simple:

- to talk about things you are not sure will happen with *perhaps* and *It's possible/probable that…* (See Lesson 4)
  It's possible that I'll be late tomorrow.

Present perfect simple

Form
You form the present perfect with *has/have* + past participle. You use the contracted form in spoken and informal written English.

Past participles

All regular and some irregular verbs have past participles which are the same as their past simple form.
Regular: *move – moved, finish – finished, visit – visited*
Irregular: *leave – left, find – found, buy – bought*

Some irregular verbs have past participles which are not the same as the past simple form.

go – went – gone   *be – was/were – been*
drink – drank – drunk   *ring – rang – rung*

For a list of the past participles of the irregular verbs which appear in **Reward Upper-intermediate,** see page 109.

Been and *gone*

He's been to America. (= He's been there and he's back here now.)
He's gone to America. (= He's still there.)

Use
You use the present perfect simple:

- to talk about an action which happened at some time in the past. We are not interested in when the action took place, but in the experience. You often use *ever* in questions and *never* in negative statements. (See Lesson 5)
  I have made other great railway journeys.
  (At some time in my life, we don't know when.)
  Have you ever been to Brazil?
  I've never been to Brazil.

  Remember that if you ask for and give more information about these experiences, actions or states, such as *when, how, why* and *how long,* you use the past simple.
  When did you travel to Brazil?   Three years ago.

- when the action is finished, to say what has been completed in a period of time, often in reply to *how much/many.* (See Lesson 5)
  Lisa has written several novels.

- to talk about a past action which has a result in the present, such as a change. You often use *just.*
  I have just arrived in Brazil.

You can use:

- *already* with the present perfect to suggest *by now* or *sooner than expected.* It's often used for emphasis and goes at the end of the clause. (See Lesson 5)
  Shall I collect the tickets?
  No, I've collected them already.

  You can put *already* between the auxiliary and the past participle. You don't often use *already* in questions and negatives.
  I've already collected the tickets.

- *yet* with the present perfect in questions and negatives. You use it to talk about an action which is expected. (See Lesson 5)
  Have you booked your flight yet?
  No, I haven't booked my flight yet.

  You usually put *yet* at the end of the sentence.

● *still* to emphasise an action which is continuing.
I'm still waiting to hear from the travel agent.

You usually put *still* before the main verb, but after *be* or an auxiliary verb. In negatives it goes before the auxiliary.
He still goes to college.   *He is still at college.*
He still hasn't gone to college.

Present perfect continuous

Form
You form the present perfect continuous tense with *has/have been* + *-ing*. You usually use the contracted form in spoken and informal English.

Use
You use the present perfect continuous:

● to talk about an action which began in the past, continues up to the present, may or may not continue into the future, and to say how long something has been in progress. You use it to talk about how long something has been happening. (See Lesson 5)
I have been waiting for the train for two hours.

You use *since* to say when the action or event began.
I've been living in Brazil since l990.

● to talk about actions and events which have been in progress up to the recent past that show the present results of past activity. (See Lesson 5)
What's Mary been doing?
She's been cleaning the car.
(The car is now clean. She may be wet.)

We can sometimes use the present perfect simple or continuous with little difference in meaning. However, as with all continuous tenses the speaker is usually focusing on activity in progress when using the continuous form.

Past continuous

Form
You form the past continuous with *was/were* + present participle. You use the contracted form in spoken and informal written English.

Use
You use the past continuous:

● to talk about something that was in progress at a specific time in the past. (See Lesson 6)
I was working at the hospital three years ago.

● to talk about something that was in progress at a specific time in the past, or when something else happened. You join the parts of the sentence with *when* and *while*. The verb in the *when* clause is in the past simple. The *The doctor was driving in the hospital grounds when he met Sister Coxall.*

The verb in the *while* clause is usually in the past continuous.
While the doctor was driving in the hospital grounds, he met Sister Coxall.

● to talk about an activity that was in progress when interrupted by something else.
The nurse was talking to the doctor when I knocked on the door.

Remember that you use *when* + past simple to describe two things which happened one after the other.
I telephoned my mother when I heard the good news.

You don't usually use these verbs in the continuous form.
believe feel hear know like see smell sound taste think understand want

Future in the past

You can use *was/were going to* + infinitive to talk about something that was planned or promised for the future at some point in the past. To express this idea, we use similar structures to the ones we normally use to talk about the future, but we change the verb forms. Instead of *am/is/are going to* we use *was/were going to*. It is usually used when the plans or promises didn't happen. (See Lesson 18)
You were going to lower taxes five years ago, but you didn't.

Past perfect simple

Form
You form the past perfect with *had* + past participle. You use the contracted form in spoken and informal written English. (See Lesson 6)

Use
You use the past perfect simple:

● to talk about an action in the past which happened before another action in the past. The second action is often in the past simple. (See Lesson 5)
Although we arrived on time, the doctor had already left.

● in reported speech or thoughts after verbs like *said, told, asked, thought.* (See Lesson 20)
'These products have been highly recommended.'
He told me that these products had been highly recommended.

- with *when, after, because* and *until* or the first of
two actions.
*After they had promoted the product, the sales
rose steadily.*

  You can use two past simple tenses if you think the
  sequence of actions is clear.
  After they promoted the product, the sales rose steadily.

Past perfect continuous

Form

You form the past perfect continuous with *had been* +
present participle. You use the contracted form in spoken and
informal written English. (See Lesson 6)

Use

You use the past perfect continuous:

- when you want to focus on an earlier past action which
was in progress up to or near a time in the past rather than
the completed event.
You often use it with *for* and *since*.
*Sister Coxall had been running Violet Ward for
many years.*
I've been working at the hospital since last year.

Future continuous

Form

You form the future continuous with *will be* + present
participle. You use the contracted form in spoken and
informal written English. (See Lesson l8)

Use

You use the future continuous:

- to talk about something which will be in progress at a
particular time in the future.
*Scientists say we will be living in a warmer world in the
next century.*

- to talk about something which is already planned or is part
of a routine.
We will be having another exam next week.

- to ask politely about someone's plans.
Will you be staying for the next few days?

Future perfect

Form

You form the future perfect with *will have* + past participle.
You use the contracted form in spoken and informal written
English.

Use

You use the future perfect:

- to talk about something which will be finished by a specific
time in the future. (See Lesson l8)
*By the year 2000 the proportion of older people will have
increased dramatically.*

Questions

Asking questions

You form questions in the following ways:

- without a question word and with an auxiliary verb. The
word order is auxiliary + subject + verb. (See Lesson 1)
Have you ever studied another foreign language?

- when a verb has no auxiliary, you use the auxiliary *do* in
the question, followed by an infinitive without *to*.
Do you write down every new word you come across?

You don't use *do* in questions with modal verbs or
the verb *be*.
Can you guess what a word means from the context?
Are you looking forward to working in groups?

You can use *who, what* or *where* and other question words to
ask about the object of the sentence.
What did you study last year?
I studied English. (= *English* is the object of
the sentence.)

You can use *who, what* or *where* and other question words to
ask about the subject of the sentence. You don't use *do* or *did*.
What gives you most help, your textbook or your dictionary?
My dictionary gives me most help. (= *My dictionary* is the
subject.)

You can form more indirect, polite questions with one of the
following question phrases.
Would you mind helping me with this activity?
Could you pass me my dictionary?
I wonder if you could tell me what these words mean?

Negative questions

You often use negative questions when you expect the
answer *yes*. For this reason, they are often used in invitations
and exclamations. (See Lesson 1)
Won't you stay a little longer?
Aren't you worried about the cost?
You can also use negative questions to express the
idea of criticism.
Hasn't Mary contacted you yet?
Aren't you supposed to be working today?

Imperative questions

You use imperative questions to give an order or to encourage someone to do something. (See Lesson 1)
Say something in Russian, will you?
Give me a hand with this heavy suitcase, will you?

Suggestions

You use *shall we* as a question tag when you make a suggestion. (See Lesson 1)
Let's go to Paris, shall we?

Reply questions

You often reply to a statement by making a short question, containing just the auxiliary verb and the personal pronoun. Reply questions do not ask for information. They express interest, contrast or surprise, depending upon the intonation. (See Lesson 1)
It takes three hours by train.   Does it? I didn't know that.

Question tags

Question tags turn a statement into a question. (See Lesson 1)

Tags after affirmative statements

If the statement is affirmative, you use a negative tag.
You speak French, don't you?
It is usual to give short answers to questions tags.
You speak French, don't you? Yes, I do./No, I don't.

Tags after negative statements

If the statement is negative, you use an affirmative tag.
You haven't forgotten that as well, have you?
Yes. (= Yes, I have forgotten it.)
No. (= No, I haven't forgotten it.)

To ask a real question, the intonation rises on the tag. To show you expect agreement, the intonation falls on the tag. You often use question tags to show friendliness or to make conversation.

Verbs patterns

Verbs of sensation

See, hear, feel, watch, listen to and *notice* are verbs of sensation.
You can put an object + *-ing* when you only feel, see or hear part of an action and the action continues over a period of time. (See Lesson 8)
I heard a child crying.
I felt someone squeezing my hand.

You can put an object + infinitive when you feel, see or hear the whole action and the action is now finished.
I felt someone grasp my hand.
I saw someone enter the bathroom.

Remember + noun/*-ing*

You can use *remember* + noun/*-ing* to talk about a memory. (See Lesson 9)
I remember meeting you last year.
Do you remember the first time we met?

When the subject of the memory is different from the subject of the sentence, you put a noun or a pronoun between *remember* and the *-ing* form.
I remember my mother reading bedtime stories every night.
I remember her reading bedtime stories every night.

Noun/adjective + *to* + infinitive

You can put *to* + infinitive after certain nouns and pronouns, usually to describe purpose. (See Lesson 11)
Where are the keys to lock this door?

You can put *to* + infinitive after these adjectives.
pleased disappointed surprised difficult easy

I was surprised to see Mary at the party.
It's difficult to concentrate when there is a lot of noise.

You can put *of* (someone) + *to* + infinitive after these adjectives.
nice kind silly careless good wrong clever stupid generous

It was stupid of Peter to forget the tickets.
It was generous of the company to give us a bonus.

You can put *for* + object + *to* + infinitive after these adjectives.
easy common important essential (un)usual (un)necessary normal rare

It's rare for men to wear a hat these days.

You can put *for* + *-ing* to describe the purpose something is used for.
It's a thing for brushing your hair.
It's a device for shaving.

Here are some ways of expressing contrast.
in spite of/despite + noun/*-ing*
Despite being a good idea, it's dangerous.
He went out in spite of feeling unwell.
In spite of the bad weather, he went out.

Clauses of purpose

You use *to/in order to* to describe the purpose of an action when the subject of the main clause and the purpose clause are the same. They can be followed by a present tense with a future meaning. (See Lesson 11)
I'll get up early tomorrow, to miss the traffic.

In order to makes a clause of purpose sound more formal.
We'll write to the lawyer in order to confirm the arrangements.

In negative sentences, you have to say *in order not to*.
In order not to disrupt the conference, I left without saying goodbye.
I'm going to leave now, in order not to miss the bus.

You use *so (that)*:

- when the subject of the main clause and the purpose clause are different.
  I'll give you my address so that you can send me a postcard.

- when the purpose is negative.
  I'll give you my address so that you don't get lost.

- with *can* and *could*.
  We arrived at the airport early, so that the children could watch the planes.

Modal verbs

The following verbs are modal verbs.
can could may might must should will would

Form
Modal verbs:

- have the same form for all persons.
  I may see you tomorrow.
  She could see you next week.

- don't take the auxiliary *do* in questions and negatives.
  Can you give him the tickets?
  You mustn't smoke in the library.

- take an infinitive without *to*.
  I'll come as soon as I can.
  I should telephone her tonight.

Use
You use *must*:

- to talk about something you are obliged to do. The obligation usually comes from the speaker and can express a moral obligation. (See Lesson 10)
  You must ring me as soon as you arrive.

  You often use it for strong advice or safety instructions. (See Lesson 10)
  You must fasten your seatbelt.

Have to has more or less the same meaning as *must* but the obligation comes from someone else. You often use it to talk about rules. (See Lesson 10)
I have to work from 9.00 am until 5.00 pm every day.
You have to drive on the left in Britain.

You can often use *have got to* instead of *have to*, especially for a specific instance. (See Lesson 10)
I've got to work from 8.30 am to 5.00 pm this week.

But you use *have to* for things which happen regularly, especially with an adverb or adverbial phrases of frequency.
We have to buy a television licence every year.

You use *can't* and *mustn't*:

- to talk about what is not possible to do or what you're not allowed to do. (See Lesson 10)
  You can't learn English in six weeks.
  You mustn't smoke in the classroom.

You can only use *must, mustn't* and *have got to* to talk about the present and future. Here is how you talk about obligation in the past.

Present	must	have to	have got to	mustn't
Past	had to	had to	had to	couldn't or wasn't/weren't allowed to

You use *must have*:

- to talk about something that probably or certainly happened in the past. (See Lesson 19)
  I haven't got my keys. I must have left them at home.

You use *can't have*:

- to talk about something which probably or certainly didn't happen in the past.
  I can't have left my keys at home, as I put them in my pocket.

You use *should* and *shouldn't*:

- to say what is right or wrong or express the opinion of the speaker. (See Lesson 10)
  I don't think the government should increase taxes.

- to give less strong advice.
  You don't look well, you should stay in bed.

You use *should have* and *shouldn't have*:

- to describe actions in the past which were wrong. (See Lesson 15)
  He should have stayed in bed, but he didn't.
  He shouldn't have got up, but he did.

● to express regret or criticism about actions in the past.
  (See Lesson 15)
  *I should have phoned the department store to check that the
  call was genuine.*
  I shouldn't have left the house.

Ought to have/ought not to have has a similar meaning to
should have/shouldn't have to express criticism.

You use *may have* or *might have*:

● to talk about something which possibly happened in the
  past. (See Lesson 19)
  *John wasn't at work yesterday. He might have been sick, or
  he may have been on holiday.*

Don't need to/needn't/needn't have/ didn't need to

You use *don't need to* + infinitive or *needn't* + infinitive to say
either what isn't necessary to do or what you don't have to do.
(See Lesson 10)
*You don't need to/needn't carry identification, but it's a good
idea.* (= It isn't necessary to carry identification.)

You use *needn't have* + past participle to say what someone
did, although it was unnecessary.
He needn't have phoned the police.
(= It wasn't necessary to phone the police, but he did.)

You use *didn't need to* + infinitive to say that something was
unnecessary. We don't know if the person did it or not.
He didn't need to phone the police. (= It wasn't necessary to
phone the police, we don't know if he did or not.)

Zero conditional

Form
You form the zero conditional with *if/whenever* + present
simple + present simple or imperative. *If* means the same
as *whenever*. (See Lesson 12)

Use
You use a zero conditional to talk about general truths, habits
or routines.
If you heat ice, it melts.
Whenever I go to the gym, I always have a shower.

You separate the two clauses with a comma.
The *if* clause can go at the beginning or end of the sentence.

First conditional

Form
You form the first conditional with *if* + present simple or
present continuous *will* + infinitive. (See Lesson 12)
If I go to the post office, I'll post the letter for you.
If I'm passing the post office, I'll post the letter for you.

Use
You use the first conditional to talk about a likely situation
and to describe its result. You talk about the likely situation
with *if* + present simple. You describe the result with
will or *won't*.
If I'm working late tonight, I'll go out and buy a sandwich.

You separate the two clauses with a comma. You often use
the contracted form in speech and informal writing. The *if*
clause can go at the beginning or end of the sentence.

Second conditional

Form
You form the second conditional with *if* + past simple or past
continuous *would* + infinitive. (See Lesson 12)
If I knew her name, I'd tell you.

Use
You use the second conditional:

● to talk about an unlikely or imaginary situation and to
  describe its result. You talk about the imaginary or unlikely
  situation with *if* + past simple. You describe the result with
  would/wouldn't. (See Lesson 12)
  If I won a lot of money, I'd travel around the world.

● to give advice.
  If I were you, I'd see the doctor.

You separate the two clauses with a comma. You often use
the contracted form in speech and informal writing. The *if*
clause can go at the beginning or end of the sentence.

Third conditional

Form
You form the third conditional with *if* + past perfect, *would
have* + past participle. (See Lesson 12)
*If Peter had seen me at the party, he would have spoken
to me.*

Use
You use the third conditional to talk about an imaginary or
unlikely situation in the past and to describe its result. You
talk about the imaginary or unlikely situation with *if* + past
perfect. You describe the result with *would have/
wouldn't have*. (See Lesson 15)
I wouldn't have met Peter, if I hadn't gone to the party.

You can use *may have, might have* or *could have* if the result is not certain.
If he had pulled out his knife, I could have been injured.

You separate the two clauses with a comma. You often use the contracted form in speech and informal writing. The *if* clause can go at the beginning or end of the sentence.

If and *when*

You use *if* in zero and first conditional sentences for actions and events which are not certain will happen.
If a waiter suggests water, I ask for sparkling.
If I go out tonight, I'll have dinner early.

You use *when* in zero and first conditional sentences for actions and events which are certain to happen.
When I drive to work, I always listen to the radio.
When we go out tonight, we'll have dinner in a nice restaurant.

Unless, even if, as long as/provided (that) or/otherwise

You can use *unless, even if, as long as/provided (that)* with zero and first conditional sentences to talk about likely situations and their results.

You can use *unless* to mean *if … not.* (See Lesson 12)
It is dangerous to swim in the sea, unless you are a good swimmer.
(= It is dangerous to swim in the sea, if you're not a good swimmer.)

You use *even if* to emphasise *if* or to express a contrast or to give some surprising information. Compare:
If they offer me the job, I won't accept it.
Even if they offer me the job, I won't accept it.

You use *as long as* and *provided (that)* to mean *on condition that.*
I'm sure you'll get the job as long as you prepare for the interview.
You can come and stay tomorrow provided (that) you telephone me first.

You can also use the expressions with second conditional sentences, when you talk about an unlikely situation and its result.

You can follow an instruction/advice with *or* or *otherwise* + clause to describe the result if you don't follow the instruction/advice.
You'd better take your sun cream on holiday or you might get sunburnt.
Make sure you take an umbrella otherwise you'll get wet.

Phrasal verbs

Phrasal verbs are verbs with a particle. They cannot necessarily be understood by knowing what the individual parts mean. Sometimes the meaning is obvious because the meaning of the verb plus particle can easily be worked out. In other words the meaning is literal. (See Lesson 16)
I looked up at the beautiful blue sky.

Sometimes the meaning is not obvious because the meaning of the verb plus particle cannot be worked out. In other words it is non-literal.
I looked up the word in my dictionary.

There are four types of phrasal verbs.

Type 1 These do not take an object.
My car has broken down.

Type 2 These take an object. The noun object goes before or after the particle.
It's cold. You'll have to put on your coat.
or *It's cold. You'll have to put your coat on.*
The pronoun object must go before the particle.
You'll have to put it on.

Type 3 These also take an object. The noun and the pronoun object go after the particle.
I drove into the wall.
I drove into it.

Type 4 These have two particles and take an object. The noun and the pronoun object go after the particle.
I get on with my parents.
I get on with them.

It is usual to use phrasal verbs, especially in spoken English. But it's usually possible to replace them with another verb or verbal phrase.
You'll have to put on your coat as the weather is cold.
You'll have to wear your coat as the weather is cold.

Used to and *would* + infinitive

Remember that you use *used to* and *would* + infinitive to talk about past habits and routines which are now finished. You often use it to contrast past routine with present state. (See Lesson 9)
Every summer we used to go to the seaside for our summer holiday. Now we go to the country.
We would meet the same people at the beach every year.

You can also use *used to* to talk about past states, but not *would.*
I used to like ice-cream when I was a child.

Be/get used to + noun/-ing

Be used to + noun/-ing has quite a different meaning from *used to* + infinitive. If someone is used to something it means it is no longer strange, but they have become accustomed to it. (See Lesson 9)
I've lived in Milan for three years now, so I am used to the busy traffic.
The weather in England can be cold in winter, if you are not used to it.

You can use *get used to* to mean *become used to*. This expresses the idea that something was difficult or unusual before, but is no longer so.
I am getting used to the cold climate in this country.
I got used to the spicy food, although it seemed strange at first.

Describing a sequence of events

Before and after

You can use *before* and *after* + -ing to describe a sequence of two events which both have the same subject. (See Lesson 6)
After graduating he moved to London.

You can use *when, as* and *while* to describe two events which happen at the same time. The second verb is often in the past simple and is used for the event which interrupts the longer action. (See Lesson 6)
When she was working in hospitals overseas, the terrible conditions made her angry.

Defining relative clauses

You can define people, things and places with a relative clause beginning with *who, that, which, where* or *whose*. The information in the defining relative clause is important for the sense of the sentence and gives essential information about the subject or object of the sentence. (See Lesson 14)

You use *who* or *that* to define people:
– as a subject pronoun.
The man who telephoned me earlier was my husband.
In this sentence *who* refers to the subject = *the man*.

– as an object pronoun.
The most interesting speaker who we met was Dr Fitouri.

In this sentence *who* refers to the object = *Dr Fitouri*.

You can leave out *who/that* when referring to the object of the relative clause.

You can use a participle clause instead of a relative clause if the noun or pronoun is the subject of the clause. You use a present participle to replace the relative pronoun + a present or past tense in a defining relative clause.
The family who lives next door are very friendly.
(= *The family living next door are very friendly.*)

You use *which* or *that* to define things.
– as a subject pronoun.
There's a large garage which belongs to the house.
– as an object pronoun.
It is the nicest place which/that we've ever seen.

You can leave out *which/that* when it is the object of the relative clause.
It is the nicest place we've ever seen.

You use a past participle to replace the relative pronoun + *be* in passive sentences in a defining relative clause.
Any house (which is) situated on the beach is in danger from storms.

You use *where* to define places.
The house where my parents live, is near the city centre.
If you leave out *where*, you have to add a preposition.
The house my parents live in is near the city centre.

You use *when* for times. You can usually leave out *when* in a defining relative clause.
The time when I get up is usually around 8 o'clock.
The time I get up is usually around 8 o'clock.

Non-defining relative clauses

You use a non-defining relative clause *who, which*, or *where* to give extra information about the subject or object of a sentence. Relative pronouns cannot be left out of non-defining relative clauses. Commas are necessary around non-defining relative clauses when written and pauses when spoken. (See Lesson 14)

You use *who* for people.
William Boyd, who has written many books, is one of my favourite authors.

You use *which* for things. You cannot use *that* in non-defining relative clauses.
I gave him a glass of water, which he drank immediately.

You can use *which* to refer back to the whole sentence.
My car is in the garage, which means I will get the bus to work.

It is also possible, but not common, to use a participle clause instead of a non-defining relative clause if the noun or pronoun is the subject of the clause.
The people, who were working so hard, are now going to have a relaxing holiday.
(=*The people working so hard, are now going to have a relaxing holiday.*)

Participle clauses

Participle clauses are often used in stories to describe background information. They focus on the action by leaving out nouns, pronouns, auxiliary verbs and conjunctions. This often creates a more dramatic effect. (See Lesson 8)

Use

You can use a participle clause:

● when two actions happen at the same time. You use it for one of the actions.
I sat in the chair watching the television.

● as a 'reduced' relative clause.
I used to walk to the bus stop with the elderly gentleman living near us.
(= I used to walk to the bus stop with the elderly gentleman who lived near us.)

● when one action happens immediately after another action. You use it for the first action.
Walking to the chair, he sat down.

● when an action happens in the middle of a longer action. You use it for the longer action.
Thinking this was another guest, I said good evening.

● to say why something happens.
Not wanting to contradict him, I said nothing.

● When it is important to show that one action has finished before another action begins, you use the perfect participle.
Having told my mother the news, I then telephoned my sister.

I wish and *if only*

You can express:

● regret about a present state with *wish* + past simple or past continuous.
I wish she spent more time with me. (See Lesson 3)
I wish I knew what I was going to do. (See Lesson 15)

● regret about the past with *wish* + past perfect.
I wish I hadn't acted so badly. (See Lesson 15)

● a wish with *could* + infinitive.
I wish I could travel more. (See Lesson 15)

You can use *if only* if the feeling is stronger.
If only it were more exciting. (See Lesson 3)
If only I had phoned the department store. (See Lesson 15)

You can use *I wish ... would* to express a wish about a definite time in the future if you think the wish is *not likely* to happen.
I wish you would help me wash my car tomorrow.
(= I know you are not going to help me.)

You can use *I hope* + present simple to express a wish about a definite time in the future if you think the wish *is likely* to happen.
I hope you help me wash my car tomorrow.
(= You said you would, and I believe you.)

The passive

You form the passive with the different tenses of *be* + past participle.
Present simple passive: *Italian is spoken here.*
Past simple passive: *The man was told to fix the television.*
Present continuous passive: *The house is being painted.*
Past continuous passive: *He was being taken to hospital.*
Present perfect passive: *The child has been sent home.*
Future passive: *It is an industry which will be encouraged.*
Modal passive: *My boss might be given a pay rise this year.*

Use

You can use the passive:

● when you do not know who or what does the action. (See Lesson 13)
The cable TV is connected to our phone.

● when you are not interested in who or what does something. (See Lesson 13)
All the electrical appliances were shut down.

● when you want to take away the focus of personal responsibility, especially in sales brochures and product information to give an 'official' tone. (See Lesson 13)
It is believed that the fault will be repaired in due course.

We usually begin a passive sentence with the known information and end the sentence with the new information. You can use a passive infinitive as the subject of a sentence for emphasis.
To be contacted by e-mail is not very sociable.

You can use a passive infinitive without *to* after modal verbs.
The Internet should be controlled by the government.

You can use a passive gerund:

● as the subject of a sentence.
Being connected to an e-mail system is very useful.

● as the object of a sentence.
Most people like being contacted by e-mail.

● with a preposition.
People are afraid of being censored by the government.

By and *with*

You use *by* to say who or what is responsible for an action.
The basement has been flooded by the washing machine.

You use *with* to talk about the instrument which is used to perform the action.
The lights were switched on with the car phone.

You also use *with* to talk about materials or ingredients.
The bedroom windows are covered with ice.

Passive constructions with *say, believe* etc.

You can use the following passive constructions with *say, believe* etc. to show that you're not sure of the truth of the statement or that you want to distance yourself from it. (See Lesson l9)
You can use *it* + passive + *that* clause.
It is believed that the government will reduce taxes.

You can use subject + passive + *to* + infinitive when the belief etc. is referring to an earlier action.
The government is said to have reduced taxes.

You use these constructions in a formal style.
Here are some of the verbs you use them with:
consider expect know report say understand think consider allege claim acknowledge

The definite and indefinite article

Here are some rules for the use of articles. (See Lesson 2)

You use *a/an:*

● when you refer to a singular countable noun when the listener/reader does not know exactly who or what is being referred to or when you talk about something for the first time.
There's a red car parked outside our house.
I watched a very good film last night.

● with nouns, especially jobs, after *be* and *become.*
I am a lawyer in a local firm.
I became a lawyer when I had completed my studies.

You use *the:*

● with singular and plural nouns when the listener/speaker both know who or what is being referred to or when you talk about something again.
(See Lesson 2)
The red car outside our house, belongs to our neighbours.
Did you like the film we watched last night?

● before a noun if there is only one.
The moon was shining very brightly last night.
I travelled round the world last year.

● before certain public places.
I went to the cinema with my sister.
Can you take this letter to the post office?

● before some geographical areas.
Portugal is on the Atlantic coast.
I visited the Sahara desert while I was on holiday.
Have you ever been to the Seychelles?

You don't use any article:

● with plural, abstract or uncountable nouns when you talk about something in general. (See Lesson 2)
Teachers are quite well paid today.
I used to drink coffee, but now I drink tea.

● before the names of most countries, towns and streets.
I lived in Brazil for five years.
The journey from Lyon to Paris took about three hours.
We walked up Regent Street towards Marylebone Road.

Countable and uncountable nouns

Countable nouns are the names of things which you can count. They have both singular and plural forms.
(See Lesson l7)
This dress is very expensive.
These dresses are very expensive.

Uncountable nouns cannot be counted and always take singular verbs.
The weather is very good today.
I think tea is a nicer drink than coffee.

Some nouns can be both countable and uncountable depending on the way they are used.
I like wine.
Burgundy and claret are wines from France.
The glass in the window is broken.
Can I have a glass of water?

Some countable nouns are seen more as a mass than a collection of separate elements.
bean(s), spice(s)

Sometimes a word is uncountable in English and countable in other foreign languages. For example, *accommodation* is uncountable in English but countable in many European languages.

Quantity words

You can use the following expressions of quantity:
(See Lesson l7)

- with countable nouns.
  *a(n) few few many both (of) several
  neither (of) a couple(of)
  I only have a few dollars in my wallet.
  I know several people who like eating fish for breakfast.*

- with uncountable nouns.
  *very little not much a little less much
  a great deal of
  I have very little money left in my wallet.
  I hope we pay less tax with the next government.*

- with both countable and uncountable nouns.
  *some any no none hardly any half all a lot of
  lots of (not) enough more most
  Could you lend me some money?
  I'm afraid I have hardly any cash in my purse.*

  Some is common in affirmative clauses, and *any* is
  common in questions and negatives. But you use *some*
  in questions if you expect, or want to encourage, the
  answer *yes.*
  Would you like some more tea?
  You can use *any* when you mean it doesn't
  matter which.
  You can get a loan from any high street bank.

Adjectives

When there is more than one adjective, you usually put
opinion adjectives before *fact* adjectives. (See Lesson 7)
She was wearing a beautiful new dress.

You can use a noun as an adjective before another noun.
car door cassette box

Nouns used as adjectives do not have a plural form. You put
a hyphen between the two parts of the noun clause.
The train journey takes two hours.
It is a two-hour train journey.

You can turn a participle + adverb phrase into a compound
adjective. You put a hyphen between the participle and the
adverb.
The landscape was whitened with snow.
It was a snow-whitened landscape.

When you want to create a word picture of the way
something looks you can use a simile – comparing one thing
with another.
The mist drew back like a set of theatre curtains.
The river was so far below us it looked like an old shoelace.

Reported speech

Reported statements

You report what people said by using
said (that) + clause.
When you put direct speech into reported speech,
you usually change:
– the tense of the verb.
– adverbs of time and place.
– the pronouns, unless the speaker is talking about
  him/herself.

You don't usually make these changes:
– when the tense of the main reporting verb is in the present
  tense.
– if the statement is still true at the time of reporting.
– when the direct speech contains a modal verb, such as,
  may, might, could, should, ought to. (See Lesson 20)

Reporting verbs

You can often use a reporting verb to describe the general
sense of what someone thinks or says.

Reporting verbs include:
*advise admit argue boast claim complain confessed
explain insist maintain offer point out promise
recommend say suggest tell threaten warn wonder*

There are several patterns for these verbs. (See Lesson 20)

Pattern	Verbs
1 verb + *to* + infinitive	*agree ask decide hope promise refuse* *He decided to go home.*
2 verb + object + *to* + infinitive	*advise ask encourage persuade remind warn* *She persuaded him to take the job.*
3 verb + *(that)* clause	*agree decide explain hope promise suggest warn* *She explained that she had lost her purse.*
4 verb + object + *(that)* clause	*advise tell warn* *He told the man that he was driving too fast.*
5 verb + object	*accept refuse* *She accepted the invitation.*
6 verb + 2 objects	*introduce offer* *She offered her a cup of tea.*

Irregular Verbs

Verbs with the same infinitive, past simple and past participle

cost	cost	cost
cut	cut	cut
hit	hit	hit
let	let	let
put	put	put
read /riːd/	read /red/	read /red/
set	set	set
shut	shut	shut

Verbs with the same past simple and past participle, but a different infinitive

bring	brought	brought
build	built	built
burn	burnt/burned	burnt/burned
buy	bought	bought
catch	caught	caught
feel	felt	felt
find	found	found
get	got	got
have	had	had
hear	heard	heard
hold	held	held
keep	kept	kept
learn	learnt/learned	learnt/learned
leave	left	left
lend	lent	lent
light	lit/lighted	lit/lighted
lose	lost	lost
make	made	made
mean	meant	meant
meet	met	met
pay	paid	paid
say	said	said
sell	sold	sold
send	sent	sent
sit	sat	sat
sleep	slept	slept
smell	smelt/smelled	smelt/smelled
spell	spelt/spelled	spelt/spelled
spend	spent	spent
stand	stood	stood
teach	taught	taught
understand	understood	understood
win	won	won

Verbs with same infinitive and past participle but a different past simple

become	became	become
come	came	come
run	ran	run

Verbs with a different infinitive, past simple and past participle

be	was/were	been
begin	began	begun
break	broke	broken
choose	chose	chosen
do	did	done
draw	drew	drawn
drink	drank	drunk
drive	drove	driven
eat	ate	eaten
fall	fell	fallen
fly	flew	flown
forget	forgot	forgotten
give	gave	given
go	went	gone
grow	grew	grown
know	knew	known
lie	lay	lain
ring	rang	rung
rise	rose	risen
see	saw	seen
show	showed	shown
sing	sang	sung
speak	spoke	spoken
swim	swam	swum
take	took	taken
throw	threw	thrown
wake	woke	woken
wear	wore	worn
write	wrote	written

Pronunciation guide

/ɑː/	park		/b/	buy
/æ/	hat		/d/	day
/aɪ/	my		/f/	free
/aʊ/	how		/g/	give
/e/	ten		/h/	house
/eɪ/	bay		/j/	you
/eə/	there		/k/	cat
/ɪ/	sit		/l/	look
/iː/	me		/m/	mean
/ɪə/	beer		/n/	nice
/ɒ/	what		/p/	paper
/əʊ/	no		/r/	rain
/ɔː/	more		/s/	sad
/ɔɪ/	toy		/t/	time
/ʊ/	took		/v/	verb
/uː/	soon		/w/	wine
/ʊə/	tour		/z/	zoo
/ɜː/	sir		/ʃ/	shirt
/ʌ/	sun		/ʒ/	leisure
/ə/	better		/ŋ/	sing
			/tʃ/	church
			/θ/	thank
			/ð/	then
			/dʒ/	jacket

Tapescripts

Lesson 1   Sounds and speaking, activity 2

PAT You speak French, don't you?

DON Yes. In fact, I speak French and Russian.

PAT Russian! You didn't learn Russian at school, did you?

DON Yes, when I was seventeen. I did Russian for a couple of years.

PAT Well, say something in Russian, will you?

DON No, I've almost forgotten it. It's easy to forget a language if you don't practise.

PAT And what about your French. You haven't forgotten that as well, have you?

DON No, I practised when I was in France.

PAT I've got an idea. Let's go to Paris, shall we?

DON For the day?

PAT Well, why not? It only takes three hours by train now, doesn't it?

DON Does it? I didn't know that. Aren't you worried about the cost?

PAT No, it'll be good fun. And there'll be plenty of opportunities to speak French, won't there?

Lesson 1   Listening, activity 2

Q Hello, Hazel.

HAZEL Hi.

Q Um...can you tell us how many languages you speak and which ones they are?

HAZEL Yes, er... I speak three languages. English, French and Welsh.

Q Good, how interesting. How did you learn them?

HAZEL Um... well, I was brought up in Wales and you had to learn Welsh, um... when you were in school. And French I chose to learn, I thought it would be, you know, useful to learn it.

Q Right. And, er... do you still remember it from school?

HAZEL Well, not really. I've forgotten most of it now because it really was a long time ago. Um ...

Q What was the most difficult aspect of learning it?

HAZEL Well, I was very embarrassed when we had to speak French in front of the rest of the class, you know. The terrible pronunciations and things. Also, I think listening, the listening comprehension was very difficult because it was always so fast...

Q Oh, yes. A common complaint.

HAZEL Yeah. Difficult to keep up, you know.

Q What do you think the most useful thing to do is?

HAZEL I think the grammatical system is the most useful because if you learn about grammar in another language you can relate it to your own native language and I think that's very helpful.

Q Do you mean structure and everything?

HAZEL Yes.

Q Thanks very much.

Q Michael.

MICHAEL Hi.

Q How many languages do you speak and, er... which ones are they?

MICHAEL Well, I speak English and I speak German.

Q Aha. And how did you learn them?

MICHAEL Um... I was living in Germany. Actually, er... my parents, er... moved to Germany and so I had to learn to speak German or not speak to anybody.

Q Right. Where did you learn? At school?

MICHAEL Aha. I went to school and I had to speak German in class, er... but always spoke English at home.

Q Right. What was the most difficult aspect of learning a foreign language?

MICHAEL Oh, I suppose getting it perfect. I mean, now even I ... I make mistakes all the time and ... and Germans would laugh at me...

Q Hmm ...

MICHAEL But they seem to understand what I'm trying to say most of the time.

Q Right. What do you think the best way to learn a language is?

MICHAEL I think to go to the country that speaks that language and then you have to throw yourself in and learn how to speak it. Um...I think it's probably a lot easier to learn a language when you're young.

Q Yes. I'd agree with that.

MICHAEL And you are maybe less afraid of making mistakes.

Q Hmm...

Q Janet.

JANET Hello.

Q Hi. Can you tell us how many languages you speak and, er... which ones they are?

JANET Um... well, I speak English, which is my native tongue, and French.

Q Oh right. And how did you learn French?

JANET Well, really by listening to cassettes in a car and video cassettes at home and then, um... I took a weekly magazine for about two years.

Q You must be more or less self-taught. Was it difficult?

JANET Um... well I must say when I met real live French people I found it quite difficult, yes, I must say that.

Q What did you think the most important aspect would be?

JANET Oh, definitely to have a very good grounding in grammar.

Q Aha.

JANET And also I always used a dictionary if I didn't understand a word as well.

Q Right. Um... did you... how did you feel about the self-study method? Was that the one you used?

JANET Oh gosh, well, it fitted in with my professional life. It's a very lonely way of doing things, the self-study um... but as I say, it fitted in with my life as a doctor.

Q Oh, right. Thanks very much.

Lesson 2   Vocabulary and speaking, activity 2

JANE You must be George Dennis.

GEORGE Yes, that's right.

JANE Hello, George, pleased to meet you. Welcome to the company! My name's Jane and I'm going to show you around the office.

GEORGE Hello, Jane. Thank you very much.

JANE I'll introduce you to everyone. Let's go and meet your boss. Ah, there he is. Bob, this is George Dennis, it's his first day. George, this is Dr Robert Crewe.

GEORGE How do you do, sir?

BOB Call me Bob, George. Everyone calls me Bob. Welcome to the company.

GEORGE Thank you, Bob.

Lesson 2   Listening, activity 2

Q Mary.

MARY Yes?

Q I hope you don't mind my calling you Mary.

MARY Er... no, no.

Q A generational difference, you know, the customs have changed so much in Britain over the last fifty years, haven't they?

MARY Yes, they certainly have.

Q Do you think children behave very differently now?

MARY From my day, yes, I do, because children in my day were supposed to be seen and not heard. And the discipline, it was very strict. I suppose you didn't want your children, you see, to let you down.

Q I see. And what do you think Peter, as a member of a younger generation? Do you think children behave very differently now?

PETER Yes, I think they do. Um... there is less discipline really. I mean, sometimes the discipline is a problem, nowadays and then you definitely... they're definitely not meant to be seen and not heard. They're a big part of family life, aren't they? So, things have changed.

Q Hmm. And I suppose the whole family structure has changed, hasn't it? Who was the head of the family in your day.

MARY Oh, it was always the father! Um... I mean, he was even served first at dinner, er... and he was the one that took all the main decisions in the family

Q Ah, yes.

MARY Hmm.

Q And Peter, do you think that's still the same in today's world?

PETER Not to the same extent, no, and I mean in a lot of families, in our family, we all take decisions together. It's not like he's the lord and master which I think is how he was seen. It's more democratic if you like. It's... it's more equally shared.

Q Hmm. I suppose, Mary, people's ideas about marriage have changed a lot too, haven't they? Did people get married at a different age in your youth?

MARY Um..., well, yes, yes, they did indeed. And certainly the girls felt that if they weren't married by the time they were twenty-one or twenty-two they'd been left on the shelf! Absolutely.

Q Do you know any twenty-one-year-olds who would feel left on the shelf, Peter?

PETER No, not at all. People leave it a lot longer now. Maybe because they live longer, I don't know. You've got a longer life so people usually don't get married until they're in their thirties.

Q Uh, uh.

PETER Yes.

Q That's a big difference.

PETER Mmm.

Q Have manners changed a great deal? Do people address each other differently?

MARY Oh, yes, certainly. I mean, you'd always call people, you know, Mister and use his surname or Mrs and use her surname. You wouldn't use their Christian names, their first names, I mean unless it was close family or friends. And your neighbours, I mean, no, you wouldn't call first names like you just called me Mary!

Q Well, I did ask! How about you, Peter?

PETER Well, nowadays you do use first names, generally, I mean, I can't think of a situation where you wouldn't.

Q There's no one that you would call Sir or Mister?

PETER Well, I don't know, a magistrate?

Q A lawyer or maybe a policeman?

PETER But no. Most people you can usually address by their first name.

Q Aha. And I suppose families used to stay together longer too, didn't they? In your youth, Mary, were parents, and grandparents and children all living together in the same house?

MARY Yes, yes.

Q Or is that a myth?

MARY No, no, no. Usually, they certainly did. They probably left home when they got married and established a family of their own but usually they would stay in the same house, yes.

Q Now, Peter, how would you like to live with your grandmother?

PETER No, well, I like to visit her but we... people generally leave home, I mean, when they go to college. That's when I left home. Um..., and even women, I mean, there's no... there's no hard and fast rule that women stay at home until they marry now, they often go and live in a flat somewhere and leave the family nest.

Q Well, I think that's shocking!

Lesson 3 **Speaking and listening, activity 2**

DAVE My dad took me to my first match when I was... oh, I can't have been more than about five. And I still support the same team...

JANE Now I go every day before work and sometimes at weekends as well and it's great. I meet my friends, have a long workout and then a shower and a drink and I like the feeling I have of, you know, really being fit.

SARAH I just wanted to go back a little way, like maybe... a hundred years or so, but the more I did it, the more interested I became. Now, I'd like to go back in the family just as far as I possibly can.

TIM Oh, they're wonderful! You get these huge insects or giant vegetables or whatever moving around the town and everyone takes it so seriously. And it doesn't matter that the special effects are lousy and it's nothing like what we can do today. That's part of the charm.

Lesson 3 **Speaking and listening, activity 3**

DAVE Well my girlfriend says I'm obsessed. She's always complaining that I spend every Saturday either at the match, or watching it on TV. I don't think I'm obsessed. I only watch football about, well, maybe three times a week. Football's great, so exciting. And it's brilliant now that they play weekday matches and on Sundays as well. I've loved football ever since I was a kid; my dad took me to my first match when I was... oh, I can't have been more than about five. And I still support the same team: Arsenal. They're the greatest!

JANE I suppose you could say I'm obsessed. It all started about five years ago when I fell off my bicycle and broke my leg. I had to stay in hospital for ages and I couldn't move and people kept bringing me chocolates and stuff and I got really fat. When finally they let me out of hospital I still couldn't do much for about six months and I felt just awful. When my leg was better, I started going to the gym to get back into shape. It took months of hard work but it was really worth it and after I got fit again, well, I just kept going. Now I go every day before work and sometimes at weekends as well and it's great. I meet my friends, have a long workout and then a shower and a drink and I like the feeling I have of, you know, really being fit.

SARAH Well, I've always loved history and visiting old country houses. And then one day I decided to find out about my family history. So I began looking up old records and finding out who my ancestors were and what kind of lives they had. It started about three years ago when my sister had a baby. At first I just wanted to go back a little way, like maybe... a hundred years or so but the more I did it, the more interested I became. Now, I'd like to go back in the family just as far as I possibly can. I'm stuck around the 16th century at the moment, but there are some records in a church in Leeds that I think might help me, so I'm going there next week to try to find out more. Some of my family think I'm mad, but I don't care. I just want to know everything I can and I'm determined to find out as much as possible.

TIM With me it's old B movies. You know those old movies they produced in the fifties to play alongside the big films. They were always about, you know, giant ants taking over the world and aliens landing from outer space and causing strange things to happen to people in small towns in America. Oh, they're wonderful! You get these huge insects or giant vegetables or whatever moving around the town and everyone takes it so seriously. And it doesn't matter that the special effects are lousy, it's nothing like what we can do today – that's part of the charm. I got hooked on B movies when I was a teenager. Now I collect them on video. They still put them on TV but usually in the middle of the night. My friends can't understand what I see in them, but for me they're just the greatest thing ever. Revenge of the Killer Tomatoes, that's my favourite.

Lesson 3   Speaking and listening, activity 6

WOMAN 1 Dave and his football? Oh, it's definitely an obsession. You know he even watches it on TV when he's seen it live – you know when he's actually been to the match! I can't understand it. It's boring. All they do is kick a ball around. I wish he spent more time with me. But no, it's football, football, football with him!

MAN 1   Oh, I couldn't agree more. But, well, you know I worry about Jane. All that exercise! It can't be good for you to do it so often. I mean, she goes to the gym every day! If only she'd do something different as well – at least at the weekend! I think you can overdo it if you're not careful.

WOMAN 1 Oh, I disagree. She's really fit. She looks great! I just wish I could be that disciplined.

WOMAN 2 Oh, so do I. But what about Tim! Those films are such a strange thing to be obsessed with. I mean, they're so old and the acting is so bad! He's always watching them. If only he were interested in something a bit more up-to-date. But Tim thinks they wonderful.

MAN 2   Yes! He's absolutely right. They are the best thing on TV.

MAN 1   Well, I try to get involved in Sarah's interests but I just can't get excited about history. I wish it were more exciting. I just can't see the point of digging up the past.

Lesson 4   Vocabulary and listening, activity 2

Conversation 1
WOMAN   Good morning, Fogg Art Museum, may I help you?
MAN   Yes, can you tell me what time you open?
WOMAN   We open at 10 in the morning, except on Saturdays when it's midday.
MAN   OK, and what time do you close?
WOMAN   We're open until 7 every evening, except on Thursdays when we stay open until 10.
MAN   OK, thanks a lot.

Conversation 2
WOMAN   Good evening, this is the East Coast Grill.
MAN   Hi, yeah, I'd like to make a reservation for a table for tomorrow night.
WOMAN   Sure, and how many people would that be for?
MAN   Six.
WOMAN   So, a table for six on Friday June 7th. OK, we can do that. What time do you want it for?
MAN   Make it 8 o'clock.
WOMAN   And your name is?
MAN   Stein.
WOMAN   OK Mr Stein, we'll see you tomorrow, Friday June 7th at 8pm. Bye.
MAN   Thanks, bye.

Conversation 3
WOMAN   Good morning, this is Bailey's Store, can I help you?
MAN   Yes, could you tell me if you have a travel service in the store?
WOMAN   Yes, sir, we have our own travel agency.
MAN   OK, and does it do flight and hotel bookings for Europe?
WOMAN   You tell them where you want to go, and they'll sort it out for you, sir.
MAN   Good, I'll try and get there this evening. You're open until 7, aren't you?
WOMAN   That's right.
MAN   Thanks. Bye.

Conversation 4
WOMAN   Could I speak to the manager?
MAN   Could I ask what it's about?
WOMAN   The music last night really went on for far too long, and I wish to speak to the manager about it.
MAN   I'm sorry that it disturbed you, madam. Are you a local resident?

WOMAN   Yes, unfortunately. I thought the club closed at 2.
MAN   It usually closes at 2, but last night and tonight it stays open until 4.
WOMAN   So it's going to be just the same tonight?
MAN   That's right.
WOMAN   (Sarcastic) Great! That's great!

Conversation 5
MAN   Can I have two tickets for the concert tonight?
WOMAN   Yes, sir. Where would you like to sit?
MAN   Oh, not too far back.
WOMAN   How about in row D?
MAN   Yes, that'll do fine.
WOMAN   It starts at 7.30. How would you like to pay?
MAN   I'll pay by AMEX. Can you tell me what time it finishes tonight?
WOMAN   About 10.30.
MAN   OK, thanks.

Lesson 4   Listening and speaking activity 1

GRAHAM Well, I guess we'd better plan an itinerary.
ANGELA   I guess so. We really need to impress him.
GRAHAM Okay. Um… well I guess we'd better start at breakfast. How about breakfast in Harvard Square?
ANGELA   Great. I love that place.
GRAHAM At 8 o'clock?
ANGELA   Yeah. 8 o'clock's great.
GRAHAM Okay. Good. Good. And that should take us what, half an hour or so… from say 8.30 to 11 we can take him sight-seeing. In Cambridge?
ANGELA   Well, why don't we start at 9? I think we should allow a little bit longer for breakfast. You know what it's like.
GRAHAM Okay, a relaxed start to the day…
ANGELA   Yeah.
GRAHAM …and then we'll just rush through Cambridge. It's just a bunch of universities, anyway. Okay…
ANGELA   Mmm….
GRAHAM …and then so noon-time we can find ourselves up on Beacon Hill. Maybe have a little stroll around there?
ANGELA   Perfect. That sounds great.
GRAHAM Okay, excellent. Which should take us right through to my favourite part of the day …
ANGELA   Lunch at the Union Oyster Bar!
GRAHAM The Union Oyster Bar!
ANGELA   Yes, let's.
GRAHAM I've never been there.
ANGELA   Oh, it's fantastic. You'll love it.
GRAHAM Are you sure he likes oysters?
ANGELA   Oh, I'm sure he will. It really has a wonderful atmosphere.
GRAHAM Okay. Oysters at what, say, 1 o'clock?
ANGELA   Perfect!
GRAHAM Excellent. Okay, so what, we need another hour for lunch, then we can walk along Commonwealth Avenue.
ANGELA   Well, shall we have an hour and a half for lunch, and say start 2.30?
GRAHAM Well, I guess so. I don't want him to think we're lazy or anything, though.
ANGELA   Well, it's just I hate pushing things and things always take longer than you imagine.
GRAHAM And you don't want to go walking on a bellyfull of oysters.
ANGELA   No, you don't!
GRAHAM Okay. Well, that'll take us all the way down to Back Bay, where we can do some shopping, say, around what, three?
ANGELA   Oh, that's wonderful!
GRAHAM Yeah?
ANGELA   Yeah, no that sounds great.
GRAHAM That'll take the afternoon. Then in the evening, how about drinks? At where?
ANGELA   The Hyatt Regency.

GRAHAM Excellent idea.
ANGELA Okay. And shall we say 7.30?
GRAHAM Well, let's make it 7.
ANGELA I don't know, I think...
GRAHAM How much shopping?
ANGELA ... well I can shop till I drop, so please can we say 7.30?
GRAHAM Okay!
ANGELA Okay.
GRAHAM You got it. But then let's not drink for long. I'd say let's go for dinner at... where? Joseph's Aquarium?
ANGELA Yes. That's a great idea.
GRAHAM 8 pm. I'll book a table.
ANGELA Oh, again, I don't know if... um...... I think we should say 8.30 to give us an hour for drinks before supper.
GRAHAM Okay.
ANGELA Okay.
GRAHAM Whatever you say.
ANGELA Great.
GRAHAM So then let's finish the evening at, um... Quincy Market.
ANGELA Oh, perfect. That's a really good idea.
GRAHAM At what, 10 o'clock?
ANGELA Yes, 10 sounds wonderful.
GRAHAM Uhuh.
ANGELA I think he's really going to be impressed with all that.
GRAHAM Yes. It's a great idea.

Lesson 5   Listening, activity 2

Speaker 1 Germaine Greer. I think she's hugely intelligent. And, er...academically pretty brilliant as well. But she has a great sense of humour. And her book *The Female Eunuch*, er… is a book that actually changed... changed me in a big way back in the 1970s. I like the way she's not afraid to say the first thing that comes into her head, even if it's wrong sometimes. Um… and she seems to have a very positive and joyous approach to life.

Speaker 2 New York for me. I toured America four years ago but didn't quite get to New York but I'd love to go there. I'd like to spend time in supposedly the city that never sleeps, that has such a... a vibrancy and is about four gears higher in... kind of pace of life than London is. I think I'd really like that.

Speaker 3 It was, er… in a beach hut on Cosamue in Thailand and I was there with my boyfriend and we were very much in love and we were staying in this little hut which was only about twenty feet from the sea. And we could just run out into the sea first thing in the morning and we just lived on fish and fruit and it was wonderful.

Speaker 4 I suppose to jump out of an aeroplane, preferably with a parachute, but I also wouldn't mind if I didn't do it because I'm so apprehensive, if not frightened of doing it. But I would like to, yes, yes, I would like to.

Speaker 5 Plastering? Yeah, I know it sounds silly but I didn't think I could do it. There was a great big wall that had to have all this old plaster taken off and a whole lot of new plaster and skimming done. And I didn't think I could do it, but I did, and I felt really good about it.

Lesson 6
Listening, activity 3
Part 1

Sister Coxall had been running Violet Ward for many years. Her pride and joy was her own little office, scrupulously clean, its walls glistening with fresh white paint. She sat at her desk, her eyes unseeing. Who was this new doctor, anyway? Some silly youth fresh from medical school? What right had he to interfere in the running of her ward?
She had met him yesterday. He had driven into the hospital grounds and almost driven over her. There were plenty of 'Go Slow' notices within sight. Besides, almost everybody who worked at the hospital knew she walked through the grounds at that time of day.
'Are you all right?' he had said, getting out of his car. 'I really wasn't concentrating.' He seemed embarrassed. 'Er, Sister, I'm frightfully sorry.'
She couldn't help smiling. 'That's all right, Mr –' she paused politely. 'Doctor – Doctor Green. I've just arrived, as you can see,' he grinned. 'I'm taking over the running of D Block.'
Sister Coxall noticeably stiffened. 'D Block?' she echoed.
'Look, get into my car, and I'll drive you to the Nurses' Home.' They sat in silence and soon were climbing the dingy staircase leading to Sister Coxall's neat room. Once inside, she took off her cape. 'Sit down, Doctor, I'll make some tea.'
Sitting drinking the sweet tea, Doctor Green explained that he had always been interested in psychiatric work and when he had finished his studies, he had applied for this post in one of the country's largest psychiatric hospitals. He had not expected to get the job, but he did, and without an interview.
He told her of the great changes and new ideas he hoped he would introduce. 'For instance,' he said, 'the sister on Violet Ward has been working there for ten years. She must have lost her identity to some extent. Her patients must be more like children to her than sick people.' He leaned forward. 'You know, Sister, she is in danger of illness herself. Tomorrow, when I begin my work, I intend to move that sister to a different ward. She may not realise it at the time, but the change will do her good.'
Sister Coxall listened, a faint pink flush tinged her ears.

Lesson 6
Listening, activity 5
Part 2

The day had arrived. She looked around her office. She was going to be removed from this, her home, and placed among strangers.
'No,' she screamed, and her fist came heavily down upon the desk, scattering pens into sudden life.
Sister Coxall's mind began to work. Now it raced. Nobody knows he is coming here except me. He said he was going to stay at a hotel last night and was coming straight to the ward this morning, before reporting to the General Office. He had no white coat or identity badge yet.
A diabolical smile drew back the corners of her thin straight mouth. 'There is only one thing to do,' she muttered, and rose and went to the door.
'Nurse,' she called, ' a new patient is expected this morning, a Mr Green. When he arrives, bring him straight to my office.' She looked down at the empty report paper she held in her hand. 'It says here that he is paranoid and greatly confused; he thinks he's a doctor. Humour him, Nurse. I'll prepare a strong sedative.'
Going to the cupboard, Sister Coxall took down a syringe and filled it with a cool orange liquid. She then took an empty file from a cabinet and began to prepare a written report on Mr Green.
She sighed. The ward was full of men, all confused, all insisting they were doctors. No one was ever going to take her ward and office away from her. No one.

Lesson 7 **Listening and speaking, activity 2**

Q Right, Terry and Kathy, we're talking about holidays. Can you… can you give me an idea of your holiday nightmare?

TERRY Oh, easy! A crowded beach! Ugh! We holidayed in Cornwall last year, St Ives, do you know it?

Q Yeah.

TERRY Absolutely dreadful! The beaches are so full of people – there were so many people, all lined up like whales on a beach. It was absolutely dreadful. We booked in for two weeks, but only stayed for one.

Q Oh no. And is that the same for you, Kathy?

KATHY Well, no, the worst thing for me is a boat trip. I really don't like sailing at all. I get very seasick so it's just miserable. I just spend the whole time sort of staring over the side and wishing it was over.

Q And is that a daytrip out on a boat?

KATHY No, any sea trip – I just can't handle it, I can't handle the movement of the boat.

Q Okay, so what's your idea of a holiday in paradise?

TERRY Oh, that's easy. We honeymooned in the Virgin Islands ten years ago. Absolutely terrific. Absolutely beautiful – the sun, the sand, the peace and quiet is just astounding and the people… the people are… the shopkeepers right… the shopkeepers have this sort of ritual of greeting you. When you go in they formally shake your hand and say 'Hello, thank you for coming to my shop'. It's amazing… amazing.

Q And what's your favourite?

KATHY That's the kind of place I've always wanted to go, you know.

Q You've been to the Virgin Islands as well?

KATHY No, I haven't. I've always wanted to go. But you know, a sunny place, palm trees, happy people, relaxed. No cars. I think that's wonderful. I once went to Sark in the… in the Channel Islands and it's not tropical of course but, there aren't any cars and everybody either walks or they go by horse and cart, and it's won… it's so peaceful.

Q It's like a trip back in time?

KATHY Yes. It's gorgeous.

Q Right, and so, when you're on this holiday, what would your favourite holiday pastime be?

TERRY Um… reading. You know, I take all my novels that I want to read, you go to the bookshop beforehand… catch up on all those novels that you wanted to read and… diving. I got into diving when we honeymooned in the Virgin Islands. That's one of the… the thing I do. I don't waterski or anything like that, just diving. It's brilliant.

Q Right. Right. And is that the same for you, Kathy?

KATHY Yes, I like reading as well but I'm not too fussy. I like thrillers – any old cheap thriller. I'm ready to read pretty well anything. I abandon all taste when I go away.

Q And so that would be one of the items that you'd take on your holidays. What other items do you always take on holiday?

TERRY The thing I cannot go without are my eye shields. You know, long-haul flights – I'm not talking about just a small flight. But long-haul flights, I cannot do without – I cannot sleep otherwise either on a plane. I mean, with my eye shields, you know, I usually fall asleep as soon as we take off but without them, you know useless. Useless.

Q All right. So I guess it's a kind of Pavlov's dog reaction.

TERRY Yes, I suppose, yes!

Q And Kathy, what do you take?

KATHY Well, apart from the books, which I've mentioned already, oddly enough I like to take my favourite perfume. You know, you go out in the evening and I always feel slightly more interesting if er… I'm wearing perfume.

Q And what is your perfume?

KATHY It's called 'Attraction'. It's by Elveda. Yeah.

Q Oh, very nice. I don't know that one, actually. What do you miss most when you're away from home?

TERRY Um… it's probably the Sunday papers. 'Cos… cos, I'm so busy during the week, the Sunday papers is a time when I can sit down, either at home or have a pint in the pub, and catch up. I love to catch up on my reading when I'm on holiday.

Q Right. It seems as though that's all you'll be doing. You'll either be diving or reading on this holiday!

TERRY Well, what else is there?

Q And Kathy?

KATHY I always miss a decent loaf of bread. At home we have a baker who bakes the bread on the premises and who opens on Sundays, too, so we get lovely fresh, crusty bread every day.

Q Oh right, okay.

Lesson 8

Listening, activity 2

Part 1

LOUISE Yeah, I want to tell you about this incredible thing that happened to me. When I was at school we went on this school visit to Scotland and we stayed in this… in this, incredible castle. It was on the edge of er… on the edge of a lake and it was beautiful but it was really spooky. You know, it kind of reminded me of something out of a horror film. Anyway, I was sharing a room with this girl called Melissa. She was a really nice girl and we were staying in this little sort of attic room at the top of the castle with an incredible view over the lake and mist and everything. And every morning we had these cookery classes in the old kitchen, and they were with this old Scottish cook – she was an absolute darling. She was brilliant, a brilliant person and she lived in the castle. Anyway, Melissa, said that she'd heard this music playing, like piano music playing, in a room, you know, right at the top of the castle. And er… she mentioned this to one of the teachers, and they told her, you know, that she was just imagining things, you know. The teacher she… she thought that Melissa was completely out to lunch, basically. Anyway, the cook heard Melissa telling the teacher and she said that Chopin had stayed in this very castle.

MAN/WOMAN (laughter) It's like one of those urban myths…

LOUISE Honest! No, no, really! And Melissa said that she recognised the music and that it was Chopin. And anyway, we checked the dates and Melissa, you won't believe this, she heard the music on the very same anniversary of his visit to the castle.

MAN I don't believe you!

WOMAN I find that very hard to believe!

Lesson 8

Listening, activity 4

Part 2

LOUISE Er… something else happened in this very same castle.

MAN Oh no.

WOMAN Here we go again!

LOUISE It was a special place. It really was. Anyway, we went to sleep one night and… er… this is still with Melissa… and we both woke up at exactly the same moment. And, er… there was this really, really strong smell of gas. You know, it was a real stench, in our room. Anyway, you know… we immediately ran out and we got one of the teachers and they …

MAN Did you open the windows?

LOUISE No, we just went straight to the teacher, okay, and the teacher just said, you know, don't be silly, I'm sure its your imaginations, you know…

WOMAN Could she not smell it, then?

LOUISE No, no! Anyway, she didn't bother even coming into the room. Um… so we went back to bed and um… we woke up twice more during the night and again smelling gas.

MAN Didn't the teachers come up to check the room?

LOUISE No, no, they just thought we were being silly. Anyway, so the next morning the teacher, you know, told everyone about what happened to us and everybody was laughing at us... you know, they just... the teacher was taking the mickey out of us. It made us... it made us really mad. She just sat there splitting her sides.

MAN The teacher did?

LOUISE Yeah. And um... anyway our lovely old cook, you know, the brilliant woman, asked what room we were sleeping in and um... we told her that it was the Rose Room. Anyway, she looked as if she'd seen a ghost.

ALL Why?

LOUISE Well, because, you see, what she told us was that we were staying in the bedroom of the son and heir of the family who owned the castle, and apparently he was killed in the First World War by gas on October the 11th, 1917. And that was the exact same date that we smelt the gas – on the anniversary of his death. They are incredible things.

Progress check Lessons 5 to 8
Listening and speaking, activity 1

I was a nurse in a London hospital going on night duty at 8pm. I went to my ward and began to check all the patients. Suddenly I heard a man's footsteps coming up the stairs and I saw a man in a chauffeur's uniform who said, 'I have come for my wife.' As this was a ward for men, I told him to go down to the office to ask where he should go, although I knew no patient would be allowed to go home at that time of night.

Then the sister on duty arrived, and said she'd been with a woman patient who was dying. An ambulance had brought her in that morning, unconscious. The police were trying to find her husband. I told her about the chauffeur, and she went to ask about the matter at the office. But she returned and said that no one had been there to enquire about their wife. And the man who operated the lift, standing in full view of the stairs said he'd not seen anyone in chauffeur's uniform.

The next day, the sister told me that she'd found out about the unknown lady who had died in the night. The woman's husband was the chauffeur for a rich family. Early on the previous morning he had set out on a long journey with his employers. But the car had been involved in an accident and the chauffeur was killed. When he left home that morning his wife was well and looking forward to spending a day in town with a friend. The friend had called to collect her and she was surprised to receive no answer to the doorbell. She looked through the letterbox and saw the poor woman lying on the floor of the hall. A neighbour called the police and an ambulance took the chauffeur's wife to hospital, where she failed to recover consciousness and died in the night.

At this stage no one knew where her husband was. The police hadn't been able to contact him. They also didn't know that he had died in a road accident five hours before his wife died in hospital. It became clear to me that the man in the chauffeur's uniform I'd spoken to had in fact been dead for some time.

Lesson 9
Listening, activity 3

Q So, you spent some time in Africa as a teacher. Whereabouts where you then?

MATTHEW I spent about a year in Sudan.

Q And, and, when was that?

MATTHEW About ten years ago.

Q And how long did you stay?

MATTHEW I stayed about er... a year.

Q Ah, and you enjoyed it... you had a good time?

MATTHEW Yes, er... it was a real experience for me. Just after university.

Q So you were what, twenty-one, twenty-two when you went there?

MATTHEW Yeah.

Q Great. And, and what subjects did you use to teach there?

MATTHEW It was English. Um... all the teachers, um..., came out from England were English teachers. So English language mainly and a bit of literature.

Q And did they just do, did they just do English and literature in English? Or did they do other subjects as well?

MATTHEW No that was all. All the other subjects were in Arabic.

Q I see. And what was a typical day like, I mean, how would you start your day when you were there as a teacher.

MATTHEW Um... well, I lived in town, and the school was about two miles out of town. We'd start in a cafe, about seven o'clock in the morning having tea. Walk out to school, um... along the Nile, I taught in a town by the Nile, um... teach a couple of lessons then have breakfast at school...

Q How long were your lessons, how long did they last?

MATTHEW Um... about forty minutes. Some times they were double classes. About forty minutes...

Q So you did two lessons, then you used to have break...

MATTHEW We used to have breakfast with the staff, um... then two more lessons, another break, two more lessons and then we stopped at around 1 o'clock.

Q So that used to be six lessons.

MATTHEW Six lessons in a day.

Q And how many pupils did you have in the class?

MATTHEW Well, the classes were large, because there was a shortage of teachers, really, so anything from forty-five to seventy, in a class.

Q Gosh, that's enormous. And what was the classroom like?

MATTHEW Well, the classrooms were okay, desks, chairs enough for the students, not enough books for all the students, um... open windows, no glass, and blackboards that were quite old, had holes in.

Q So, the equipment wasn't really...

MATTHEW There wasn't really any equipment, no, blackboards and chalk.

Q Blackboards and chalk... And er... were you used to this kind of equipment? When you began teaching?

MATTHEW I knew what to expect, but um... I trained as teacher with equipment you'd find in a classroom here, overhead projectors and so on...

Q Yes, yes, so, I suppose, after a year you got used to using that kind of equipment, not having overhead projectors... there didn't used to be overhead projectors or anything like that at all...

MATTHEW No, there wasn't any electricity during the day for a start. And we had to get used to adapting what we wanted to teach, how we wanted to work with the class...

Q So you had lessons that used to be about forty minutes long. Were there any exams at the end of the semester or...?

MATTHEW Yes, every class had exams at the end of the year, and the top year had national exams to sit, um... which were actually quite important...the equivalent of O'levels in England.

Q Hmm... Hmm... And was there anything that er... that happened that you... you were embarrassed about or that you found amusing...was there any amusing incidents.

MATTHEW Well, it was very interesting working and living in a different culture, we used to have breakfast together as staff and you eat with your hands, so it was quite important that you wash your hands. Um... the first time... the first day at school, I remember washing my hands in the water, the bowl of water that was actually the drinking water...

Q Oh dear...

MATTHEW And, er... luckily, everybody laughed.

Q Good, good, yes... People are very kind to visitors to a foreign culture, aren't they? Thank you.

Lesson 10
Vocabulary and listening, activity 3

WOMAN   Something that really intrigues me is the difference between the American legal system and the British legal system. For instance, in Britain are you innocent until you're proved to be guilty, or the other way around?

MAN   No, that's actually on the Continent. You find in France that you're guilty until proven innocent. Here, you're innocent until proven guilty.

WOMAN   Right. What about if you're convicted of drug dealing? Are always sent to prison or is there sometimes a fine?

MAN   Um… well, it's different in Scotland… I don't know exactly the laws there, their laws are slightly different, but here it's quite often something… it's quite often a fine, yes.

WOMAN   Right. And weaponry? Is it an offence to carry a weapon, such as a gun or a knife?

MAN   Oh most definitely, yeah. I mean, guns are pretty much illegal and very much frowned upon, and so are knives. Yes, it's definitely an offence.

WOMAN   Gosh. It's so incredibly different, isn't it? And if the police arrest you, are you allowed to call a lawyer?

MAN   I believe so, yes, yes, as soon as you get to the station you're given the option to call a lawyer. Obviously you don't have to, but I should think in some cases it's quite a good idea.

WOMAN   Absolutely. And if the police suspect you of a crime, is it legal to remain silent when they question you?

MAN   I think you do, yes you do have the right to remain silent. Although I believe the law's changed slightly, and um… the fact that you remain silent may be used against you in court.

WOMAN   Oh my goodness. Right. Okay. And how about if you're charged with a crime? Do you always go into custody while you wait for a trial?

MAN   No. You can get bail, either… either a cash bond bail, which someone has to post for you, or you just get police bail, which is free, and they'll release you on that until they want to call you up again.

WOMAN   Right. Okay. What about if you confess to a crime? Do you always get a lighter sentence?

MAN   No. It's not like in the States where you get plea bargaining. Here, um… just because you confess to a crime, it doesn't mean you're going to get a lighter sentence. It depends on the seriousness of the crime.

WOMAN   Oh, right. And how about, are there any crimes which you can be executed for?

MAN   [laughs] Er… not any more. Oh yes! No, no, there is one actually. I think it's treason which they would probably use in time of war, but I don't know.

WOMAN   See again, that's a huge difference because …

MAN   Absolutely. Absolutely. But not for murder. I mean if you just murder someone, if you bump someone off, then you can't be hung, but if it's against the State, I think you can still, you know, theoretically have your head lopped off and put on a pole above the Tower of London.

WOMAN   Oh, scary, scary. And is there always a trial by jury for serious crimes?

MAN   Yes. Minor crimes tend to go to Magistrate's Courts, but Crown Court is, er… with a jury is always reserved for serious crimes, yes.

WOMAN   Wow. And who is the person who decides on a sentence? Is it the jury or is it the judge?

MAN   Um… usually in most crimes the jury will give a decision on whether they're guilty or innocent, but it's usually the judge who does the sentencing, saying how long it is and what term, and so on.

WOMAN   It's amazing. You know, there's just so many differences between the two systems.

MAN   Really?

WOMAN   Yeah.

MAN   How interesting.

Lesson 11
Speaking and listening, activity 2

WOMAN   These are amazing inventions. But these illustrations here, now this first one, what's this?

MAN   That first one is a baby patting device designed by Thomas V Zelenka in California in 1968. In the night it's difficult for the parents to stay awake and to help the baby fall asleep. And, so Mr Zelenka designed this device to do it for them.

WOMAN   Oh, I see.

MAN   Um… the possible disadvantage is that it could actually harm the baby.

WOMAN   How?

MAN   Well, if the baby moved around and the patter patted it on the head, it could injure it. It's a nice idea, but it's careless of the inventor to use electricity.

WOMAN   Dangerous, isn't it?

MAN   You should never have electricity in a baby's bedroom.

WOMAN   Right. And this second one, a saluting device?

MAN   A saluting device. It's to raise your hat when you meet someone in the street and your hands are full. When your hands are full it's not always easy to raise your hat. Of course, it's always important to greet people politely. But it's rare for men to wear hats these days.

WOMAN   Yes, that's true, that's true.

MAN   It's an old-fashioned device.

WOMAN   And what about this next one, this kitchen fork?

MAN   It's a fork hook, actually, designed in 1919, for picking up a hot bucket. When you're boiling something it's sometimes difficult to lift the bucket without burning your hands.

WOMAN   I know, but what about eating?

MAN   Well, yes, you'd eat with a fork, but it's essential for you to be careful when you use it as a fork. I mean, it's useless as a fork for putting food in your mouth, because of the huge spike on it!

WOMAN   Goodness! And then we have a knife mirror?

MAN   Yes, the knife mirror, which was designed in 1908, is to let you look at your teeth and inspect them after eating to see if you've got any bits of food stuck. After a meal we're often surprised to find a bit of food stuck on our teeth.

WOMAN   Indeed!

MAN   But it would be unusual for you to clean it off at the table.

WOMAN   Yes. And I find this amazing… this grape fruit shield.

MAN   The grape fruit shield was to protect you from the juice when you cut into a grapefruit.

WOMAN   That's sensible.

MAN   It tends sometime to squirt out all over the place. When eating grapefruit, it's essential for you to avoid getting the juice in your eyes because the grapefruit juice can sting. But it might be easier for you to cut the grapefruit into pieces, I would have thought. The strange thing about this invention is the shield, if you look at it, is on the wrong side.

WOMAN   Oh, so it is!

Lesson 12
Reading and listening, activity 3

JOSIE   It's nice here, isn't it?

PHILIP   Yes. It's great. I really like it.

JOSIE   It's quite busy.

PHILIP   Yes.

JOSIE   Have you been here before?

PHILIP   No, no. I heard it was good, though.

JOSIE   Right.

PHILIP   I heard the main thing about the place was the quality of the food. You know, it's the one thing I'm prepared to pay for – if the food's, you know, good quality, that's the most important thing.

JOSIE   It's expensive then, is it?

PHILIP Yeah, but I also like the way you can see from where it's coming round. The appearance of the food is gorgeous. You know, it really looks like the chef's taken a great deal of care to prepare it and I think that's important.

JOSIE I'm not really that bothered about quality, I must admit.

PHILIP Really?

JOSIE No, I'm not. I like the price to be quite low. You know, I think it's a shame to spend a lot of money on food, really. But I think for me, what's important when I go out for a meal is the company. And I think you can have really good meals, it doesn't really matter what the food is like. If you've got good company, with your family or your friends, that's the important thing. It's an occasion, isn't it?

PHILIP Well, yeah, I know. But I think if I go out for a meal, you can always have that at home or at a party. If I go out for a meal, the most important thing is the food for me.

JOSIE Yeah. Do you try lots of different things, then... or...?

PHILIP Yes. I love it. Especially anything I haven't had before or if it's remotely exotic and I can't pronounce it, that's the best thing! That's ideal. I really like to experiment, especially with new tastes.

JOSIE Oh, really? Oh, you're far more adventurous than I am! I couldn't even... I could never try anything that I'd never had before. I'm very conservative in my tastes.

PHILIP Really?

JOSIE Yes, I'm afraid so.

PHILIP So you like quick things, simple things?

JOSIE Yeah, well...

PHILIP For me a quick meal's a sandwich.

JOSIE Oh really?

PHILIP That's the quickest thing, yes.

JOSIE Oh, a sandwich is lunch for me. I mean ...

PHILIP Really?

JOSIE I don't like hamburgers or fast food. No, it makes me feel a bit yucky.

PHILIP Right.

JOSIE But do you think... would you ever give anything up?

PHILIP What do you mean?

JOSIE Is there any food that you would give up? I'm thinking about giving up meat, for example. I'd quite like to be a vegetarian.

PHILIP Yeah. Yeah.

JOSIE But would you give anything up, like desserts, or something like that?

PHILIP I love desserts! I love desserts! Would I give anything up? I don't know, I mean I love fruit and I love bananas, they're my favourite.

JOSIE Do you?

PHILIP I don't think I'd ever be able to give that up. I would be able to give up most things, but not fruit, because I just love the taste and the texture.

JOSIE Yes, me too. I always like to finish a meal by eating an apple because it makes my mouth taste nice and fresh.

PHILIP Yes, lovely.

Progress check Lessons 9 to 12
Listening and writing, activity 1

MAN A man tried to smuggle four baby parrots, worth £8,000, from Thailand to Australia. When he got to Adelaide airport, he took the birds from his suitcase and put them in his trousers. When customs officers heard chirping noises coming from his trousers, they searched him. He was fined £10,000.

WOMAN A man in England claimed he had lost his court case over an accountancy dispute because the loud snoring of the judge's dog had distracted him from conducting his own defence. The judge said the dog was guilty of nothing more than breathing noisily.

MAN A Norwegian ambulance crew who went to the wrong address took a healthy man 50 kilometres to hospital. 'I tried to protest,' said the man, 'but they said that from then on, they were making the decisions and that I had no say in it.'

Lesson 13
Vocabulary and listening, activity 2

RICHARD Anna, I wonder if you could help me in explaining what these different things are? First of all, a CD-ROM. What's that?

ANNA A CD-ROM. Okay. It's a way of keeping information on a disk, which can then be read by a computer.

RICHARD So you put it into the computer...

ANNA Yes...

RICHARD ...And then the computer reads it. I see. Right. Now, a fax. I know that that's a way that you send or receive printed material down the phone line in an electronic form. But how does that differ from e-mail?

ANNA Well, e-mail is actually a system which is used by computer users so messages can be sent from computer to computer, but a fax actually uses the telephone.

RICHARD Right.

ANNA And a fax machine.

RICHARD Right. I see. Right, so it's like two computers talking to one another.

ANNA That's right.

RICHARD I see.

ANNA And a fax isn't computer operated. It's using a fax machine and a phone line.

RICHARD Down the phone talking to the fax machine?

ANNA Yes.

RICHARD Right. And what exactly is the Internet?

ANNA Right. Well I suppose, you know, like with the e-mail you've got computer to computer. It's a bit like that. It's a network which allows computer users from anywhere in the world actually, to actually communicate with each other.

RICHARD Right.

ANNA People usually pay a subscription to a company ...

RICHARD Yeah...

ANNA And they go on-line.

RICHARD Right.

ANNA That's the term.

RICHARD So there's... like... loads of computers all talking to each other.

ANNA That's right, yes.

RICHARD Oh right.

ANNA It's fascinating, actually.

RICHARD And what exactly is satellite TV?

ANNA Well, it's a way of broadcasting television using a satellite that's up in space.

RICHARD Right.

ANNA Rather than using, you know, a transmitter...

RICHARD Like a transmitter on the ground?

ANNA Transmitters and aerials here on the ground, it's actually using a satellite up in space to pick up all the airwaves.

RICHARD So the signal's sent up to the satellite...

ANNA ... and then sent back down.

RICHARD I see. So what is Cable TV, then?

ANNA Well, that kind of works, I suppose, in the opposite way. It's a system, again of broadcasting television, but instead of having a satellite up in the air, you've got cables that run under the ground along maybe phone lines, that kind of thing. It gives viewers... sort of... more access to more channels.

RICHARD It's a physical connection...

ANNA That's right, yeah.

RICHARD ... from wherever they're sending the programme to your television, so it's actually one long cable.

ANNA Yes.

RICHARD Oh, right.

Lesson 13

Vocabulary and listening, activity 5

ANNA The thing is, Richard, CD-ROMs are actually much better than books.

RICHARD Why's that?

ANNA Well, you can store so much more information on the disks. I mean, not just stories, but you can have pictures from galleries, you can have say portraits from the Louvre in Paris or the National Gallery in London, there's so much...

RICHARD I have to disagree. I don't think anything will ever replace the book as a means of storing information in the way that you actually look through a book to find it, and when it comes to art, there's no substitute for the real thing. Nothing will replace a visit to Paris or London to see...

ANNA Of course not, but you can have it in your own home, can't you?

RICHARD I know, but people are always saying this. Every few years something comes along and everybody says, "Oh, this is the way of the future. This is going to replace..." I mean, a few years ago a friend convinced me that LPs and tapes were out, that CD-ROMs would replace them and that hasn't happened yet.

ANNA No.

RICHARD You see, there's nothing more convenient than a book, is there?

ANNA Well, I think you're a bit frightened of change, aren't you? I mean... I expect you've got a fax machine, haven't you, but actually e-mail is far better because it's much faster than a fax machine. And I bet you thought you'd never have anything as advanced as a fax machine, but...

RICHARD No, but yes, I use the fax, but I think E-mail is a rather expensive form of sending letters because you've got to pay the subscription to the company and everything, whereas...

ANNA Yeah...

RICHARD ...with a fax you're just paying for a simple phone call.

ANNA Yeah, I agree. And a fax is still a good way of sending visual information, such as drawings and diagrams. But, you know, a lot of people like to be... kind of... contacted by e-mail.

RICHARD Really?

ANNA Yeah. Oh yeah!

RICHARD I can't believe that!

ANNA It's quite a sociable thing, you know, because you can actually...

RICHARD I think it's much better to have a handwritten letter, surely?

ANNA Well...

RICHARD It sounds horribly cold to me.

ANNA Well, no... not really, because you can be quite sociable, you can... you know you can chat to people, rather than, you know... you send something, somebody sends something back, you know, you can do an odd line here, an odd line there. It's good.

RICHARD No, I disagree. I don't think it's very sociable to be contacted by e-mail and be talking to a computer screen. I mean, it's like talking to a robot.

ANNA Well, I think it's good to be connected to e-mail, because it is a very spontaneous way of communicating with people all over the world.

RICHARD What about the Internet? I mean, you're a huge fan of that, at the moment, aren't you?

ANNA Well, I am actually. I mean, I don't think it should be government controlled, because then, you know, you lose your freedom of speech, you lose...

RICHARD Well...

ANNA ...your rights, you know...

RICHARD I can *see* what you're saying, but I do believe there should be some control over the Internet, otherwise it could be used as a way of sending political propaganda, or pornography. There's a huge amount of pornography, and it goes to anyone with a computer. I think that's wrong.

ANNA Yeah... there are a lot of people that are afraid of being censored by the government...

RICHARD Well, people are being censored right now... And... in lots of different ways. Why do we just use the Internet as an argument there?

ANNA I see your point, but what about TV then, what are your views on that? Because I think... you know... that if you can watch TV stations from anywhere in the world then obviously it's going to help you to find out about other cultures. You know, being connected to cable and satellite and TV isn't as expensive as you might imagine these days.

RICHARD No., but if there's a lot of satellite television coming in and it's all in different languages, it's not much use if... because you won't understand it!

ANNA Yes, I suppose so. But you can still look at the pictures!

Lesson 14

Vocabulary and listening, activity 3

Q I'm here in California and I'm interviewing Don Wright. He's a computer programmer and he lives in a very elegant ranch-style house here in California. And this house is surrounded by vineyards, it's not far from the beach, which is situated close to the town and which is used by most people at least once a day. Now, Don, tell me, what I'd like to know is, and what my listeners would like to know is, what's your attitude towards your possessions? Do you consider yourself to be a wealthy person?

DON Oh, I wouldn't call myself wealthy no, but I guess I'd have to say I'm pretty well off here. It's a nice place to live, don't you think?

Q Yes, I do indeed.

DON And the family next door, I'd say they were quite wealthy. They've got vineyards and everything. But just because they're rich doesn't mean they're not friendly. They're very friendly people, like most of the people in the neighborhood.

Q Oh, that's nice.

DON I mean, I don't feel particularly materialistic. I don't feel the need to have an expensive limousine parked in my driveway for instance, but I guess my lifestyle is fairly expensive. Um... I'd like to have a house right down on the beach, but at the moment that's too expensive.

Q Is it? Right. And what are your leisure pursuits?

DON Well, I like to go surfing and I like rock-climbing and I like roller-blading, you know, that kind of thing.

Q Yeah?

DON And I like going camping, sometimes.

Q And... I mean, with all these things, with your camping and your rock-climbing, and everything, what about then your physical fitness? That's important, isn't it?

DON Absolutely. I feel I can't even relax unless I feel fit. I think you'll find that's true of a lot of people in California. I like to go jogging every day, and so do my neighbors. You meet the whole neighborhood out before 8am, running around in all the right gear!

Q Yeah.

DON It... it... means that I can go into my working day feeling relaxed because my muscles have been worked.

Q Good, so you're not tense?

DON I'm not tense at all.

Q That's great! One of the things that seems to be sort of... a new thing, er... certainly amongst almost everybody really, is a kind of feeling of spiritual development and mental development. I mean... how... What's your attitude towards that? Is it important?

DON It's very important. I used to, in my younger days, I used to live in a hippy community and um...

Q Did you?

DON Yeah, and there was a change of attitude there towards mental and spiritual development and I find myself now turning to Buddhism and looking to the east, to the eastern mysticism for a... for a way of life.

Q And does this affect your working pattern? Your work?

DON Well, I suppose it affects everything I do. It's a matter of being in tune with the world instead of fighting against it, I suppose. I'm a computer programmer and um... and... my work is very important to my self-esteem, and so it's important to me that I um... enjoy my work and that I'm not struggling against it.

Q Right.

DON And... and I find that the working environment here in California is fairly laid back. Sometimes there's a little bit of stress at work, but er... I'd say everything goes pretty smoothly, as long as you're in the spiritual flow.

Q And what are your attitudes towards visitors, people who are not part of your immediate community?

DON Well, I really like the cosmopolitan....

Q ...you do?

DON ... aspects of California. I think you'll find if you talk to most of the people in the neighborhood, not many were actually born here. California's... is a place that all kinds of different backgrounds come to and there's a real... the area's really ethnically diverse and I find that particularly um... particularly pleasant as a place to live. I think you'll find very little racism in this area and I really hate racist attitudes.

Q Yes, yes. So do I. Thank you very much, Don Wright.

Lesson 15

Listening, activity 1

JANET Well, I certainly had a lucky escape last summer. I had been on holiday in Tanzania. I'd had a wonderful time, and for my last three days I'd travelled down to Zanzibar, which is this wonderful tropical island off the coast. And, well, people had warned me that flights out of Zanzibar were very unreliable, you know, they got cancelled all the time and that sort of thing. But the man in the airline office assured me that I definitely would get a plane on the Thursday morning. You see I had to be in Nairobi to get my flight back to Europe that night. Well, anyway, he said that cancellations were a thing of the past and that all their flights now left on time and there were no problems. Well, on the Thursday morning I got up early, you know, to get to the airport in plenty of time, but there was no-one there. No one at all – it was all shut up. It was 7 in the morning and my flight was supposed to leave at 8.30 so I was a bit worried, but I thought, OK, keep calm, maybe someone will come along soon. So I managed to stay calm... and at a quarter to eight a few people did come but they didn't know anything about an 8.30 flight. In the end at about half past <u>nine</u> someone from the airline company arrived but he just said he didn't know whether there would be a flight that day or not. I was really anxious by now because I just had to be in Nairobi by 10 o'clock in the evening or I would miss my flight home. No one seemed to have <u>any</u> idea what was going on. By 12 o'clock I got really frustrated because they wouldn't give me any information, and I didn't know what to do. There were no phones working and I didn't know who I could call for help anyway. Well, in the end, I sat at that miserable little airport for <u>8 hours</u>! A small plane did eventually come and I got to Nairobi about 30 minutes too late. I was furious. I had to spend the night in Nairobi and wait for a plane the following afternoon. But the next morning, I heard on the news that the plane I should have taken from Nairobi to Frankfurt had crashed. I was totally shocked. If I hadn't been delayed in Zanzibar I would have been on that plane. I would have been in the plane crash. It was a very lucky escape!

PAUL Well, I had a lucky escape just the other night. I was having a drink down at my local pub, when these two youths came in and they started having a fight with another man who was just sitting there, not causing any trouble or anything. Anyway, a couple of other blokes and I tried to stop the fight, and we pulled the two youths away from the man, but one of them managed to swing round and hit me in the face. I've still got a black eye. Well, in the end the police came and they arrested them. And I found out afterwards that the one who had

hit me had a knife in his pocket. So I suppose I was lucky that he didn't do more damage. If he'd pulled out his knife, I could have been seriously injured. But what really makes me furious is that I found out a couple of days later that the police just let them go. They didn't charge them or anything because they were only 16. I think that's disgraceful. They should have locked them up! In fact I'm going down to the police station this evening to complain.

FIONA I was involved in a really bad traffic accident a few months ago. In fact, I'm lucky to be alive. And if I hadn't been wearing my seat belt I certainly wouldn't be alive. I was driving down the road on my way home from work behind this big lorry with a load of hay bales, you know a farm lorry and the hay was piled up really high. I was thinking, how nice it was that you still see country scenes like this, you know, farmers with loads of hay for their cattle driving down the road and... suddenly the lorry swerved sharply to the left. I don't know if he was trying to avoid something on the road or what, but he swerved and a load of hay started to fall off the lorry and there were all these bales of hay falling down on my car. And well, I braked as hard as I could, but I couldn't see where I was going because there was all this hay on the bonnet of my car, blocking the windscreen. Well, I ran into the back of the lorry and the whole of the front of my car was completely crushed in and I ended up in hospital with broken bones. I think if I hadn't been wearing my seat belt and if I had been driving faster, I would certainly have been killed. I was extremely lucky.

Lesson 16

Vocabulary and listening, activity 4

STEVE Francesca, what's your favourite piece of music, would you say?

FRANCESCA I think it's 'Pie Jesu' by Andrew Lloyd-Webber.

STEVE Really?

FRANCESCA Yeah, I really like that.

STEVE When did you first hear it?

FRANCESCA Oh, about five years ago my sister was in a choir concert and that was the first time I heard it, and I thought it was really beautiful. What about you? What's your favourite?

STEVE Well, it's a big piece. It's Mahler's second symphony.

FRANCESCA Oh! What, the whole thing?

STEVE Oh yeah, yeah!

FRANCESCA When... when did you first hear that?

STEVE Um... about 1978, I think, when I was eighteen.

FRANCESCA A long time ago.

STEVE Yeah. But it stays with me and I've seen it, performed, several times since then.

FRANCESCA Why do you like it?

STEVE It's just an immense work and it's like everything is in there, the life, the universe, everything, and... and it's just amazing music.

FRANCESCA You can't really say that about Pie Jesu, I suppose.

STEVE I don't know... why do you like it... why do you like that piece?

FRANCESCA I just think it's very gentle and soothing and I just like the tune.

STEVE (laughter) Well, you could say that about the Mahler. It's lots of nice tunes, I suppose. What about a book, a favourite book. What would you say?

FRANCESCA Um... well, I think it has to be *Wuthering Heights* by Emily Bronte.

STEVE Oh yeah!

FRANCESCA Oh, yes. Because there's such passion in there... and it's such an exciting story.

STEVE Yes. And when did you first read the book?

FRANCESCA Well, I had to read it when I was doing my A-levels at school. That was the first time I read it, and I've read it a few times since then. What about you? What's yours?

STEVE   Um…, it's one I read about four years ago and I've gone back to it since. It's called *A History of the World in Ten and A Half Chapters* by Julian Barnes.

FRANCESCA   Oh! Is it a comedy?

STEVE   Well, there's humour in it but it's basically ten stories, all supposedly quite separate from one another…

FRANCESCA   Right.

STEVE   …but running through them there's lots of common little ideas.

FRANCESCA   Oh, I see.

STEVE   The first story's about these woodworm that were on Noah's Ark and then they keep reappearing…

FRANCESCA   Oh, I see. Oh that's good.

STEVE   One of the stories is about a pope… and his throne was eaten by the woodworm.

FRANCESCA   Yeah. So you must have read it a few times, then?

STEVE   Yeah. Yes… I mean, you can read it in any order, as well, really.

FRANCESCA   Yes.

STEVE   You can read the chapters in any order, so… yes, it's a good book.

Lesson 17

Grammar, activity 1

WOMAN   Can you lend me some money? I forgot to go to the bank.

MAN   Well, I've only got a few pounds left.

WOMAN   Oh, dear. I need quite a lot. Don't worry. I'll go to the bank when I go shopping.

MAN   If you're going shopping, can you get me a couple of bottles of water? You can get bottled water at any shop on the high street.

WOMAN   Yes, and we need some tins of tomatoes. I'm making spaghetti bolognese tonight. We've got hardly any beans. Shall I get some beans as well?

MAN   All right.

Lesson 17

Listening and speaking, activity 2

Q   Good morning. Do you have a few minutes to answer a questionnaire about shopping trends?

MEHMET AND NANTHAPA   Sure.

Q   Thank you very much. First of all, may I ask your names and where you are from?

MEHMET   I'm Mehmet and I come from Turkey.

NANTHAPA   My names Nanthapa and I'm from Thailand.

Q   Great. Now can you tell me how often you go shopping? Mehmet?

MEHMET   Well, in my country I suppose most people go shopping about once or twice a week. For food, I mean. We go to the supermarket and buy everything we need for about a week. There are a few things we might buy more frequently, like say bread, but on the whole I think about once a week.

NANTHAPA   Oh. In my country I think people go shopping every day because there are lots of markets and you, well, if you buy things at the market every day you know that they are really fresh.

Q   I see. So that's quite a big difference! What would you say you spend most money on?

MEHMET   Well, food of course. And personally I spend a lot of money on CDs. I'm very keen on music and I buy a lot of CDs. Also clothes. I spend quite a lot on clothes. I probably buy something every week.

NANTHAPA   Yes, I think food and clothes for me too, really. But I don't buy clothes regularly – only when I see something I like.

Q   And what about other things? Do you buy things for the home?

MEHMET   What do you mean?

Q   Well, things like carpets, chairs, you know furniture and, well, pictures…

NANTHAPA   I don't buy things like that very often.

MEHMET   I sometimes buy things for the home, but only every few months, certainly not often.

Q   I see. Now which of the items you buy are necessities?

MEHMET   Well, food of course. That's definitely a necessity. Oh, and things like a newspaper and,er… well, clothes. I think clothes are a necessity. Well, if you're buying them because you need them and not just because you want something fashionable.

Q   What about you Nanthapa?

NANTHAPA   Necessities? Well, as Mehmet said, food is a necessity. I'm not sure about a newspaper… maybe clothes… but really I think just food.

Q   And how often do you buy presents for other people?

MEHMET   Oh, sometimes. If it's someone's birthday or at Christmas. But it has to be a special occasion.

NANTHAPA   Well, I buy presents if I am going to someone's house. And sometimes I might buy something for a friend, just for fun because I know they will like it. So I guess I buy presents quite often.

Q   And what about paying for things you buy? Do you usually use cash or credit cards or cheques? Which do you prefer?

NANTHAPA   Oh, I always use cash.

MEHMET   It depends. For something big I would probably use a credit card. Otherwise I prefer cash.

Q   Right. OK. What about borrowing money? Do you ever borrow money from friends or from a bank?

MEHMET   Not from a bank, no. And friends… well, not very much. I might borrow a little money, you know, if I hadn't got enough for my bus fare or something like that. But not just because there's something expensive I want to buy. And I would never ask a friend to lend me a lot of money, no.

Q   And you, Nanthapa, do you borrow money?

NANTHAPA   No. I don't. I don't like to borrow money at all. If I want to buy something expensive then I wait until I have got enough money to buy it.

Q   So do you like to save money?

NANTHAPA   Well, I try to save money, but it's very difficult. There are so many nice things I would like to buy; but if there's something special I want, then, yes, I'll save up for it. But then I'm saving to buy something particular. Not saving to have lots of money in the bank. I'm no good at that!

MEHMET   Yes, I'm pretty much the same. I would really like to be able to save money and get interest on it, but usually I spend my money as soon as I've earned it.

Q   Well, that's all the questions. Thank you both very much.

MEHMET AND NANTHAPA That's OK. You're welcome

Lesson 18

Listening, activity 1

Q   In our radio car we have Geraldine Faulkes who is on the campaign trail in the constituency of Liverpool north east. Good morning, Mrs Faulkes.

MRS FAULKES   Good morning, John.

Q   Now, Mrs Faulkes. It's only three weeks till the general election. How's the campaign going?

MRS FAULKES   I am fully confident that the Conservative Party will win this general election and that the people of this country will welcome five more years of good Conservative Government.

Q   I see. Now I believe that your party is promising tax cuts if it wins the election.

MRS FAULKES   That's right, John. We are the party of low taxation and we believe that our economic policies over the past five years have been the right policies. Our economy is growing stronger and now is the right time for income tax cuts.

Q   But Mrs Faulkes, you said that five years ago when you were campaigning for the last general election. You said you would lower taxes five years ago, but you didn't, did you?

MRS FAULKES   Our economic policies over the last five years have given us one of the strongest economies in Europe with some of the lowest interest rates. We said that we were going to lower interest rates at the last election and we have delivered our promise. And what's more we believe that interest rates will remain low if we are elected for another term.

Q But I don't think low interest rates are the same as lower taxes. You said you would lower taxes and you didn't. Why should we believe you this time?

MRS FAULKES The economy of the country is now very healthy thanks to good government, and I believe that now is the time for tax cuts.

Q Some people might think that you're just saying that so that you get re-elected... But what about your other policies? What is your policy on health? With hospitals closing down and people having to wait years for hospital treatment. Will there be more government spending on healthcare?

MRS FAULKES This country enjoys the finest healthcare system in the world. The healthcare system is safe in the hands of the Conservative party.

Q But five years ago you said you were going to spend more money on healthcare, and you didn't. Now we have fewer hospitals and waiting lists are enormous. Hospitals are also understaffed because there isn't enough money to pay the doctors and nurses...

MRS FAULKES In the last five years we have spent more on the healthcare system than the Labour government spent in their last 10 years.

Q But the Labour Party was in power over 12 years ago and with inflation and the higher cost of living you can't really compare spending 12 years ago and today can you? And what about money for medical research. Will you be spending more money on medical research if you win the election?

MRS FAULKES Yes, we will. Part of our increased spending on healthcare will go towards medical research.

Q I see. Now unemployment has been an on-going problem. How about unemployment and poverty. What would a new Conservative government do to tackle these problems?

MRS FAULKES Unemployment has been falling steadily over the last five years thanks to our training schemes for young people.

Q But those training schemes just keep young people out of the unemployment statistics for a few months. Very few of them get jobs at the end of the schemes. At the last election you said you were going to cut unemployment. In fact, all you did was to play with the statistics to make it look as if unemployment was falling.

MRS FAULKES We provided good training schemes for the unemployed.

Q Well what about more action on poverty? Five years ago you said you were going to make this a fairer society with less poverty. But in fact you have reduced government spending on the poor...

MRS FAULKES I firmly believe that people are happier when they have earned what money they have. By reducing government handouts we have encouraged people to find themselves jobs. We believe in making people independent and we believe that is what they want.

Q But if there are no jobs for them to go to, what are they to live on?

MRS FAULKES There are jobs if they look hard enough.

Q And what about your party's attitude to Europe? There's been a lot of argument in the party recently about whether we should have closer links with Europe. Is the party still divided on this issue?

MRS FAULKES There are no divisions within the Conservative Party. We are united in our belief that we will maintain close links with Europe in the future. But a close relationship with Europe doesn't mean that we will hand over government of this country to a central European government.

Q Mrs Faulkes. We have run out of time. Thank you very much.

MRS FAULKES Thank you.

Q Now in our Leeds studio we have Alan Greenwood, leader of the Opposition…

Lesson 19
Vocabulary and Listening, activity 3

STEPHEN Moving on now to other places in our tour of Legendary Britain, Lyonesse is said to be a drowned land to the west of Land's End, stretching as far as the Scilly Isles. There's nothing to be seen there today of course, just cliffs and an expanse of very beautiful sea. In fact, the legend has it that the Scilly Isles were attached to the mainland of Britain, a land where King Arthur's Knights once rode, and where Tristram, whose love affair with Iseult is part of the Arthurian legend, was born. One day there was an earthquake and a tidal wave which covered Lyonesse so that all you can see today is a few dramatic rocks above the surface of the sea. One of these rocks is St Michael's Mount, off the coast of Penzance. Lyonesse had many cities and they say that on certain days you can hear the bells ringing from the spires of the 140 churches beneath the sea.

The next picture shows Sherwood Forest, which is not far from Nottingham in the East Midlands. The forest itself is quite small these days, but in the past it was huge, stretching over many miles. It's said, of course, to be the home of Robin Hood. The legend of Robin Hood is well-known and is the story of an outlaw who stole money from the rich to give to the poor, and it was this which made him particularly popular with local people, although not with the Sheriff of Nottingham. His band was said to number more than a hundred men. But no one knows for certain if Robin Hood really existed. The character may have come from a number of different people, and so it's far from certain that he lived in Sherwood Forest. But the legend remains stronger than the facts about Robin Hood, and Sherwood Forest keeps the memory of the legend alive in the minds of its visitors today.

The next photo shows Stonehenge, which is of course the world-famous circle of prehistoric stones on Salisbury Plain. The construction was begun before 1800 BC, so it's one of the oldest structures in existence. The extraordinary thing is that the stones were brought from the Presecelly Hills in Pembrokeshire, more than three hundred kilometres away, and some people believe that it could only have been built by aliens from outer space. However, there is a more realistic school of thought which believes that the stones were floated on rafts across the Bristol Channel, then dragged over tracks of logs to Salisbury Plain. The largest stone is 7 metres high, so you can only imagine the effort and the manpower required to do this. The legend says that Stonehenge was built for sunworshipping, because on June the 21st of each year, the longest day of the year, the sun rises directly above a line drawn between two of the most important stones, and even today, there is a ceremony of sunworshipping at sunrise on Midsummer's Day.

And finally, we have a view of the Holy Island of Lindisfarne, which lies five kilometres off the coast of Northumberland. The legend is that St Aidan founded a monastery here in the seventh century, to establish a base for his mission to bring Christianity to England, and in fact, the region was one of the first Christian kingdoms in England. It's a wild, windswept island and it's recommended that you keep an eye on the tide as you take the causeway which links it with the mainland. The monastery was attacked and destroyed twice by Norse raiders but was rebuilt again in the 13th century, although it is now, once again, a ruin. The building you can see is Lindisfarne Castle, which was built in the 16th century to protect the island from an attack by the Scots, although it was never in fact needed.

Lesson 20

Speaking and listening, activity 5

MAN So tell me something about these brands and the image they project. What about Mercedes for example? What kind of image and appeal do they wish to convey to the consumer?

WOMAN Well, Mercedes is one of the world's best known brands for motor vehicles, of course, and Mercedes is famous for its image of excellent engineering, of safety of its cars, and of its German reliability, you know, you should buy a Mercedes because it won't let you down. Now, all this, you might think, could make it a very expensive product, designed to appeal to only the very rich, and it's true that in the past, drivers of Mercedes Benz cars belonged to the richest social class. But while it's true that a Mercedes is an expensive car, its appeal is much broader than one might imagine. It has what might be described as an *aspirational* appeal, which attracts people of all incomes and backgrounds. It's quite unlike most luxury cars, such as Rolls Royce, which deliberately set out to appeal only to a very small, select group of people, the aristocracy and the extremely rich. It's truly egalitarian in its image and appeal.

MAN How about Benetton?

WOMAN Benetton, yes. You could say that because of its controversial advertising campaigns, its image is better known than the product the brand represents. Well, Benetton is known for its fashion products, of course, and there's no question that the clothes are well-made, look very good and are relatively cheap, with Italian style and flair. Benetton began its advertising campaign a few years ago with a multicultural, international image of its slogan, the United Colours of Benetton. But after a while, they decided the image they wanted to give its products was slightly different, somehow, slightly less... how shall I put it... run of the mill. And now they set out to shock people with their advertising, while at the same time still stressing that the images all belong to the same kind of broad, all-embracing international community of fashion wear. And the appeal is very much to the young consumers, who feel different, who feel special, who feel they could change the world, or at least shake the world out of their complacency. It gives an interesting, exciting angle on what is frankly a rather uninteresting product.

MAN And what about Gillette? What image do they want to project?

WOMAN Well, in the beginning Gillette was as American as apple pie, but one of those products which not only everyone knew around the world, but everyone could actually buy around the world as well, even if they didn't have much money. The product is of course personal care for men, razors, aftershave, shaving cream. And unlike say Mercedes and Benetton, the product is now not a luxury one but an essential, at least in those cultures where men shave every day. So we have an essential product used every day by men all around the world. Not much scope for any excitement in its image, you might think. Wrong. Gillette's image is one of freshness, of love of life. 'Gillette – the best a man can get' is the slogan and its appeal is to every man, young at heart even if not in years. But recently Gillette has slightly adapted this image so that it appeals to 'today's' man, the 'new man' if you like, who is in touch with his emotions, someone who takes his responsibilities as a father very seriously, since being a father is being a part of this love of life I mentioned earlier. So there are pictures of today's Gillette man tenderly holding his son in his arms, his son a member, presumably, of the next generation of Gillette users. Freshness, love of life and fatherhood. That's what Gillette stands for.

Lesson 20

Vocabulary and listening, activity 2

MAN It's Henry Purcell week, this week on Classic FM and in tonight's evening concert, you can hear some of his finest chamber works and also some of his vocal music which you have probably never heard before. So keep your ears pinned, it's all tonight on Classic FM.

MAN 1 How's the new Jaguar radio commercial coming on, then?

MAN 2 I don't know it's a bit tricky. There's so many things to say about the new XJS series, and I've only got fifty seconds.

MAN 1 Fifty seconds is an absolute age! Now here we go, this is a good quote. 'The best riding and handling Jaguar to date'. *Autocar & Motor.* And here's another. 'Jaguar's miraculous chassy dishes up plenty of surprises.' *Performance Car.* Excellent magazine.

MAN 2 I know but...

MAN 1 Ah... now this is a gem! 'Far and away the best saloon car in the world.' *The Sunday Times.* I mean, the commercial virtually writes itself.

MAN 2 I know but you can't just string a load of quotes together, can you?

MAN 1 No! No, of course not, you've got to add that little extra sparkle at the end.

MAN 2 What er...this bit...

WOMAN The new Jaguar XJ series, for more information or to arrange a test drive call Freephone 0800 70 80 60.

MAN 1 Yes... well... sort of...

MAN Tower Records bring you any two titles from the Sony Essentials Classics range for only £5.99 per single disc or £10 for two or double CD set.
With over a 125 titles and featuring many of the greatest names in classical music such as cellist Yo-Yo Ma, violinist, Isaac Stern and the conductors, George Solti and Eugene Ormandy. Essential Classics is the foremost budget label. Essential Classics - great recordings, great music and at these prices, great value. At all Tower Stores now!

MAN The King may well be mad but it's the critics who are raving... 'Nigel Hawthorne's performance is colossal' says the *Evening Standard...* 'A brilliant film' says *The Daily Mail.* 'Rush to see it, it's a real gem' says Barry Norman.
Nigel Hawthorne and Helen Mirren star in 'The Madness of King George' nominated for four academy awards. 'The Madness of King George' written by Alan Bennett in the West End now and in selected cinemas across the country from Friday, rated PG.

Lesson 20

Listening and vocabulary, activity 3

SALESPERSON Can I help you, sir?

CUSTOMER Yes, I bought this watch from you last week and I've been having a few problems with it.

SALESPERSON What seems to be the trouble?

CUSTOMER Well, the salesperson said it was waterproof, but when I wore it at the swimming pool it just filled with water.

SALESPERSON Let me see. Oh, yes. We have had some problems with this brand. Would you like me to replace it with a similar model?

CUSTOMER I think I'd rather have my money back, actually.

SALESPERSON Of course. We can do that for you. Do you have your receipt?

CUSTOMER Yes, here it is.

SALESPERSON Thank you.

CUSTOMER By the way, I think you should check what you sell more carefully.

SALESPERSON I'm very sorry this has happened.

Wordlist

The first number after each word shows the lesson in which the word first appears in the vocabulary box.
The numbers in italics show the later lessons in which the word appears again.

a la carte /æ læ kɑːt/ 4
adjective /ˈædʒɪktɪv/ 1
admit /ədˈmɪt/ 20
agreement /əˈgriːmənt/ 5
agricultural /ˌægrɪˈkʌltʃər(ə)l/ 7
aisle /aɪl/ 4
album /ˈælbəm/ 16
alcohol /ˈælkəhɒl/ 14
alien /ˈeɪlɪən/ 19
alpha /ˈælfə/ 1
amazing /əˈmeɪzɪŋ/ 20
ambulance /ˈæmbjʊləns/ 6
amusing /əˈmjuːzɪŋ/ 15
ancestor /ˈænsestə(r)/ 14
anti-conformist /ˌænti kənˈfɔːmɪst/ 14
anxious /ˈæŋkʃəs/ 15
apologise /əˈpɒlədʒaɪz/ 20
apple /ˈæp(ə)l/ 12
appointment /əˈpɔɪntmənt/ 6
argue /ˈɑːgjuː/ 20
arrest /əˈrest/ 10
arson /ˈɑːs(ə)n/ 10
assembly /əˈsembli/ 18
assembly hall /əˈsembli hɔːl/ 9
athletics /æθˈletɪks/ 3
aubergine /ˈəʊbəʒiːn/ 12
audience /ˈɔːdɪəns/ 4

bail /beɪl/ 10
bake /beɪk/ 12
band /bænd/ 16, *19*
bandage /ˈbændɪdʒ/ 6
bang /bæŋ/ 8
bank /bæŋk/ 7
baptism /ˈbæptɪz(ə)m/ 14
bark /bɑːk/ 8
baseball /ˈbeɪsbɔːl/ 3
bass /beɪs/ 16
beach /biːtʃ/ 7
beckon /ˈbekən/ 2
bell /bel/ 19
bench /bentʃ/ 9
biography /baɪˈɒgrəfi/ 16
bitter /ˈbɪtə(r)/ 8
bizarre /bɪˈzɑː(r)/ 15
blackboard /ˈblækbɔːd/ 9
blackmail /ˈblækmeɪl/ 10
bleep /bliːp/ 8
blood pressure /blʌd ˈpreʃə(r)/ 6
blow /bləʊ/ 2
boil /bɔɪl/ 12
boring /ˈbɔːrɪŋ/ 5, *15*

bossa nova /ˌbɒsə ˈnəʊvə/ 16
boutique /buːˈtiːk/ 1, *4*
bow /baʊ/ 2
box office /bɒks ˈɒfɪs/ 4
boxing /ˈbɒksɪŋ/ 3
breadboard /ˈbredbɔːd/ 11
bribery /ˈbraɪbəri/ 10
bright /braɪt/ 20
bring up /brɪŋ ʌp/ 5
broom /bruːm/ 11
brush /brʌʃ/ 11
buggy /ˈbʌgi/ 14
building society /ˈbɪldɪŋ səˈsaɪəti/ 17
bullfighting /ˈbʊlfaɪtɪŋ/ 3
bungalow /ˈbʌŋgələʊ/ 1
burglary /ˈbɜːgləri/ 10
butter /ˈbʌtə(r)/ 12
buzz /bʌz/ 8

cable TV /ˈkeɪb(ə)l tiː viː/ 13
café /ˈkæfeɪ/ 4
cake /keɪk/ 12
calm /kɑːm/ 14
camcorder /ˈkæmˌkɔːdə(r)/ 13
camera /ˈkæmrə/ 13
candidate /ˈkændɪdət/ 18
candle /ˈkænd(ə)l/ 14
canteen /kænˈtiːn/ 9
canyon /ˈkænjən/ 7
caretaker /ˈkeəˌteɪkə(r)/ 9
carrot /ˈkærət/ 12
carving knife /ˈkɑːvɪŋ naɪf/ 11
cash /kæʃ/ 17
cash desk /kæʃ desk/ 4
castle /ˈkɑːs(ə)l/ 19
casualty /ˈkæʒʊəlti/ 6
cathedral /kəˈθiːdr(ə)l/ 7
CD player /ˌsiːdiː ˈpleɪə(r)/ 13
CD-ROM /ˌsiːdiː rɒm/ 13
centre /ˈsentə(r)/ 7
chain store /tʃeɪn stɔː(r)/ 4
chalk /tʃɔːk/ 9
charged with /tʃɑːdʒd wɪð/ 10
charming /ˈtʃɑːmɪŋ/ 15
chart /tʃɑːt/ 16
chemist /ˈkemɪst/ 6
cheque /tʃek/ 17
chess /tʃes/ 3
chew /tʃuː/ 2
chisel /ˈtʃɪz(ə)l/ 11
choir /ˈkwaɪə(r)/ 16
chop /tʃɒp/ 12

chopping board /tʃɒpɪŋ bɔːd/ 11
chord /kɔːd/ 16
Christianity /ˌkrɪstræⁿɪti/ 19
circle /ˈsɜːk(ə)l/ 4
city /ˈsɪti/ 7
clang /ˈklæŋ/ 8
clap /klæp/ 2
classic /ˈklæsɪk/ 20
classroom /ˈklɑːsruːm/ 9
clatter /ˈklætə(r)/ 8
cliff /klɪf/ 7
clinic /ˈklɪnɪk/ 6
cloakroom /ˈkləʊkruːm/ 4
coastline /ˈkəʊstlaɪn/ 7
coffee /ˈkɒfi/ 12
coffee grinder /ˈkɒfi ˈgraɪndə(r)/ 11
collection /kəˈlekʃ(ə)n/ 4
colossal /kəˈlɒs(ə)l/ 20
comic /ˈkɒmɪk/ 4
complain /kɒmpleɪn/ 20
company /ˈkʌmpəni/ 4
composer /kəmˈpəʊzə(r)/ 16
compromise /ˈkɒmprəˌmaɪz/ 5
computer /kəmˈpjuːtə(r)/ 13
concerto /kənˈtʃeətəʊ/ 1, *16*
confess /kənˈfes/ 10
confident /ˈkɒnfɪd(ə)nt/ 5
confused /kənˈfjuːzd/ 15
constituency /kənˈstɪtjʊənsi/ 18
consultant /kənˈsʌlt(ə)nt/ 6
cool /kuːl/ 16
corkscrew /ˈkɔːkskruː/ 11
cosmopolitan /ˌkɒzməˈpɒlɪt(ə)n/ 14
cough /kɒf/ 8
councillor /ˈkaʊnsələ(r)/ 18
country /ˈkʌntri/ 7
course /kɔːs/ 4
crash /kræʃ/ 8
creak /kriːk/ 8
credit card /ˈkredɪt kɑːd/ 17
crime /kraɪm/ 10
crutches /ˈkrʌtʃɪz/ 6
cry /kraɪ/ 8
cuddle /ˈkʌd(ə)l/ 2
currency /ˈkʌrənsi/ 17
custody /ˈkʌstədi/ 10
custom /ˈkʌstəm/ 14
cut /kʌt/ 6, *12*

dancing /dɑːnsɪŋ/ 3
deafening /ˈdef(ə)nɪŋ/ 8
delicatessen /ˌdelɪkəˈtes(ə)n/ 1
delightful /dɪˈlaɪtfʊl/ 15
delta /ˈdeltə/ 1
dentist /ˈdentɪst/ 6
department store
 /dɪˈpɑːtmənt stɔː(r)/ 4
deposit /dɪˈpɒzɪt/ 17
depressed /dɪˈprest/ 15
deputy /ˈdepjʊti/ 18
degree /dɪˈgriː/ 5
desert /ˈdezɜːt/ 7
desk /desk/ 9
devastated /ˈdevəˌsteɪtɪd/ 15
dialect /ˈdaɪəˌlekt/ 14
diary /ˈdaɪəri/ 16
dice /daɪs/ 12
diner /ˈdaɪnə(r)/ 4
dinner lady /ˈdɪnə(r) ˈleɪdi/ 9
diploma /dɪˈpləʊmə/ 5
disabled /dɪsˈeɪb(ə)ld/ 6
disappointed /ˌdɪsəˈpɔɪntɪd/ 15
disc /dɪsk/ 16
disease /dɪˈziːz/ 6
display /dɪˈspleɪ/ 4
district /ˈdɪstrɪkt/ 7
diverse /daɪˈvɜːs/ 14
dizzy /ˈdɪzi/ 6
drag /dræg/ 19
drama /ˈdrɑːmə/ 1
dream /driːm/ 5
drill /drɪl/ 11
drowned /draʊnd/ 19
drug dealing /drʌg ˈdiːlɪŋ/ 10
dustbin /ˈdʌstbɪn/ 11

e-mail /ˈiːmeɪl/ 13
earthquake /ˈɜːθkweɪk/ 19
eccentric /ɪkˈsentrɪk/ 15
ecstatic /ɪkˈstætɪk/ 15
ethnic /ˈeθnɪk/ 4
elect /ɪˈlekt/ 18
elegant /ˈelɪgənt/ 14
emergency /ɪˈmɜːdʒənsi/ 6
enthusiastic /ɪnˌθjuːzɪˈæstɪk/ 15
escalator /ˈeskəˌleɪtə(r)/ 4
essential /ɪˈsenʃ(ə)l/ 20
estuary /ˈestjʊəri/ 7
excellent /ˈeksələnt/ 20
excited /ɪkˈsaɪtɪd/ 15
exciting /ɪkˈsaɪtɪŋ/ 5, 15
executed for /ˈeksɪˌkjuːtɪd fə(r)/ 10
exercise book /ˈeksəˌsaɪz bʊk/ 9
exhibit /ɪgˈzɪbɪt/ 4
explain /ɪkˈspleɪn/ 20

fail /feɪl/ 5
failure /ˈfeɪljə(r)/ 5
fall in love /fɔːl ɪn lʌv/ 5
family /ˈfæmɪli/ 5
far-fetched /fɑː(r) fetʃt/ 15
fare /feə(r)/ 4
farmer /ˈfɑːmə(r)/ 14
fascinating /ˈfæsɪneɪtɪŋ/ 15
fax /fæks/ 13
feature /ˈfiːtʃə(r)/ 16
fed-up /fed ʌp/ 15
fee /fiː/ 17
fertile /ˈfɜːtaɪl/ 7
fez /fez/ 1
fiction /ˈfɪkʃ(ə)n/ 16
field /fiːld/ 7
finest /faɪnɪst/ 20
fishing /fɪʃɪŋ/ 3, 7
flat /flæt/ 7
float /fləʊt/ 19
food processor /fuːd ˈprəʊsesə(r)/ 13
footpath /ˈfʊtpɑːθ/ 7
forest /ˈfɒrɪst/ 7
forgery /ˈfɔːdʒəri/ 10
fork /fɔːk/ 11
fortune /ˈfɔːtjuːn/ 14
foyer /ˈfɔɪeɪ/ 4
fragrant /ˈfreɪgrənt/ 8
frantic /ˈfræntɪk/ 15
fraud /frɔːd/ 10
frown /fraʊn/ 2
frustrated /frʌˈstreɪtɪd/ 15
fry /fraɪ/ 12
furious /ˈfjʊərɪəs/ 15

gambling /ˈgæmb(ə)lɪŋ/ 3
gasp /gɑːsp/ 8
gaze /geɪz/ 8
gem /dʒem/ 20
general election
 /ˈdʒenər(ə)l ɪˈlekʃ(ə)n/ 18
glance /glɑːns/ 8
glasnost /ˈglæznɒst/ 1
glimpse /glɪmps/ 8
gloomy /ˈgluːmi/ 15
goal /gəʊl/ 5
golf /gɒlf/ 3
government /ˈgʌvənmənt/ 18
grab /græb/ 8
grant /grɑːnt/ 17
grasp /grɑːsp/ 8
grate /greɪt/ 12
grateful /ˈgreɪtfʊl/ 15
grater /ˈgreɪtə(r)/ 11
grill /grɪl/ 12
grin /grɪn/ 2
grind /graɪnd/ 12
groan /grəʊn/ 8

guest /gest/ 14
guided tour /gaɪdɪd tʊə(r)/ 4
guilty /ˈgɪlti/ 10
guitar /gɪˈtɑː(r)/ 16
guitarist /gɪˈtɑː(r)ɪst/ 16
gym /dʒɪm/ 9

hall /hɔːl/ 7
hammer /ˈhæmə(r)/ 11
happy /ˈhæpi/ 5, 15
hate /heɪt/ 5
headteacher /hedˈtiːtʃə(r)/ 9
heart attack /hɑːt əˈtæk/ 6
hedge /hedʒ/ 7
herb /hɜːb/ 14
hiccup /ˈhɪkʌp/ 8
hijacking /ˈhaɪdʒækɪŋ/ 10
hilarious /hɪˈleərɪəs/ 15
hill /hɪl/ 7
hiss /hɪs/ 8
hit /hɪt/ 16
home /həʊm/ 5, 14
horse /hɔːs/ 14
hospital /ˈhɒspɪt(ə)l/ 6
hug /hʌg/ 2
hum /hʌm/ 8
hunting /ˈhʌntɪŋ/ 3
hymn /hɪm/ 14

Impressionist /ɪmˌpreʃəˈnɪst/ 4
in credit /ɪn ˈkredɪt/ 17
income tax /ˈɪnkʌm tæks/ 17
industrial /ɪnˈdʌstrɪəl/ 7
injection /ɪnˈdʒekʃ(ə)n/ 6
innocent /ˈɪnəs(ə)nt/ 10
insist /ɪnˈsɪst/ 20
inspired /ɪnˈspaɪə(r)d/ 15
interest /ˈɪntrəst/ 17
interval /ˈɪntəv(ə)l/ 4
ironing board /ˈaɪənɪŋ bɔːd/ 11
island /ˈaɪlənd/ 7

jazz /dʒæz/ 16
job /dʒɒb/ 5
jogging /dʒɒgɪŋ/ 3, 14
judge /dʒʌdʒ/ 10
jug /dʒʌg/ 14
jungle /dʒʌŋg(ə)l/ 7
junta /ˈdʒʌntə/ 1
jury /ˈdʒʊəri/ 10

karate /kəˈrɑːti/ 1
kebab /kɪˈbæb/ 1
key /kiː/ 16
kidnapping /ˈkɪdnæpɪŋ/ 10
kindergarten /ˈkɪndəˌgɑːt(ə)n/ 1
kiosk /ˈkiːɒsk/ 4
kiss /kɪs/ 2

kneel /niːl/ 2
knight /naɪt/ 19
knitting /ˈnɪtɪŋ/ 3

ladle /ˈleɪd(ə)l/ 11
laid-back /leɪd ˈbæk/ 14
lamp /læmp/ 14
landmark /ˈlændmɑːk/ 4
Latin /ˈlætɪn/ 4
laugh /lɑːf/ 2
lawnmower /ˈlɔːnˌməʊə(r)/ 11
lawyer /ˈlɔɪə(r)/ 10
lead singer /liːd ˈsɪŋə/ 16
legal /ˈliːg(ə)l/ 10
libel /ˈlaɪb(ə)l/ 10
limousine /ˈlɪmʊˌziːn/ 14
limp /lɪmp/ 6
literary /ˈlɪtərəri/ 16
loan /ləʊn/ 17
log /lɒg/ 19
loud /laʊd/ 8
love /lʌv/ 5
low-lying /ləʊ ˈlaɪɪŋ/ 7
LP /el ˈpiː/ 16
lyrics /ˈlɪrɪks/ 16

mad /mæd/ 20
magical /ˈmædʒɪk(ə)l/ 20
magistrate /ˈmædʒɪstrət/ 10
mainland /ˈmeɪnlənd/ 19
manslaughter /ˈmænˌslɔːtə(r)/ 10
market /ˈmɑːkɪt/ 7
marry /ˈmæri/ 5
mascara /mæˈskɑːrə/ 1
materialistic /məˈtɪərɪəˌlɪstɪk/ 14
matron /ˈmeɪtrən/ 6
mayor /meə(r)/ 18
meadow /ˈmedəʊ/ 7
mellow /ˈmeləʊ/ 16
melody /ˈmelədɪ/ 16
menu /ˈmenjuː/ 4
microwave /ˈmaɪkrəʊˌweɪv/ 13
mild /maɪld/ 14
milk /mɪlk/ 12
minister /ˈmɪnɪstə(r)/ 18
ministry /ˈmɪnɪstrɪ/ 18
miraculous /mɪˈrækjʊləs/ 20
missing word /ˈmɪsɪŋ ˈwɜːd/ 1
mop /mɒp/ 11
mortgage /ˈmɔːgɪdʒ/ 17
motor racing /ˈməʊtə(r) reɪsɪŋ/ 3
mountain /ˈmaʊntɪn/ 7
mountaineering /ˌmaʊntɪˈnɪə(r)ɪŋ/ 3
mountainous /ˈmaʊntɪnəs/ 7

MP /em ˈpiː/ 18
mugging /ˈmʌgɪŋ/ 10
murder /ˈmɜːdə(r)/ 10
music /ˈmjuːzɪk/ 5
mysterious /mɪˈstɪərɪəs/ 20

nail /neɪl/ 11
nervous /ˈnɜːvəs/ 15
new /njuː/ 20
nod /nɒd/ 2
noisy /ˈnɔɪzi/ 8
notice /ˈnəʊtɪs/ 8
noun /naʊn/ 1
novel /ˈnɒv(ə)l/ 16
nudge /nʌdʒ/ 2
number /ˈnʌmbə(r)/ 16
nurse /nɜːs/ 6
oasis /əʊˈeɪsɪs/ 7
obligation /ˌɒblɪˈgeɪʃ(ə)n/ 5
observe /əbˈzɜːv/ 8
offence /əˈfens/ 10
offer /ˈɒfə(r)/ 20
oil /ɔɪl/ 12
ointment /ˈɔɪntmənt/ 6
onion /ˈʌnjən/ 12
opening hours /ˈəʊpənɪŋ aʊə(r)z/ 4
optimistic /ˈɒptɪˈmɪstɪk/ 5
outer space /ˈaʊt(r) speɪs/ 19
outlaw /ˈaʊtlɔː/ 19
outpatients /ˈaʊtˌpeɪʃ(ə)nts/ 6
overcrowded /ˌəʊvəˈkraʊdɪd/ 7
overdrawn /ˌəʊvəˈdrɔːn/ 17

pain /peɪn/ 6
painting /ˈpeɪntɪŋ/ 5
panorama /ˌpænəˈrɑːmə/ 1
paperback /ˈpeɪpəˌbæk/ 16
parliament /ˈpɑːləmənt/ 18
pass /pɑːs/ 5
pasta /ˈpæstə/ 1
pat /pæt/ 2, 8
pathetic /pəˈθetɪk/ 15
patient /ˈpeɪʃ(ə)nt/ 6
peak /piːk/ 7
peculiar /pɪˈkjuːlɪə(r)/ 15
peel /piːl/ 12
peeler /ˈpiːlə(r)/ 11
peer /pɪə(r)/ 8
pen /pen/ 9
pension /ˈpenʃ(ə)n/ 17
pepper /ˈpepə(r)/ 12
pessimistic /ˈpesɪˈmɪstɪk/ 5
photocopier /ˈfəʊtəʊˈkɒpɪə(r)/ 13
piano /ˈprænəʊ/ 1
picturesque /ˌpɪktʃəˈresk/ 7
pill /pɪl/ 6
pinch /pɪntʃ/ 2
pizza /ˈpiːtsə/ 1

plain /pleɪn/ 7
plaster /ˈplɑːstə(r)/ 6
playground /ˈpleɪgraʊnd/ 9
playing field /ˈpleɪɪŋˌfiːld/ 9
plot /plɒt/ 16
point /pɔːnt/ 2
point out /pɔɪnt aʊt/ 20
policy /ˈpɒlɪsɪ/ 18
politician /ˌpɒlɪˈtɪʃ(ə)n/ 18
portrayal /pɔːˈtreɪl/ 16
potato /pəˈteɪtəʊ/ 12
pottery /ˈpɒtərɪ/ 3
pour /pɔː(r)/ 12
premiere /ˈpremɪə(r)/ 4
preposition /ˌprepəˈzɪʃ(ə)n/ 1
prescription /prɪˈskrɪpʃ(ə)n/ 6
president /ˈprezɪd(ə)nt/ 18
press /pres/ 8
prime minister /praɪm ˈmɪnɪstə(r)/ 18
prison /ˈprɪz(ə)n/ 10
profound /prəˈfaʊnd/ 15
promise /ˈprɒmɪs/ 20
punch /pʌntʃ/ 8
punctuation /ˌpʌŋktjʊˈeɪʃ(ə)n/ 1

quadrangle /ˈkwɒdˌræŋg(ə)l/ 4
quiet /kwaɪət/ 20

racist /ˈreɪsɪst/ 14
raft /rɑːft/ 19
raider /ˈreɪdə(r)/ 19
range /reɪndʒ/ 7
rate of exchange
   /reɪt ɒv ɪksˈtʃeɪndʒ/ 17
rattle /ˈræt(ə)l/ 8
raving /ˈreɪvɪŋ/ 20
receipt /rɪˈsiːt/ 17
referendum /ˌrefəˈrendəm/ 18
refrigerator /rɪˈfrɪdʒəˌreɪtə(r)/ 13
region /ˈriːdʒ(ə)n/ 7
register /ˈredʒɪstə(r)/ 9
reliable /rɪˈlaɪəb(ə)l/ 20
rent /rent/ 17
reservation /ˌrezəˈveɪʃ(ə)n/ 4
rhythm /ˈrɪð(ə)m/ 16
riding /ˈraɪdɪŋ/ 3
river /ˈrɪvə(r)/ 7
roar /rɔː(r)/ 8
roast /rəʊst/ 12
rock /rɒk/ 16, 19
romantic /rəʊˈmæntɪk/ 20
route /ruːt/ 1
row /rəʊ/ 4
rugged /ˈrʌgɪd/ 7
rumble /ˈrʌmb(ə)l/ 8
rustle /ˈrʌs(ə)l/ 8

sad /sæd/ 5, 15

Progress Test 1 Lessons 1 – 5

SECTION 1: VOCABULARY (30 marks)

1a Underline the odd-one-out and leave a group of three related words. (10 marks)

b Add one other word to the groups of words. (10 marks)

Example: her my our <u>they</u> *their*

1 fez kebab pasta sushi _____

2 adjective noun preposition spelling _____

3 baseball golf knitting tennis _____

4 aisle circle foyer sculpture _____

5 beckon point wave wink _____

6 goal opera league pitch _____

7 company politician manager
   neighbour _____

8 elbow head foot male _____

9 English Germany Portuguese
   Russian _____

10 boutique ethnic museum restaurant _____

2 Complete these sentences with ten verbs from the box. (10 marks)

> book bring chew clap fall feed feel give
> guess look make nod shake stare take

Example: I ___*feel*___ at home in Brazil.

1 Please do not _____ the animals.

2 Do you usually _____ forward to your
   holidays?

3 You can often _____ what a word means
   from the context.

4 The journey will only _____ three hours.

5 You should _____ your food a hundred times.

6 I'll phone the restaurant and _____ a table.

7 Shall I _____ you a lift to the station?

8 I often _____ hands when I meet someone for
   the first time.

9 I don't easily _____ friends.

10 I'd like to _____ in love with someone.

PHOTOCOPIABLE

© Macmillan Publishers Limited 1996.

Progress Test 1 Lessons 1 – 5

SECTION 2: GRAMMAR (30 marks)

3a Choose ten of these words to complete the first ten spaces in the conversation. (10 marks)

Example: a) are   b) do   c) <u>did</u>

1   a) far   b) good   c) well

2   a) aren't   b) don't   c) isn't

3   a) go   b) going   c) to go

4   a) been   b) gone   c) went

5   a) make   b) making   c) to make

6   a) didn't   b) shouldn't   c) won't

7   a) been studying   b) studied   c) study

8   a) am studying   b) study   c) will study

9   a) always   b) just   c) only

10   a) listen   b) listening   c) to listen

b Complete the last ten spaces with ten of your own words or verb forms. (10 marks)

MARIA: How _did_ you get on in your exam yesterday?

PETER: Not very (1) _____ . I'm not very good at French.

MARIA: (2) _____ you? I didn't know that. They say that the best way to learn a language is (3) _____ to the country where it is spoken.

PETER: Yes, it's true. I've (4) _____ to France. But I kept (5) _____ mistakes all the time.

MARIA: You (6) _____ worry about making mistakes. It's more important to make yourself understood. Have you ever (7) _____ another foreign language?

PETER: Yes, I (8) _____ Spanish at the moment. But the teacher is (9) _____ talking English. All we do is (10) _____ to him. I (11) _____ we spent more time speaking Spanish.

MARIA: What do you like (12) _____ about learning foreign languages?

PETER: I think listening's very hard.

MARIA: (13) _____ do I. Pat and I (14) _____ to the cinema this evening. Why (15) _____ you come with us?

PETER: Yes, that (16) _____ be nice.

MARIA: I'm going to get the tickets at lunchtime. (17) _____ I get you one?

PETER: Yes, please. Er ... what's the film?

MARIA: *Les Misérables.*

PETER: Oh no! It's in French, (18) _____ it?

MARIA: Yes, but it's got English subtitles. You'll (19) _____ it! And you'll have (20) _____ opportunity to listen to French!

4 Underline the mistakes in these sentences and correct them. (10 marks)

Example: <u>Do you can</u> swim?   *Can you*

1   How long are you studying English? _____

2   Who does help you with your homework? _____

3   Show me your photos, do you? _____

4   Let's have a drink, let us? _____

5   I think fishing is bored. _____

6   If only this book is more interesting. _____

7   I don't tell you if you won't be quiet. _____

8   Today I go to a football match. _____

9   When you saw the film? _____

10   I've been knowing Tom since 1992. _____

© Macmillan Publishers Limited 1996.

PHOTOCOPIABLE

Progress Test 1 Lessons 1 – 5

SECTION 3: READING (20 marks)

5 Read the passage *Grüezi, Grüezi, Everybody*. Write down five facts about the writer, for example, his surname, his job etc. (5 marks)

_____

_____

_____

_____

_____

6 Answer these questions. (6 marks)

1 What is the writer's main problem when greeting people?

_____

_____

2 What is not the ideal solution to his problem? Why not?

_____

_____

_____

3 Why does the writer suggest that perhaps he should become a doctor?

_____

_____

_____

7 What three techniques does the writer use in order to reduce his problem? What are the advantages of these? (9 marks)

_____

_____

_____

_____

_____

Grüezi, Grüezi, Everybody

The main thing that confuses me as a foreigner in Switzerland is the idea of greeting everybody by their family name. The reason for this is that I personally have considerable difficulty remembering names – even my own. Perhaps this has something to do with my upbringing in America, where greetings such as 'Hello, folks' and 'Hi, neighbour' were sufficient. But the American form of address is considered most impolite in Switzerland.

So the first thing to learn in German-speaking Switzerland is that 'Grüezi', meaning 'greetings' or 'hello', is the standard greetings. But – and here's the point – it is considered most impolite to say 'Grüezi' without using a person's name. For example, when you enter your local grocery store, you are expected to greet Frau Stirnimann, the owner's wife. So you say 'Grüezi, Frau Stirnimann' and Frau Stirnimann replies with a warm 'Grüezi, Herr Epstein,' if that happens to be your name – which is doubtful in your case.

When I can't remember a particular person's name, I mumble what I consider the approximate number of syllables in that name. This is obviously not the ideal solution.

During the ten years I have lived here, I have devised a set of rules. First of all, I try to frequent grocery stores where there is more than one person on duty. In this instance, I could say 'Grüezi, mitenand' which means 'Greetings, all together' and it is quite acceptable. My terrible memory forces me to sneak up to stores like a thief, peering in windows and around corners, just to see whether one or – let us pray – two people are serving. Fortunately I don't have to shop very frequently.

Another technique is to go about with a person who knows the name of anyone we're likely to meet on the street. I usually get along fine when I'm out with my wife. I always walk three steps behind her and when she greets Frau Schuppisser, I just repeat her greeting.

My personal speciality is a simple one. If I meet someone with a title – a doctor or the director of a company – I can get away with 'Grüezi, Herr Doktor' or 'Grüezi, Herr Direktor.' Now the strange thing about Switzerland – and Europe generally – is that wives may also use their husband's titles. I love this system, because I can say 'Grüezi, Frau Doktor' most of the time. And if the lady in question is not a doctor's wife, she's usually pleased that I consider that she may be. I mean, it's certainly better to use a title than to forget a name, isn't it?

There are, of course, other rules to be learned, particularly for me. For example, I am not quite sure how to ask my wife to join me for a walk. I can't say 'Would you join me, Frau Direktor?' since neither she nor I are directors. Nor can I call her Frau Stirnimann since I know who she isn't. Perhaps I should give up journalism and become a doctor.

Adapted from *Lend me your Alphorn* by Eugene V Epstein

PHOTOCOPIABLE

© Macmillan Publishers Limited 1996.

Progress Test 1 Lessons 1 – 5

PHOTOCOPIABLE

SECTION 4: WRITING (20 marks)

8 Write a biography of yourself. What have been your achievements? Do you have any ambitions?
Write 15 – 20 sentences. (20 marks)

_____

_____

_____

_____

_____

_____

_____

_____

_____

_____

_____

_____

_____

_____

_____

_____

_____

_____

_____

_____

_____

Progress Test 2 Lessons 6 – 10

SECTION 1: VOCABULARY (30 marks)

1a Underline the odd-one-out and leave a group of three related words. (10 marks)

b Add one other word to the groups of words. (10 marks)

Example: fragrant <u>noisy</u> scented smelly ___*musty*___

1 dentist journalist medicine politician _____

2 aunt matron nurse sister _____

3 industrial picturesque unspoilt

   village _____

4 bitter deafening sour spicy _____

5 gaze glance glimpse grab _____

6 confident optimistic sad talent _____

7 ambulance car interview train _____

8 cut ointment pain temperature _____

9 canteen classroom gym staff _____

10 arson fraud libel pollution _____

2 Complete these compound nouns with ten words from the box. (10 marks)

assistant attack city curtains field floor food formation hall home lady market nightmare pressure ward

Example: rock <u>formation</u>

1 hospital _____   6 playing _____

2 heart _____   7 nurses' _____

3 blood _____   8 dinner _____

4 cathedral _____   9 canyon _____

5 shop _____   10 theatre _____

PHOTOCOPIABLE
© Macmillan Publishers Limited 1996.

Progress Test 2 Lessons 6 – 10

SECTION 2: GRAMMAR (30 marks)

3a Choose ten of these words or verb forms to complete the first ten spaces in the conversation. (10 marks)

Example: a) <u>can</u> b) must c) will

1 a) had played b) have played c) was playing

2 a) fell b) fall c) fallen

3 a) didn't b) hadn't c) wasn't

4 a) did I realise b) I realised c) I had realised

5 a) drip b) dripping c) to drip

6 a) cut b) had cut c) had been cutting

7 a) a b) any c) the

8 a) three hour b) three-hour c) three-hours

9 a) want b) wanting c) to want

10 a) After b) Before c) While

b Complete the last ten spaces with ten of your own words or verb forms. (10 marks)

Squash is a very fast and enjoyable game but it _can_ be dangerous too. One day last year I (1) _____ against a friend of mine when I tripped. I (2) _____ over and hit my head against the wall. I felt OK. I (3) _____ feel dizzy. Not until I looked down (4) _____ what I had done. I could see blood (5) _____ onto the floor. I (6) _____ my head quite badly. My friend drove me to (7) _____ casualty department of the local hospital. I spoke to a nurse. She told me that there was a (8) _____ wait. Not (9) _____ to stay there three hours, I went home. (10) _____ having dinner, I returned to the hospital. It (11) _____ eleven o'clock at night by now. I took a seat and looked around (12) _____ the other patients. A man (13) _____ was sitting by me had broken his arm. Another looked (14) _____ if he had hurt his leg. In another room I (15) _____ hear a child crying.

I (16) _____ waiting two more hours when the doctor called my name. After he (17) _____ looked at my cut, he took me to the operating theatre. I (18) _____ down on the bed. After the doctor had (19) _____ me an injection, he stitched up my wound. It was two o'clock in the morning (20) _____ I finally got home.

4 One word is missing in each of these sentences. Indicate where the word is missing and what it is. (10 marks)

Example: The room smelt ⟨ gas.   _of_

1 The Thames is 200 mile-long river. _____

2 Oxford is the west of London. _____

3 They aren't here – they've to the shops. _____

4 We all enjoyed at the party. _____

5 What the buildings like in Budapest? _____

6 Our house is surrounded fields. _____

7 A little way there's a small village. _____

8 I remember him saying liked music. _____

9 She have to bring her passport. _____

10 It should be the caretaker locks the doors. _____

© Macmillan Publishers Limited 1996.

PHOTOCOPIABLE

Progress Test 2 Lessons 6 – 10

SECTION 3: READING (20 marks)

5 Read the passage. In which state was the writer travelling? In which month was he travelling? (2 marks)

_____

_____

6 Answer the questions. (9 marks)

1 *I was ... entering the Manistee National Forest almost before I knew it.*

Did the first part of the journey pass quickly or slowly? _____

2 *Michigan is shaped like an oven glove and is often about as exciting.*

Does the writer paint a positive or negative picture of Michigan? _____

3 *... people could buy their own little bit of ugliness and take it out into the woods.*

What is the writer referring to? _____

4 *The sun came out ... like a shy guest.*

Was the sun quite strong when it first came out?

_____

5 *I drove transfixed.*

Was the writer affected positively or negatively?

_____

6 *The young guy ... looked surprised to have a customer.*

Why did he look surprised? _____

7 *... everybody's gone out to dinner ...*

Who was everybody? _____

8 *He seemed to snatch a figure from the air. 'Twenty dollars?' he said.*

Was he sure that the price should be twenty dollars?

_____

9 *It was odd to be in a place ... so dead.*

Why did the place seem dead? _____

7 How many times do we know that the writer got out of his car? Where? What did he do in these places? What was the weather like in each place? (9 marks)

_____

_____

_____

_____

I left Dearborn and drove north and west across Michigan. I was past Lansing and Grand Rapids and entering the Manistee National Forest, 100 miles away, almost before I knew it. Michigan is shaped like an oven glove and is often about as exciting. Towns were rare and mostly squalid – scattered dwellings and ugly prefab cabins where they made and sold ugly prefab cabins, so that people could buy their own little bit of ugliness and take it out into the woods.

After Baldwin, the road became wider and emptier and the commercialism grew sparser. At Manistee, the highway ran down the Lake Michigan, and then followed the shoreline going through rather more pleasant little communities of mostly boarded up summer homes. At Empire I stopped to look at the lake. The weather was surprisingly cold. I tried to go for a stroll, but I was only out for about five minutes before the wind blew me back to the car.

I went on to Traverse City, where the weather was milder. Traverse City looked to be a wonderful old town that seemed not to have changed since about 1948. It still had a Woolworth's, a J.C.Penney, an old-fashioned movie theatre called The State and a wonderful old restaurant, with black booths and a long soda-fountain. I had coffee and felt very pleased to be there. Afterwards I drove on north on a road running up one side of Grand Traverse Bay and down the other, so that you could always see where you were going or where you had been. As the afternoon progressed, the wind settled and the sun came out, tentatively at first, like a shy guest, and then stayed on, giving the lake bright patches of silver and blue. Far out over the water, perhaps twenty miles away, dark clouds dumped rain on the lake. It fell in a pale grey curtain. And high above a faint rainbow reached across the sky. It was inexpressibly beautiful. I drove transfixed.

In the early evening I reached Mackinaw City on the tip of the oven glove. Mackinaw City was a scattered and unsightly little town, full of gift shops, motels and ice cream parlours. Almost every place of business, including the motels, was boarded up for the winter. The Holiday Motel seemed to be open so I went inside and rang the desk bell. The young guy who came out looked surprised to have a customer. 'We were just about to close up for the season,' he said. 'In fact, everybody's gone out to dinner to celebrate. But we've got rooms if you want one.'

'How much?' I asked.

He seemed to snatch a figure from the air. 'Twenty dollars?' he said.

'Sounds good to me,' I said and signed in. The room was small but nice and it had heating, which was a good thing. I went out and had a walk around to look for something to eat. It was only a little after seven, but it was dark already and the chill air felt more like December than October. It was odd to be in a place so full of buildings and yet so dead. Even the McDonald's was closed, with a sign in the window telling me to have a good winter.

Adapted from The Lost Continent, by Bill Bryson

 PHOTOCOPIABLE

© Macmillan Publishers Limited 1996.

Progress Test 2 Lessons 6 – 10

SECTION 4: WRITING (20 marks)

8 Write about some of the laws in your country. Do you agree with them all? Do you think that some of them should be changed? Write 15 – 20 sentences. (20 marks)

_____

_____

_____

_____

_____

_____

_____

_____

_____

_____

_____

_____

_____

_____

_____

_____

_____

_____

_____

_____

_____

© Macmillan Publishers Limited 1996.

PHOTOCOPIABLE

Progress Test 3 Lessons 11 – 15

SECTION 1: VOCABULARY (30 marks)

1a Underline the odd-one-out and leave a group of three related words. (10 marks)

b Add one other word to the groups of words. (10 marks)

Example: cap skirt <u>straw</u> suit _hat_

1 chisel corkscrew hammer

   screwdriver _____

2 grater ladle lawnmower sieve _____

3 boil butter fry roast _____

4 aubergine onion potato trout _____

5 cake coffee milk water _____

6 camcorder channel computer

   video _____

7 ecstatic happy rich thrilled _____

8 devastated frantic stress upset _____

9 daughter driver husband uncle _____

10 airport buggy limousine lorry _____

2 Add prefixes to give these adjectives an opposite or negative meaning. (10 marks)

Example: fair _unfair_

1 literate _____   6 probable _____

2 suitable _____   7 convenient _____

3 licensed _____   8 willing _____

4 reversible _____   9 edible _____

5 usual _____   10 patient _____

PHOTOCOPIABLE
© Macmillan Publishers Limited 1996.

Progress Test 3 Lessons 11 – 15

SECTION 2: GRAMMAR (30 marks)

3a Choose ten of these words or verb forms to complete the first ten spaces in the conversation. (10 marks)

Example: a) fry b) <u>prepare</u> c) roast

1 a) am used b) used c) would

2 a) what b) which c) who

3 a) ate b) had eaten c) have eaten

4 a) had b) has had c) was having

5 a) didn't b) don't c) hadn't

6 a) can't b) couldn't c) shouldn't

7 a) After b) Before c) Then

8 a) use b) using c) to use

9 a) use b) using c) to use

10 a) If b) Unless c) When

b Complete the last ten spaces with ten of your own words or verb forms. (10 marks)

I'm going to tell you how to *prepare* one of my favourite desserts. It's an Italian speciality and I (1) _____ to eat it a lot when I lived in Italy. Its name is Tiramisu, (2) _____ means pick me up. Someone will have to pick you up after you (3) _____ it! My brother (4) _____ it for the first time last week. If he (5) _____ eaten so much beforehand, he could have eaten more dessert. He (6) _____ have eaten so much pizza! First of all, put some sponge fingers into a bowl. (7) _____ make a small amount of coffee. It's silly (8) _____ instant coffee if you've got real coffee. I remember (9) _____ instant coffee once – the taste wasn't the same. (10) _____ the coffee is cold, pour it over the fingers. Then take three eggs, large ones (11) _____ possible. Separate them carefully so (12) _____ you get none of the white in with the yolks. You (13) _____ now beat the white until it is stiff. Use a mixer (14) _____ beating the egg white. Then add in a tub of mascarpone, a soft white Italian cheese, and the egg yolks to the egg white. Don't forget to add some sugar, (15) _____ the dessert won't be sweet enough. The mixture should then (16) _____ poured over the fingers. Finally, put some cocoa over the top of the dessert. You (17) _____ need to use a sieve, but it looks better. Then put the dessert in the refrigerator, (18) _____ it can keep cold. It will taste delicious as long (19) _____ you make it several hours before you want to eat it. If you can't wait, then it (20) _____ still taste pretty good!

4 One word is missing in each of these sentences. Indicate where the word is missing and what it is. (10 marks)

Example: I had such ⁁ good time at school. __a__

1 It wasn't necessary you to go there. _____

2 The mistake will corrected as soon as possible. _____

3 In order not make a noise, we spoke quietly.

_____

4 You use a saucepan cook food. _____

5 If I see you this evening, I tell you. _____

6 The system has attacked by a virus. _____

7 People are often afraid technology. _____

8 The woman I spoke was a doctor. _____

9 If only I called him yesterday. _____

10 I wish I knew what I going to do. _____

© Macmillan Publishers Limited 1996.

PHOTOCOPIABLE

Progress Test 3 Lessons 11 – 15

SECTION 3: READING (20 marks)

5 Read the passage *A lucky escape* and decide if these sentences are true or false. (8 marks)

1 The girl liked flying. ☐

2 She worked as an air-hostess. ☐

3 This was her first trip in a two-seater. ☐

4 The pilot showed her how to use the controls. ☐

5 Pressing the pedals turned the plane. ☐

6 The plane crashed into some trees after hitting the ground. ☐

7 The girl saved the pilot's life. ☐

8 She escaped unhurt from the crash. ☐

6 Answer these questions. (6 marks)

1 Why did the girl take the flight?

_____

2 Why did she take the controls?

_____

3 Why didn't she try to land on a road?

_____

7 How was the girl saved in the end? What might have happened if no one had seen or heard the plane? (6 marks)

_____

_____

_____

_____

_____

_____

A lucky escape!

I had a very lucky escape on my twenty-fifth birthday. What began as a pleasure flight, arranged as a birthday present by my parents, ended up as the most terrifying experience of my life.

I had flown many times before. I had been abroad on several holidays. I had even, when I was younger, thought about becoming an air hostess. So, when my parents, offered me the opportunity to fly over our town in a two-seater, I was thrilled! I had never been in such a small plane before!

It was Friday afternoon when I got into the small plane with Bill, the pilot, at the local airfield. I sat down in the passenger seat next to him and fastened my safety belt. I was very excited as we took off.

We had been flying for about ten minutes when things suddenly went wrong. I was looking out of the window, at the tiny cars and people below, when suddenly Bill fell forward over the plane's controls.

I thought it was a joke. Perhaps he wanted to frighten me. At first I laughed. But when Bill's head stayed down, I realised that this was no joke. He had had a heart attack. The pilot was dead and, if I didn't do something, I would soon be dead too.

The plane was, by this time, completely out of control. What could I do? How could I help myself? In front of me was a set of controls. I soon found that if I pulled the wheel towards me, the plane went up. If I pushed it away from me, the plane went down. Two pedals on the floor turned the plane left and right. Somehow I had to use the wheel and the pedals to land the plane.

I looked down again as I had done before. But this time I didn't just look out of interest. I needed to find a place where I could land – and land safely. But everywhere I looked there were houses, shops and schools – and lots of people. Perhaps I could find an empty road. I turned the plane to the right and saw a road ahead of me. But the traffic was too heavy.

In the distance, away from the town, I could see an empty field. I would have to land there. There was nobody in the field. I might be killed but nobody else would be in danger.

The plane dropped very fast. I tried to slow it down but suddenly I was very close to the ground. I would be killed if I hit the ground at this speed. So, at the last moment, I pulled the wheel back and the nose of the plane rose into the air again. The plane bounced on its wheels as it hit the ground, turned over two or three times and then hit some trees. I hit my head hard on the front window. That's the last thing I remember.

I woke up later that day in hospital. I had broken both legs and one arm. I found out later from my parents that a farmer had been working in the next field. He had seen the plane going overhead dangerously out of control and had heard it hit the ground. He had then rushed to the scene of the crash and pulled me from the plane – about one minute before it exploded. Without him I would never have survived.

PHOTOCOPIABLE

© Macmillan Publishers Limited 1996.

Progress Test 3 Lessons 11 – 15

SECTION 4: WRITING (20 marks)

8 Write about a day in which you or someone you know had a lucky escape. (The story doesn't have to be true!) Write 15 – 20 sentences. (20 marks)

_____

_____

_____

_____

_____

_____

_____

_____

_____

_____

_____

_____

_____

_____

_____

_____

_____

_____

_____

_____

_____

_____

_____

_____

_____

© Macmillan Publishers Limited 1996.

PHOTOCOPIABLE

Progress Test 4 Lessons 16 – 20

SECTION 1: VOCABULARY (30 marks)

1a Underline the ten singular countable nouns in the list. (10 marks)

advice analysis bead biography children clothing
dress feet information knight lightning luggage
money music myth news people service shampoo
shoe smoke supply teeth tin women

b Write countable equivalents of the ten uncountable nouns. (10 marks)

_____

_____

_____

_____

_____

_____

_____

_____

_____

_____

2 Complete these sentences with ten different nouns. (10 marks)

1 While I was at the bank, I ordered some foreign _____ for my trip to Europe.

2 The _____ for the flat I have bought is expensive.

3 Shall I write you a _____ or do you prefer cash?

4 There are five _____ in this constituency. Only one can become our MP.

5 We live on an island but we go to the _____ about once a week.

6 An enormous tidal _____ drowned some local people.

7 He floated across the sea on a _____ made of logs.

8 I hope there isn't too much _____ on the motorway.

9 Would you like a bread _____? They're quite nice.

10 I'd like to see money spent on medical _____ into cancer and other diseases.

PHOTOCOPIABLE
© Macmillan Publishers Limited 1996.

Progress Test 4 Lessons 16 – 20

SECTION 2: GRAMMAR (30 marks)

3a Choose ten of these words or verb forms to complete the first ten spaces in the conversation. (10 marks)

Example: a) doing b) making c) dealing

1 a) As b) In c) On
2 a) when b) where c) which
3 a) didn't b) haven't c) wasn't
4 a) go b) going c) to go
5 a) have been setting b) have set c) set
6 a) is said b) says c) was said
7 a) an b) any c) some
8 a) can't have b) might have c) must have
9 a) up b) off c) down
10 a) her b) him c) them

b Complete the last ten spaces with ten of your own words. (10 marks)

I've been *making* arrangements for this year's holiday.

(1) _____ general, I like to go to a different place every year. However, last year I went to Egypt and I liked it very much. I went to Cairo, (2) _____ I saw the pyramids. I was going to sail down the Nile to Luxor but I (3) _____ . So this year I have decided (4) _____ to Egypt again – I (5) _____ my sights on visiting Luxor and the south. It (6) _____ that this is the most interesting part of Egypt.

About a month ago I went to the travel agent's and asked for (7) _____ information.

I (8) _____ booked something but I didn't have my cheque book with me. So the girl wrote (9) _____ some flight times and prices and sent me away with some brochures. The next day I went back. I asked (10) _____ to book me one of the holidays I was interested in. She told me that all the cheap flights to Luxor (11) _____ fully booked.

But she found me something that was only a (12) _____ more expensive. The accommodation (13) _____ much better – I (14) _____ be staying in one of the smartest hotels. I (15) _____ I get a nice view!

I (16) _____ forward to my holiday already! The girl also (17) _____ that I ordered some traveller's cheques. I think I (18) _____ to the bank tomorrow and do that. I don't need (19) _____ because I won't be spending very much. But, of course, money (20) _____ go as far as it used to!

4 Underline the mistakes in these sentences and correct them. (10 marks)

Example: <u>Do you can</u> swim? *Can you*

1 He turned up the invitation to dinner. _____
2 I want her to be elect as chairperson. _____
3 Her new job took out the best in her. _____
4 I've got hardly some cash. _____
5 By the year 2020 I will have live here for 30 years.
_____
6 He must has missed his train. _____
7 She told she ought to go home. _____
8 He's always quick at the mark. _____
9 What do you spend most money for? _____
10 Our MP is a member of the oppose party.
_____

© Macmillan Publishers Limited 1996.

PHOTOCOPIABLE

Progress Test 4 Lessons 16 – 20

SECTION 3: READING (20 marks)

5 Read the passage and answer these questions about the Ridgeway. (4 marks)

1 What is special about it? _____

2 How old is it? _____

3 How long is it? _____

4 Where is its most western point? _____

6 What facts do you know about the passage of Uffington? (4 marks)

1 Where is it exactly? _____

2 What words does the writer use to describe its size?

_____

3 How was it made? _____

4 How easy is it to see from the Ridgeway?

_____

7 Answer these questions about the passage. (6 marks)

1 Why does the writer say that no one who walks along the Ridgeway need feel ignorant about its origins?

_____

_____

2 What does tradition say about its origins?

_____

_____

3 What do the experts say?

_____

_____

8 Which famous writer grew up near the Ridgeway? What was the name of his most successful book? What did he think of the area in which he grew up? (3 marks)

_____

_____

_____

9 When was the White Horse last cleaned by the local people? What did cleaning it involve? Who cleans it today? (3 marks)

_____

_____

The Ridgeway

The Ridgeway, running along the escarpment of the Berkshire and Wiltshire Downs, dates from about 2,000 BC and is said to be the oldest road in Europe. From Streatley in the Thames valley to the famous stone circles of Avebury, the path runs for approximately 40 miles from east to west and passes many earthworks and burial mounds that are a visible legacy of the ancient British past.

The White Horse of Uffington lies almost exactly halfway between Streatley and Avebury. Like all prehistoric survivals it puzzles the historian, the expert and other professional providers of information. Nobody knows for certain what its purpose is, what it commemorates or even who put it there. In the modern world when every secret is known, such lack of information is reassuring. No one who walks along the Ridgeway need feel ignorant. He is just as knowledgeable as the professional archaeologist.

There is another difficulty attaching to the White Horse, namely that it is quite hard to see it clearly. Perhaps the best view is from the train between Didcot and Swindon. At a distance you can see its long lean outline, drawn as if with a few bold strokes of a giant's crayon. It gives no answers to questions about its origins, including the especially interesting one of how its ancient creators were able to cut out of the chalk such a precise and stylish shape on such a huge scale.

Tradition, as opposed to the experts, has always claimed that the White Horse commemorated the battle of King Alfred over the Danes at the battle of Ashdown in 870. The experts, however, insist that it is much older; and they are probably right. But tradition should not be dismissed as if it were just a collection of fairy stories. In the case of the White Horse common sense alone suggests that such an elaborate and magnificent monument must have been inspired by some important event. The Ridgeway country is historically associated with two great victories over heathen invaders: Alfred's over the Danes and the much earlier battle of Mount Badon in about 490. The site of the battle cannot be precisely located in either case, but it might not, however, be inappropriate to regard the White Horse of Uffington as a symbol of Christian England victorious over invading pagans.

The White Horse is linked also with *Tom Brown's Schooldays*. Its author Thomas Hughes (1822-96) was born and brought up in the village of Uffington which lies below the downs. He describes the country in the first chapter of this, his best-known book, and rebukes his fellow Englishmen for travelling all over Europe and ignoring the beauties of their own country. In a later but less successful book, *The Scouring of the White Horse*, published in 1859, Hughes described the fun and games that took place two years earlier when the White Horse was cleaned for the last time by the villagers of Uffington. Scourings had been held since the early eighteenth century, the custom being for the villagers to climb the hill, remove all the grass from the chalk areas of the horse and then celebrate the event with a day or two of various sports, involving races of all kinds and other unusual competitions. Today the Horse is the responsibility of the Department of the Environment, who carry out the necessary restoration work in less colourful style.

Adapted from *The Ridgeway, Europe's Oldest Road*, by Richard Ingrams

© Macmillan Publishers Limited 1996.

Progress Test 4 Lessons 16 – 20

SECTION 4: WRITING (20 marks)

10 Write about one of your favourite TV series or films. Say something about the plot and the characters. Explain why you like the programme or film. Write 15 – 20 sentences. (20 marks)

_____

_____

_____

_____

_____

_____

_____

_____

_____

_____

_____

_____

_____

_____

_____

_____

_____

_____

_____

_____

_____

_____

_____

PHOTOCOPIABLE

Answers Progress Test 1 Lessons 1 – 5

SECTION 1: VOCABULARY [30 marks]

1a (10 marks: 1 mark for each correct answer.)
1	fez	6	opera
2	spelling	7	company
3	knitting	8	male
4	sculpture	9	Germany
5	wink	10	ethnic

b (10 marks: 1 mark for each appropriate answer.)
1 a foreign word for something to eat, eg *pizza*
2 a part of speech, eg *verb*
3 a sport, eg *boxing*
4 a part of a cinema or theatre, eg *stage*
5 a verb which describes an action done with the hand, eg *scratch*
6 a word connected with football, eg *stadium*
7 a person, eg *supporter*
8 a part of the body, eg *arm*
9 a language or nationality adjective, eg *Italian*
10 a place in a town or city, eg *university*

2 (10 marks: 1 mark for each correct answer.)
1	feed	6	book
2	look	7	give
3	guess	8	shake
4	take	9	make
5	chew	10	fall

SECTION 2: GRAMMAR [30 marks]

3a (10 marks: 1 mark for each correct answer.)
1	c) well	6	b) shouldn't
2	a) aren't	7	b) studied
3	c) to go	8	a) am studying
4	a) been	9	a) always
5	b) making	10	a) listen

b (10 marks: 1 mark for each appropriate answer.)
11	wish	16	will/would
12	least	17	Shall
13	So	18	isn't
14	are going	19	enjoy/like/love
15	don't	20	an/the

4 (10 marks: ½ mark for each mistake and ½ mark for each correction.)
1	have you been	6	was/were
2	helps	7	won't
3	will	8	am going
4	shall we	9	did you see
5	boring	10	known

SECTION 3: READING [20 marks]

5 (5 marks: 1 mark for each of the following points.)
surname: Epstein
country (in which he grew up) or nationality: America(n)
marital status: married
country in which he lives: Switzerland
time he has lived there: ten years
job/profession: journalist

6 (6 marks: 2 marks for each answer.)
1 He cannot remember people's names.
2 Mumbling (the approximate number of syllables) is not the ideal solution.
3 He could then address his wife as 'Frau Doktor'.

7 (9 marks: 3 marks for each technique.)
1 He greets more than one person at the same time. This means that he can use the greeting 'Grüezi, mitenand' rather than greet each person by name.
2 He goes about with his wife, who knows the name of anyone they're likely to meet.
3 He uses titles for men such as 'Herr Doktor'; he uses 'Frau Doktor' for their wives. The advantage of this is that people like being addressed by a title even if they do not have one.

SECTION 4: WRITING [20 marks]

8 (20 marks)
Tell students what you will take into consideration when marking their written work. Criteria should include:
– efficient communication of meaning (7 marks)
– grammatical accuracy (7 marks)
– coherence in the ordering or the information or ideas (3 marks)
– layout, capitalisation and punctuation (3 marks)

It is probably better not to use a rigid marking system with the written part of the test. If, for example, you always deduct a mark for a grammatical mistake, you may find that you are over-penalising students who write a lot or who take risks. Deduct marks if students haven't written the minimum number of sentences stated in the test.

PHOTOCOPIABLE
© Macmillan Publishers Limited 1996.

Answers Progress Test 2 Lessons 6 – 10

SECTION 1: VOCABULARY [30 marks]

1a (10 marks: 1 mark for each correct answer.)

1	medicine	6	talent
2	aunt	7	interview
3	village	8	ointment
4	deafening	9	staff
5	grab	10	pollution

b (10 marks: 1 mark for each appropriate answer.)
1 a job or profession, eg *lawyer*
2 a person who works in a hospital, eg *specialist*
3 an adjective for describing the landscape, eg *rugged*
4 an adjective for describing taste, eg *sweet*
5 a verb for talking about sight, eg *observe*
6 an adjective for describing character, eg *practical*
7 a means of transport, eg *bus*
8 a medical complaint, eg *disease*
9 a place in a school, eg *playground*
10 a crime, eg *burglary*

2 (10 marks: 1 mark for each correct answer.)

1	ward	6	field
2	attack	7	home
3	pressure	8	lady
4	city	9	floor
5	assistant	10	curtains

SECTION 2: GRAMMAR [30 marks]

3a (10 marks: 1 mark for each correct answer.)

1	c) was playing	6	b) had cut
2	a) fell	7	c) the
3	a) didn't	8	b) three-hour
4	a) did I realise	9	b) wanting
5	b) dripping	10	a) After

b (10 marks: 1 mark for each appropriate answer.)

11	was	16	had been
12	at	17	had
13	who	18	lay/sat
14	as	19	given
15	could	20	when

4 (10 marks: ½ mark for each indication of a missing word and ½ mark for each correct word.)

1 is ∧ 200 *a*
2 is ∧ the *to*
3 they've ∧ to *gone*
4 enjoyed ∧ at *ourselves*
5 What ∧ the *are*
6 surrounded ∧ fields *by*
7 way ∧ there's *off*
8 saying ∧ liked *he*
9 She ∧ have *doesn't*
10 caretaker ∧ locks *who*

SECTION 3: READING [20 marks]

5 (2 marks: 1 mark for each answer).
The writer was travelling in the state of Michigan in the month of October.

6 (9 marks: 1 mark for each answer.)
1 quickly
2 negative
3 prefab cabins
4 no
5 positively
6 because he didn't expect any customers at that time of year
7 the people who worked at the hotel
8 no
9 because all the buildings were closed

7 (9 marks: 3 marks for each of the three places.)
1 Empire: he tried to go for a stroll. It was very windy.
2 Traverse City: he had coffee. The weather was milder (than at Empire).
3 Mackinaw City: he got a room in a hotel and had a walk around, to look for something to eat. The weather was chilly; it felt more like December than October.

SECTION 4: WRITING [20 marks]

8 (20 marks)
Tell students what you will take into consideration when marking their written work. Criteria should include:
 – efficient communication of meaning (7 marks)
 – grammatical accuracy (7 marks)
 – coherence in the ordering or the information or ideas (3 marks)
 – layout, capitalisation and punctuation (3 marks)

It is probably better not to use a rigid marking system with the written part of the test. If, for example, you always deduct a mark for a grammatical mistake, you may find that you are over-penalising students who write a lot or who take risks. Deduct marks if students haven't written the minimum number of sentences stated in the test.

© Macmillan Publishers Limited 1996.

PHOTOCOPIABLE

Answers Progress Test 3 Lessons 11 – 15

SECTION 1: VOCABULARY [30 marks]

1a (10 marks: 1 mark for each correct answer.)

1	corkscrew	6	channel
2	lawnmower	7	rich
3	butter	8	stress
4	trout	9	driver
5	cake	10	airport

b (10 marks: 1 mark for each appropriate answer.)

1 a tool, eg *drill*
2 an item of kitchen equipment, eg *peeler*
3 a verb which describes cooking, eg *stew*
4 a vegetable, eg *carrot*
5 something to drink, eg *wine*
6 an item of technology, eg *photocopier*
7 an adjective for describing positive feelings, eg *inspired*
8 an adjective for describing negative feelings, eg *confused*
9 a family member, eg *mother*
10 a means of transport, eg *plane*

2 (10 marks: 1 mark for each correct answer.)

1	illiterate	6	improbable
2	unsuitable	7	inconvenient
3	unlicensed	8	unwilling
4	irreversible	9	inedible
5	unusual	10	impatient

SECTION 2: GRAMMAR [30 marks]

3a (10 marks: 1 mark for each correct answer.)

1	b) used	6	c) shouldn't
2	b) which	7	c) Then
3	c) have eaten	8	c) to use
4	a) had	9	b) using
5	c) hadn't	10	c) When

b (10 marks: 1 mark for each appropriate answer.)

11	if	16	be
12	that	17	don't
13	must/should	18	where
14	for	19	as
15	otherwise	20	will

4 (10 marks: ½ mark for each indication of a missing word and ½ mark for each correct word.)

1 necessary ⌄ you *for*
2 will ⌄ corrected *be*
3 not ⌄ make *to*
4 saucepan ⌄ cook *to*
5 I ⌄ tell *will ('ll)*
6 has ⌄ attacked *been*
7 afraid ⌄ technology *of*
8 spoke ⌄ was *to*
9 I ⌄ called *had*
10 I ⌄ going *was*

SECTION 3: READING [20 marks]

5 (8 marks: l mark for each answer.)

1	T	5	T
2	F	6	T
3	T	7	F
4	F	8	F

6 (6 marks: 2 marks for each answer.)

1 it was a birthday present from her parents
2 because the pilot had died
3 the traffic was too heavy

7 (6 marks in total.)

A farmer saw the plane going overhead and heard it hit the ground.
He had pulled her from the plane.
She might have been killed when the plane exploded a minutes later, if he hadn't pulled her out.

SECTION 4: WRITING [20 marks]

8 (20 marks)

Tell students what you will take into consideration when marking their written work. Criteria should include:
- efficient communication of meaning (7 marks)
- grammatical accuracy (7 marks)
- coherence in the ordering or the information or ideas (3 marks)
- layout, capitalisation and punctuation (3 marks)

It is probably better not to use a rigid marking system with the written part of the test. If, for example, you always deduct a mark for a grammatical mistake, you may find that you are over-penalising students who write a lot or who take risks. Deduct marks if students haven't written the minimum number of sentences stated in the test.

PHOTOCOPIABLE

© Macmillan Publishers Limited 1996.

Answers Progress Test 4 Lessons 16 – 20

SECTION 1: VOCABULARY [30 marks]

1a (10 marks: 1 mark for each correct answer.)

1	analysis	6	myth
2	bead	7	service
3	biography	8	shoe
4	dress	9	supply
5	knight	10	tin

b (10 marks: 1 mark for each appropriate answer.)

1	a piece of advice	6	a sum of money
2	an item of clothing	7	a piece of music
3	a piece of information	8	an item of news
4	a flash of lightning	9	a bottle of shampoo
5	an item/a piece of luggage	10	a puff of smoke

2 (10 marks: 1 mark for each correct answer.)

1	currency/money	6	wave
2	mortgage	7	raft
3	cheque	8	traffic
4	candidates	9	roll
5	mainland	10	research

SECTION 2: GRAMMAR [30 marks]

3a (10 marks: 1 mark for each correct answer.)

1	b) In	6	a) is said
2	b) where	7	c) some
3	a) didn't	8	b) might have
4	c) to go	9	c) down
5	b) have set	10	a) her

b (10 marks: 1 mark for each appropriate answer.)

11	were	16	am looking
12	little	17	suggested
13	is	18	may/might/will ('ll) go
14	will	19	many
15	hope	20	doesn't

4 (10 marks: ½ mark for each mistake and ½ mark for each correction.)

1 <u>up</u> down
2 <u>elect</u> elected
3 <u>took</u> brought
4 <u>some</u> any
5 <u>live</u> lived
6 <u>has</u> have
7 <u>told</u> said
8 <u>at</u> off
9 <u>for</u> on
10 <u>oppose</u> opposition

SECTION 3: READING [20 marks]

5 (4 marks: 1 mark for each answer.)

1 it is said to be the oldest road in Europe
2 (about) 4,000 years old
3 (about) 40 miles long
4 Avebury

6 (4 marks: 1 mark for each answer.)

1 halfway between Streatley and Avebury or 20 miles from Streatley/Avebury
2 huge scale
3 it was cut from the chalk
4 not easy

7 (6 marks: 2 marks for each answer.)

1 No one – including the experts – can be certain about its origins. So no one need feel that they know less than they should.
2 It is said that the White Horse commemorated the battle of King Alfred over the Danes and the battle of Ashdown in 870.
3 The experts think that the White Horse was made before 870, ie it is older.

8 (3 marks: 1 mark for each answer.)

1 Thomas Hughes
2 *Tom Brown's Schooldays*
3 He thought that it was beautiful/wonderful etc.

9 (3 marks: 1 mark for each answer.)

1 1857
2 removing the grass from the chalk areas
3 the Department of the Environment

SECTION 4: WRITING [20 marks]

10 (20 marks)

Tell students what you will take into consideration when marking their written work. Criteria should include:
  – efficient communication of meaning (7 marks)
  – grammatical accuracy (7 marks)
  – coherence in the ordering or the information or ideas (3 marks)
  – layout, capitalisation and punctuation (3 marks)
It is probably better not to use a rigid marking system with the written part of the test. If, for example, you always deduct a mark for a grammatical mistake, you may find that you are over-penalising students who write a lot or who take risks. Deduct marks if students haven't written the minimum number of sentences stated in the test.

© Macmillan Publishers Limited 1996.

PHOTOCOPIABLE